Social Mobility in Late Antique Gaul

Strategies and Opportunities for the Non-elite

In *Social Mobility in Late Antique Gaul*, Allen E. Jones explores the situation of the non-elite living in Gaul during the late fifth and sixth centuries. Drawing especially on evidence from Gregory of Tours' writings, Jones formulates a social model based on people of all ranks who were acting in ways that were socially advantageous to them, such as combining resources, serving at court, and participating in ostentatious religious pursuits such as building churches. Viewing the society as a whole and taking into account specific social groups, such as impoverished prisoners, paupers active at churches, physicians, and wonder-working enchanters, Jones creates an image of Barbarian Gaul as an honor-driven, brutal, and flexible society defined by social mobility. Jones's work also addresses topics such as social engineering and competition, magic and religion, and the cult of saints.

Allen E. Jones is associate professor of history at Troy University.

D1418775

To Patricia

SOCIAL MOBILITY IN LATE ANTIQUE GAUL

STRATEGIES AND OPPORTUNITIES FOR THE NON-ELITE

ALLEN E. JONES

TROY UNIVERSITY

CAMBRIDGE
UNIVERSITY PRESS

32 Avenue of the Americas, New York NY 10013-2473, USA

Cambridge University Press is part of the University of Cambridge.

It furthers the University's mission by disseminating knowledge in the pursuit of
education, learning and research at the highest international levels of excellence.

www.cambridge.org
Information on this title: www.cambridge.org/9781107629929

First published 2009
First paperback edition 2013

A catalogue record for this publication is available from the British Library

Library of Congress Cataloguing in Publication data
Jones, Allen E., 1963–
Social mobility in late antique Gaul : strategies and opportunities for
the non-elite / Allen E. Jones.
p.   cm.
Includes bibliographical references and index.
ISBN 978-0-521-76239-7 (hardback)
1. Social mobility – Gaul – History – 5th century.   2. Social mobility – Gaul – History –
6th century.   3. Social classes – Gaul – History – 5th century.   4. Social classes –
Gaul – History – 6th century.   5. Social structure – Gaul – History – 5th century.
6. Social structure – Gaul – History – 6th century.   7. Gaul – Social conditions –
5th century.   8. Gaul – Social conditions – 6th century.   9. Gaul – Religious life and
customs – 5th century.   10. Gaul – Religious life and customs – 6th century.   I. Title.
HN425.J664   2009
305.5'1309364–dc22   2008048945

ISBN 978-0-521-76239-7 Hardback
ISBN 978-1-107-62992-9 Paperback

CONTENTS

✿ ✿ ✿

ACKNOWLEDGMENTS

This book is the result of research done over ten years. I am happy to be at the point where I may thank friends, scholars, and associates who have advised, counseled, and otherwise contributed to my scholarship efforts.

First I thank Ralph Mathisen, who was advisor for my dissertation while I was at the University of South Carolina, and who today teaches at the University of Illinois at Urbana-Champaign and of course is editor of the *Journal of Late Antiquity*. Thanks to Ralph I was able to access much biographical material from the *Biographical Database for the Late Antiquity Project*. I am of course grateful for that and for a decade and more of his mentoring. I also want to thank Ralph since it is he who introduced me to that Gregory of Tours fellow, whose brain I've been trying to pick for nearly half my life now, much to the amusement and bewilderment of friends and family. I thank several other South Carolina faculty who contributed ideas while serving on my dissertation committee – namely, Robert Patterson, Jeremiah Hackett, Scott Gwara, and the late Peter Becker.

As anyone who has used Mathisen's *Biographical Database* knows, anonymous people matter. This maxim certainly applies in regard to the making of my manuscript, for it simply would not have become what it is without the expertise of three anonymous readers. The first read my dissertation some years ago and offered both welcomed encouragement and a vision for how I might develop an effective book. Much has happened in the field of Late Antiquity in the decade between the dissertation's completion and the book's publication. Here the advice of two readers selected by Cambridge University Press came into play. They made several specific and excellent suggestions pertaining to matters such as changing some content, updating the bibliography, and taking into account some recent scholarship such as that involving material evidence. I am truly grateful for these readers' advice and invaluable insights. I also would like to thank Publishing Director Beatrice Rehl and her staff at Cambridge University Press for their role in converting the manuscript into a book. Special thanks goes to manuscript editor Ronald Cohen for generously giving of his expertise, for many helpful suggestions, and for his cordiality. Of course, whatever shortcomings remain within the text are entirely my own.

I found time to accomplish a goodly amount of writing on the manuscript thanks to a sabbatical in fall 2006 granted by Troy University. A string of travel grants provided by Troy's faculty development office have enabled me to attend conferences, especially the Medieval Congress at Kalamazoo, where I was able to meet with eminent scholars, which in turn has contributed to my growing understanding of Gregory of Tours' world and Late Antiquity in general. I would like to thank the library and interlibrary loan staff at the Thomas Cooper Library at the University of South Carolina, and also the librarians, and notably Belinda Edwards and Jill McLaney, at the interlibrary loan office at Troy. Thanks also to Keiko Clark at Troy for applying her artistry to the map on page xi.

I have benefited from being able to move between two congenial environments: the history department at Troy and home. My thanks to all of my colleagues perched in the attic of Bibb Graves, past and present, and also to friends and students who have shared in the anticipation of this book's completion. I thank my parents Allen and Deana, and the boys. And I thank Patricia, to whom this book is dedicated.

ABBREVIATIONS

Amm. Marc.	Ammianus Marcellinus
Caes. Arel.	Caesarius of Arles
Carm.	*Carmen* (poem)
CCL	*Corpus Christianorum, Series Latina*
Chron.	*Chronicon* (chronicle)
CSEL	*Corpus Scriptorum Ecclesiasticorum Latinorum*
CTh	*Codex Theodosianus*
Ep.	*Epistula* (letter)
Greg. Tur.	Gregory of Tours
GC	*Liber in gloria confessorum*
GM	*Liber in gloria martyrum*
Hist.	*Decem libri historiarum*
VJ	*Liber de passione et virtutibus s. Iuliani martyris*
VM	*Libri quattuor de virtutibus s. Martini episcopi*
VP	*Liber vitae patrum*
LCL	Loeb Classical Library
Mar. Avent.	Marius of Avenches
MGH	*Monumenta Germaniae Historica*
AA	Auctores antiquissimi
LL	Leges nationum germanicarum
SRM	Scriptores rerum merovingicarum

PL	*Patrologia Latina*, ed. J.-P. Migne
PLRE	*The Prosopography of the Roman Empire*, 3 vols.
PLS	*Pactus legis Salicae*
Sid. Ap.	Sidonius Apollinaris
Sirm. Const.	*Constitutiones Sirmondianae*
SC	*Sources chrétiennes*
Sulp. Sev.	Sulpicius Severus
TTH	Translated Texts for Historians
TRW	Transformation of the Roman World
Ven. Fort.	Venantius Fortunatus

0   100   200 km

Gaul in the Late Sixth Century. Adapted with permission from M. Heinzelmann, *Gregory of Tours: History and Society in the Sixth Century,* Cambridge University Press, copyright © 2001, Cambridge University Press. [Map drawn by Keiko Clark, Troy University, Troy, Alabama. Source: Original map, M. Heinzelmann after A. Longnon and E. Ewig. Version: U. Hugot (DHIP), Model map: H. Atsma (DHIP).]

INTRODUCTION: BARBARIAN GAUL

CHAPTER ONE

The historian is generally occupied far more with great events and imposing characters than with the quiet, dim life which flows on in silent, monotonous toil beneath the glare and tumult of great tragedies and triumphs. It is natural that it should be so.

SAMUEL DILL, *Roman Society in Gaul in the Merovingian Age*[1]

Late Antiquity, stretching roughly from the late third through seventh centuries, was an age characterized by transition.[2] In that period, Europe experienced dramatic political and social changes: Western imperial rule disappeared, replaced by smaller kingdoms, trade and taxation declined, aristocrats concentrated on more proximate interests,

1. Samuel Dill, *Roman Society in Gaul in the Merovingian Age* (London: Macmillan, 1926), 235.
2. The theme of "transition" is emphasized in a continuing series of interdisciplinary conferences in the U. S. called "Shifting Frontiers" and also in a recent interdisciplinary and collaborative effort among international (mostly European) scholars called the Transformation of the Roman World Project. Editors of the latter expect seventeen publications to result; Ian Wood, "Report: The European Science Foundation's Programme on the Transformation of the Roman World and Emergence of Early Medieval Europe," *Early Medieval Europe* 6 (1997): 217–27. Initial publications of the two projects are, respectively, Ralph W. Mathisen and Hagith Sivan, eds., *Shifting Frontiers in Late Antiquity* (Aldershot and Burlington, VT: Ashgate, 1996); and Leslie Webster and Michelle Brown, eds., *The Transformation of the Roman World, AD 400–900* (London and Berkeley: British Museum and University of California Press, 1997).

and Roman and indigenous cultures merged.[3] Furthermore, Christian thought and practice increasingly infiltrated and influenced European politics, society, and culture.[4] Inhabitants of Gaul were in the forefront in experiencing these important societal shifts.[5] Gallic society forever changed with the introduction of peoples whom the sources label "barbarians." Sizeable migrating groups passed through and/or settled in Gaul from the first decade of the fifth century.[6] According to the chronicle tradition, bands of Vandals, Sueves, and Alans moved westward over the Rhine River from December 406. By 409, some had proceeded to Spain and North Africa, while others stayed. The Empire responded to these movements by expanding a policy of settling the "barbarians" as *foederati*, federate soldiers. In 413, the Western government settled Burgundians along the upper Rhine, and in 418 it placed Visigothic *foederati* in the province of Aquitania Secunda. By then, Franks had long been serving a similar purpose in northern Gaul. But even before the death of the last legitimate Western emperor, barbarian military leaders donning Roman military titles had begun treating parts of Gaul as if they were their own.[7] Between 465 and 480, King Childeric, leader of Salian Frankish federates stationed in Belgica, took territory in

3. General narrative histories include J. B. Bury, *History of the Later Roman Empire from the Death of Theodosius I to the Death of Justinian*, 2 vols. (New York: Dover, 1958); Averil Cameron, *The Mediterranean World in Late Antiquity, AD 395–600* (London and New York: Routledge, 1993); and Stephen Mitchell, *A History of the Later Roman Empire, AD 284–641: The Transformation of the Ancient World* (Malden, MA, and Oxford: Blackwell, 2007). For broad approaches to the era, see Averil Cameron, Bryan Ward-Perkins, and Michael Whitby, eds., *The Cambridge Ancient History*, vol. 14, *Late Antiquity: Empire and Successors, A.D. 425–600* (Cambridge: Cambridge University Press, 2000); and Paul Fouracre, ed., *The New Cambridge Medieval History*, vol. I, *c. 500–c. 700* (Cambridge: Cambridge University Press, 2005).

4. Judith Herrin, *The Formation of Christendom in Late Antiquity* (Princeton, NJ: Princeton University Press, 1987); Peter Brown, *The Rise of Western Christendom, Triumph and Diversity, A.D. 200–1000* (2nd ed., Malden, MA, and Oxford: Blackwell, 2003).

5. John F. Drinkwater and Hugh Elton, eds., *Fifth-Century Gaul: A Crisis of Identity?* (Cambridge: Cambridge University Press, 1992); Ralph W. Mathisen and Danuta Shanzer, eds., *Society and Culture in Late Antique Gaul: Revisiting the Sources* (Aldershot and Burlington, VT: Ashgate, 2001).

6. In general see J. B. Bury, *The Invasion of Europe by the Barbarians* (London: Macmillan, 1928); Lucien Musset, *The Germanic Invasions: The Making of Europe, A.D. 400–600*, trans. by E. and C. James (University Park, PA: Pennsylvania State University Press, 1975); Walter Pohl, ed., *Kingdoms of the Empire: The Integration of Barbarians in Late Antiquity*, TRW 1 (Leiden: Brill, 1997); Matthew Innes, *Introduction to Early Medieval Western Europe, 300–900: The Sword, the Plough and the Book* (London: Routledge, 2007), 63–137.

7. When the exiled emperor Julius Nepos died in 480, the barbarian Odovacar, who was already ruling Italy as *rex*, ended any pretense of imperial rule in the West; Cassiodorus, *Chron.*, s. a., 476.

the Seine basin.[8] After 480, Childeric's son, the warrior-king Clovis (reigned ca. 481–511), enjoyed more military successes than failures and thereby consolidated power in northern Gaul and expanded his authority south of the Loire River.[9] Following up on these advances, Clovis's sons and grandsons established complete Frankish control over the southern Gallic regions previously held by Burgundians, Visigoths, and Ostrogoths.[10]

This familiar story of "Germanic" conquest of "Roman" Gaul has undergone considerable scholarly revision in recent decades. To begin, modern studies of ethnogenesis dismiss biological distinctions between "Romans" and "barbarians" and among the separate so-called "Germanic" groups. New models tend to abandon credence in ethnographic concepts that had been proposed by late ancient writers themselves, such as Jordanes, who culled ancient Greek and Roman texts and then identified contemporary sixth-century Goths with the ancient *Getae*, about whom he had read. In place of discarded theories, recent analyses in general explain how a "barbarian people" could result from a lasting coalescing of troops around the nucleus of a successful warlord, to which group institutions (e.g., laws) and traditions (e.g., legendary origins) might attach themselves.[11]

> This critical mass of warriors under a successful commander is converted into a people through the imposition of a legal system. Peoplehood is the end of a political process through which individuals with diverse backgrounds are united by law. So conceived, a people

8. Edward James, *The Franks* (Oxford and New York: Blackwell, 1988), 64–77.

9. Ibid., 78–91. For an alternative to traditional interpretations of Childeric and Clovis advancing out of Belgica, see Guy Halsall, "Childeric's Grave, Clovis' Succession, and the Origin of the Merovingian Kingdom," in *Society and Culture in Late Antique Gaul: Revisiting the Sources*, ed. Ralph W. Mathisen and Danuta Shanzer (Aldershot and Burlington, VT: Ashgate, 2001), 116–33.

10. On specific barbarian peoples, for the Burgundians, see Justin Favrod, *Histoire politique du royaume burgonde, 443–534* (Lausanne: Bibliothèque historique vaudoise, 1997). On the Goths, see Peter Heather, *The Goths* (Oxford and Cambridge, MA: Blackwell, 1996); Herwig Wolfram, *History of the Goths* (Berkeley: University of California Press, 1988). For the Franks, see Patrick Geary, *Before France and Germany: The Creation and Transformation of the Merovingian World* (New York and Oxford: Oxford University Press, 1988); Edward James, *The Franks* (op. cit.); John M. Wallace-Hadrill, *The Long-Haired Kings and Other Studies in Frankish History* (New York: Barnes and Noble, 1962); and Ian Wood, *The Merovingian Kingdoms, 450–751* (New York: Longman, 1994).

11. Patrick J. Geary, "Barbarians and Ethnicity," in *Late Antiquity: A Guide to the Postclassical World*, ed. G. W. Bowersock, Peter Brown and Oleg Grabar (Cambridge, MA, and London: Harvard University Press, 1999), 108.

is constitutional, not biological, and yet the very imposition of law makes the opposite appeal: it is the law of the ancestors. The leader projects an antiquity and a genealogy onto this new creation.[12]

For illustration, considering the Franks, even before Clovis's reign his father Childeric had become a dominant politico-military figure around Tournai. The presence of a sizeable amount of Byzantine coinage in Childeric's grave, discovered in 1653, suggests that one reason Childeric could sustain his position was Byzantine financial support; soldiers latched onto Childeric not only because of the likelihood of his succeeding in battle but also to partake in his lucre.[13] A factor that contributed to the lasting prominence of the warlord's family was cooperation with members of local power structures, including ecclesiastical aristocrats such as Bishop Remigius of Reims.[14] When Clovis inherited his father's position, sufficient numbers of aristocrats such as Remigius apparently were willing to accept the king's authority so long as he continued to heed their advice. Clovis did not intend to establish or maintain separate identities for Franks and Romans. While the Frankish royal family – the Merovingians – perhaps distinguished themselves from others by wearing long hair and claiming descent from a sea monster called the quinotaur, Frankish people at large adopted a legendary Trojan ancestry.[15] The latter claim actually linked Franks and Romans, for people identifying themselves as the latter had been touting the same ancestry for centuries.[16] Another potential difference between Franks and Romans disappeared when Clovis and many of his soldiers famously converted to the brand of Christianity prevalent among the Gallic populace at large – Catholicism.[17] So for inhabitants of the Frankish sub-kingdoms of the sixth century, as already for residents of the Gothic

12. Ibid.
13. James, *The Franks*, 58–63.
14. Greg. Tur., *Hist.* 2.31; *Epistulae Austrasicae* 2.
15. Fredegar, *Chron.* 2.4–6, 3.2, 9.
16. For Frankish legends, see Wood, *Merovingian Kingdoms*, 33–38; Geary, "Barbarians and Ethnicity," 124–25.
17. Avitus of Vienne, *Ep.* 46; Greg. Tur., *Hist.* 2.31. For dating Clovis's baptism, it is advisable to rely on contemporary sources rather than on Gregory. See Danuta Shanzer, "Dating the Baptism of Clovis: The Bishop of Vienne vs the Bishop of Tours," *Early Medieval Europe* 7 (1998): 29–57.

and Burgundian realms in the late fifth, one cannot speak properly of ethnically distinct Romans and "barbarians."

According to new models of ethnogenesis, ethnicity becomes less a matter of biology than one of selected identity.[18] For example, small-scale farmers from late fifth-century Pannonia and Moesia who tossed fortune to the wind and joined Theodoric the Great on his campaigns into Italy by 493 would have changed identity from "Roman" to "Goth."[19] Thus, mentions of ethnicity in legal sources such as the word "Burgundian" in the Burgundian law code would pertain not to a culture distinguishable from the "Romans" but rather to individuals participating in the military.[20] Otherwise, litterateurs could use the term "barbarian" rhetorically to denote a person with a "barbaric" penchant for violence, or a "barbaric" persistence in heresy, or even one who used "barbarous" speech.[21]

So why maintain the term "barbarian," as I do in the subtitle of this chapter? In something of a nostalgic spirit akin to that sometimes expressed in the rhetoric of our sources, the present study will use "barbarian" (e.g., preceding "era" or "Gaul") to connote a century-and-a-half long period when Western kings were supplanting imperial rule and replacing each other. Some have used the term "sub-Roman" to denote these years, but that term even more than "barbarian" may be read to suggest a concept of cultural "decline and fall," which many scholars have abandoned for the aforementioned notion of "transition."[22]

---

18. Walter Pohl with Helmut Reimitz, eds., *Strategies of Distinction: The Construction of Ethnic Communities, 300–800*, TRW 2 (Leiden: Brill, 1998).
19. Patrick Amory, "Names, Ethnic Identity, and Community in Fifth- and Sixth-Century Burgundy," *Viator* 25 (1994), 5.
20. Ibid., 3.
21. Patrick Amory, "Ethnographic Rhetoric, Aristocratic Attitudes and Political Allegiance in Post-Roman Gaul," *Klio* 76 (1994), 440–47.
22. See Glen W. Bowersock, "The Vanishing Paradigm of the Fall of Rome," in idem, *Select Papers on Late Antiquity* (Bari: Edipuglia, 2000), 187–97; and Richard Gerberding, "The Later Roman Empire," in *The New Cambridge Medieval History*, vol. I, *c. 500-c. 700*, ed. Paul Fouracre (Cambridge: Cambridge University Press, 2005), 25–26. However, for arguments in favor of maintaining the "fall," one relying principally upon archaeology and a second upon military narrative, see respectively, Bryan Ward-Perkins, *The Fall of Rome and the End of Civilization* (Oxford: Oxford University Press, 2005); and Peter Heather, *The Fall of the Roman Empire: A New History of Rome and the Barbarians* (Oxford: Oxford University Press, 2006). Likewise, see Peter Heather, "The Western Empire, 425–476," in *The Cambridge Ancient History*, vol. 14, *Late Antiquity: Empire and Successors, A.D. 425–600*, ed.

Others prefer "late ancient," but that term properly refers to a more extensive period stretching further back than the fifth century. More than a decade ago, when the scholarly notion of Late Antiquity still was "in the making," one study offered the adjective "barbarian" to demarcate Gallic society in the fifth century, with forays into adjacent decades.[23] The present work likewise maintains the designation, but it will focus upon a later range of years, the latter fifth through the end of the sixth centuries. These years constitute a period of foundation and stabilization of Western realms, which it is perhaps more appropriate to call "barbarian" rather than "Germanic."[24] One cohesive feature for the time frame under review is a prolonged effort on the part of Gallic aristocrats to increase their control over local society. Even before the establishment of independent kingdoms, Gallic landed nobles had begun to concentrate their efforts on improving their local position. Disruption caused by migrations and subsequent creation of smaller political units with regularly "shifting frontiers" denied Gallic magnates the benefit of participating in Roman imperial service. Aristocrats, particularly to the south, clung tenaciously to traditional "defining" practices such as land management and literary pursuits.[25] For example, after his homeland came under the control of Burgundians and then Visigoths, the aristocrat and former imperial office holder Sidonius Apollinaris continued to communicate with fellow nobles and impress them by publishing books of letters and poetry in an elegant Latin style. A century later, the Italian-born poet Venantius Fortunatus composed books of verse extolling the nobility of fellow socially prominent Gauls. The careers of Sidonius and Fortunatus represent another grand feature of the Barbarian era, the preeminence of Christian leadership. Like many

A. Cameron, B. Ward-Perkins, and M. Whitby (Cambridge: Cambridge University Press, 2000), 1–32, esp. at 18–30.

23. Ralph W. Mathisen, *Roman Aristocrats in Barbarian Gaul: Strategies for Survival in an Age of Transition* (Austin: University of Texas Press, 1993).

24. On the inadequacy of terms such as "Germans" or "Germanic" for describing barbarians of the Migration Age, see Walter Goffart, *Barbarian Tides: The Migration Age and the Later Roman Empire* (Philadelphia: University of Pennsylvania Press, 2006), 1–12.

25. For aristocratic survival strategies, see Walter Goffart, *Barbarians and Romans (A.D. 418–584): The Techniques of Accommodation* (Princeton, NJ: Princeton University Press, 1983); and especially Mathisen, *Roman Aristocrats in Barbarian Gaul* (op. cit.).

other ambitious men they became bishops. From the fifth century on, acquiring episcopal office became a principal means by which aristocrats maintained and augmented local influence.[26] Sidonius, Fortunatus, and others used their literary talents to promote fellow ecclesiastical aristocrats' efforts at social empowerment. Not only did Fortunatus pen songs extolling episcopal virtues; he also composed books to convince fellow Christians that God preordained saintly bishops to hold their influential posts. Even more profuse in hagiographical output was Fortunatus's patron and friend, Bishop Gregory of Tours, who wrote multiple tomes that presented the miraculous deeds and extolled the dedication and faith of dozens of Christian martyrs and confessors, most of them from Gaul. Presiding over a diocese in the Loire valley and writing toward the end of the sixth century, Gregory's depiction of a Gaul overrun with Christian shrines does not constitute the wishful thinking of a bishop living on some cultural periphery; instead, it rather accurately attests to the virtual completion of a process of widespread Christian saturation that had been largely accomplished a century earlier.[27] Thus, mine is not the Barbarian Gaul of those who once perceived the region divided into two culturally distinct zones – a southern "Roman" and northern "Frankish" Gaul.[28] Neither is it a "frontier" land brimming with

26. Claudia Rapp, *Holy Bishops in Late Antiquity: The Nature of Christian Leadership in an Age of Transition* (Berkeley, Los Angeles, and London: University of California Press, 2005), 194.
27. See Yitzhak Hen, *Culture and Religion in Merovingian Gaul, A.D. 481–751* (Leiden, New York, and Cologne: Brill, 1995), 7–18. Recent critical analyses of funerary inscriptions, including graffiti, indicate that Gallic and Spanish saints cults were likely even more numerous and varied than previously imagined; Mark A. Handley, *Death, Society and Culture: Inscriptions and Epitaphs in Gaul and Spain, AD 300–750*, BAR International Series 1135 (Oxford: Archaeopress, 2003), 164. Likewise, archaeology on remains of edifices such as the early fourth-century basilica of Saint Peter outside Autun attests to the early presence of Christian sacred spaces distinct from pagan topography, and calls into question the survival of large pagan shrines beyond the third century; Bailey Young, "Sacred Topography: The Impact of the Funerary Basilica in Late Antique Gaul," in *Society and Culture in Late Antique Gaul: Revisiting the Sources*, ed. Ralph W. Mathisen and Danuta Shanzer (Aldershot and Burlington, VT: Ashgate, 2001), 169–86.
28. Pierre Riché, *Education and Culture in the Barbarian West, Sixth through Eighth Centuries*, trans. by John J. Contreni (Columbia, SC: University of South Carolina Press, 1976), 177–83. This is not to deny that differences, most subtle but some pronounced, between north and south persisted, such as a greater degree of stability for southern aristocrats than for northern ones in the fifth and sixth centuries; Guy Halsall, *Settlement and Social Organization: The Merovingian Region of Metz* (Cambridge: Cambridge University Press, 1995), 33–39. Chris Wickham, *Framing the Early Middle Ages: Europe and the Mediterranean, 400–800* (Oxford and New York: Oxford University Press, 2005), 181, while acknowledging the greater strength of southern aristocracies, downplays any notion of a

prominent pagans stalwartly persevering among masses of "half-Christian" peasants.[29] Rather, this Barbarian Gaul is a thoroughly Christianized social entity suitable for investigation as such. Analysis will prejudice sources pertaining to a Gallic "heartland" consisting of Neustria, Burgundy, Aquitaine, Provence, and western Austrasia. It will not rely on evidence from peripheral zones such as Thuringia and Frisia.[30] While I acknowledge the merits of regional studies that have highlighted local distinctions and emphasized societal shifts in different places at different moments, nevertheless, I contend that Gaul, from Arles to Vienne to Trier to Nantes, constitutes a region viable for scholarly analysis by virtue of its deep-seated cultural unity.[31] This viability applies especially for the topic upon which the present study will focus: the *milieux* of non-elites.

I propose to investigate how participants in diverse groups mostly ranking below aristocrats fared in affecting their own strategies to survive and even prosper. While the study takes into account recent literature pertaining to archaeological and material evidence, the sources upon which it chiefly relies are narrative texts, especially history and saints' lives. Scarcely any modern analysis of Gallic society could stand without reference to hagiographical works, for saints' lives make up

---

serious north-south socio-political disparity, opposing what he calls "the north Frankish meltdown theory." Wickham, ibid., 43–44, 675–76, divides Gaul ecologically into a Mediterranean zone reaching up to around Lyons, and a northern zone with economic activity akin to that for England and northern Germany. Still, he estimates that Gallic physical topography never seriously impeded communications or an ability to establish political control over "the whole territory from the Rhine to the Pyrenees"; ibid., 43.

29. Valerie Flint, *The Rise of Magic in Early Medieval Europe* (Princeton, NJ: Princeton University Press, 1991), 47; and see Ramsay MacMullen, *Christianity and Paganism from the Fourth to Eighth Century* (New Haven: Yale University Press, 1997). Once widespread interpretations of the interment of burial objects as evidence for the presence of pagan "Germans" fearful of death being active in Gaul through the sixth century have been soundly rejected; Bonnie Effros, *Merovingian Mortuary Archaeology and the Making of the Early Middle Ages* (Berkeley, Los Angeles, and London: University of California Press, 2003), 80–85, 133, 147.

30. Even Gaul's peripheral zones, however, are suspected of having been Christianized earlier than what once was believed – e. g., Thuringia in the sixth century; Ian Wood, *The Missionary Life: Saints and the Evengelisation of Europe, 400–1050* (Harlow, UK: Longman, 2001), 9.

31. Excellent regional studies include Patrick Geary, *Aristocracy in Provence: The Rhone Basin at the Dawn of the Carolingian Age* (Philadelphia: University of Pennsylvania Press, 1986); Halsall, *Settlement and Social Organization: The Merovingian Region of Metz*; Matthew Innes, *State and Society in the Early Middle Ages: The Middle Rhine Valley, 400–1000* (Cambridge: Cambridge University Press, 2000).

much of the surviving literature for the age.[32] They also contain many references to people from the lower social echelons. It is therefore most fortunate that recent generations of scholars have reaffirmed hagiography's worth as a historical source. Into the mid-twentieth century, many historians valued saints' lives only to the extent that they might squeeze from such texts a few facts that might be added to some grand narrative. An earlier scholarly willingness to dismiss literature about saints stemmed in part from an elitist presupposition that powerful late ancient people only wrote miracle stories to appease a superstitious *populus*. But a modern revolution of sorts in interpreting late ancient hagiography has turned this assumption on its head, emphasizing instead how upper-class persons fostered saints' cults and composed saints' lives partly to improve their control over society. Two features that scholars following Peter Brown have accepted as fundamental to late ancient society are "the predominance of the holy man" and the establishment of episcopal *potentia*.[33] Regarding the latter, analysis of Gallic saints' lives, notably those from Gregory of Tours' corpus, reveals how bishops did not simply inherit power from absentee Western emperors; rather, ecclesiastical prelates worked hard to establish their authority.[34] One element in the augmentation of episcopal power was control of saints' cults, which became formidable institutions in the fifth and sixth centuries.[35] By then, the *locus* of divine power in the Mediterranean world had shifted from average people, objects, and institutions to a few exceptional humans – especially martyrs, bishops, and anchorites.[36] The ascetic

---

32. See Thomas F. X. Noble and Thomas Head, *Soldiers of Christ: Saints and Saints Lives from Late Antiquity and the Early Middle Ages* (University Park, PA: Pennsylvania State University Press, 1995), 1–50.

33. Peter Brown, *Society and the Holy in Late Antiquity* (Berkeley, Los Angeles, and Oxford: University of California Press, 1982), 103–52. On Brown's influence and impact, see, e.g., the dozen essays contained in James Howard-Johnston and Paul Anthony Hayward, eds., *The Cult of Saints in Late Antiquity and the Middle Ages: Essays on the Contribution of Peter Brown* (Oxford and New York: Oxford University Press, 1999). While all of the contributors say how they have benefited from Brown's work and a few of the articles are panegyrical, several articles offer poignant criticisms of the scholar's methods and conclusions.

34. Ibid., 246.

35. For the rising importance of saints' cults selected from sample cities spread about all Gaul, see Hen, *Culture and Religion in Merovingian Gaul*, 82–120.

36. Peter Brown, *The Making of Late Antiquity* (Cambridge, MA, and London: Harvard University Press, 1978), 11–12.

lifestyle of the anchorite, and afterward the monk, was so distinct that he became the "friend of God" *par excellence*.[37] In the West, deceased saints assumed the dominant position among Christian guardian angels and spirits.[38] It was asserted that a martyr's *praesentia* was to be found in his or her corpse or remains.[39] Martyrs' relics were argued to contain divine power – *potentia* – and prominent ecclesiastics who possessed them wielded this *potentia* too.[40] Furthermore, should anyone receive some benefit from this power – for example, should one be cured of some illness at a saint's tomb – he would become indebted to the saint in terms of a patron–client relationship.[41]

It is analyses of changes to the social ordering in the late ancient West that have inspired the present study. Part and parcel of Peter Brown's realization of the value of saints' lives as a source was the denial of a once-common assumption that Christian reverence for grave and corpse was the creation of credulous and superstitious masses, which ecclesiastical elites reluctantly accepted. Brown's contrary view, that socially prominent Christians introduced the cult of saints "from above" to dominate their communities, caused questioning of another assumption, that late ancient Western societies possessed "two tiers," one a "learned elite" and the other "popular."[42] Brown's theory was met with widespread support and complaint.[43] One appeal for maintaining a "two-tiered" model points out how ancient and medieval authors them-selves, from Cicero to Origen to Guibert of Nogent, recognized two

---

37. Ibid., 81–101.

38. Peter Brown, *The Cult of the Saints: Its Rise and Function in Latin Christianity* (Chicago: University of Chicago Press, 1981), 56; idem, *Society and the Holy in Late Antiquity*, 166–95. While Western rev-erence for dead saints was dominant, it was not complete. On the perseverance of Western "living saints," see Joan M. Petersen, "Dead or Alive? The Holy Man as Healer in East and West in the Late Sixth Century," *Journal of Medieval History* 9 (1983): 91–98.

39. Brown, *Cult of the Saints*, 86–105.

40. Ibid., 106–27.

41. Ibid.; 113; John H. Corbett, "The Saint as Patron in the Work of Gregory of Tours," *Journal of Medieval History* 7 (1981), 1–13.

42. Brown, *Cult of the Saints*, 12–22, 121.

43. For support, see, e. g., Luce Pietri, *La ville de Tours du IVe au VIe siècle: Naissance d'une cité chré-tienne* (Rome: École française de Rome, 1983), 485–86; and J.-M. Wallace-Hadrill, *The Frankish Church* (Oxford: Clarendon Press, 1983), 78. For criticism, see especially Jacques Fontaine, "La culte des saints et ses implications sociologiques. Réflexions sur un récent essai de Peter Brown," *Analecta Bollandiana* 100 (1982), 37–38.

tiers in religious thought.[44] Another defense of "two tiers" asserts the existence of an elite culture, the ideals of which were advanced primarily by prominent ecclesiastics, at odds with a popular culture epitomized by "peasant masses."[45] Jacques Le Goff imagined that proponents of ecclesiastical culture intentionally refuted folkloric culture usually through heavy-handed methods such as destroying pagan temples, superimposing Christian over pagan rituals, and adulterating folkloric themes with Christian meanings.[46] In contrast to these aggressive measures, Le Goff characterized ecclesiastical participation in saints' cults as an instance of elites "co-opting" an element of popular culture to advance their own agenda, that being to evangelize the masses.[47] A thesis that occupies something of a middle ground between Brown and Le Goff by emphasizing a sharing of responsibility for the operation of saints' cults is that of Raymond Van Dam, who posits that it is misleading to conceive of autonomous elite and popular cultures and then speculate on which influenced the other. Van Dam suggests it would prove more fruitful for scholars to investigate the interactions among individual people and social classes.[48] Incorporating anthropological techniques into studies focusing particularly upon inhabitants of sixth-century Touraine, he perceives members of the community to have developed a "collective consciousness" out of a multiplicity of images of its patron, Saint Martin, which images originated from both ecclesiastical leaders and commoners.[49] While Van Dam's methodology serves as a laudable balance against Brown's heavy emphasis on struggle between members of different social classes participating in the cult of saints, I would suggest caution lest one overemphasize concepts such as diplomatically generated "consensus" and "collective consciousness." For Barbarian

---

44. Alexander Murray, "Peter Brown and the Shadow of Constantine," *Journal of Roman Studies* 73 (1983), 201.
45. Jacques Le Goff, *Time, Work, and Culture in the Middle Ages*, trans. by Arthur Goldhammer (Chicago: University of Chicago Press, 1980), 154–55.
46. Ibid., 157.
47. Ibid., 156–57.
48. Raymond Van Dam, "Images of Saint Martin in Late Roman and Early Merovingian Gaul," *Viator* 19 (1988), 17–18.
49. Ibid., 18.

Gaul was an honor-based, violent society whose participants commonly made use of coercion:

> Actually, in most honour-structured societies … a man's value is assessed according to his ability to multiply interventions in the social scene and then to extend the cycle of social exchanges, such as marriage, funerals, banquets, and donations to church and monasteries. The more he participates actively, visibly and successfully in these social events, the more he will be approached for and with advice, contributions and rewards. In so doing, he not only gains material income, but he also brings about the growth of symbolic capital. Among these social interactions, the function of violence seems crucial.[50]

In such a violent world, changes frequently resulted from intimidation and force as individuals of means achieved social objectives through bald displays of strength and imposing rituals of power.[51] One needs only think of Clovis's dramatic production of the burial of King Childeric: the massive burial mound, the display of grave goods teeming with symbolism of Roman and barbarian leadership, the surrounding horse graves, the attendant dinners and distribution of gifts. Per the king's design, this pageantry enabled Clovis to appear so formidable that he was able to gather allies and sustain his father's

---

50. Nira Gradowicz-Pancer, "De-Gendering Female Violence: Merovingian Female Honour as an 'Exchange of Violence,'" *Early Medieval Europe* 11.1 (2002), 6. As will be seen, Gallic women also participated in these exchanges. On early medieval honor and vengeance, see Julia H. Smith, *Europe after Rome: A New Cultural History, 500–1000* (Oxford and New York: Oxford University Press, 2005), 100–14. Smith, ibid., 101, comments that *Pactus legis Salicae*'s mentions of various spoken insults "suggest a world of touchy pride that turned on women's sexual propriety and men's aggressive valour."

51. On Gallic violence, see Mathisen, *Roman Aristicrats in Barbarian Gaul*, 139–43; and Wolf Liebeschuetz, "Violence in the Barbarian Successor Kingdoms," in *Violence in Late Antiquity: Perceptions and Practices*, ed. H. A. Drake (Aldershot and Burlington, VT: Ashgate, 2006), 37–46, both of whom contend that the Merovingian era was more violent than the late Roman period. Walter Pohl, "Perceptions of Barbarian Violence," in ibid., 15–26, acknowledges Gallic violence, but he is not inclined to speculate on one age's being more brutal than another. Neither is Guy Halsall, "Violence and Society in the Early Medieval West: An Introductory Survey," in *Violence and Society in the Early Medieval West*, ed. Guy Halsall (Woodbridge: Boydell, 1998), 1–45. On the role of rituals in establishing power and confirming social relationships, see Frans Theuws, "Introduction: Rituals in Transforming Societies," in *Rituals of Power: From Late Antiquity to the Early Middle Ages*, TRW 8, ed. Frans Theuws and Janet T. Nelson (Leiden, Boston and Cologne: Brill, 2000), 1–13, especially at 8–9.

kingdom-building momentum, and thus he set the stage for more than two centuries of Merovingian dominion.[52] In a society where endless competitions for social distinction predominated, pronouncements of "consensus" coming from Gallic authors are as likely to have been misleading as was their rhetoric about uncouth "barbarians." For example, a foreign, newly elevated and unpopular bishop might quickly proclaim that his new locale's saint has accepted him as leader, and he might even convince himself that the community has welcomed him too, only to discover years after the fact that his imagined consensus was something of an illusion; in fact, a hostile faction had been biding its time, awaiting an opportune moment to strike against the episcopal interloper. Such was the predicament for none other than Gregory of Tours early in his episcopacy.[53] Thus in communities across Barbarian Gaul, consensus could be a will o' the wisp.

Building upon a base of remarkable scholarship, from Brown to Van Dam and Mathisen and beyond, I perceive that what a study of Gallic society needs is a more rigorous analysis of the aspirations and actions of people from all social quarters, but especially those situated toward society's bottom.[54] It has been four generations since Sir Samuel

---

52. Halsall, "Childeric's Grave, Clovis' Succession," 129–30. Halsall, ibid., 121–22, 129, also interprets the "exceptional nature of Childeric's burial" to reflect the pressure and difficulty Clovis faced as he attempted to succeed his father in a politically unstable environment.

53. The leader of clerical resistance against Gregory at Tours was an archdeacon named Riculf, who was passed over for Gregory as bishop. See William C. McDermott, "Felix of Nantes: A Merovingian Bishop," *Traditio* 31 (1975), 10–13. Alternatively, perhaps Gregory was aware of the precariousness of his situation throughout his first seven years as bishop, and so his talk of consensus was completely rhetorical. For conflict abounding behind texts extolling the "rhetoric of concord," see Walter Pohl, "The Construction of Communities: An Introduction," in *The Construction of Communities in the Early Middle Ages*, TRW 12, ed. Richard Corradini, Max Diesenberger, and Helmut Reimitz (Leiden and Boston: Brill, 2003), 6.

54. Principal inspirations for this monograph include Brown, *The Cult of the Saints* (op. cit.); Van Dam, *Saints and their Miracles in Late Antique Gaul* (Princeton, NJ: Princeton University Press, 1993); Mathisen, *Roman Aristocrats in Barbarian Gaul* (op. cit.). Of course, important work on non-elites has already begun in earnest. For relations among Western haves and have-nots, see Peter Brown, *Power and Persuasion in Late Antiquity: Towards a Christian Empire* (Madison: University of Wisconsin Press, 1988); and idem, *Poverty and Leadership in the Later Roman Empire* (Hanover, NH: Brandeis University Press/University Press of New England, 2002). For a presentation of sources showing Western people of all ranks active in various social contexts, see Ralph W. Mathisen, *People, Personal Expressions, and Social Relations in Late Antiquity*, 2 vols. (Ann Arbor: University of Michigan Press, 2003). See further the excellent bibliographical compilation by Lukas Amadeus Schachner, "Social Life in Late Antiquity: A Bibliographical Essay," in *Social and Political Life in Late Antiquity*, Late

Dill attempted a similar feat for an English reading audience. Writing eighty years ago (1926), Dill exhibited an interest in persons from the lower echelons of Gallic society that scarcely surpassed the virtually complete indifference some Gallic letter writers offered social inferiors. As the introductory quote for this chapter attests, Dill concluded that the historian's dismissal of "the quiet, dim life which flows on in silent, monotonous toil beneath the glare and tumult of great tragedies and triumphs" was "natural."[55] As if to prove Dill's statement, many in the past few decades have performed yeoman's work in reconsidering the "imposing characters" of Western societies, Gaul included.[56] Of course, we would attribute the preponderance of recent studies on late ancient aristocrats less to some innate human propensity than to a logical "leaping at the chance" for scholars to utilize universally available, exceptional biographical compendiums of magnates and social elites, especially the *Prosopography of the Later Roman Empire (PLRE)*.[57] But no amount of scholarly revision for Gallic society can be complete without a reconsideration of persons from the lower social ranks. Questions must be asked anew for them as well. Just who exactly were the people whom some have denied, either wholly or in part, a meaningful contribution to the cult of saints? Did there exist below multiple aristocracies a homogeneous group whom scholars may appropriately characterize as the "superstitious masses"? How would an effort to consider the opportunities and socially advantageous actions of individuals within different groups of the so-called "popular tier" affect an understanding of Gallic society?

Antique Archaeology 3.1, ed. W. Bowden, A. Gutteridge and C. Machado (Leiden and Boston: Brill, 2006), 41–93.

55. Dill, *Roman Society in Gaul in the Merovingian Age*, 235.

56. On late ancient aristocrats, see, e. g., M. T. W. Arnheim, *The Senatorial Aristocracy in the Later Roman Empire* (Oxford: Clarendon, 1972); John W. Matthews, *Western Aristocracies and Imperial Court, A.D. 364–425* (Oxford: Clarendon, 1975); Michele R. Salzman and Claudia Rapp, eds., *Élites in Late Antiquity, Arethusa* 33.3 (Baltimore: Johns Hopkins University Press, 2000). For Gaul, see, e. g., Brian Brennan, "Senators and Social Mobility in Sixth-Century Gaul," *Journal of Medieval History* 11 (1985): 145–61; Frank D. Gilliard, "The Senators of Sixth-Century Gaul," *Speculum* 54 (1979): 685–97; and Mathisen, *Roman Aristocrats in Barbarian Gaul*.

57. A. H. M. Jones and J. R. Martindale, eds., *The Prosopography of the Later Roman Empire*, vol. 1, *A.D. 260–395* (Cambridge: Cambridge University Press, 1971); J. R. Martindale, ed., *The Prosopography of the Later Roman Empire*, vol. 2, *A.D. 395–527* (Cambridge: Cambridge University Press, 1980); idem, ed., *The Prosopography of the Later Roman Empire*, vol. 3, *A.D. 527–641* (Cambridge: Cambridge University Press, 1992).

What would become of the "two-tiered" model if one were to discover that important social behaviors and activities among people from Gaul's various social ranks differed only by a matter of degrees? And finally, how might one go about attempting to address such questions?

GOALS OF THE BOOK

I explore aspects of the situation of people who were not part of the power structure of Barbarian Gaul, but who nevertheless had an impact on society. I propose to begin my approach to Gallic society in a manner that rather emulates those scholars who have been reconsidering ethnicity, by taking an initial step of suspending assumptions of duality: "elite" versus "popular," "Roman" versus "barbarian."[58] Otherwise, I shall construct a social model that is in keeping with recent research and based on a firm textual foundation.[59] To borrow from Ian Wood borrowing from Peter Brown: "It is necessary to reconstruct microcosms. Individual microcosms can then be compared synchronically and diachronically with other microcosms, thus building up a more inclusive picture."[60] This study essentially will constitute the first part of Wood's

58. On the inadequacy of thinking in terms of polarities when assessing late ancient societies, see Peter Garnsey and Caroline Humfress, *The Evolution of the Late Antique World* (Cambridge: Orchard Academic, 2001), 84. One long-lasting and overly dualistic assumption being rejected by recent archaeologists and scholars proposed that the presence of burial goods, commonly found in row grave cemeteries (*Reihengräberfelder*) in northern Gaul, identified the deceased as "Germanic," while an absence of objects, or a presence of inscriptions, indicated the dead to have been "Gallo-Romans." For this tradition and its abandonment in favor of theories that emphasize the role of social strategizing in the production of early medieval funerals, see Effros, *Merovingian Mortuary Archaeology*, 100–110, 192–96. Effros, ibid., 110, writes, "Rather than particular customs being uniquely Gallo-Roman or Frankish, funerary symbolism represented a constantly evolving form of political, social, personal, and religious expression."

59. Two recent works that contain model efforts for constructing social overviews are Smith, *Europe after Rome*, and Innes, *State and Society in the Early Middle Ages*. While the former is broad in scope and the latter a local analysis, both eschew the study of institutions *per se* and instead build their models upon examinations of local patterns and developments in social structuring, community building, and political strategizing. See Smith, ibid., 3–7; Innes, ibid., 4–12. Guy Halsall, "Social Identities and Social Relationships in Early Merovingian Gaul," in *Franks and Alemanni in the Merovingian Period: An Ethnographic Perspective*, ed. Ian Wood (Woodbridge, Suffolk: Boydell, 1998), 141–65, proposes another behaviorally based social model for which individuals look to benefit socially by "playing" one or more aspects of their identities. These include "ethnicity, religious belief, age, gender, family, other 'fictive' kinship group, settlement location, position in a 'vertical' hierarchy of power ('rank' or 'class'), and so on"; ibid., 141.

60. Ian Wood, "Conclusion: Strategies of Distinction," in *Strategies of Distinction: The Construction of Ethnic Communities, 300–800*, ed. W. Pohl and H. Reimitz (Leiden, Boston, and Cologne: Brill, 1998), 301.

method; it will construct a microcosm. One aspect of my development of a model for society thus will be to build around the writings of a singular author, Gregory of Tours. This approach should prove beneficial not only because no text offers more data about the wide array of participants in Gaul than Gregory's, but also because no Gallic author has received the degree of scrutiny from recent historians that the Bishop of Tours has. While the present exercise will privilege the microcosm that is "Gregory's world," nevertheless it also will incorporate data from other literary sources, mostly clerical writings. The heavy ecclesiastical slant of the surviving evidence will direct the reader's attention frequently to behavior at churches, especially activities involving saints' cults, but other aspects of life will also be explored. Additional context will come from taking into account recent scholarship on Gallic epigraphic and material evidence. Data from epigraphy and material remains can be used to corroborate, or challenge, evidence from literary texts, and it can reveal aspects of society that literary sources do not address.[61] Otherwise, the present microcosmic exercise will benefit from incorporating insights from several recently available macrocosmic studies of early medieval Europe that have synthesized recent scholarship utilizing literary, documentary, and archeological evidence.[62]

In some respects, this study was initially envisioned as a complement to Ralph Mathisen's *Roman Aristocrats in Barbarian Gaul*. That tome addressed the variety of ways that fifth-century aristocrats strove to remain atop society as Gaul passed from imperial to barbarian control.[63] Mathisen identified aristocratic strategies, including acquiring high church office, establishing elite identity through literary studies, serving in barbarian governments, and even adopting violence as a means of "self help." My reading of *Roman Aristocrats* has caused me to question,

61. Mark A. Handley, "Beyond Hagiography: Epigraphic Commemoration and the Cult of the Saints in Late Antique Trier," in *Society and Culture in Late Antique Gaul: Revisiting the Sources*, ed. Ralph W. Mathisen and Danuta Shanzer (Aldershot and Burlington, VT: Ashgate, 2001), 188, 196; Patrick Périn, "Settlements and Cemeteries in Merovingian Gaul," in *The World of Gregory of Tours*, ed. Kathleen Mitchell and Ian Wood (Leiden, Boston, and Cologne: Brill, 2002), 89.

62. E. g., Smith, *Europe after Rome*; Matthew Innes, *Introduction to Early Medieval Western Europe*; Wickham, *Framing the Early Middle Ages*.

63. For Mathisen, *Roman Aristocrats in Barbarian Gaul*, xi, the "fundamental question" is: "What kinds of conscious and positive responses did the resident Romans make to the changes in their world?"

and to try to discover, how non-elites of that transitional age might have developed strategies to cope and/or prosper. Again, because a greater amount of literary evidence about people of low rank survives within more sixth-century sources than fifth, I deemed it necessary to situate the present study approximately a century after the period analyzed by Mathisen. Having done so, it turns out that this study is now able to complement a more recent offering by the same author, *People, Personal Expression, and Social Relations in Late Antiquity.* In that work, Mathisen offers more than 100 extended excerpts from 70 sources, the selections intended to illustrate features of, and changes within, late ancient Western societies.[64] Mathisen selects numerous passages that reveal how "nonelite groups, be they the less socially privileged, the economically disadvantaged, or those marginalized because of their ethnicity or gender, were able to find niches of opportunity provided by the changing times."[65] The present study has adopted much the same goal of illuminating the social stratagems and possibilities for social achievement of various inhabitants of Gaul; however, it pursues this end through a methodology more akin to that used in *Roman Aristocrats.* Ultimately, this study relies upon interpretations of collective biographical data extracted from literary sources. Regarding collective biography, as Alan V. Murray has succinctly put it, "The aim of prosopography is to compile accurate data on a defined group – that is, a set of individuals – and to interrogate this data with the objective of illuminating our understanding of a particular historical society."[66] Undeniably, when it comes to "illuminating" late ancient societies, prosopography best serves analyses of social elites, especially, for example, when one has at hand a myriad of noble names with which to reconstruct social networks.[67]

---

64. Mathisen, *People, Personal Expression, and Social Relations,* 2: 1.
65. Ibid., 1: 3.
66. Alan V. Murray, "Prosopography," in *Palgrave Advances in the Crusades,* Helen Nicholson, ed. (Basingstoke and New York: Palgrave Macmillan, 2005), 109.
67. See, e. g., Ralph W. Mathisen, *The Ecclesiastical Aristocracy of Fifth-Century Gaul: A Regional Analysis of Family Structure,* PhD diss. (University of Wisconsin, 1979; repr. Ann Arbor, MI: University Microfilms, 1980); Christian Settipani, "L'apport de l'onomastique dans l'étude des généologies carolingiennes," in *Onomastique et Parenté dans l'Occident médiéval,* ed. K. S. B. Keats-Rohan and C. Settipani (Oxford: Occasional Publications of the Unit for Prosopographical Research, 2000), 185–229. For historiography on late ancient prosopography and methodological suggestions, see

But as Robert Kaster's masterful analysis of grammarians demonstrates, worthwhile prosopographical studies of late ancient groups whose members were not mostly aristocratic can result.[68] As for the present study, two chapters (Seven and Eight on Physicians and Enchanters, respectively) employ a prosopographical approach; Chapter Seven even draws heavily on material from *PLRE*. As for other chapters, although they rely upon analysis of collective biographical material, the analytical exercise admittedly cannot be termed prosopography so much as interpretation of case studies. Still, not a small amount of the evidence derived for use throughout this work has been selected from biographical entries contained in the *Biographical Database for Late Antiquity* project.[69] Even material pertaining to groups (e.g., a band of prisoners liberated during a saint's festival) might have been derived from a "group entry" (anonymous group: prisoners) relating "biographical data" (released from jail by a saint). This data is susceptible to analysis with collective biographical material about other individuals and groups who share common characteristics.

The prosopographically based methodology for this study shares with prosopography proper two assumptions: (1) that one can extract accurate biographical data from text, and (2) that this data can be used to craft a meaningful representation of people engaged in certain behaviors in a past society. These assumptions require some comment in an era of ongoing debate about the relationship between text and past reality.[70] I acknowledge that no text constitutes a perfect mirror of

the collected articles in Averil Cameron, ed., *Fifty Years of Prosopography: The Later Roman Empire, Byzantium, and Beyond* (Oxford: Oxford University Press, 2003).

68. Robert A. Kaster. *Guardians of Language: The Grammarian and Society in Late Antiquity* (Berkeley and Los Angeles: University of California Press, 1986).

69. On the flexibility of the computer-based Biographical Database for Late Antiquity, and on applications, see Ralph W. Mathisen, "Creating and Using a Biographical Database for Late Antiquity," *History Microcomputer Review* 5.2 (1989): 7–22; and idem, "La base de données biographique pour l'antiquité tardive," in *Onomastique et Parenté dans l'Occident médiéval*, ed. K. S. B. Keats-Rohan and C. Settipani (Oxford: Occasional Publications of the Unit for Prosopographical Research, 2000), 262–66.

70. Walter Pohl, "The Construction of Communities," 2, in the introduction to the twelfth offering for the TRW series, writes: "the old model of the text as a simple mirror of objective reality has been superseded, even as the impulse of the linguistic turn is beginning to fade." Averil Cameron, "History and the Individuality of the Historian," in *The Past before Us: The Challenge of Historiographies of Late Antiquity*, ed. Carole Straw and Richard Lim (Paris: Brepols, 2005), 73–74, comments on the lack

the past, and neither can a scholarly social model make such a claim, this one included. But that does not mean that social historians should not offer their best efforts at composing representations of past realities. In attempting to do this, I try to remain ever cognizant of the difficulties that accompany retrieving social data from texts. It is important to assess the reliability and suitability of particular texts for obtaining certain kinds of information. One must take account of circumstances that might cause an individual author to be more or less forthcoming with different sorts of data. I have tried to be aware of the *mentalités*, social and political circumstances, social agendas, and literary techniques of the writers whose texts are being analyzed.[71] It is with this in mind that, again, I have purposefully designed this study to hinge upon what I argue to be a solid foundation, the voluminous text of a *mentalité* with which I and others strive to be very intimately familiar, the writings of Gregory of Tours.[72]

The investigation begins in Chapter Two with a consideration of the sources, most of which originated from the hands of ecclesiastical aristocrats. This chapter will note how control of written evidence by the powerful, especially clerics, makes understanding the situation of non-elites harder. Be they writers of legislation, letters and poems, sermons or saints' lives, aristocratic litterateurs used their writings to promote agendas complementary to their theologies and beneficial to their social order, families, and selves. This chapter will point out certain obstacles that arise from a dependence upon written sources. Nevertheless, it also will justify how scholars can regard certain passages within these texts as viable for extracting reliable biographical data.

---

of theory coming out of the TRW books in particular and out of European studies on late antiquity in general. She is more optimistic about prospects for theory from North America. On contingencies of text with past, and of today's historians' theories with their own circumstances, see the other contributions in the same volume. Likewise, for further suggestions on scholarly directions utilizing theory, see also Elizabeth Clark, *History, Theory, Text: Historians and the Linguistic Turn* (Cambridge, MA, and London: Harvard University Press, 2004), 156–85.

71. Ian Wood, "Continuity or Calamity?: The Constraints of Literary Models," in *Fifth-Century Gaul: A Crisis of Identity?* ed. John Drinkwater and Hugh Elton (Cambridge: Cambridge University Press, 1992), 9–18.

72. See the discussion in Chapter Two between pp. 62 and 63.

Chapters Three and Four will advance a multi-layered model for representing Gallic society. Chapter Three will address Gallic aristocrats and aristocracies. It begins with a presentation of two elitist visions of how society should be devised, one based on law and the other on literary works. While Salic lawmakers intended a society devoid of a hereditary nobility and centered upon people's reliance on royal courts for institutional privileges, elite Gallic litterateurs envisioned maintaining and strengthening aristocratic identities. Despite differences, the perceptions contained in the legal and literary sources concur in their producers' desire for society to be hierarchical. That it was, but Gallic society was complicated by aristocratic participation in fierce factionalism and competition for patronage, and by the persistent efforts of ambitious social inferiors. Furthermore, despite harboring elitist sensibilities, aristocrats were not averse to allowing social advancement for individuals on the lower end of society, especially their own clients and protégés. Chapter Three will present a model (continued throughout Chapter Four) that reflects how Gallic society in the Barbarian era was fluid within a recognizably hierarchical paradigm. This model will emphasize how individual enterprise affected social structure as people from all ranks "played" the system. The chapter will examine how members of Gallic noble families participated in multiple aristocracies. They maintained and improved their social situation by marrying and by combining material resources, acquiring prestigious posts at royal courts, and becoming involved in prestigious activities at church. Chapter Four will address how individuals from the lower social ranks improved socially by engaging in similar strategies. Regardless of whether they were free people with considerable properties, paupers or slaves, many humble Gauls followed well-trodden secular social stratagems, attempting to improve upon their condition by marrying and/or by becoming soldiers or court functionaries. The best evidence for people of low ranks' seeking a more meaningful and/or socially advantageous lifestyle pertains to persons affiliated with churches. It was a varied lot that joined the growing ranks of clerics and ascetics. Chapter Four will conclude that the resultant model shows that the most relevant divide among participants in Gallic society was not some ostensible barrier between aristocrats and "the rest."

To consider in greater detail how less socially powerful Gauls strategized to succeed in the Barbarian age, Chapters Five through Eight will address four distinct groups whose members enjoyed various degrees of social opportunity and success. The seemingly eclectic groups have been selected in part because each is well represented in the written sources, especially saints' lives. Chapter Five examines the most passive (temporarily at least) among society's participants, a group that was powerless to do anything but appeal to patrons: prisoners. Gaul's inmates almost always originated from the lowest socio-economic strata. Some were fortunate to obtain a new lease on life by participating in the "ritual of miraculous release," one of several means by which leaders of clerical establishments displayed social authority and amassed clients. Chapter Six considers a broad, economically disadvantaged group, *pauperes* active at churches. This large but rather well-delineated throng included small farmers, lowly urban laborers, and beggars. Among these, those most closely associated with churches were the registered poor and low-level clerics. The *pauperes* of this chapter found refuge, and otherwise strove to cause positive change in their lives by associating closely with prominent ecclesiastics and saints.

Chapters Seven and Eight will examine the lively contest for authority among Gaul's healers. Chapter Seven's consideration of physicians dispels erroneous notions about Gallic aristocrats harboring negative attitudes toward doctors. The chapter begins by establishing a context; it offers a prosopographical consideration of physicians in the late ancient world. It then shows how doctors in Gaul enjoyed prestige and were able to prosper by plying their craft. Not unlike many physicians throughout the late ancient Mediterranean, Gallic doctors mostly were of "middling" status; they were very literate and highly skilled in their area of expertise and they could demand high prices from a well-to-do clientele. Despite the presence of literary passages (especially from Gregory of Tours) that relate clerical concerns about people seeking physical remedies from physicians instead of saints, this chapter concludes that there was no rivalry between these two kinds of healer. Chapter Eight addresses the efforts of *incantatores*, mostly folk healers and diviners, whom clerical authors commonly demeaned as *malefici*. Despite frequently being demonized in clerically inspired literature, and although some endured censure in the form of expulsion and even exorcism, these healers persisted in their endeavors, especially in rural districts where Gallic residents deemed their attention a necessity. The chapter concludes that many *incantatores* shared the same social predicament as their predominantly impoverished clientele, while a few enjoyed a modicum of prestige and wealth. Furthermore, enchanters were Christians, not pagans.

Chapter Nine offers concluding remarks that in effect argue that subsequent studies of Gallic society need to offer the same rigorous regard for persons of the lower social echelons that scholarship presently confers upon aristocrats. An exacting examination of the socially less privileged reveals that any theory that attempts to separate late ancient people into "elite" and "popular" tiers is overly general and errant. In the end, this book aims to offer an accurate and meaningful model for the way various elements of Gallic society may be effectively analyzed.

EVIDENCE AND CONTROL

CHAPTER TWO

"[Martin's] relatives were not the lowest in worldly terms, but nevertheless were pagans."
SULPICIUS SEVERUS, *Vita Sancti Martini* 2.1.[1]

"Then the highest dignity was advanced [upon Martin], so although [he seemed] poor by his clothing, contemptible by his tunic, he was like a senator in his heavenly seat."
VENANTIUS FORTUNATUS, *Vita Sancti Martini* 3.51–52.[2]

The written sources for Barbarian Gaul are numerous, varying according to genre and the individual litterateurs' agendas. One unifying feature for nearly all surviving literature of the age is composition by upper class persons, especially ecclesiastics. This control of written evidence by a sub-group among the powerful makes an understanding of the situation of non-elites problematic. This chapter will begin by considering briefly the variety among available sources and the difficulties they pose for the

---

1. Sulp. Sev., *Vita Martini* 2.1 (*CSEL* 1, 111): "parentibus secundum saeculi dignitatem non infimis, gentilibus tamen."
2. Ven. Fort., *Vita Martini* 3.51–52 (*MGH*, AA 4.1, 331): "processit tum summus honor, sed pauper amictu, despectus tunica, caelesti in sede senator."

study of society. Because personal aspirations and social agendas were peculiar even among the narrow group of literarily active ecclesiastics, and because single authors expressed themselves by writing in multiple genres, the last part of the chapter will examine in greater detail the literary production of four writers: Avitus of Vienne, Caesarius of Arles, Venantius Fortunatus, and Gregory of Tours. The careers of these litterateurs cover the full span of the Barbarian era, and so this exercise will provide a brief but cohesive narrative for the period under review.[3] More importantly, it will reveal how writing constituted an element of the strategies by which powerful people attempted to fashion society to their advantage.

Sources and Aristocrats

The principal written genres that survive for Gaul include letters, poetry, hagiography, historiography, doctrinal texts, and legislation.[4] Two endeavors maintained by upper class Gauls throughout the Barbarian era were letter writing and poetry. Authors produced epistles in part to convey a sense of continuity with the Roman and Christian past. By writing letters, Gauls could imagine themselves operating in the classical tradition of Cicero, Pliny, and Symmachus, and the Christian tradition of Paul, Augustine, and Jerome. Likewise, by composing poetry, they could perceive themselves imitating not only Virgil and Horace but also the Psalmist and Prudentius. Both letter writing and poetry provided opportunities for litterateurs to show off their rhetorical abilities, a skill that held especial significance for Gauls, because their region once bore a reputation as a cradle for rhetoricians.[5] In the fourth century, the emperor Theodosius I had filled educational posts as far as Constantinople with graduates from the schools of Gaul. The greatest Gallic rhetorician was

3. For concise narratives covering much the same timeframe, see Raymond Van Dam, "Merovingian Gaul and the Frankish Conquests," in *The New Cambridge Medieval History*, vol. 1, *c. 500–c. 700*, ed. Paul Fouracre (Cambridge: Cambridge University Press, 2005), 193–231; and Innes, *Introduction to Early Medieval Western Europe*, 265–313, with bibliography at 303–11.

4. See Guy Halsall, "The Sources and Their Interpretation," in *The New Cambridge Medieval History*, vol. 1, *c. 500–c. 700*, ed. Paul Fouracre (Cambridge: Cambridge University Press, 2005), 56–90, for an overview of late ancient literary, documentary, and archaeological sources.

5. Hagith Sivan, *Ausonius of Bordeaux: Genesis of a Gallic Aristocracy* (London and New York: Routledge, 1993), 74–93.

Ausonius of Bordeaux, whom Emperor Valentinian I invited to the imperial capital at Trier to tutor the prince Gratian. When Gratian assumed his imperial rule in 367, Ausonius used the court connection to enhance his standing even more. He supplemented his family's recently achieved nobility with prestigious imperial posts for himself, relatives, and friends. Ausonius's literary efforts at familial and self-promotion included mention of his origins in a *Gratiarum Actio* delivered publicly at Gratian's court, and independently of that a series of commemorative poems, the *Parentalia*, dealt in detail with the author's own relations.[6] The example of Ausonius's ostentatious literary production to proclaim before aristocratic peers that he belonged in society's highest echelons offered a behavioral model that powerful Gauls would not forget.

As opportunities to climb the imperial *cursus honorum* waned in the fifth century, upper-class Gauls clung tenaciously to literary pursuits, especially correspondence.[7] Senatorial aristocrats and their descendents formed literary circles so that through their epistles, writers might maintain an identity as members of the most prominent social rank. Aristocrats fostered solidarity through letters and poetry that emphasized friendship, *amicitia*. The most significant epistolary circle of the fifth century was a group centered about the erudite Sidonius Apollinaris, Bishop of Clermont (ca. 469–ca. 480). As Sidonius exchanged letters of *amicitia* with fellow aristocrats, his region fell under the control successively of Burgundians and Visigoths. His 148 epistles are crucial for revealing how Gallic aristocrats initially reacted to the establishment of the barbarian kingdoms.[8] Informative for the subsequent generation are the letters and poems of two relatives of Sidonius. The first, Bishop Ruricius of Limoges (ca. 485–ca. 510), wrote his epistles (83 survive) when it seemed the Visigoths would remain the supreme power in Gaul,[9] while the second, Avitus, Bishop of Vienne (ca. 495–ca. 518),

6. Ausonius's poetry offers the most detailed genealogical stemma for any Gallic aristocratic family; see ibid., 49–73.
7. Mathisen, *Roman Aristocrats in Barbarian Gaul*, 105–18.
8. W. B. Anderson, ed. and trans., *Sidonius, Poems and Letters*, 2 vols., Loeb Classical Library (Cambridge, MA, and London: Harvard University Press, 1936–65).
9. Ralph W. Mathisen, *Ruricius of Limoges and Friends: A Collection of Letters from Visigothic Gaul*, TTH 30 (Liverpool: Liverpool University Press, 1999).

composed letters (96 survive), poems, and homilies during the apogee of Burgundian royal fortunes.[10] Recent considerations of Ruricius's and Avitus's correspondence have debunked an errant picture of Gallic society continually beset by "marauding barbarians," the latter image being partly a result of past scholarship placing too much credence in Sidonius and earlier fifth-century writers' opining, and too readily interpreting their ethnic rhetoric as evidence for a society actually divided into "conquering barbarian" and "despondent Roman" groups.[11] Throughout the sixth century, not only the heirs of large landowning families, but also upwardly mobile magnates active in royal courts, wrote letters and poetry in a florid Latin style to convince peers that they too possessed an air of nobility. The *Epistulae Austrasicae*, a late sixth-century collection of 48 letters by multiple authors, seems to have been a production of the Austrasian court at Metz. It attests to the continuing significance of letter writing for the Gallic powerful.[12]

Like letter writing and poetry, hagiography is a genre, or more properly a "multiplicity" of genres, which aristocrats dominated from its inception in Gaul.[13] The first and most influential Gallic saint's life was the *Life of Saint Martin* by Sulpicius Severus. In the last decades of the fourth century, the provincial aristocrat Sulpicius became mesmerized by the activities of the apocalyptic, ascetic thaumaturge Martin, who despite becoming Bishop of Tours in 371 continued a monastic regimen at the monastery of Marmoutiers. Even before Martin's death

---

10. Danuta Shanzer and Ian Wood, *Avitus of Vienne: Letters and Selected Prose*, TTH 38 (Liverpool: Liverpool University Press, 2002).

11. Much of Ruricius of Limoges' correspondence can be read to suggest that for aristocrats in late fifth-century Aquitaine under the Visigoths, "life went on." This very amicable state of affairs would change only toward 507 as the Franks approached; Ralph W. Mathisen, "The Letters of Ruricius of Limoges and the Passage from Roman to Frankish Gaul," in *Society and Culture in Late Antique Gaul: Revisiting the Sources*, ed. Ralph W. Mathisen and Danuta Shanzer (Aldershot and Burlington, VT: Ashgate, 2001), 101–15.

12. Wood, *Merovingian Kingdoms*, 26.

13. Late ancient writings about saints served a variety of functions, liturgical and otherwise. A hagiographical work could be used to promote a saint's cult, to encourage a particular kind of pious behavior, to legitimize a church or monastery's claim to property, or to present a political or theological viewpoint. See Ian Wood, "The Use and Abuse of Latin Hagiography in the Early Medieval West," in *East and West: Modes of Communication*, ed. Evangelos Chrysos and Ian Wood (Leiden and Boston: Brill, 1999), p. 93–109, quoted at 93.

in 397 Sulpicius, influenced by Athanasius of Alexandria's seminal hagiographic portrayal of Anthony of Egypt, decided to commemorate in literature the wonderworking deeds of the *apostolus Galliarum*, Martin. Sulpicus wrote the *Life* and supplementary *Dialogues* (ca. 400) about Saint Martin in a fluent style of Latin intended to impress upper-class confreres. While the *Vita Martini* constitutes a principal stylistic model for subsequent western hagiography, Sulpicius's Gallic imitators in the sixth century abandoned his literary pretensions, opting instead to write in a simpler style akin to the general spoken Latin, so that their message could influence a broader audience.[14] Most subsequent Gallic writers of *Lives* also differed from Sulpicius in that their preferred subjects were native Gauls with aristocratic pedigrees. For example, two early saints' lives from the region are the *Vitae* of Germanus of Auxerre and Geneviève of Paris. Around 475, Constantius, a priest of Lyons, wrote a *Life* about Germanus, a general in Roman imperial service, perhaps *dux tractus Armoricani et Nervicani*, who by virtue of his title would have possessed senatorial status.[15] In 418, the people of Auxerre, likely taking advantage of the protection a politically connected former military officer could afford in a potentially disruptive age, swiftly elevated Germanus to priest and then bishop (418–ca. 448). Constantius's text assured the people of Auxerre that their patron's *potentia* would continue to protect the community, as evidenced by miracles occurring about Saint Germanus's corpse.[16] A second distinguished Gaul who became the object of a cult was Geneviève of Paris. Geneviève's suitability for a *Vita* was predicated in part by her apparent senatorial origins; judging by the names of her parents, Severus and Gerontia, the family might have participated in the same ecclesiastical faction as Germanus of Auxerre.[17] Interestingly, in addition to depicting Germanus supporting the young

14. Richard Collins, "Observations on the Form, Language and Public of the Prose Biographies of Venantius Fortunatus in the Hagiography of Merovingian Gaul," in *Columbanus and Merovingian Monasticism*, ed. H. B. Clarke and M. Brennan (Oxford: BAR, 1981), 107–08.
15. Constantius of Lyons, *Vita Germani* 2; *PLRE* 2, 504, s. v., "Germanus 1."
16. Constantius of Lyons, *Vita Germani* 45.
17. Martin Heinzelmann and Joseph-Claude Poulin, *Les Vies anciennes de sainte Geneviève de Paris: Études critiques* (Paris: Librairie Honoré Champion, 1986), 81–86; Allen E. Jones, "The Family of Geneviève of Paris: Prosopographical Considerations," *Medieval Prosopography* 24 (2003): 73–80.

woman's leadership efforts in and about Paris, the *Vita Genovefae* also portrays an aged Geneviève still pursuing her family's role as the locale's premier patron during the Frankish ascendancy.[18] Like Constantius of Lyons, the anonymous author of the *Vita Genovefae* (composed ca. 520) invited readers and listeners to accept the notion that a deceased socially prominent figure was capable of acting as the community's patron. As hagiographical production increased throughout the sixth century, a high percentage of the *Lives*' commissioners, composers, and saints would remain aristocrats.

As they were with hagiography, aristocrats were also the producers of Gaul's historical writings. Scholars once drew a sharp distinction between hagiography and history, but increasingly this is not the case.[19] Beginning more than a century ago, historians tended to dismiss writings that pertained to saints for being fraught with *topoi* and for failing to address what to their minds were more "significant" matters than miracles – that is, politics and state-building. More recently, historians look to accomplish more than merely build political narratives. They also have come to realize how the composition of saints' lives, especially late ancient ones, did not occur without political and social considerations; so, given careful analysis, these writings may prove "historically" valuable as sources for episodes of local disputes and resolution.[20] Similarly, it now is recognized that late ancient "historical" narratives, including both histories and chronicles, are neither primarily "political" nor can their apparently factual material be taken at face value. Gallic chroniclers, for example, regularly included certain details in their texts, and excluded others, according to whether the information was supportive or

---

18. Geneviève and Germanus: *Vita Genovefae* 2–6, 11; Geneviève and the Franks: 26, 35, 56.
19. Felice Lifshitz, "Beyond Positivism and Genre: 'Hagiographical' Texts as Historical Narrative," *Viator* 25 (1994), 95–113, identifies the present concept of "hagiography" as a nineteenth-century construct, and she assesses the application of a modern distinction between "hagiography" and "history" to early medieval composers to be anachronistic and unhelpful.
20. Paul Fouracre, "Merovingian History and Merovingian Hagiography," *Past and Present* 127 (1990): 3–38. See also Thomas Pratsch, "Exploring the Jungle: Hagiographical Literature between Fact and Fiction," in *Fifty Years of Prosopography: The Later Roman Empire, Byzantium, and Beyond*, ed. Averil Cameron (Oxford: Oxford University Press, 2003), 59–72, who marshals evidence to demonstrate that the presence of *topoi* and authorial bias need not mean that certain passages within hagiographical texts do not contain historical information.

harmful to their theological leanings.[21] For present purposes, it suffices to note here that chroniclers and historians of Barbarian Gaul were few, and, not surprisingly, they were prominent ecclesiastics.

Another genre dominated by aristocrats was doctrinal writings, by which texts authors both promoted theological positions and furthered ecclesiastical agendas. In the days of Germanus of Auxerre and Geneviève's parents, a theological matter over which Gallic ecclesiastical aristocrats quarreled fiercely was the reception of an Augustinian interpretation of grace and free will. Opponents of a dominant faction of writers that perceived Augustinian predestination as a "foreign" theology belittled the independent-minded group by misleadingly associating their beliefs with that of a condemned heretic, Pelagius. Popes such as Leo I the Great (440–461) also opposed the so-called "Semi-Pelagians," and so, not surprisingly, the very Gauls who were trying to thwart the "foreign" theological intrusion also were opposing papal interference in Gallic ecclesiastical matters. This entwined nature of theology and church politics, which consumed the minds of powerful Gallic bishops, betrays an "ecclesiastical aristocratic" character to the tracts that promoted one side or the other of such debates.[22] While sixth-century theological disputes do not appear to have been as heated as those of previous years, contests of words continued, for example, as in the increasingly lopsided debate between ultimately triumphant Nicene and eventually moribund Arian interpretations of the godhead.[23] The very aristocrats

21. Ian Wood, "Continuity or Calamity?: The Constraints of Literary Models," in *Fifth-Century Gaul: A Crisis of Identity?* ed. John Drinkwater and Hugh Elton (Cambridge: Cambridge University Press, 1992), 14–15.

22. For the theology, see Rebecca Harden Weaver, *Divine Grace and Human Agency: A Study of the Semi-Pelagian Controversy* (Macon, GA: Mercer University Press, 1996). For the complementary ecclesio-political infighting, see Ralph W. Mathisen, *Ecclesiastical Factionalism and Religious Controversy in Fifth-Century Gaul* (Washington, DC: Catholic University Press, 1989).

23. See, e.g., Greg. Tur., *Hist.* 6.40, 9.15. Gregory of Tours neither narrated nor commented about the Three Chapters, a sixth-century controversy initiated in Byzantium with the intent to reconcile eastern and western Christians over lingering differences of opinion about the nature(s) of Christ. One mid-century Gallic prelate seemingly interested in the matter was Nicetius of Trier, who penned a letter to Justinian and interestingly mistook the emperor's position to be that Christ had one fully human nature; *Epistulae Austrasicae* 7. On the enduring impact that a haphazard nature in the dissemination of theological ideas especially from Rome had for Gallic prelates attempting to participate in the Mediterranean discourse, see Ian Wood, "The Franks and Papal Theology, 550–660," in *The Crisis of the Oikoumene: The Three Chapters and the Failed Quest for Unity in the Sixth-Century Mediterranean*, ed. Celia Chazelle and Catherine Cubitt (Turnhout: Brepols, 2007), 223–41.

who penned politically charged theological pamphlets also hashed out debates at church councils, from whence a victorious party attempted to impose its will upon Christian communities by promulgating canons.

Whether legal sources were sacred or secular, law as a written medium was a production of upper-class authors. On the secular side, a significant development in fifth- and sixth-century legislation was the public commissioning of law codes. The principal Roman codes are the *Theodosian Code*, first issued at Constantinople in 438 by Theodosius II, and the more ambitious *Justinian Code*, published in 534.[24] By the latter date, rulers of Gaul's barbarian states had begun commissioning codes for their own realms. Kings emulated the imperial practice of promulgating written law in part to impress upon their subjects an air of political legitimacy, a necessary precondition if they were to secure effective control over newly conquered lands and establish an orderly society. The Visigothic King Euric (ca. 466–484) produced the first barbarian legal compilation, the *Codex Euricianus*, while his successor Alaric II (484–507) commissioned in 506 the so-called *Breviarium Alaricianum*, the main part of which preserves legislation from the *Theodosian Code*.[25] In 517, the Burgundian ruler Sigismund (516–523) published the *Liber Constitutionum*, sometimes wrongly called the *Lex Gundobada*.[26] Before this, probably between 507 and 511, Clovis published the *Pactus legis Salicae*, a Frankish legal compendium the original of which probably consisted of sixty-five titles.[27] While several revised editions of *Pactus legis Salicae* followed in the Merovingian age, individual laws recorded early on tended not to change. This benefits our purposes in that the code reads today as it would have applied throughout the sixth century. But the legislative process in Gaul was not static; rather, kings regularly

---

24. Into the twentieth century, scholars traditionally interpreted codification as evidence for a decline in Roman legal practice and Roman culture in general. More recent scholarship about late ancient codes offers a more positive assessment. One recognizes, for example, that the Theodosian Code did not "petrify" Roman law so much as it served a corrective purpose, providing "a starting point for legal and forensic deliberations." See Garnsey and Humfress, *The Evolution of the Late Antique World*, 52–82, quoted at 60.

25. Wolfram, *History of the Goths*, 193–97.

26. Wood, *Merovingian Kingdoms*, 10–11, 51–52.

27. Katherine Fischer Drew, trans., *The Laws of the Salian Franks* (Philadelphia: University of Pennsylvania Press, 1981), 57–167; Ian Wood, *Merovingian Kingdoms*, 108–15.

supplemented and revised the legal corpus by publishing edicts. Extant examples from Salic law were commissioned by Clovis's many sons and grandsons.[28] Tellingly, kings often published secular legislation in tandem with the promulgation of new church law, the latter being a process dominated by the clerical establishment. While Gallic bishops of the mid-fifth century had enjoyed an era of unprecedented liberty, able to produce church legislation free from royal and papal involvement, kings in the sixth century, not bishops, actually summoned church councils, just as emperors continued to do in Byzantium.[29] Nevertheless, Gallic monarchs almost certainly convened councils at the prompting of bishops, and episcopal motives early influenced some secular constitutions.[30] Therefore one should regard the composition of both secular and church law as emerging in an atmosphere of general cooperation between secular and ecclesiastical magnates.

Given the predominance of an aristocratic hand in the surviving literature, it follows that the content of most of our sources will reflect the values of people with high rank, especially prominent ecclesiastics. Regarding letters, for example, nearly every surviving epistle was written by and addressed to an aristocrat. Litterateurs widely dispersed across Gaul maintained contact by attaching epistles to poems, gifts, and even the books they swapped. Writers sent letters along with clients whom they commended to one another. A principal concern for the illustrious correspondents was to overcome the distance separating them and maintain solidarity. Some letters consist of lengthy displays of nothing more than rhetorical pretension, while others are very short, just a sentence.[31] What mattered most was that writers kept in touch; the intent of friendship letters has been likened to that of Christmas cards.[32]

---

28. Wood, *Merovingian Kingdoms*, 102–08.

29. Sixth-century bishops also needed kings to help enforce canonical decisions, sometimes to the prelates' consternation. In 573, bishops attending the Council of Paris condemned the uncanonical elevation of a certain Promotus as bishop of Châteaudun, but King Sigibert refused to enforce the ruling, and so Promotus was able to maintain his episcopal dignity until the king's death; Greg. Tur., *Hist.* 7.17.

30. *PLS* 65b, a constitution included in the original Salic code, concerns burning churches, an obvious clerical concern.

31. E.g., Ruricius of Limoges, *Ep.* 2.5.

32. Shanzer and Wood, *Avitus of Vienne: Letters*, 60.

As with the letters they wrote, aristocrats also composed poems, in part to encourage a sense of unity. While some poems were meant to be read privately, others – namely, panegyrics – were to be read aloud to proclaim a dignitary's merit, and even to convince an assembled crowd that an individual belonged among society's leaders. One occasion at which a Gallic writer might use a composition to promote the social significance of powerful friends and patrons was a church dedication. Public readings of poetic descriptions of religious edifices and prose dedication sermons accompanied the opening of churches. Given the scant amount of archaeological remains from Barbarian Gaul, these productions are helpful for imagining how Gallic churches actually looked.[33] But such poems and homilies were not intended merely to describe; rather, authors invariably directed the attention of a listening or reading audience to the upper-class founders and benefactors who contributed to the building projects.[34] Composers lauded prominent figures for contributing materials to the construction efforts. These materials constituted the fruits of the labor of the litterateurs' friendship letters, because the resultant churches would provide the very setting where clerical magnates would cause the community to render obeisance. Dedicatory sermons listed powerful ecclesiastics in attendance to impress a public assembly by asserting its patron's connection with other men of resources. For the dedication of the cathedral at Nantes by Bishop Felix, for example, the crowd was "honored" by the presence of five bishops, and according to the author of the dedicatory poem, the assembly high and low ought to have regarded the church builder as a "new Solomon."[35]

In addition to calling attention to distinguished persons, authors used literary media to convince audiences that the rightful kind of patron was one of aristocratic rank. For example, as the introductory quotes for this chapter attest, an interesting phenomenon involving Saint Martin was a refashioning of the saint's image that increasingly conformed to

---

33. Ian Wood, "The Audience of Architecture in Post-Roman Gaul," in *The Anglo-Saxon Church: Papers on History, Architecture, and Archaeology in Honour of Dr. H. M. Taylor*, ed. L. A. S. Butler and R. K. Morris (London: Brill, 1986), 74–79.
34. Ibid., 75.
35. Ven. Fort., *Carm.* 3.6; Wood, "Audience of Architecture in Post-Roman Gaul," 76.

an ecclesiastical aristocratic ideal. In fact, Martin had been the son of a Pannonian soldier, and had himself participated in the Roman military before becoming a monk and then bishop. Martin's first hagiographer, Sulpicius Severus, admitted that his hero's family was not aristocratic; he rather accurately recorded that Martin's "relatives were not the lowest in worldly terms" (*parentibus secundum saeculi dignitatem non infimis*).[36] Sulpicius did venture somewhat into the realm of hyperbole, however. By declaring Martin an *apostolus*, he claimed that spiritual authority in Gaul rested only with him, not with fellow bishops for whom Martin and Sulpicius had little regard.[37] While Sulpicius and Martin apparently cared as little for *episcopalis auctoritas* as they did for *saeculi dignitas*, subsequent patrons of hagiographers were not of such a mind, and so the image of Martin had to change. In the 460s, the senatorial aristocrat Bishop Perpetuus of Tours commissioned Paulinus of Périgueux to write a verse account of Sulpicius's *Vita Martini* and *Dialogi*. In this rendition, the poet adjusted aspects of the saint to conform to his patron's sense of where authority ought to lie – with bishops. Paulinus deemphasized potentially embarrassing features such as Martin's apocalyptic sensibilities and his opposition to other bishops.[38] At the end of the sixth century, another versifier of Sulpicius's *Vita Martini* went a step further in the "aristocratization" of the monk-bishop by omitting any mention of the saint's actual social status and writing instead about how Martin belonged to the "heavenly senate" (*super astra senatus*).[39] Changing images of Martin thus reveal how Gallic writers over time could and did willingly distort past reality to placate sensibilities of contemporary aristocrats.

Yet another potential problem for understanding Gallic society through available sources is indifference on the part of some authors toward diurnal matters. Although epistles and poetry constitute a large part of what survives, rarely did letter writers comment on daily

36. Sulp. Sev., *Vita Martini* 2.1 (*CSEL* 1, 111).
37. E.g., Sulp. Sev., *Vita Martini* 7.7.
38. Van Dam, "Images of Saint Martin," 5.
39. Ven. Fort., *Vita Martini* 2.457 (*MGH*, AA 4.1, 329); and see Van Dam, "Images of Saint Martin," 11.

life.[40] Even for a litterateur who did such as Sidonius Apollinaris, the literary images can be imbued with distorting rhetoric. As has been mentioned, one aspect of Sidonius's writings that scholars once regularly misinterpreted was his ethnic terminology. For example, in one poetic epistle, Sidonius offered a famous description of his unwanted predicament living among the "barbarians": "Placed as I am among long-haired hordes, … praising oft with wry face the song of the gluttonous Burgundian who spreads rancid butter on his hair. … Driven away by barbarian thrumming the Muse has spurned the six-footed exercise ever since she beheld these patrons seven feet high."[41] On the one hand, this passage perhaps betrays a truthful prejudice on the part of the author, who like other late fifth-century aristocrats bristled at the thought of relinquishing some of their lands to newly situated soldiers. But on the other hand, the notion of "smelly barbarians" itself was a fiction drawn from a classical stereotype. The author chose a negative image of uncouth savages not because it accurately depicted the Burgundians, but because it fit a momentary sour disposition caused by the poet's having lost his muse. Conversely, whenever Sidonius was of a different mind, as when once he was in need of royal patronage, he could portray a barbarian king possessing all the qualities of a Roman emperor.[42] Liberal use of stereotypes thus complicates interpretation of what may appear to be depictions of actual social conditions. Another dilemma arises from the fact that Gallic litterateurs used writings not simply to describe events but also to advance broad visions for society at large and to facilitate personal agendas. These schemes were as varied as the authors themselves and therefore need individual treatment. Thus we shall turn now to a consideration of the literary production of four writers to see how singular motives affected what can be known about Gallic society.

40. Shanzer and Wood, *Avitus of Vienne: Letters*, 65–66.
41. Sid. Ap., *Carm.* 12 (Anderson, ed. and trans., 1: 212–13): "… inter crinigeras situm catervas…, laudantem tetrico subinde vultu, quod Burgundio cantat esculentus, infudens acido comam butyro? … ex hoc barbaricis abacta plectris spernit senipedem stilum Thalia, ex quo septipedes videt patronos."
42. Amory, "Ethnographic Rhetoric, Aristocratic Attitudes," 446. See Sid. Ap., *Ep.* 7.9, for a depiction of Euric's court, replete with ancient imagery, intended for one of the king's courtiers from whom Sidonius was seeking a favor.

AVITUS OF VIENNE

Alcimus Ecdicius Avitus was born to a Gallic senatorial family connected to that of Sidonius Apollinaris's. Maintaining bishoprics and other high church office had become regular business for late fifth-century aristocratic families, and Avitus's clan was no different. In 494/96, Avitus succeeded his father as Bishop of Vienne, a metropolitan see in the Burgundian kingdom. Avitus's city endured a siege in 500 when one Burgundian king squared off against another. The victor of the contest was Gundobad (ca. 474–516), a monarch whose legitimacy benefited from his having held high Roman military titles, *magister utriusque militae* and *patricius*.[43] While he was an Arian Christian, Gundobad was noted for his toleration of Catholics; he and Avitus were amicable. Gundobad was arguably the most powerful ruler in Gaul between Clovis's death in 511 and his own in 516.[44] He granted his son Sigismund the title of king during his lifetime. Sigismund converted from Arianism to Catholicism and early patronized the latter confession in 515 by founding the monastery of St. Maurice at Agaune, an occasion for which Avitus composed and recited the dedicatory homily.[45] Avitus's proximity to Gundobad and Sigismund is attested by letters the bishop wrote on behalf of both to foreign dignitaries.[46] Others of Avitus's epistles express his ambition to spread Catholicism, a goal facilitated by Sigismund's sole control of the throne after 516. Sigismund immediately used the law to promote his authority and reorganize the realm. In 517, he commissioned the secular code, the *Liber Constitutionum*, and he convened the Council of Epaon. Avitus presided over this synod and set the criteria for dismantling the Arian church.[47] Avitus probably died on 5 February 518, five years before a Frankish invasion snuffed out the life of Sigismund and the political reality of the Burgundian kingdom.[48]

---

43. *PLRE* 2: 524–25, s. v. "Gundobadus 1."
44. Wood, *Merovingian Kingdoms*, 51.
45. Shanzer and Wood, *Avitus of Vienne: Letters*, 379–81.
46. Ibid., 8.
47. Ibid., 9–10.
48. Ibid., 10. Avitus died in 522 at the latest.

Avitus traditionally is hailed for his poetic works, most notably a five-book Augustinian inspired versification of tales from Genesis and Exodus entitled *On Acts of Spiritual History*, but it is his letter writing and legislation that demand our attention.[49] Typical of surviving Gallic correspondence, Avitus's epistles are addressed to society's most powerful participants: rulers, bishops, and secular aristocrats. Most of his correspondence pertains to ecclesio-political business; notable are several writings on behalf of the Burgundian kings to Emperor Anastasius at Constantinople.[50] Avitus's most famous letter includes the bishop's congratulations to the Frank King Clovis on the occasion of his Catholic baptism.[51] Its subject matter, like that of other epistles, betrays Avitus's most earnest agenda, promotion of the orthodox faith against what was perhaps a momentarily ascendant Arianism. One letter addressed to the Arian Gundobad forcefully argues a Catholic position on the Trinity. It reveals not only the considerable extent of Avitus and the king's theological sophistication but also a high degree of toleration for debate in the Burgundian realm.[52] But Avitus perhaps was less in a mood to haggle about theology than he was in a position to impose it. His principal concern to foster a unified front for the fight against heresy was accomplished in part by adopting an Augustinian theology pertaining to human agency in the matter of salvation. This program ran afoul of Semi-Pelagianism, that independent Gallic position that had remained popular throughout the previous century.[53] Avitus's agenda for Catholic unity also envisioned securing a more effective hierarchical church with the papacy as the unquestionable head. Writings were integral to formulation and implementation of Avitus's vision for a Christian society. Thus he circulated the *On Acts of Spiritual History* among fellow erudite ecclesiastics to coax them toward his preferred Augustinian stance on

---

49. Ibid., 59.
50. Ibid., 141–53.
51. Ibid., 362–73.
52. Ibid., 162–86.
53. Carrying the torch for the still dominant Gallic *via media* between Pelagius and Augustine into the final decade of the fifth century was the aged Bishop Faustus of Riez, author of *De Gratia*; see Weaver, *Divine Grace and Human Agency*, 165–80.

agency.[54] Otherwise, his homilies attest that the Bishop resorted to the increasingly commonplace methods of church building and promotion of saints' cults to enhance his status as a local patron.[55] While Avitus hardly seems as dedicated to the cult of saints as subsequent Gallic ecclesiastics would be, his association with the cult of Peter was a notable exception.[56] Vienne's church of St. Peter had become the usual burial site for the city's bishops, but Avitus himself likely was responsible for promoting devotion to Peter to the point where the apostle's cult became the most popular one in the vicinity.[57] While these building and cultic activities testify to Avitus's general effort to amass prestige at Vienne, his leadership in encouraging reverence for the pope's favorite saint in particular evinces further a design to promote papal authority and orthodoxy in Gaul. When Sigismund ascended the throne, the ambitious prelate wasted no time in plotting the downfall of Arianism. In one letter to Bishop Victorius of Grenoble likely written in 516/17, Avitus broached the potentially sticky topic of what to do with the Arian churches. He advocated restoring Catholic churches that the Arians had taken, but he discouraged converting "tainted" edifices that the Arians had built.[58] Within the year, Avitus was presiding over the Council of Epaon. Its

54. Ian Wood, "Avitus of Vienne: The Augustinian Poet," in *Society and Culture in Late Antique Gaul: Revisiting the Sources*, ed. Ralph W. Mathisen and Danuta Shanzer (Aldershot and Burlington, VT: Ashgate, 2001), 275–76, writes: "[*On Acts of Spiritual History*] could have introduced the reader to an Augustinian reading of Genesis and Exodus, while at the same time providing literary pleasure. Coming at the moment at which the Gallic church opted for an Augustinian stance, Avitus' poetry reflected a mood and had a role to play. This was a particularly pleasurable way to learn one's Augustine ..." Close to this, I suspect that the *Spiritual History* had more of a role in establishing a mood than reflecting one, other than the author's. Weaver, *Divine Grace and Human Agency*, 181, remarks that it is unclear how widespread the Gallic challenge to Faustus would have been at this stage in the debate.

55. Wood, "Audience of Architecture in Post-Roman Gaul," 77–78.

56. Avitus of Vienne, *Ep.* 29, 50.

57. Ibid. Mamertus of Vienne (died. ca. 475) was the first bishop buried in the funerary basilica of Saint Peter connected to the south western extra-mural cemetery. All of the city's bishops would be buried in this church into the eleventh century; Handley, *Death, Society and Culture*, 156. Epigraphic and literary evidence attest that Vienne's late ancient options for burials near saints' relics included cemeteries associated with Gervasius and Protadius, Ferreolus and Julian of Brioude, Peter, and Severus; ibid., 155–60. Mark Handley's comparison of a chronological distribution of epitaphs in Vienne's cemeteries, ibid., 157, suggests that Peter's cemetery had become the most popular by the turn of the sixth century, and esteem for the apostle's cult absolutely skyrocketed from the time of Avitus's episcopal tenure.

58. Shanzer and Wood, *Avitus of Vienne: Letters*, 295–302.

canons reveal how attendant bishops readily adopted almost to the letter the Bishop of Vienne's scheme for dismantling Arian churches.[59] Not only did Avitus's agenda directly affect ecclesiastical legislation, but it might also have influenced secular law. In 517, a case involving a royal courtier prompted further correspondence between Avitus and Victorius in which the two pondered what constituted incestuous marriage.[60] One result of this meeting of the minds was a canon at Epaon (canon 30), but perhaps another was proclamation of a ruling on incest included in the *Liber Constitutionum*.[61] Whether or not Avitus participated in drafting the constitution, its publication reveals how a piece of secular legislation could reflect a matter of ecclesiastical interest at a given moment. The case of Avitus typifies how Gallic ecclesiastics tried to convert their visions for Christian society into a legally based reality, and used writings to do it. Another Gallic litterateur who shared aspects of Avitus's dream for a unified Catholic society was Caesarius of Arles.

Caesarius of Arles

The significance of the literary corpus of Caesarius of Arles for understanding sixth-century Gallic society ranks second only to the writings of Gregory of Tours. But regarding his design for Christian society, Caesarius's vision was closer to that of Avitus. Caesarius hailed from an aristocratic family with estates in the Burgundian kingdom. He became a cleric at Chalon-sur-Saône in 486/87, but after two short years he abandoned his *patria* to become a monk at the prestigious island monastery of Lérins.[62] Caesarius relied on occupational acquaintances and family ties to ascend the clerical ranks. In 499, his relative, Bishop Aeonius of Arles, removed the notoriously ascetic young monk from Lérins and established him as abbot over the men's monastery at Arles. Following Aeonius's death, Caesarius won a heated contest for control of the

59. Ibid., 296.
60. Ian Wood, "Incest, Law and the Bible in Sixth-Century Gaul," *Early Medieval Europe* 7 (1998), 297–98.
61. Ibid., 298.
62. William E. Klingshirn, *Caesarius of Arles: The Making of a Christian Community in Late Antique Gaul* (Cambridge: Cambridge University Press, 1994), 18–23.

prestigious see in 502.[63] For the next forty years, he would attempt to realize an ambitious, and somewhat zealous, vision for Christian society, a design intended to change not just the diocese of Arles but potentially the entire of Gaul. Caesarius's writings constitute an important element of the very reform effort to which they attest.

Upon becoming bishop, Caesarius maintained an ascetic regimen, and he encouraged others of his station to do the same. He intended to turn the southern Gallic episcopacy away from a lifestyle of luxurious and secular pursuits (e.g., hunting, feasting, and doting over church properties), which had accompanied the previous century's growing aristocratic control of the office.[64] This reform reflected the influence of Augustine, as did Caesarius's equally ambitious program to exhort his entire congregation to adopt a monastically modeled behavior including increased prayer, church attendance, almsgiving, and tithing.[65] Among the first of many impediments to Caesarius's ambitions was the fact that his new see belonged to the Arian Visigothic kingdom, ruled by Alaric II. Around 504/05, Alaric acted on a charge that the Burgundian-born prelate was plotting to hand the city over to Gundobad, and he exiled the bishop to Bordeaux. But a year later, Alaric, perhaps cognizant of a need for indigenous aristocratic support in the face of an impending Frankish invasion, released Caesarius. The king further tried to bolster Provençal loyalties by commissioning the *Breviarium Alaricianum* and by requesting that Caesarius preside over a Catholic synod, the Council of Agde (506). Despite the king's efforts to secure his subjects' loyalty, Alaric lost the decisive battle against the Frank King Clovis at Vouillé in 507.[66] For the better part of 508, Franks and Burgundians besieged Arles, but the siege was lifted by the intervention of Ostrogothic soldiers from Italy. Thereafter, Caesarius's see came under the control of Theodoric the Great (reigned 488–526), who restored Arles as the seat of a praetorian prefecture. Although the new monarch was an Arian Christian, having his

63. Ibid., 82–87.
64. William E. Klingshirn, *Caesarius of Arles: Life, Testament, Letters*, TTH 19 (Liverpool: Liverpool University Press, 1994), xiii.
65. Ibid., xiv.
66. Greg. Tur., *Hist.* 2.37.

province rest in the mostly Italian Ostrogothic realm actually facilitated Caesarius's efforts to achieve greater Catholic unity by allowing contact with the pope. In 513, the bishop incurred another treason charge, and so he traveled to Ravenna, where he dazzled Theodoric's court and immediately overcame any suspicion.[67] He then marched to Rome and personally petitioned Pope Symmachus to restore to his authority several Provençal dioceses.[68] This venture initiated a long lasting and fruitful correspondence between Arles and Rome.[69] Not only did the pope support restoration of the dioceses; Symmachus also elevated Caesarius as papal vicar (*vicarius*) of Gaul. Thereafter, the Bishop of Arles alone had the right to wear the *pallium* signifying extra-metropolitan status.[70] Under Ostrogothic rule, Caesarius further advanced his reforms and at the same time extended his authority in Arles by founding new institutions. His best model for fostering "the perfect Christian life" was the women's monastery at Arles, rededicated in 512.[71] Caesarius himself determined the nuns' holy regimen by composing the *Regula ad virgines*, which would prove arguably the most influential rule produced in Barbarian Gaul.[72] The bishop ensured familial control of the socially influential convent by making his sister Caesaria abbess.

Another way by which he tried to realize his vision was by regularly convening church councils. Between 524 and 529, Caesarius presided over synods at Arles (524), Carpentras (527), Orange (529), and Vaison (529). The canons from these synods reflect Caesarius's determination to fulfill his reform agenda. For example, a ruling from the Council of Arles (524) insists that laymen who would enter the higher clergy undergo a one-year probationary period living the life of an ascetic before ordination.[73] When a bishop who himself had signed the canons at Arles improperly elevated a cleric, ignoring Caesarius's stringent standard in the process,

---

67. Cyprian of Toulon et al., *Vita Caesarii* 1.36.
68. Klingshirn, *Caesarius of Arles: Life, Testament, Letters*, 87.
69. Of twenty-five letters that pertain to Caesarius (seven by the bishop, fifteen addressed to him, and three addressed to Gallic bishops and churches), sixteen are exchanges with popes; ibid., 77.
70. Caes. Arel., *Ep.* 8b; Klingshirn, *Caesarius of Arles: The Making of a Christian Community*, 130.
71. Ibid., 104–10, 117.
72. Ibid., 118–22.
73. Council of Arles (524), canon. 2; Klingshirn, *Caesarius of Arles: Life, Testament, Letters*, 100.

the latter encouraged prelates attending Carpentras (527) to forbid the negligent prelate from taking mass for a year.[74] Caesarius sought backing for his zealous vision of an upright clergy by petitioning the papacy to confirm the decision. A letter from Pope Felix IV to Caesarius in 528 did just that and thus attests to the smooth operation of a Roman–Arlésien ecclesiastical machine.[75] Caesarius scored what scholars generally regard as his greatest theological triumph, the defeat of Semi-Pelagianism, at the Council of Orange (529).[76] Before the synod, Pope Felix IV had sent Caesarius a collection of *capitula* detailing Augustinian views on grace and predestination. The bishops at Orange proposed twenty-five canons that read almost verbatim from the papal *capitula*, but the proceedings especially reflect Caesarius's own pastorally motivated theology: "In fact, Orange espoused what Caesarius had preached: Christians have only God to thank for the gifts that they have already received, of faith, forgiveness, and the freedom to do good. They must act on the basis of this grace to attain salvation."[77] But nearly two years later, Pope Boniface II had to send a letter confirming the acts of Orange. This epistle reveals that even at the height of his power Caesarius continued to meet with opposition, and it also attests to the bishop's usual recourse when faced with such a dilemma, to appeal for papal support.[78] In the subsequent decade the Roman–Arlésien connection eroded, as did the Bishop of Arles' tenuous authority. For example, Caesarius failed to convince prelates attending a synod at Marseilles (533) to punish harshly a fellow bishop, Contumeliosus of Riez, who had admitted to sexual misconduct. Furthermore, the errant bishop was able to maintain control of his see by appealing to Pope Agapetus, whose decision contradicted the will of Caesarius.[79] Meanwhile, Clovis's progeny finally managed to set aside internecine bickering and resumed the Frankish

74. Ibid., 122–23.
75. Ibid., 100–02.
76. Klingshirn, *Caesarius of Arles: The Making of a Christian Community*, 141–42.
77. Weaver, *Divine Grace and Human Agency*, 232.
78. Klingshirn, *Caesarius of Arles: Life, Testament, Letters*, 124–27.
79. Klingshirn, *Caesarius of Arles: The Making of a Christian Community*, 249: "In the affair of Contumeliosus we have perhaps the clearest indication of Caesarius's incapacity to impose his own vision of church reform and church order upon his suffragan bishops."

offensive into southern Gaul. As a result, Childebert I, Chlothar I, and Theudebert I partitioned away the Burgundian kingdom in 534.[80] The next year, Emperor Justinian initiated what would constitute the most brutal series of campaigns in Late Antiquity, a twenty-year "re-conquest" of Ostrogothic Italy. The new Ostrogothic king, Vitigis, realizing his inability to battle the Byzantines and maintain control of southern Gaul, ceded Provence to the Franks.[81] Childebert I took control of Arles in 536/37, but unfortunately for Caesarius, parts of his province were distributed between two rulers, Childebert and Theudebert. Thus, although the Bishop of Arles' lands finally rested within realms of Catholic rulers, the change did not prove beneficial to his ecclesiastical authority. Now the aging prelate was merely one of some fifteen metropolitans within the Frankish church, none of whom would be keen to acknowledge Caesarius's claim to primacy in Gaul.[82] Furthermore, the center of the Gallic church now shifted northward as evidenced by the next two general councils convened at Orléans (538 and 541), neither of which Caesarius attended.[83] With his authority reduced to a point where it scarcely reached beyond his own city walls, Caesarius composed a final text, his testament. His will takes the form of a letter, and although it resembles other late ancient wills in that it offers the usual bequeathals, the author's principal purpose for writing the document was to maintain the integrity of the women's monastery, especially against future episcopal interference.[84] Perhaps comforted by the notion that his cherished institution was secure, Caesarius died 27 August 542.

While letters and canons confirm the powerful bishop's efforts to effect change and the strong reactions that they engendered, the impact of Caesarius's reform upon local society is best appreciated through his sermons. As with other Gallic sources, interpreting this evidence is not without difficulties. First, many of Caesarius's sermons contain borrowed material; for example, some derive partly, and others wholly, from

---

80. Wood, *Merovingian Kingdoms*, 51–54.
81. Klingshirn, *Caesarius of Arles: The Making of a Christian Community*, 256.
82. Ibid., 257.
83. Ibid., 258–59
84. Klingshirn, *Caesarius of Arles: Life, Testament, Letters*, 67.

Augustine's sermons among other texts.[85] Second, what survive are not the sermons Caesarius actually delivered to his congregation; instead, they are texts that the bishop edited and sent to clerics as models for recitation in preaching.[86] Third, the sermons include the zealous reformer's rhetoric, and so one cannot imagine them always conveying how people were actually behaving.[87] Despite all this, the sermons, if considered critically, can provide invaluable insights for understanding the thought and behavior for different elements of the bishop's congregation:

> In expressing what he thought his audience agreed with or took for granted, Caesarius's sermons point to the issues on which a consensus existed. In expressing what he thought they disagreed with, they provide evidence of points of dissent. In describing behaviors he disapproved of, they provide evidence of what people were actually doing.[88]

As with other sources, recognizing that Caesarius's sermons project an author's image of society necessitates that one be wary of the text, but it does not preclude an ability to discover valuable information about how society actually functioned. This lesson applies not only to Caesarius's writings but also to writings about him. Around 548, three bishops and two of Caesarius's clerical disciples collaborated to produce a two-book *Life of Saint Caesarius of Arles*, in which the authors portray the prelate not only as the tireless ecclesiastic that he obviously was, but also as a wonder-worker. While some have been quick to dismiss characterizations of prominent ecclesiastics healing others as nothing more than the necessary literary embellishments of hagiographers, the ritualistic behavior behind some miracle stories from Caesarius' *Life* finds solid corroboration in the bishop's preaching about helping the infirm. Tales of Caesarius's wonder-working efforts were not pure fiction, for the bishop's sermons attest that he did advocate trying to heal sickly members of his congregation through prayer, unction, and making the sign of the

85. Klingshirn, *Caesarius of Arles: The Making of a Christian Community*, 11–12.
86. Ibid., 9–10.
87. Ibid., 14.
88. Ibid.

cross.[89] Corroboration of sources – literary, documentary, and material – is a helpful expedient for the social historian attempting to ascertain when a text may be depicting a person's actual behaviors rather than merely offering *topoi*.[90]

VENANTIUS FORTUNATUS

If the Frankish ascendancy signaled an end to effective implementation of Caesarius of Arles' dream, it occasioned a new life for our next litterateur, the poet Venantius Fortunatus. Unlike the other three writers highlighted in this chapter, the exact social status to which Venantius was born is unclear. Given that he received a quality education but that he early on depended on the patronage of others to make his way in life, it has logically been proposed that Venantius's family were middling landowners.[91] There is no way to confirm this, however, so his relations might as well have been provincial aristocrats. Venantius Honoratus Clementianus Fortunatus was born at Duplavis near Treviso in northern Italy probably in the 530s.[92] He received an education in law and rhetoric at Ravenna, which city already had fallen to Justinian, whose generals continued to press against the Ostrogoths until the kingdom succumbed in 555.[93] Venantius's earliest surviving poems presage what would become the poet's lifelong manner of availing his literary talent to ecclesiastical patrons. He lauded a certain Bishop Vitalis, probably bishop of Altinum, in a poem likely recited before a crowd of local dignitaries.[94] Next he commemorated the same bishop's foundation of the church of St. Andrew with verses, which would have ornamented a wall and thereby advertised the patron's dignity.[95] Perhaps it was some personal contact or correspondence between an Italian patron and a

---

89. Ibid., 162–63.
90. Pratsch, "Exploring the Jungle: Hagiographical Literature," 62–64.
91. Dominique Tardi, *Fortunat. Étude sur le dernier représentant de la poésie latine dans la Gaule mérovingienne* (Paris: Boivin, 1927), 27–28.
92. Brian Brennan, "The Career of Venantius Fortunatus," *Traditio* 41 (1985), 50.
93. On Venantius's education, see Judith George, *Venantius Fortunatus: A Latin Poet in Merovingian Gaul* (Oxford: Clarendon, 1992), 20–22.
94. Ven. Fort., *Carm.* 1.1; Brennan, "Career of Venantius," 53.
95. Ven. Fort., *Carm.* 1.2.

Gallic bishop that enabled Venantius to consider striking out for Gaul.[96] With the fall of the Ostrogoths, if the poet intended to seek royal patronage he likely would do so either in Spain or Gaul. Upon the death of King Childebert I in 558, all Frankish lands reverted to a single ruler, Clovis's last surviving son, Chlothar I. After the latter died in 561, his surviving sons divided Gaul among themselves: Charibert, Guntram, Sigibert, and Chilperic.[97] Thus Gaul now had four centers of patronage to attract ambitious characters. To strengthen their political positions, the Frankish kings not only resorted to violence but also ventured to secure diplomatic ties through marriage. In 566, word spread that Sigibert intended to marry the Visigothic princess Brunhild. Perhaps it was the opportunity this wedding presented that enticed Venantius to cross the Alps in 566/67.[98]

Venantius established his reputation in Gaul by singing a celebration song (*epithalamium*) to magnates assembled at Metz for Sigibert and Brunhild's nuptials.[99] Afterward, the poet bandied among the Austrasian aristocracy. This networking resulted in several lasting friendships, including one with Gogo, another literarily adept courtier who later would become tutor for the royal couple's son, Childebert II.[100] Perhaps no one in Sigibert's court offered the lasting or lucrative kind of patronage that the poet sought, or perhaps Venantius simply wanted to consider all options that Gaul might present. Regardless, within the year he abandoned Metz for Paris, site of the court of King Charibert,

---

96. For Nicetius of Trier as the likeliest candidate to have welcomed Venantius to Gaul, see Brennan, "Career of Venantius," 57–58; George, *Venantius Fortunatus: A Latin Poet*, 27. Alternatively, Venantius may have struck out for Gaul to visit the basilica of Saint Martin, as he claimed in his verse *Vita Martini*, in thanks for the saint's having healed him at Ravenna; Ven. Fort., *Vita Martini* 4.630–701. See Handley, *Death, Society and Culture*, 141–42, for epigraphic evidence corroborating the presence of Martin's cult in sixth-century Ravenna.

97. Greg. Tur., *Hist.* 4.22. Political circumstances following Chlothar's demise were complicated. On the king's death, his youngest son, Chilperic, who had a different mother from his siblings, seized the treasury, distributed wealth among aristocrats, and took Paris. Had Chilperic not made this preemptive move, perhaps his half-brothers would have excluded him from the succession. Instead, Guntram, Childebert, and Sigibert forced Chilperic out of Paris and then divided the realm among the four, perhaps not as equally as Gregory of Tours suggested. On the wars of this generation of Merovingians, see Wood, *Merovingian Kingdoms*, 89–93.

98. Brennan, "Career of Venantius," 56.

99. Ven. Fort., *Carm.* 6.1.

100. *PLRE* 3: 541–42.

to whom he delivered a panegyric.[101] But Charibert died suddenly in 567, and so Venantius next ventured through the Touraine, where he likely met Bishop Eufronius, and thence into Poitou. At Poitiers, Venantius discovered two promising patrons, not only a grateful bishop, Pascentius, but also an influential former queen turned nun, Radegund.[102] Radegund had been a Thuringian princess captured in war and married at an early age to King Chlothar I. Disgusted that her mate had killed her brother, Radegund separated from the king and established an abbey peopled with prominent nuns.[103] Perhaps Chlothar's willingness to permit Radegund to pursue her ascetic regimen arose from recognition of the prestige his family might acquire through control of a convent filled with daughters of socially significant families, a principal model being Caesarius's convent under the care of his female relations. Radegund adopted for her nuns the *Regula ad virgines* that Caesarius had composed for the Arlésien abbey. The queen apparently had a good relationship with Bishop Pascentius, who previously held the post of abbot at the city's monastery of Saint Hilary. Venantius lent his literary talent on Pascentius's behalf by associating the bishop's merits with those of the principal Poitevin holy patron, Hilary, and thereby declaring the bishop's spiritual authority.[104] It is uncertain exactly when Venantius became a priest, but perhaps this happened during the episcopacy of the grateful Pascentius.[105] Otherwise, Fortunatus's pen contributed mightily to Queen Radegund's agenda to bolster the prestige of her convent. To this end, Radegund used her royal influence to acquire from Constantinople a piece of the True Cross. This effort demanded delicate diplomacy, including gaining King Sigibert's permission. With that given, a Frankish delegation traveled to the Byzantine capital, where Emperor Justin II and Empress Sophia honored Radegund's request. Granting a piece of the True Cross could have involved strengthening an imperial–Austrasian alliance against the two regimes' common foe,

101. Ven. Fort., *Carm.* 6.2.
102. *PLRE* 3: 1072–74.
103. On Radegund's convent, see Van Dam, *Saints and their Miracles*, 28–41.
104. Ven. Fort., *Vita Hilarii* 1 (*MGH*, AA 4.2, p. 1); Collins, "Observations on the Form, Language, and Public of the Prose Biographies of Venantius," 108.
105. Brennan, "Career of Venantius," 67, thinks this time the most likely.

the Lombards.[106] For his part, Venantius wrote a panegyric conveying thanks to the imperial couple, and he composed hymns, including the famous *Pange lingua* and *Vexilla regis prodeunt*, sung on the occasions of the relic's advent and installation in the convent.[107] Celebrating the arrival of the Cross was problematic, however, owing to the demise of Pascentius and the accession of Bishop Maroveus, an apparent foe of Radegund who would have regarded the queen's presence as a challenge to his religious authority.[108] The new bishop reportedly refused to preside over the relic's installation, and so conducting the ceremony fell to Radegund and Venantius's friend, Bishop Eufronius of Tours.[109]

Despite a seemingly amicable situation at Poitiers, Venantius ventured from his home frequently in the early 570s and availed his literary talents to other ecclesiastical patrons. An enjoyable stay at Bordeaux with Bishop Leontius II (ca. 549–573) and his wife Placidina, for example, resulted in several occasional poems and a lengthy panegyric idealizing the prelate.[110] Time spent with Bishop Domitianus of Angers resulted in the composition of a *Life of Saint Albinus*. This *Vita* reveals much about aristocratic intentions in the composition of hagiography; not only did the episcopal patron direct the production, but he even provided Venantius with a cleric who gathered information for the poet to weave into the text.[111] The *Life of Albinus* typifies Venantius's portrayals of male saints, all of whom were bishops. Venantius depicted each as being predestined to become bishop and as deserving of the community's loyalty and support by virtue of their holding the office. Each *Life* is prefaced with a letter to the episcopal patron who commissioned the work, and whom readers also were expected to regard as being predestined to his

106. Ibid., 62.
107. Ven. Fort., *Appendix carminum* 2; *Carm.* 2.2, 6.
108. The usual negative impression of Maroveus, derived as it is from the viewpoints of Radegund's hagiographers, is likely somewhat unfair. For an estimation of Maroveus's sensitive pastoral side, see Barbara Rosenwein, "Inaccessible Cloisters: Gregory of Tours and Episcopal Exemptions," in *The World of Gregory of Tours*, ed. Kathleen Mitchell and Ian Woods (Leiden, Boston, and Cologne: Brill, 2002), 193–94.
109. Greg. Tur., *Hist.* 9.40.
110. Ven. Fort., *Carm.* 1.16, 18–20.
111. Ven. Fort., *Vita Albini* 1–2.

leadership role.[112] Interestingly, one man would prove to be both patron and subject for Venantius. Bishop Germanus of Paris secured the poet to write a *Life of Saint Marcellus of Paris*, and after the pontiff's death in 576, a successor urged Venantius to compose a *Life of Saint Germanus*. "Fortunatus's hagiography is, then, a case in which the writer, episcopal commissioner, saint, and text are all intimately linked, and the portrait of sanctity in itself mirrors the aspirations and ambitions of that small group of men who directly assist in the production and dissemination of the *Vitae sanctorum*."[113]

What may have been Venatius's greatest boon happened in 573 with the accession of Eufronius's nephew Gregory as Bishop of Tours. Gregory's elevation was not welcomed by all at Tours, and so the new bishop required literary promotion to help convince the Tourangeaux that he was the proper person for the job. Venantius eagerly obliged the new prelate by composing an *adventus* poem for recital upon Gregory's entry at Tours. In addition to heralding Gregory as Saint Martin's choice to direct the faithful, and God's choice too, this poem encouraged members of the community to unite under the bishop's lead.[114] Over the next few years, Venantius composed for Gregory a poetic rendering of Sulpicius Severus's *Life of Saint Martin*. In this work, the poet recast the monk-bishop with an otherworldly senatorial pedigree that conformed to his aristocratic patron's ideal image of the bishop.[115] By 576, Gregory had joined Radegund and Agnes, Abbess of the monastery of the Holy Cross, as one of Venantius's principal patrons. It was Gregory who encouraged Venantius to publish his verses, a feat that resulted in ten volumes, which the poet in turn dedicated to the Bishop of Tours. From these poems, one learns that Gregory presented to Venantius a *villa* and fields along the Vienne River, perhaps located between Tours and Poitiers.[116] Venantius's poems attest to precious moments shared with friends, and thus remind us that not every moment of Barbarian

---

112. John Kitchen, *Saints' Lives and the Rhetoric of Gender* (New York and Oxford: Oxford University Press, 1998), 48–49.
113. Ibid., 49.
114. Ven. Fort., *Carm.* 5.3.
115. Van Dam, "Images of Saint Martin," 11–12.
116. Ven. Fort., *Carm.* 8.19.

Gaul involved violence and mayhem. But they also reveal how much of the poet's literary output was intended to benefit a patron – the poems now helping Gregory cope with one scrape and another – from surviving a treason charge to avoiding paying taxes.[117] When Radegund died in 587, Venantius played an important part in promoting her sanctity by composing a *Life of Saint Radegund*. Upon the death of Maroveus in 591, the episcopal successor at Poitiers was Gregory's archdeacon, Plato. This appointment suggests that Gregory's ecclesiastical influence was strong and growing, especially given that Poitiers did not lie within the metropolitan's province. When Plato died, his successor was Venantius. Unfortunately, dates for Fortunatus's consecration and death cannot be determined precisely; traditional years for his episcopal tenure are ca. 595 to 605. Nor do we know whether Gregory played a part in his friend's elevation, although the late date makes this unlikely.

Venantius's verses provide a much-needed means to contrast the harsh images of Gallic society contained in Gregory's pages. Ironically, a difficulty in using Venantius's writings to understand society arises from the very education that made possible the poet's illustrious reputation. Because of his classical training, Venantius was especially prone to pepper his text, both the prose hagiography and poetry, with rhetoric-laden literary conventions, whether describing aristocrat or pauper.[118] Thus, a considerable portion of any portrait of a holy bishop from one of his *Vitae* consists of stock "saintly" tropes that likely amount to little in the way of evidence for a subject's actual personality.[119] Likewise, the attributes of any bishop presented in one of Venantius's episcopal panegyrics represent idealized features that a commissioning bishop expected the poet to emphasize, and thereby impress an audience. In his occasional verses, Venantius might offer a rare stock characterization for a person of low rank. For example, one poem purportedly details how Sigibert's court once was punting along a river when a cook absconded with the author's boat. The poet wrote, "Did he who snatches food from the flames with

---

117. See the next section about Gregory of Tours.
118. Van Dam, "Images of Saint Martin," 9: "… Fortunatus's poem [*Vita Martini*] made Saint Martin more of a classical than an ecclesiastical and biblical hero."
119. Kitchen, *Saints' Lives and the Rhetoric of Gender*, 25–57.

fiery hand not know to keep faith on the waters and to keep his hands off a boat? Black hearted, smoke-fed, soot-dyed; his face is another cooking pot which his own implements have painted a filthy colour."[120] One can hardly imagine these verses to describe an actual person or event, and even if this incident did actually happen, the poet's casting of the event still constitutes little more than a chance for Venantius to display his skill at "kitchen humor" in the tradition of the Roman satirists.

However, certain among Fortunatus's poems are very well suited for ascertaining behaviors and proclivities among the Gauls, especially socially prominent ones. A number of poems that pertain to figures at court prove useful in revealing aristocratic tastes and attitudes.[121] For example, a panegyric to King Sigibert portrays the ruler as simultaneously a victorious warrior and a lover of peace.[122] The poet's selection of these motifs indicates how these would have been important values among participants at the Austrasian court with its mixture of bellicose secular officials and clerics. Similarly, several poems contain flattering lines intended to supplement aristocrats' efforts at proclaiming their magnanimity, such as pieces written to ornament church walls. Regardless of the extent of the poet's flattery, such works constitute evidence for powerful individuals' engaging in actual socially advantageous behavior, such as building churches and promoting saints' cults.[123] The occasional opportunity to corroborate evidence further enables one to appreciate circumstances and motives and confirm events touched upon in Venantius's poetry and hagiography. For example, Fortunatus's second longest poem is a consolation-lamentation written on the occasion of the demise of Galswintha, sister of Brunhild and Visigothic princess who died (ca. 570) within weeks of marrying King Chilperic.[124] Years

---

120. Ven. Fort., *Carm.* 6.8; Judith George, *Venantius Fortunatus: Personal and Political Poems*, TTH 23 (Liverpool: Liverpool University Press, 1995), 53.

121. Judith W. George, "Portraits of Two Merovingian Bishops in the Poetry of Venantius Fortunatus," *Journal of Medieval History* 13 (1987), 190: "Fortunatus is writing for patrons, if not for friends, and so reflects back to them the characteristics and virtues they pride themselves on, what they consider their achievements …"

122. Ven. Fort., *Carm.* 6.1a; Nira Pancer, *Sans peur et sans vergogne: De l'honneur et des femmes aux premiers temps mérovingiens* (Paris: Albin Michel, 2001), 98.

123. On these actions see the discussion in Chapter Three between pp. 124 and 126.

124. Ven. Fort., *Carm.* 6.5; George, *Venantius Fortunatus: Personal and Political Poems*, 40–50.

later, Gregory of Tours would describe in the *Historiae* how the king himself had garroted the princess.[125] The poet's failure to mention the particulars of Galswintha's death has resulted in what once was a traditional charge of cowardice, which itself accompanied a more general voice of indignation coming from scholars frustrated with Venantius's seeming unreliability as a source for historical nuggets.[126] But now, rather than being used to excoriate the poet, the *De Galsuintha* is recognized as having had a possible propagandistic purpose for its intended listeners, Brunhild and an Austrasian audience. It has been proposed that the piece was meant to foster a shared sensibility between Austrasian Metz and Visigothic Toledo.[127] Although Venantius does not denounce the king, "the pathetic coloring he gives to Galswintha's fate is well suited to win sympathy for her and prepares the ground for a correspondingly negative portrayal, in pro-Austrasian propaganda, of Chilperic's role in the affair."[128] Much of Venantius's corpus attests to how the Poitevin shared with Gregory of Tours a fierce loyalty to the Austrasian regime. While this pair's political agendas largely coincided, the unabashedly celebratory, oft worldly demeanor of so many of Venantius's lines differ markedly from the Bishop of Tours' theologically oriented writings. Another difference arises in that the latter's text affords much more material with which to consider the *milieux* of non-elites, so let us turn now to Gregory.

Gregory of Tours

Georgius Florentius Gregorius was born in 538/39 to a southern Gallic aristocratic family with ecclesiastical connections.[129] On his father Florentius's side, Gregory was related to Bishop Gallus of Clermont (525–551), and by his mother, Armentaria, he was related to Bishops

---

125. Greg. Tur., *Hist.* 4.28.
126. Michael Roberts, "Venantius Fortunatus' Elegy on the Death of Galswintha (*Carm. 6.5*)," in *Society and Culture in Late Antique Gaul: Revisiting the Sources*, ed. Ralph W. Mathisen and Danuta Shanzer (Aldershot and Burlington, VT: Ashgate, 2001), 198–99.
127. Ibid., 311.
128. Ibid.
129. For a brief, informative biography, see Ian Wood, *Gregory of Tours* (Bangor, Gwynedd, UK: Headstart History, 1994), 4–21.

Nicetius of Lyons (551/2–73), Gregorius of Langres (506/7–539/40), and Tetricus of Langres (539/40–72).[130] The paternal family claimed descent from Vettius Epagatus, one of forty-eight second-century martyrs of Lyons, and Gregory asserted that he was related to all but five of his episcopal predecessors at Tours.[131] Because Florentius died while Gregory was but a boy (before age eleven years), the youth acquired his education among clerical relatives. Gregory first resided at Clermont with his father's brother, Bishop Gallus, and then at Chalon-sur-Saône with his mother's uncle Nicetius. Apparently the classical education that southern Gallic aristocrats such as Sidonius Apollinaris and Avitus of Vienne had acquired was no longer available by the 540s. Under relatives and tutors Gregory studied "ecclesiastical writings."[132] This upbringing as much as any other factor would have influenced Gregory's determination to forego a lofty "Sidonian" style of writing for a "rustic" idiom that people from all levels of society could comprehend.[133] Besides simply following in the family business – elder brother Peter had become a deacon at Langres – Gregory's decision to enter the clergy apparently entailed completion of a vow to Saint Illidius of Clermont to become a cleric in the event that he survived an illness.[134] Gregory's text provides numerous expressions of a personal conviction that everyone, like him, should rely upon saintly *potentia*.[135] But this author's stories are not mere literary encouragement; rather, tales about family saints often pertain to actual behaviors his aristocratic kin had been practicing for generations, activities that Gregory fully took to heart.

Gregory's writings reveal a variety of methods whereby ecclesiastical aristocrats established spiritual authority by presiding over saints'

130. For genealogy, see Martin Heinzelmann, *Gregory of Tours: History and Society in the Sixth Century*, trans. Christopher Carroll (Cambridge: Cambridge University Press, 2001), 7–22.
131. Greg. Tur., *Hist.* 1.29, 31, 5.49. On Gregory's claim to be related to most of his predecessors, see Ralph W. Mathisen, "The Family of Georgius Florentius Gregorius and the Bishops of Tours," *Medievalia et Humanistica* 12 (1984), 83–95.
132. Greg. Tur., *VP* 2, *praef.*
133. Helmut Beumann, "Gregor von Tours und der Sermo rusticus," in *Spiegel der Geschichte. Festgabe für Max Braubach zum 10. April 1964*, ed. K. Repgen and S. Skalweit (Münster: Aschendorff, 1964), 69–98.
134. Greg. Tur., *VP* 2.2.
135. Ian Wood, "The Individuality of Gregory of Tours," in *The World of Gregory of Tours*, ed. Kathleen Mitchell and Ian Wood (Leiden, Boston, and Cologne: Brill, 2002), 38.

cults.[136] First, they commemorated cults by regularizing celebrations of saints' festivals. For example, Gregory's father Florentius and paternal uncle Gallus promoted Saint Julian's cult by leading relatives on annual pilgrimages to the church at Brioude, where they celebrated the martyr's festival on 28 August.[137] Second, they built edifices as physical testaments to the family's association with the saints. Thus, when Bishop Gregorius of Langres "realized" that a large sarcophagus that was being revered by country folk outside Dijon was "in fact" the tomb of Saint Benignus, he immediately repaired the vaulting and embellished the crypt, and later, amid the pomp of a clerical assemblage, he transferred the saint's body to a church.[138] This episode represents a blatant aristocratic appropriation of control of an already established sacred space. The addition of buildings and rituals will have helped legitimize and justify, visually and lastingly, the powerful family's seizure and adaptation of the cult.[139] Third, ecclesiastics asserted control over cults and otherwise generally publicized their ability to understand sacred mysteries by proclaiming visions. Thus, Bishop Gregorius was able to convince his congregation of the identity of the aforementioned unknown corpse because, he claimed, Benignus appeared in a dream and told the bishop who he was.[140] Similarly, Armentaria, Gregory's mother, along with two women and a priest, "understood" by way of a vision that an adulterous deacon who could not perform a mass was unable to do so because a hidden sin prevented him.[141] Because this last event happened at a village church at Riom during a ceremony in honor of Benignus's teacher Polycarp, the vision likely constituted part of Armentaria's strategy to introduce the Burgundian cults of Polycarp and Benignus into her husband's *patria*, the Auvergne.[142] Fourth, aristocrats used relics to physically represent the presence of the saintly powers they promoted beyond the limited

---

136. See Raymond Van Dam, *Leadership and Community in Late Antique Gaul* (Berkeley, Los Angeles, and Oxford: University of California Press, 1985), 202–29.
137. Greg. Tur., *VJ* 24–25.
138. Greg. Tur., *GM* 50.
139. Rosenwein, "Inaccessible Cloisters," 186–87.
140. Greg. Tur., *GM* 50.
141. Greg. Tur., *GM* 85. For Armentaria as visionary, see Isabel Moreira, *Dreams, Visions, and Spiritual Authority in Merovingian Gaul* (Ithaca, NY, and London: Cornell University Press, 2001), 82–85.
142. Heinzelmann, *Gregory of Tours: History and Society*, 14–15.

confines of holy tombs. For example, Gregory's father carried about his neck the ashes of unknown saints in a golden medallion to protect him from assaults and flood on long journeys. Florentius's widow Armentaria later used the same reliquary to douse a fiery field, and Gregory subsequently employed it to miraculously avoid a thunderstorm.[143] Fifth, prominent ecclesiastics organized religious ceremonies to direct the attention of the faithful toward cult sites controlled by powerful families. Thus, when plague swept over the Auvergne in 543, Bishop Gallus instituted an annual Lenten procession from Clermont to the church of Saint Julian of Brioude.[144] Sixth, aristocrats ensured the longevity of cults by commissioning and composing hagiography. Gregorius of Langres allocated a *Passio* of the holy martyr Benignus from visiting Italians.[145] Similarly, it likely was a family member who commissioned an extant but anonymous sixth-century *Life of Saint Nicetius of Lyons*, although, surprisingly, Gregory professed unfamiliarity with the author.[146] Furthermore, Gregory admitted that it was Armentaria herself who prompted him to write about contemporary miracles happening at Saint Martin's tomb at Tours.[147] Gregory also expressed the saintliness of at least five relatives in his hagiography. Thus, by virtue of his family's example, young Gregory by the mid-sixth century would have become an undeniably adept manipulator of all these media to amass spiritual authority over a locale.[148]

---

143. Greg. Tur., *GM* 83.
144. Greg. Tur., *Hist.* 4.5, *VP* 6.6.
145. Greg. Tur., *GM* 50.
146. Greg. Tur., *VP* 8, *praef.*
147. Greg. Tur., *VM* 1, *praef.*
148. Because information for Gregory's relatives is strewn about his entire corpus, it must be asked to what extent the author expected readers to appreciate these illustrious individuals as his own relatives? Ian Wood, "Individuality of Gregory of Tours," 40, suspects that Gregory's early readers, unlike modern scholars intent upon building genealogical reconstructions, would not have realized that certain characters were his relatives, for Gregory was usually "strategically silent" about such relationships. But Helmut Reimitz, "Social Networks and Identities in Frankish Historiography. New Aspects of the Textual History of Gregory of Tours' *Historiae*," in *The Construction of Communities in the Early Middle Ages: Texts, Resources and Artefacts*, TRW 12, ed. Richard Corradini, Max Diesenberger, and Helmut Reimitz (Leiden: Brill, 2003), 245–53, contends that Gregory anticipated contemporaries' being able to combine information about his kin with other data such as material pertaining to the bishops of Clermont and Tours, and thereby understanding his literary strategies to assert his family's significance and thus to emphasize his own political and religious importance and establish spiritual authority. For Reimitz, ibid., 253, Gregory's contemporaries would have an

Upon Chlothar I's demise in 561, the Auvergne fell to the control of King Sigibert. Two years later, Gregory, already a deacon, fell ill, and so he made a pilgrimage with several clerics to the basilica of Saint Martin of Tours, which see then belonged to mother Armentaria's cousin Eufronius.[149] Other travels in the 560s likely brought the youthful cleric to the Austrasian court. Perhaps Gregory was present at Metz when Venantius sang the *epithalamium* at Sigibert and Brunhild's wedding.[150] Upon the demise of Eufronius in 573, the Austrasian royal couple selected Gregory to succeed to the cathedra. His uncanonical consecration took place at Metz, not Tours, under the supervision of Bishop Egidius of Reims.[151]

It was during Gregory's twenty-one years as bishop that he composed his history and hagiography. Toward the end of the *Historiae*, he summarized his most important literary achievements: "I have written ten books of *Histories*, seven of *Miracles* and one *On the Life of the Fathers*. I wrote one book of *Commentaries on the Psalms* and one book on the *Offices of the Church*."[152] The seven books of *Miracula* include one book, *On the Glory of the Martyrs*, and another, *On the Glory of the Confessors*, each containing more than one hundred anecdotes, most of which highlight the *virtutes* of Gallic saints. One book, *On the Passion of Saint Julian of Brioude*, details mostly posthumous miracles performed by that martyr, while four books, *On the Miracles of the Bishop Saint Martin of Tours*, do the same for the patron saint of Gregory's diocese. *On the Life of the Fathers* is a collection of twenty short saints' lives, three of which exalt relatives: Gallus of Clermont, Gregorius of Langres, and Nicetius of Lyons.[153] Recent scholarship tends to deem

---

advantage over scholars today, for "[d]espite the fact that early medieval readers lacked the tools of modern historical research, they inhabited the world of the quarrels which finally led to the production of Gregory's work."

149. Greg. Tur., *VM* 1.32.

150. Heinzelmann, *Gregory of Tours: History and Society*, 33.

151. Ven. Fort., *Carm.* 5.3. Gregory made no mention of his consecration in his writings. See Heinzelmann, *Gregory of Tours: History and Society*, 40.

152. Greg. Tur., *Hist.* 10.31 (*MGH*, SRM 1.1, 535–36): "Decem libros Historiarum, septem Miraculorum, unum de Vita Patrum scripsi; in Psalterii tractatu librum unum commentatus sum; de Cursibus etiam Ecclesiasticis unum librum condidi."

153. Greg. Tur., *VP* 6–8.

efforts to date when Gregory composed particular parts of his corpus as futile, for the author edited, augmented, and cross-referenced his text up to the last years of his episcopacy. Still, much material pertains to the later years of Gregory's life. The last three of the four books about Martin address events during the author's episcopacy, while Books Five to Ten of the *Historiae* cover a mere eighteen years, from 575 to 592. As mentioned, the author's writing style betrays a desire to address a broad audience, although Gregory certainly anticipated kings, bishops, and aristocrats lending an especially attentive ear to his message.[154] Like Caesarius's before him, Gregory's literary agenda constituted nothing less than an appeal for Christians to alter radically their behavior and live in accordance with an understandable and achievable "law of God."[155] His Christianizing effort was both pastoral and theological; he was especially wont to proclaim a need for the Gauls to obey their church leaders – bishops and saints – for to not do so would jeopardize their souls.[156] Although he distinguished between *libri historiarum* and *libri miracularum*, both media constituted for Gregory two sides of the same coin. His hagiography brought to the forefront the holy patrons whom he wanted readers to revere, and it provided examples of how the faithful should defer properly to Christian leaders.[157] Gregory expected his miracle tales to be understood not as mere behavioral *exempla* but rather as descriptions of actual events. He hoped that a narration of diurnal miraculous occurrences would overwhelm his audience with "proof" that the saints were effective patrons ever ready to provide believers actual physical and spiritual well-being.[158] Gregory intended the *Historiae* to provide commentary on the world "following

---

154. For comments directed at kings and bishops, see, e. g., Greg. Tur., *Hist.* 5, *praef.*, 10.31.

155. See Kathleen Mitchell, History *and Christian Society in Sixth-Century Gaul: An Historiographical Analysis of Gregory of Tours' Decem Libri Historiarum* (Ph.D. diss., Michigan State University, 1982), 142–66.

156. Gregory asserted that to disobey one's bishop was to commit heresy. See Martin Heinzelmann, "Heresy in Books I and II of Gregory of Tours' *Historiae*," in *After Rome's Fall: Narrators and Sources of Early Medieval History. Essays presented to Walter Goffart*, ed. A. C. Murray (Toronto, Buffalo, and London: University of Toronto Press, 1998), 67–82.

157. Heinzelmann, *Gregory of Tours: History and Society*, 172–81.

158. See Walter Goffart, *The Narrators of Barbarian History (A. D. 550–800), Jordanes, Gregory of Tours, Bede, and Paul the Deacon* (Princeton, NJ: Princeton University Press, 1988), 127–53.

the condition of the times, mixed and confused."[159] Whereas in the *Miracula* he focused only upon saintly heroes and deeds, he designed the *Historiae* to detail a litany of both good and bad events, "miracles of the saints" (*virtutes sanctorum*) and "slaughters of the people" (*strages gentium*).[160] Gregory portrayed Gaul like Israel of old, full of sinners but benefiting from God's providence thanks to the presence of blessed heroes such as the "apostolic" Martin and "David-like" King Clovis. He hoped contemporary kings would emulate Clovis's example of reserving warfare for heretical foes.[161] Furthermore, rulers should practice proper (canonically approved) sexual behavior, abandon internecine warfare, which for Gregory was tantamount to sinful patricide and fratricide, and most importantly, give due respect to God's truly appointed leaders of society, the saints and their earthly representatives, the bishops. In a properly functioning Christian world, the remainder of society would obey good kings who abided the advice of good bishops. While Gregory included in the *Historiae* several miniature *vitae*, which he acknowledged as digressions, he designed even the principal narrative to cause readers to realize their need to defer to bishops and saints, although here the examples are often of a censuring variety.[162] Gregory intended graphic portrayals of one bloody incident after another, again, to "overwhelm" readers with "real life" examples of a divinity ready to mete justice. He intended this "proof" to attest that unrepentant opponents of bishops and saints will suffer God's wrath, often in the form of violent or humiliating death, which prefigures an eternal punishment to come.[163]

159. Greg. Tur., *Hist.* 2, *praef.* (*MGH*, SRM 1.1, p. 36): "Prosequentes ordinem temporum, mixte confuseque."
160. Greg. Tur., *Hist.* 2, *praef.* (*MGH*, SRM 1.1, p. 36); Goffart, *Narrators of Barbarian History*, 152–53.
161. I do not think that Gregory's famous portrayals of Clovis using duplicitous methods to bring about the deaths of several Frankish kings are satirical; *pace* Goffart, *Narrators of Barbarian History*, 218–19. For Gregory, Clovis was a divinely favored king fighting just warfare against pagans and heretics; Phillip Wynn, "Wars and Warriors in Gregory of Tours' *Histories* I-IV," *Francia* 29.1 (2001), 21–28. Besides Clovis, two additional model rulers for Gregory were the Frank Theudebert I and the Emperor Tiberius II; Greg. Tur., *Hist.*, 3.25, 4.40.
162. For small *vitae*, see, e.g., Greg. Tur., *Hist.* 6.6, 8.15, 10.29.
163. Allen E. Jones, "Death and Afterlife in the Pages of Gregory of Tours," (forthcoming).

Gregory's writings offer the most details for the political narrative of sixth-century Gaul. Two years after the episcopal elevation, his royal supporter Sigibert assailed Chilperic. Sigibert was on the verge of capturing his brother when an assassin stabbed him to death. Gregory suspected that Chilperic's wife Fredegund sent the murderer.[164] Chilperic, who previously had contested Sigibert's control of Tours, now claimed the city outright and imposed upon it a former *comes* named Leudast, who along with the new ruler would prove to be the bishop's principal bane. Gregory imagined Chilperic's treatment of bishops to fall especially short of the ideal. In 577, Chilperic assembled the prelates of his realm, Neustria, in Paris to try Bishop Praetextatus of Rouen, a friend of Gregory's who had lent support to the ruler's rebellious son, Merovech.[165] Chilperic wanted to humble Praetextatus further in a secular court, but this action would have run counter to Gregory's conception of the proper relationship between royal and episcopal authority, so he led an effort that thwarted the procedure.[166] In 578/79 Chilperic also tried to impose unwanted taxes upon the Touraine,[167] and in 580, he summoned Gregory to a council at Berny-Rivière to answer charges leveled by Count Leudast and rebellious clerics at Tours that the bishop had conspired to invite King Guntram to take the city. The conspirators also charged that Gregory had accused Queen Fredegund of adultery.[168] The tension at Berny might have been less than what has sometimes been assumed, for before the synod transpired, Chilperic had already switched blame to Leudast and achieved some amicability with Gregory.[169] For his part, Gregory helped smooth relations with the sovereign by having Venantius sing a panegyric on Chilperic and Fredegund's behalf.[170]

164. Greg. Tur., *Hist.* 4.51.
165. Greg. Tur., *Hist.* 5.18. Merovech, along with brothers Theudebert and Clovis were Chilperic's sons through an earlier wife, Audovera; Greg. Tur., *Hist.* 4.28. Their stepmother Queen Fredegund would have perceived them as an obstacle to her security.
166. See Heinzelmann, *Gregory of Tours: History and Society*, 45, who comments on the importance of this trial for Chilperic as an expression of power and for Gregory "as a paradigm of the bishop's place in Merovingian society and the episcopate's relationship to its king ..."
167. Greg. Tur., *Hist.* 5.26, 28.
168. Greg. Tur., *Hist.* 5.49.
169. Heinzelmann, *Gregory of Tours: History and Society*, 46–48.
170. Ven. Fort., *Carm.* 9.2.

Despite this temporary lull in animosity, Gregory's loathing for the king and his allegedly murderous wife never faltered. In 584, Chilperic fell victim to assassination, and again Gregory posited Fredegund as the likely instigator.[171] Gregory concluded Chapter 6 of the *Historiae* by spewing venom on the deceased monarch; he famously condemned Chilperic as the "Nero and Herod of our day" and accused him of greed and malice. He charged the king with murdering clerics and hating bishops, and to top it off he insinuated that Chilperic's soul was already burning in hellfire.[172] As historian, Gregory intended the example of Chilperic to attest to the way Merovingian monarchs ought not to act toward God's bishops and saints and to show what they should expect if they did misbehave.[173]

Upon Chilperic's demise, his last surviving half-brother, Guntram, ruler of Burgundy, became by default the dominant Merovingian leader. Because Guntram had no heir, he was compelled to favor a nephew; but he had two, Fredegund's newly born son Chlothar II of Neustria, and Brunhild's teenaged son Childebert II of Austrasia. Initially, Guntram adopted both.[174] For his part, Gregory, whom we recall was a partisan for the Austrasian court, all but insinuated in his writings that Chlothar II was not Chilperic's son.[175] One pressing matter for Guntram and

---

171. Greg. Tur., *Hist.* 6.45. A Burgundian chronicler traditionally called Fredegar, writing around 660, posited a more likely scenario – that Queen Brunhild dispatched Chilperic's assassin; Fredegar, *Chron.* 3.93.

172. Greg. Tur., *Hist.* 6.45, 8.5; Jones, "Death and Afterlife in the Pages of Gregory of Tours" (forthcoming).

173. Heinzelmann, *Gregory of Tours: History and Society*, 41, sees the entire of *Historiae* Books 5 and 6 as "a moralizing judgment on a ruler." However, for an argument that Gregory's criticisms of Chilperic were dishonest appraisals meant to protect himself from an even more sinister king, Guntram, see Guy Halsall, "Nero and Herod? The Death of Chilperic and Gregory's Writing of History," in *The World of Gregory of Tours*, K. Mitchell and I. Wood, eds. (Leiden, Boston, and Cologne: Brill, 2002), 337–50.

174. Greg. Tur., *Hist.* 7.13.

175. Ian Wood, "Deconstructing the Merovingian Family," in *The Construction of Communities in the Early Middle Ages: Texts, Resources and Artefacts*, TRW 12, ed. Richard Corradini, Max Diesenberger, and Helmut Reimitz (Leiden, Boston, and Cologne: Brill, 2002), 163–64. Similarly, an anonymous chronicler writing in 727 questioned Chlothar's legitimacy, insisting that Fredegund had murdered Chilperic after the king learned of her affair; *Liber Historiae Francorum* 35. Based on this and Gregory's testimony, Ian Wood, ibid., 164, offers: "[T]he almost inevitable conclusion is that Chlothar was not Chilperic's biological heir." *Pace* Wood, but without DNA evidence, it is impossible to assess anyone's patrimony. Nor can one estimate the likelihood of any late ancient person's legitimacy, even if one had the friendliest of sources, much less one very hostile witness and a second writing more than a century after the fact!

Fredegund involved avenging Chilperic's death. Duke Eberulf, a principal murder suspect to Guntram and Fredegund's minds, sought sanctuary at Saint Martin's basilica at Tours. Guntram sent his agent Claudius with armed retainers to the church, where eventually they slew Eberulf in the vestibule. But Claudius, too, was butchered with a number of his men at the hands of Gregory and Saint Martin's vengeful minions.[176] Another concern for Guntram in 585 was the second arrival in Gaul of a usurper named Gundovald, who claimed to be the long lost son of Chlothar I. Gundovald's appearance posed a quandary for Gallic aristocrats such as Gregory in that the claimant constituted another figure about whom a noble faction might arise. Even as Gundovald received the loyalty of certain aristocrats, some of whom were former friends of Gregory such as Egidius of Reims, Guntram acted decisively. He sent to the south a force that rapidly dispatched the pretender.[177] Afterward, Guntram summoned bishops to a general council at Orléans. Several of Gregory's anecdotes depicting time spent with Guntram, including attending a banquet and a hunting jaunt, offer the bishop's most favorable portrayal of a contemporary ruler.[178] One is left with the impression that Gregory was on the whole an admirer.[179] But this fondness for the king stemmed at least in part from Guntram's facilitation of Tours being restored to the Austrasian realm. In 587, Guntram allied with Childebert II and Brunhild. Gregory preserved in full in the *Historiae* a copy of the Treaty of Andelot, which sealed the deal.[180] Gregory, who had always been a proponent of Brunhild, visited the Austrasian court in 588 with Venantius accompanying to offer flattering verses and grease the wheels of the long-neglected relationship between bishop and crown.[181] Despite a happy return to the Austrasian fold, Gregory faced several difficulties during the young king's tenure. In 589, Childebert II sent

176. Greg. Tur., *Hist.* 7.21–22, 29.
177. Greg. Tur., *Hist.* 7.34–38. On Gundovald's power play and the involvement of Austrasian aristocrats, see Wood, *Merovingian Kingdoms*, 93–98.
178. Greg. Tur., *Hist.* 8.1–7.
179. Heinzelmann, *Gregory of Tours: History and Society*, 51–75, contends that Guntram was Gregory's model for the ideal king, a "new Hezekiah."
180. Greg. Tur., *Hist.* 9.20.
181. Ven. Fort., *Carm.* 10.7–9; *Appendix carminum* 5–6; Brennan, "Career of Venantius," 76.

officials to levy taxes upon the Touraine. The bishop quickly pointed out how kings traditionally had exempted Tours from such treatment out of respect for Saint Martin. Gregory again resorted to Venantius's verses by inviting the offending royal officials to an Easter dinner where the poet sang the merits of Saint Martin while they ate.[182] Childebert subsequently confirmed the city's tax-exempt status.[183] In 589/90, the king also proved helpful by sending soldiers at Gregory's request to restore order at Poitiers, where nuns at the convent of the Holy Cross rebelled against their abbess.[184] In 592, King Guntram died, but rather than eulogizing him in the *Historiae*, Gregory mentioned his death only in passing in the last of his books on Saint Martin's miracles.[185] What likely mattered most for Gregory was that the old king's possessions fell to his royal patron Childebert II, not to Fredegund and Chlothar II, the latter now eight years of age. Late in his life, Bishop Gregory stood secure as a respected ecclesiastical aristocrat in the mighty Austrasian kingdom. In 590, Gregory celebrated the completion of a long-term restoration of the cathedral at Tours. Venantius not only provided verses for the dedicatory festivities, but also he penned the poetic *tituli* attached to the mural imagery.[186] One *titulus*, which accompanied an image probably depicting Gregory entering Paradise alongside the "heavenly senator" Martin, reads in part: "Through your intercession, oh Gregory, may the holy pastor [Martin] take away so many stains from the guilty Fortunatus."[187] This triumphant celestial imagery was put to the test when the Bishop of Tours died, traditionally given as 17 November 594. Gregory could not have imagined that just two years after his death, the sudden demise of Childebert II would precipitate other unforeseen events and result in the ascendancy of Chlothar II's Neustria.[188]

182. Ven. Fort., *Carm.* 10.11.
183. Greg. Tur., *Hist.* 9.30.
184. Greg. Tur., *Hist.* 10.14–16.
185. Greg. Tur., *VM* 4.37.
186. Ven. Fort., *Carm.* 10.6; Herbert L. Kessler, "Pictorial Narrative and Church Mission in Sixth-Century Gaul," in *Pictorial Narrative in Antiquity and the Middle Ages*, ed. H. L. Kessler and M. Shreve Simpson (Washington, DC: Gallery of Art, 1985), 76, 80.
187. Ibid., 76–77: "… qui sacer ipse mihi te, pastor, agente, Gregori, Fortunato adimat tot maculosa reo."
188. Upon Childebert II's death, his sons Theudebert and Theuderic ruled Austrasia and Burgundy, respectively; Fredegar, *Chron.* 4.16. Fredegund died in 597; Fredegar, *Chron.* 4.17. In 613, Theuderic

While much of Gregory's narrative focuses upon power politics, his pages also offer the most vivid vignettes for Gallic society. As kings led armies against kings, bishops appealed to saints for vindication against greedy secular magnates, well-to-do and poor people took up the ascetic lifestyle, and slaves fled to churches to escape violent masters. Such scenes admittedly are limited, confined to the concerns of a politically astute ecclesiastical aristocrat.[189] Scholars certainly can no longer consider Gregory a naïve recorder of events.[190] The Bishop of Tours was capable of fashioning literature to his own advantage every bit as much as his friend Venantius did for his many patrons. But just what kind of information would Gregory likely have concealed or distorted when writing his text, and what would he not bother to hide or augment? And which among his many anecdotes and books, if any, might be deemed reliable for reflecting to some extent actual social conditions and behaviors? One benefit to privileging the pages of this author, whose writings have so much potentially to offer an analysis of Gallic society, is the fact that Gregory has become in recent years the object of much scholarly scrutiny.[191] Many have become intent upon honing in on this historian's *mentalité*. The result is that, as if one were now able to peer at multiple facets of a single gem, many Gregorys, diverse but all contributing to the fuller image of a whole, have come to light:

> For Michael Wallace-Hadrill he was a propagandist of the shrine of Saint Martin at Tours, for Peter Brown and Ray Van Dam in their different ways a key witness to the meanings of the cult of the saints, for Giselle de Nie a poet of the spiritual imagination, for Walter Goffart an expert religious commentator working through a

defeated his brother Theudebert in battle and captured him; Fredegar, *Chron.* 4.32. Then Chlothar II's Neustrian army decisively defeated the Austrasian and Burgundian forces and thereby united the Frankish realms. It was ordered that the aged Queen Brunhild be trampled to death beneath the hooves of a wild horse; Fredegar, *Chron.* 4.42.

189. See Ian Wood, "The Secret Histories of Gregory of Tours," *Revue Belge de Philologie et d'Histoire* 71 (1993), 253–70, on the inability of Gregory to give a frank presentation of "all the facts," especially those pertaining to court life, due to the dangerous political environment.

190. See Goffart, *Narrators of Barbarian History*, 112–27, for consideration of a century and more of scholarly commentary on Gregory as historian.

191. See Allen E. Jones, *Gregory of Tours and His World: A Bibliography*, http://spectrum.troy.edu/~ajones/gotbibl.html (2002).

medium of irony, for Martin Heinzelmann a theologian expressing ideas through narrative, and for [Ian Wood] a sly manipulator of religious and political information.[192]

To these one might add a pair of recent Gregorys: for Barbara Rosenwein, he was a member of an Austrasian emotional community uninhibited in its affirmation of feelings, and for Danuta Shanzer, an accomplished prose litterateur whose "drive for completeness" contended with "an eagerness to polish and perfect a well-wrought urn," albeit probably "a poet *manqué*."[193] We shall never see the entire gem, the complete Gregory, but today's images are far superior to that composer of a nationalistic *History of the Franks*, to which bogus impression most scholars were attached as recently as two generations ago.[194] Now that Gregory himself has become a more understandable commodity, one may ask anew what kind of information he would have been likely to hide, distort, or share openly within his pages. What parts of Gregory's text can be regarded as representations of people engaged in actual behaviors? What sections can be plausibly thought to convey biographical data?[195]

In light of a new consensus for Gregory as a shrewd manipulator of text, one might first ponder the accuracy of writings that pertain to events that happened before the author's lifetime. Although Gregory consulted, and occasionally cited, earlier sources pertaining to the distant past, this does not mean his word on this material can be taken for granted. Gregory probably took advantage of faded memory, and

---

192. Wood, *Gregory of Tours*, ii–iii. See also idem, "Individuality of Gregory of Tours," 29–30.
193. Barbara H. Rosenwein, *Emotional Communities in the Early Middle Ages* (Ithaca, NY: Cornell University Press, 2006), 100–29; Danuta Shanzer, "So Many Saints – So Little Time … The Libri Miraculorum of Gregory of Tours," *Journal of Medieval Latin* 13 (2003), 24; and idem, "Gregory of Tours and Poetry: Prose into Verse and Verse into Prose," in *Aspects of the Language of Latin Prose*, ed. T. Reinhardt, M. Lapidge, and J. N. Adams (Oxford and New York: Oxford University Press, 2005), 319.
194. See Goffart, *Narrators of Barbarian History*, 119–27.
195. My ultimate interest is to ascertain past behavior rather than simply to find "fact." Nevertheless, I find the "fact-finding" remarks of Thomas Pratsch, "Exploring the Jungle: Hagiographical Literature," 59–72, helpful. Pratsch, ibid., 62, rightly argues that scholars trying to distinguish "fact" and "fiction" need to address the matter not only on the level of genre and author but also for singular parts of individual works. This rationale applies equally well for one looking to identify behavioral patterns, and furthermore, it is equally applicable to history as well as hagiography.

fashioned temporally distant personas to fit theological and ecclesiastical assumptions more boldly than what he would have attempted for contemporary characters. A case in point is a presentation of seven third-century Gallic apostles reportedly sent from Rome during the reign of Emperor Decius.[196] Because our author wrote about these figures in an ostensibly "realistic" style in the *Historiae,* and because alternate Gallic apostolicity theories stem from hagiographies that earlier scholars deemed "unrealistic," Gregory's tale long has been accepted as the "real" version.[197] But now his story has collapsed under critical analysis, and it becomes apparent how the astute bishop offered this tale to convince readers that the sees of his paternal homeland and episcopacy, Clermont and Tours, were of equal age with the bishopric of Arles, and hence should hold equal prestige.[198] A more famous pre-contemporary for whom many still turn to Gregory's *Historiae* in search of a historical person is King Clovis. As mentioned, Gregory portrayed Clovis as a Gallic David; the latter becomes an exemplar for having adopted Catholicism and waging war against heretic rulers and unscrupulous (presumably pagan) relations. When one compares the Clovis of *Historiae* Book Two with contemporary evidence for the ruler, it becomes necessary to regard Gregory's representation as chronologically flawed and highly distorted by theologizing.[199] Gregory even proves somewhat unreliable when writing about early political events happening in his native Auvergne. For example, regarding King Theuderic's devastating assault on the region, a topic about which the author was rather obsessive, he confusedly made the campaign contemporaneous with Theuderic's conquest of Burgundy in 534.[200] But more reliable temporal factors provided within the text enable one to situate the actual date for the Auvergne invasion as 523 or 524.[201] Despite Gregory's chronological inconsistency, however, this does

---

196. The seven are Gatianus of Tours, Trophimus of Arles, Paul of Narbonne, Saturninus of Toulouse, Denis of Paris, Stremonius of Clermont, and Martialis of Limoges; Greg. Tur., *Hist.* 1.30.

197. Felice Lifshitz, "Apostolicity Theses in Gaul: The *Histories* of Gregory and the 'Hagiography' of Bayeux," in *The World of Gregory of Tours,* ed. K. Mitchell and I. Wood (Leiden, Boston, and Cologne: Brill, 2002), 213–14.

198. Ibid., 217–18.

199. Ian Wood, "Gregory of Tours and Clovis," *Revue Belge de Philologie et d'Histoire* 63 (1985), 249–72.

200. See Greg. Tur., *Hist.* 3.11–13, *VP* 4.2–3, 5.2, *VJ* 13, 23.

201. Wood, *Merovingian Kingdoms,* 53.

not mean that Theuderic did not actually assail the Auvergne, nor need it deter one from making an accurate reconstruction of events during the campaign.[202] As for extracting data about persons active prior to the author's lifetime, obviously one needs to use extreme caution.

Fortunately, the vast majority of events Gregory wrote about happened during his lifetime, and much of that during the years of his episcopacy. For this period, Gregory's chronology becomes reliable, even if the author had reasons for not always keeping to strict chronological order. Very few would question the "actuality" of important actors and events described in the latter parts of his account (e.g., that an assassin struck a fatal blow to Bishop Praetextatus in the cathedral at Rouen in 586, or that nuns rebelled at the convent of the Holy Cross at Poitiers in 589).[203] Because Gregory was an interested party in many of the high-level political machinations that he detailed, one certainly needs be wary of how partisanship impacted his interpretation of events. Likewise, one should also suspect that Gregory felt constrained about what he could write about certain powerful people, since some of these people frequently responded to challenges to their authority violently and fatally.[204] But despite a use of discretion when commenting upon current events, this did not stop the bishop from insinuating a great deal that he expected readers to discern.[205]

Among the more tumultuous of contemporary events that Gregory depicted was the rise and fall of the pretender Gundovald.[206] On this matter, historians theorize about whether, as Gregory seems to have believed, Gundovald actually was a son of Chlothar I.[207] What scholars

202. Ibid.
203. Greg. Tur., *Hist.* 8.31, 9.39–43. Paul Fouracre, "Why Were So Many Bishops Killed in Merovingian Francia?" in *Bischofsmord im Mittelalter: Murder of Bishops*, ed. Natalie Fryde and Dirk Reitz (Göttingen: Vandenhoeck and Ruprecht, 2003), 15, writes, "… no-one seriously argues that Gregory invented important events."
204. Wood, "The Secret Histories of Gregory of Tours," 256, estimates that it was especially dangerous for Gregory to write during the years of Chilperic's reign.
205. Ibid., 270: "… there are moments when Gregory does allow the reader to see below the surface of his work … and appears to invite the audience to unwrite some of the history that he wrote."
206. Greg. Tur., *Hist.* 6.24, 7.10–11, 26–32, 34–38.
207. For consideration of Gregory's acceptance of Gundovald's claim to be a Merovingian, see Bernard S. Bachrach, *The Anatomy of a Little War: A Diplomatic and Military History of the Gundovald Affair (568–586)* (Boulder, CO, San Francisco, and Oxford: Westview, 1994), 1–30; and Ian Wood,

do not deny are Gundovald's actions: that he came to Gaul in response to aristocratic overtures, and that he twice attempted to establish himself in southern Gaul as a legitimate Merovingian. Gregory's admission and lamentation on how certain aristocrats, including fellow Austrasians, supported the pretender's bid for power evinces how the author could be forthcoming with sensitive and even potentially embarrassing information. The reason Gregory was so forthright in divulging unseemly conduct among Gallic elites in regard to episodes such as the Gundovald affair lies in the author's combined literary, pastoral, and political objective to convince socially prominent readers of his works to forego subsequent similar worldly stratagems, lest they too suffer dishonorable death and damnation. As for Gregory's depictions of the behaviors of powerful participants in such incidents, these may be regarded as reliable evidence, which the modern historian is at liberty to interpret as fairly accurate biographical data for how certain Gauls went about social strategizing.

If Gregory is trustworthy when offering details of contemporary warfare, he is not always unbiased when it comes to commenting on personal politics. A more localized situation involving a prominent Gaul pertains to Bishop Priscus of Lyons (d. ca. 586). What can be gathered from other sources that Gregory's writing do not admit is how Priscus played a prominent role in King Guntram's effort to reform the Burgundian clergy and laity. Priscus presided over two councils of Mâcon (581/83 and 585), and he may have had a hand in producing a canon law compilation, the *Collectio Vetus Gallica*.[208] Gregory wrote in favorable terms about Guntram's concern for the welfare of the church, and he also dedicated an anecdote of the *Historiae* to the proceedings at the Council of Mâcon (585). But Gregory's only mention of Priscus

---

"Deconstructing the Merovingian Family," 161–62. Wood, ibid., 62, proposes that Gregory's mention (*Hist.* 7.11) of prodigies prior to Gundovald's death supports the notion that the pretender was of royal blood. While that may be, Gregory's vocabulary in this instance further indicates that the author interpreted the signs to portend Gundovald's damnation; Allen E. Jones, "Death and Afterlife in the Pages of Gregory of Tours" (forthcoming).

208. Rob Meens, "Reforming the Clergy: A Context for the Use of the Bobbio Penitential," in *The Bobbio Missal: Liturgy and Religious Culture in Merovingian Gaul*, ed. Yitzhak Hen and Rob Meens (Cambridge: Cambridge University Press, 2004), 162.

at the council did not pertain to his desire for reform or the presiding role; instead, it depicted how the bishop was forced to pay restitution for an unseemly row between the prelate's servants and those of a duke.[209] Gregory elsewhere insinuated that Priscus and his wife did not remain celibate, that their kin were insane, and that the bishop showed no reverence for his holy predecessor, Saint Nicetius, Gregory's great uncle.[210] Indeed, Gregory and Priscus's families were rivals for the cathedra at Lyons. While our author complained that Priscus did not revere Saint Nicetius, he also conveniently left out of his writings how Priscus, too, was honored *post mortem* as a saint and buried alongside Nicetius![211] Here we see Gregory's prejudice affecting how he portrayed an individual, causing him to omit the fact that Priscus was a reformer, and to some minds a holy man. But this prejudice need not deter us from realizing how Gregory has provided important evidence on aspects of actual social interaction. In particular, one may interpret details such as Priscus's refusal to support Nicetius's cult and reports that Priscus's supporters assailed Gregory's kin as revealing just how partisan, violent, and lasting ecclesiastical factionalism could become whenever families clashed over holy turf.[212]

Gregory's writings on Merovingian politics are also potentially subject to partisan coloring. Yet another politically charged event depicted in the *Historiae* involves two antagonists, both of whom Gregory despised. In 584, Queen Fredegund, having been accused of adultery by Count Leudast four years earlier, sent forth men who publicly wounded the count in a Parisian market.[213] Because Gregory took almost every opportunity to criticize Fredegund, this anecdote gives one pause, for one must wonder whether the queen actually was the casual murderer and adulterer that the bishop implied. Despite the fact that Gregory harbored obvious animus for the woman, historians scarcely doubt the author's assertion that she commonly ordered assassinations. Rather,

---

209. Greg. Tur., *Hist.* 8.20.
210. Greg. Tur., *Hist.* 4.36.
211. Wood, *Gregory of Tours*, 45.
212. For more on Priscus, see the discussion in Chapter Three at pp. 115 and 116.
213. Greg. Tur., *Hist.* 6.32.

they use the example of Fredegund as an opportunity to understand general social behavior – for instance, how queens had reason to fear bishops' charges of illegitimacy, and how royal women were every bit as capable as their spouses at employing vendetta to maintain their power and reputations.[214] I do not think that Gregory, despite a real risk of harm, did much shying away from informing readers about his opinions on the behavior of powerful and dangerous people. He plainly shared his estimation that the soul of King Chilperic was damned, and he was in the process of making a solid case that Fredegund's soul deserved the same fate when he concluded the *Historiae*.[215] Although Gregory's representations of contemporary characters are certainly fabrications in that the author emphasized their participation in certain activities and omitted other details, always necessarily and sometimes maliciously, I contend that most of what he did divulge about the actions of people of recent memory constitutes reliable material for use as biographical data. One can interpret this data while at the same time remaining aware that the author is denigrating some and lauding others.

The *Historiae* tend to focus upon momentous events and extraordinary circumstances, and so for scenes of more quotidian life one must turn to the *Miracula*. Gregory should not be regarded as less dependable when writing *Miracula* than *Historiae*. To borrow from, and admittedly somewhat misappropriate, Felice Lifshitz: "[I]f Gregory of Tours is reliable, then Gregory of Tours is reliable."[216] With Lifshitz I agree that there is no good reason to "believe" Gregory as "historian" and doubt him as "hagiographer."[217] For our present purposes, I would extrapolate from

---

214. Fouracre, "Why Were So Many Bishops Killed," 21–22; Nira Gradowicz-Pancer, "De-Gendering Female Violence: Merovingian Female Honour as an 'Exchange of Violence,'" *Early Medieval Europe* 2.1 (2002), 1–18.

215. Jones, "Death and Afterlife in the Pages of Gregory of Tours" (forthcoming).

216. Lifshitz, "Apostolicity Theses in Gaul," 213.

217. Goffart, *Narrators of Barbarian History*, 152, writes that Gregory used the "same mode of storytelling" in the *Miracula* and *Historiae*. Wood, *Gregory of Tours*, 23, points out that Gregory conveyed an "appreciation of the workings of the divine" in both the *Historiae* and *Miracula*. The contention of Lifshitz, "Beyond Positivism and Genre," 102–04, that it is unhelpful to anachronistically impose a distinction between historical and hagiographical genres to study ninth- through eleventh-century texts works as well for Gregory's writings. Although he distinguished between *Historiae* and *Miracula*, Gregory did not intend the books for different audiences, nor did his presentation of subject matter vary substantially. His manner of gathering anecdotes for the *Historiae* and *Miracula*

this that, as with the *Historiae*, one generally can rely on descriptions of contemporary actors in the *Miracula* as conveying accurate biographical data. Furthermore, whether taking from the *Historiae* or *Miracula*, this reliability applies regardless of a person's social rank. Thus, if one is not going to doubt that Guntram's army killed Gundovald in 585, or that Fredegund's thugs killed Leudast in 580, then there is no reason to question that a runaway slave turned would-be saint paraded across Gaul in 580, that two Saxons in service to a merchant killed and robbed their master near Orléans in 585, or that, to use Gregory's linguistic idiom, Saint Martin healed the knee of a slave who visited the saint's tomb in 592.[218] Many of the contemporary miracles depicted in the *Historiae* and *Miracula* are likely to constitute literary representations of people engaged in biblically modeled behaviors rather than biblically modeled fictions.[219] Gallic hagiographers exhibited marked variety as they represented the saints in their literature, and so social historians have to reassess each writer's motives and methods independently. I am far more doubtful about there being historical antecedents for Venantius Fortunatus's miracle stories than most of Gregory's. Otherwise, I am not denying that Gregory did not include legends in his writings about saints and miracles. We already have mentioned the legend of the seven Gallic apostles, and how this story would have supported claims to spiritual authority for Clermont, Tours, and ultimately Gregory himself.[220] A quainter legend described in both the *Historiae* and *Miracula* pertains to "two lovers" from Clermont whose tombs sadly were placed along separate walls, but they miraculously situated themselves adjacently.[221] Gregory intended his rendition of the tale to praise the chaste lifestyle.

were much the same; both included family tales, oral traditions, stories gathered from earlier writings, and much personal experience. Where notable variation did arise in the author's story-telling, it was for two kinds of hagiography. Gregory relied heavily on miracle registers for his "shrine-based" books about Saints Martin and Julian, whereas he was not constrained by such "existing and mandatory material" for composition of the "composite" books on martyrs and confessors; Shanzer, "So Many Saints – So Little Time," 23, 37.

218. Slave turned saint: Greg. Tur., *Hist.* 9.6; murderers: *Hist.* 7.46; Martin healing slave: *GM* 4.41.
219. Cf. Richard Finn, "Portraying the Poor: Descriptions of Poverty in Christian Texts from the Late Roman Empire," in *Poverty in the Roman World*, ed. Margaret Atkins and Robin Osborne (Cambridge: Cambridge University Press, 2006), 141.
220. Greg. Tur., *Hist.* 1.30.
221. Greg. Tur., *Hist.* 1.47, *GC* 31.

Likewise, he offered several unhistorical, comedic legends to demean heretics. For example, he explained that an Arian husband once determined to insult his wife and her dinner guest, a Catholic priest, by having his own guest, an Arian priest, bless the dinner as the courses arrived. But in the end, the Arian priest consumed a portion of food, flatulated, and died.[222] Similarly, it is told that when a band of Arians forced a Catholic girl to be re-baptized, she pronounced the Trinity and defecated in the font, and the heresiarch Arius himself reportedly perished by loosing his entrails and soul into a privy.[223] These yarns do not typify Gregory's miracle stories; more frequent and standard are barebones accounts of healings at saints' shrines, such as the following complete anecdote: "A blind man attending the same festival [of Saint Martin] was begging as a suppliant that he recover his vision. He then touched a curtain hanging outside from the wall to the feet of the saint. Soon blood was gushing from his eyelids, and he recovered his vision with the people watching."[224] Gregory almost certainly culled this story about a pilgrim actually attending one of Martin's festivals from the miracle register kept at that saint's basilica. As for the author's principal intention for portraying *miracula*, Gregory provided representations for many actual incidents – in the case of miracles, mostly people coming to a church, revering a saint, and recovering some measure of health – in order to convince readers that they would enjoy similar benefits should they modify their faith.

Like many other Gallic writings, Gregory's text constitutes an element of a strategy to fashion a society within which, incidentally, the elite litterateur would benefit socially. But I think that Gregory, perhaps more than any other Gallic author, felt obligated to portray people

---

222. Greg. Tur., *GM* 79.
223. Greg. Tur., *Hist.* 2.2, 3, *praef.* On Gregory's low humor, see Shanzer, "So Many Saints – So Little Time," 48–50, particularly 48–49 for the priest's flatulence, and 49 n. 208 for her original reading of the girl's having diarrhea. Furthermore on comedy in hagiography, see idem, "Laughter and Humour in the Early Medieval Latin West," in *Humour, History and Politics in Late Antiquity and the Early Middle Ages*, ed. Guy Halsall (Cambridge: Cambridge University Press, 2002), 25–47, with reference to Gregory at 31–35.
224. Greg. Tur., *VM* 2.50 (*MGH*, SRM 1.2, 176): "Sic et caecus in eadem festivitate supplex inplorans receptionem visionis, ut pallulam adtigit, qui a foris ad pedes sancti de pariete dependit, mox erumpente a palpebris sanguine, teste populo, visum recepit."

involved in actual activities. He selected events in which ostensibly holy or villainous people participated in either constructive or destructive behavior and then underwent certain consequences including blessedness, violent death, and much in between. Gregory thought the presentation of a barrage of *miracula* and *strages* the best way to prove his point about the need for people to obey their bishops and saints so that they could stand a chance at salvation. As it turns out, then, the text with the most abundant material for witnessing a diverse lot of Gauls acting in a limited but not insignificant variety of activities also constitutes a fairly reliable source for gathering biographical data. I have one last justification for relying heavily upon Gregory's text. There is, of course, a risk to claiming that one bishop's writings can apply as evidence for the better part of Gaul. Here, use of other written sources and consideration of recent studies on material culture will provide considerable context. But as to my assertion that Gregory makes an excellent witness for his times and for an extensive region, I would emphasize that he was educated but not aloof, a celibate bishop well familiar with the mores of an honor-driven, secular world pressing down upon him. He had an expansive knowledge commensurate with his own wide travels, and varied familial, ecclesiastical, and political connections. He was a native of the Auvergne with landed interests in Burgundy, and despite expressing befuddlement, he knew well why contemporaries did not regard the fortified town (*castrum*) of Dijon as a city (*civitas*).[225] He visited courts at Soissons, Orléans, and Metz, fraternized with their courtiers, and preferred those from the last place the most.[226] He had a possible relation named Gundulf who was an abbot, later bishop, at Metz.[227]

225. Gregory had visited Dijon and offered a glowing appraisal of the site in the *Historiae*, remarking especially about its huge wall circuit; Greg. Tur., *Hist.* 3.19. His uncle Gregorius of Langres promoted the cult of Saint Benignus at Dijon and was buried there, as was Gregory's brother, Peter; Greg. Tur., *GM* 50, *VP* 7.3, *Hist.* 5.5. The family's interests in the town most likely resulted from their possession of estates there. They probably were trying to relocate the cathedra and *civitas* status from Langres to Dijon, which would not have been a popular move, especially for the residents in and about Langres. Thus, Gregory was feigning dismay about the status of Dijon. For this interpretation, see Wood, *Gregory of Tours*, 42–43.
226. Gregory is critical not only of Chilperic's but also of many kings' courtiers. Despite his fairly positive estimation of King Guntram, he has little positive to write about Burgundian courtiers.
227. Ven. Fort., *Vita Radegundis* 13; Halsall, *Settlement and Social Organization*, 15.

A great uncle with the same name was stationed at Marseilles, and through him Gregory would have been well aware that that city was a great port of extreme importance for the Merovingians.[228] One of Gregory's closest acquaintances was an abbot at Limoges, and he would have learned much about events at Trier from that friend's disciple who dwelt near that city.[229] On a mission from Guntram to Childebert II, Gregory ventured as far eastward as Coblenz.[230] As Bishop of Tours, his own diocese extended to the westernmost edge of woolly Brittany. If he rarely referenced Provence and never mentioned Caesarius of Arles, it likely was not on account of a lack of knowledge about either.[231] Tours was important as an ecclesiastical center, much less so for economics, but Gregory admired its physicality much as he did other urban centers for their walls and "the bishop within them and the saints outside."[232] While he undoubtedly delighted in writing about the Auvergne and Touraine, his references to Clermont and Tours were central to an ambitious project of literary self-promotion.[233] Thus, if Gregory's historiography was parochial, the man was anything but. Therefore the Bishop of Tours becomes an extremely well-informed social commentator for Barbarian Gaul. I conclude that despite there being obstacles to interpreting our

228. Greg. Tur., *Hist.* 6.11; Simon T. Loseby, "Marseille and the Pirenne Thesis, I: Gregory of Tours, the Merovingian Kings, and 'Un Grand Port,'" in *The Sixth Century: Production, Distribution and Demand*, TRW 3, ed. Richard Hodges and William Bowden (Leiden, Boston, and Cologne: Brill, 1998), 203–29. Wickham, *Framing the Early Middle Ages*, 172, proposes that Gregory was not as familiar with his maternal, Burgundian relations as with his paternal kin, and he imagines that Gregory erred in estimating that Gundulf was his great uncle. Wickham's estimation of Gregory's ignorance about Burgundy and his "Aquitanian orientation" does not sufficiently take into account the writer's historiographical program of emphasizing Clermont with Tours to legitimize his position, about which see, Reimitz, "Social Networks and Identities in Frankish Historiography," 246–48. Also I think it highly unlikely that Gregory would have been unfamiliar with a contemporary relative who shared with the bishop the experience of serving simultaneously in high-profile roles for the same two courts, King Guntram's followed by Childebert II's; Greg. Tur., *Hist.* 6.11, 26.

229. Aredius of Limoges; Greg. Tur., *Hist.* 10.29; Vulfolaic at Trier: *Hist.* 8.15–16. On Gregory's sources for Trier, see Handley, "Beyond Hagiography: Epigraphic Commemoration," 191.

230. Greg. Tur., *Hist.* 8.13–14.

231. I suspect that the oft-noted silence about Caesarius stemmed from Gregory's having a "Semi-Pelagian" sensibility. This is not an original assertion, but it has yet to be put to critical analysis.

232. Simon T. Loseby, "Gregory's Cities: Urban Functions in Sixth-Century Gaul," in *Franks and Alemanni in the Merovingian Period: An Ethnographic Perspective*, ed. Ian Wood (Woodbridge, Suffolk: Boydell, 1998), 256. On a general lack of economic activity for late ancient Tours, see Henri Galinié, "Tours de Grégoire, Tours des archives du sol," in *Grégoire de Tours et l'espace gaulois*, ed. Nancy Gauthier and Henri Galinié (Tours: Association Grégoire 94, 1997), 67–80.

233. Van Dam, *Saints and their Miracles*, 13–28; Wood, "Individuality of Gregory of Tours," 36.

sources, the writings that survive, especially Gregory's corpus, have much to reveal about our authors' perceptions of, and their characters' actual behaviors within, society. In the next two chapters, therefore, we shall construct a model for that society according to an interpretation of biographical data derived from these works. There we shall witness a hierarchical world with a diversity of options and opportunities for social advancement for many.

SOCIAL STRUCTURE I: HIERARCHY, MOBILITY, AND ARISTOCRACIES

CHAPTER THREE

Three days ago there departed from us amid general mourning the Lady Philomathia, a dutiful wife and a kind mistress, a busy mother and a devoted daughter, one to whom in social and domestic life her inferior owed respect, her superior consideration, her equal affection.

SIDONIUS APOLLINARIS, *Epistula* 2.8.1[1]

The previous chapter addressed how any understanding of Gallic society will be made difficult because most of the sources derive from a small segment of society, male ecclesiastical aristocrats. While this control of the evidence demands caution in interpretation, it does not negate the possibility of gaining much insight about how society was structured and how people acted and interacted. Using evidence for Gallic activity – that is, biographical data – over this and the next chapter we shall attempt to construct a model for the society of Barbarian Gaul. A first step toward that model will be to regard images for the structure of society

---

1. Sid. Ap., *Ep.* 2.8 (Anderson, ed. and trans., 1: 446–47): "Decessit nudius tertius non absque iustitio matrona Philomathia, morigera coniux domina clemens, utilis mater pia filia, cui debuerit domi forisque persona minor obsequium, maior officium, aequalis adfectum."

74

that the producers of our sources advanced. In particular, we shall consider briefly what may be characterized as two independent efforts at "envisioning" society. The first was motivated by secular, indeed royal, concerns, and derives from legal sources, while the second was heavily influenced with ecclesiastical ideas and comes from literary texts. Although the visions expressed in these two kinds of source disagree in particulars, it becomes apparent that socially prominent composers of law and literature shared an opinion that a proper society should be orderly and hierarchical. Along these lines, the introductory quote for this chapter, in which Sidonius bemoans the demise of a noblewoman named Philomathia, reflects how Gallic litterateurs envisioned a hierarchical society in which superiors owed "consideration" to inferiors within the same social rank, while inferiors of every rank owed "respect" to their superiors. Here, the fact that Sidonius and company were willing to share opinions of how they thought society ought to be implies that litterateurs were not necessarily attempting to disguise actual conditions of the world in which they operated. One aspect of those conditions would have been the existence of some semblance of the hierarchical social structure the authors imaged, and so this will have to be figured into the model. But much data from the literary evidence indicates that Gallic society was not static, and neither were social ranks monolithic. Patronage was a feature that complicated society and enabled individuals to climb into higher social ranks. Factionalism occasioned frequent shifts in the makeup of various social groups, including separate clusters of aristocrats. This social suppleness needs to be emphasized, too. Thus, as we construct the model, each of these aspects will be included: hierarchy, fluidity, and diversity.

One trick to building a social model is to avoid falling prey to authors' rhetorical devices, while another involves not distancing oneself overly much from the *mentalités* of participants in a society under investigation. The latter sometimes happens through the introduction of terminology inconsistent with what writers of an age used.[2] The present

---

2. A classic example is the study of "feudal" society. The word "feudalism" has become virtual anathema for medievalists in the last decade or so. See especially Susan Reynolds, *Fiefs and Vassals: The Medieval Evidence Reinterpreted* (New York and Oxford: Oxford University Press, 1994).

model's structure will therefore be based on rankings and other social terminology offered by the authors themselves. Relying upon our lit- terateurs' vocabulary, and admittedly mainly that of Gregory of Tours, I propose to consider Gallic society according to four vertical group- ings that existed among three ranks: (1) aristocrats, (2a) well-to-do free people (*ingenui*), (2b) free paupers (*pauperes*), and (3) slaves. Addressing one group and then the next, from the top down, this model will build itself upon analysis of evidence for individual actors of all ranks' strat- egizing toward social improvement.

Upward social mobility in Gaul could involve several possible changes to a person's circumstances including improvement in one's economic situation, social rank, and/or social influence. A person could improve economically through an increase in material goods, either moveable wealth or land. Acquiring land especially would enable one more effec- tively to achieve greater social power, for example, through being able to lord it over more dependents.[3] With more resources, one might display power more effectively, for example, though ostentatious expenditure such as building a large church, which in turn could suggest that one was "deserving" of greater social influence. Shows of economic worth and power could result in social mobility in the form of movement into a higher rank. This would be accomplished when established members of an upper social tier recognized an individual as belonging among their numbers. But advancement need not be limited to an increase in rank, nor was it usually so. One simply could improve his place in a pecking order by moving up an established *cursus honorum*, either secular (e.g., *comes, dux, maior domus*) or ecclesiastical (e.g., doorkeeper, exorcist, priest). Such a move could be accompanied by increased influence and/ or wealth. In a world where many were susceptible to economic loss due to sudden catastrophe (e.g., crop failure or the death of a family's pri- mary provider) and even downward mobility (e.g., being captured in a raid and reduced to slavery), another aspect of social mobility entailed a

---

3. On the virtual inseparability of lordship over land and people for early medieval societies, see Smith, *Europe after Rome*, 151–52.

person's decreasing the likelihood of falling into destitution.[4] One could do this by becoming attached to a powerful established institution (e.g., a royal court or church) that privileged its members and protected them from such straits. Such are the stratagems one witnesses Gauls attempting in the literary sources. In this and the next chapter, we shall concentrate upon members of the four social groupings (aristocrats, *ingenui*, *pauperes*, and slaves) participating in three strategies: (1) marrying and combining family resources, (2) pursuing secular office, and (3) pursuing clerical office and/or religious authority.[5] The second half of this chapter will present details of how aristocrats used each of these strategies to maintain and enhance social status. It also will attend to examples of individuals who attempted to infiltrate the noble ranks. But to begin, let us approach our model by considering how the elite composers of our sources imagined society.

THE VIEW(S) FROM ABOVE: HIERARCHICAL SOCIETY

A first step toward building a model for Gallic society will be to consider perceptions about that world advanced by the producers of our texts. Fortunately, such an effort benefits from the survival of one kind of source for which ecclesiastics were not the principal propagators – secular legislation. Inhabitants of Barbarian Gaul lived with a diversity of legal systems.[6] In Caesarius of Arles' lifetime, he and fellow Arlésiens were subject to laws decreed by Visigothic, then Ostrogothic, then Frankish kings. Gregory of Tours, who was ever subject to Frankish governance, distinguished between secular and church law, *lex romana* and *lex catholica*.[7] Over the better part of the sixth century, Salic law applied to all within the Frankish realms whether they were legally categorized

---

4. See Brown, *Poverty and Leadership*, 49, who contends that late ancient societies included the same "widespread 'shallow poverty' that had always characterized an ancient society."
5. By no means is this an exhaustive list of the ways Gauls attempted to improve their social lot. One stratagem that will not be examined separately, but will receive some consideration, is use of intimidation and violence for economic or social gain.
6. See T. M. Charles-Edwards, "Law in the Western Kingdoms between the Fifth and Seventh Century," in *The Cambridge Ancient History*, vol. 14, *Late Antiquity: Empire and Successors, A.D. 425–600*, ed. Averil Cameron, Bryan Ward-Perkins, and Michael Whitby (Cambridge: Cambridge University Press, 2000), 260–87.
7. Greg. Tur., *VP* 8.5, *Hist.* 5.38.

as *romani* or *franci*; however, Alaric's *Breviarium* and the Theodosian Code remained in use.[8] Although one family continued to rule Gaul, by the mid-seventh century different law codes again applied for separate regions: *Pactus legis Salicae* in Neustria, *Lex Ribuaria* in Austrasia, and the *Liber Constitutionum* in Burgundy.[9] While bishops, kings, and secular magnates commonly worked in concert to create legislation, one may characterize sixth-century lawmaking (outside the production of canons) as an essentially secular affair.[10] Furthermore, although lawmakers instilled ideas of proportional fairness within their text, the resultant legislation invariably assumed a hierarchical social structure with a king at the top.[11] Gallic law codes and edicts, therefore, as much as any other written genre, may be interpreted as projecting ideal images for society, visions for which a royal interest predominates. Of course, the particulars of these visions will have differed according to the variety of edicts and codes – Visigothic, Burgundian, and Frankish. For the sake of brevity, and given the early appearance and lasting significance of the last, it is only the Salic law that our analysis will consider.

The makers of Salic law included two systems to divide society – liberty and wergild. The more basic of the dividing principals was that between free and slave. This distinction had deep roots in ancient cultures. The Roman jurist Gaius had written, "And indeed the highest division of persons by law is that all men are either free or slave."[12]

---

8. Ian Wood, "The Code in Merovingian Gaul," in *The Theodosian Code*, ed. Jill Harries and Ian N. Wood (Ithaca, NY: Cornell University Press, 1993), 159–77; Antti Arjava, "The Survival of Roman Family Law after the Barbarian Settlements," in *Law, Society and Authority in Late Antiquity*, ed. Ralph W. Mathisen (Oxford and New York: Oxford University Press, 2001), 37–38.

9. Wood, *Merovingian Kingdoms*, 114–15.

10. Nira Pancer, *Sans peur et sans verogne: De l'honneur et des femmes aux premiers temps mérovingienne* (Pais: Albin Michel, 2001), 104–21, characterizes *Pactus legis Salicae* as reflecting a code of honor that was worldly and, indeed, aggressive.

11. On fairness, Salic law contains more food-related constitutions than any other barbarian legal corpus, which can be interpreted to mean that these laws reflect "a governmental sensitivity to local needs" primarily beneficial for food producing peasants; Kathy Pearson, "Salic Law and Barbarian Diet," in *Law, Society and Authority in Late Antiquity*, ed. Ralph W. Mathisen (Oxford and New York: Oxford University Press, 2001), 285. Salic law also included constitutions that discouraged theft of goods from the (presumably) defenseless, especially women, but also the deceased, including slaves. Receiving composition could enable an aggrieved family of any social level to recover a degree of honor. See Effros, *Caring for Body and Soul*, 28–32.

12. Gaius, *Institutes*, 1.9 (Francis Zulueta, ed., *The Institutes of Gaius*, 2 vols. [Oxford: Clarendon, 1946], 1: 4): "Et quidem summa divisio de iure personarum haec est, quod omnes homines aut liberi sunt aut servi."

During the late Empire, Christianization had not deterred the Roman practice of keeping slaves; instead, influential ecclesiastics proposed that slavery was an institution divinely decreed and deservedly meted upon sinful humankind.[13] One witnesses the continued relevance for a legal category of slavery in the titles of dozens of constitutions within *Pactus legis Salicae*.[14] According to the letter of the law, the disparity between the treatment of slave and free was extreme; whereas a free man was his own person under the law, Salic law regarded a slave as property.[15] Salic legislation afforded free people privileges not available to slaves, the most obvious involving torture, proof of innocence, and punishment.[16] While the law prescribed monetary fines for convicted free people, it imposed potentially debilitating corporal punishment for slaves found guilty of identical offenses.[17] The prevalence of the free/slave dichotomy in laws for ascertaining guilt and meting punishments for all manner of crimes suggests that the makers of *Pactus legis Salicae* could not conceive of society without such a distinction. They perceived slavery as an essential component for a rightly hierarchical society that needed to be maintained to assure continued orderliness.[18]

13. E.g., Augustine, *De civitate dei* 19.15–16. This is not to say that manumission did not become a significant Christian charitable activity. See Rapp, *Holy Bishops in Late Antiquity*, 239–42.

14. The slave population could be perpetuated not only through birth, war, and trade, but also through legal means. Persons unable to pay property judgments or legal fines could be reduced to slavery; *PLS* 58. Furthermore, a free man who married the female slave of another could be subject to slavery, as could a thief apprehended in a locked house; *PLS* 25.4, 85. For the continued relevance of slavery in Barbarian Gaul, see the section on *Servi* in Chapter Four.

15. See, e.g., *PLS* 10.1, on the theft of a slave, maidservant, horse or ox. If a slave were injured, composition for damages went not to the inflicted individual, but to his master. Likewise, if a person convicted of a crime were free, he paid damages, whereas if the offender were a slave, the lord was required to pay; e.g., *PLS* 35.

16. Torture and proof by lot (*sors*) for slaves: *PLS* 40.4, 82.2, 83.2. Contrast for free: *PLS* 53.1–8. Free persons accused of petty theft might face the ordeal of boiling water (*inius*), by which one had to retrieve a ring from scalding liquid. The failure of abrasions to appear could prove God's favor and hence determine the innocence of the accused. Although potentially more painful than the *sors*, the *inius* relied on God's justice instead of blind chance, and so the Gauls might have thought the procedure less humiliating. See Ian Wood, "Disputes in Late Fifth- and Sixth-Century Gaul: Some Problems," in *The Settlement of Disputes in Early Medieval Europe*, ed. Wendy Davies and Paul Fouracre (Cambridge: Cambridge University Press, 1986), 19, for the *inius* and its possible origins.

17. See, e.g., *PLS* 40.1, in which a captured thief, if a freeman, pays composition, but if a slave, receives twenty lashes. For the opportunity of a slave owner to pay a fee, or "buy the back" of the slave, see *PLS* 40.2.

18. This essential legal division of people expressed in secular law did not necessarily mirror a corresponding actual difference in patterns of exploitation of slave and free. About early medieval slavery, Chris

A second conspicuous method for legally distinguishing subjects of the Frankish kingdoms was according to "wergild," the amount a killer must pay a victim's relations.[19] Perhaps even more than the free/slave dichotomy, laws assigning wergild reveal clearly how Frankish kings perceived a rightly hierarchical world. According to Salic law, some people simply were worth more than others. Interestingly, wergild did not distinguish social ranks among free persons; rather, the system involved a complex assessment that depended on several criteria including liberty, sex, age, service to the king, and even "ethnicity." The basic wergild was that for a free "Frank" (*francus*), whether man or woman, two hundred *solidi*.[20] A cautious interpretation for the meaning of *francus* in Salic law is a person from a family whose men were liable for military service.[21] The wergild of a *francus* was double that for a "Roman" (*romanus*).[22] Makers of Salic law divided *romani* into landlords and renters, and apparently they intended the term in general to identify people who "did not usually fight."[23] The double value of wergild for a Frank versus a Roman evinces the kings and their lawmakers' concern to privilege the soldiery, which was after all the base for royal power. Along that line of thinking, military service was for males the principal criterion for augmenting wergild. Thus, a man killed while serving in the army was worth 600 *solidi*.[24] Likewise, a boy under twelve years of age, because he potentially offered a full lifetime of military service, had a wergild of 600 *solidi*.[25] For females, fertility was the central criterion; a woman of childbearing age had a value of 600 *solidi*, while a woman who reached an age at

Wickham, *Framing the Early Middle Ages*, 262, writes: "… the [plantation-based] slave mode was only a minor survival, everywhere marginal to the basic economic structure, the landlord-peasant relationship (where there were landlords at all)."

19. James, *The Franks*, 216–18.
20. *PLS* 15.1.
21. Halsall, *Settlement and Social Organization*, 28, elucidates: "Those Franks who migrated across the Rhine and settled in northern Gaul had always been subject to military service; those who adopted Frankish ethnicity as a result of fighting on the winning side doubtless regarded themselves as subject to the same dues."
22. See, e.g., *PLS* 42.4.
23. Halsall, *Settlement and Social Organization*, 28.
24. *PLS* 8.1 (*MGH*, LL sectio 1, 4.1, 273): "Si quis hominem ingenuum in hoste occiserit et in mortridam mittitur, solidos MDCCC culpabilis iudicetur." Composition for murder was three times a victim's wergild. Here, *ingenuus* would equate with *francus*, a person subject to the military levy.
25. *PLS* 24.1, 4; 41.18.

which she likely could no longer bear offspring was worth 200 *solidi*.[26] These adjustments for men and women by age betray the legislators' central concern to maintain numbers from which future soldiers could be drawn. The king's authority and the security of the realm depended upon it.

Wergild values in Salic law were prohibitive, and in practice few would have been capable of paying recompense to the surviving kin of a murder victim. In one respect, then, high wergild may have served as a privilege in the form of a deterrent for a potential attacker; the higher the wergild, the greater the safeguard.[27] In this sense, differentiation among wergild values reflects legislators' intentions to make the king's court a place for people to turn for privilege and honor. Royal judicial and military leaders were declared worthy of an augmented wergild. For example, Salic law prescribed values of 600 *solidi* for counts (*comites*),[28] royal retainers (*antrustiones*),[29] and royal justices (*sagibaroni*).[30] By virtue of a late sixth-century edict, bishops too received a value of 600 *solidi*.[31] Importantly, lawmakers augmented wergild for dignitaries specifically by occupation, not according to social rank. By so doing, legislators were able to acknowledge a degree of honor for prominent individuals without recognizing the existence of a hereditary nobility.[32] Because the highest wergilds were reserved for persons in regular proximity to kings,

26. *PLS* 24.8–9; 41.17, 19; 65e.1–4. On wergilds for women, see Suzanne Fonay Wemple, *Women in Frankish Society: Marriage and the Cloister, 500 to 900* (Philadelphia: University of Pennsylvania Press, 1981), 28–29. The value to kin and community of women of marrying and childbearing age (up to around age forty), and the high and longer lasting value of males, is further reflected by patterns of deposition of grave goods (e. g., jewelry and weapons); Halsall, *Settlement and Social Organization*, 248; idem, "Social Identities and Social Relationships," 154–55. Likewise, gender and age distribution for epitaphs indicates an identical assessment for the worth of men and women; Handley, *Death, Society and Culture*, 81.

27. Setting wergild, with other kinds of compensation, high also could serve to convince Gauls that this was an honorable alternative to seeking vengeance against an attacker, which could potentially spark an episode of retributive violence. On the honorability of accepting composition for persons of low rank but not necessarily for aristocrats, see Pancer, *Sans peur et sans vergogne*, 116–18.

28. *PLS* 54.1.

29. *PLS* 41.5.

30. *PLS* 54.3.

31. *PLS, septem causas* 8.5 (*MGH*, LL sectio 1, 4.1, 273). Deacons and priests would not receive individual wergilds until the Carolingian age; *Lex Salica S* 6 [58], 3–4 (*MGH*, LL sectio 1, 4.2, 202).

32. The lack of legal regard for aristocrats within Salic law likely constituted an aspect of Merovingian policy designed to forestall institutional recognition of a noble class; Halsall, *Settlement and Social Organization*, 35–37.

especially people in royal service, it seems that Frankish rulers intended them as a privilege and honor that the powerful were to acquire only in exchange for loyalty to the court. Hence, a secular landowning *romanus* could achieve his highest wergild by becoming one of the king's closest confidants, a member of the *conviva regis*.[33] Thus, the legal record, by virtue of the free/slave dichotomy and the variable wergild privilege, betrays a secular vision of a hierarchical society centering about king and court and devoid of a hereditary nobility.

If Salic law did not recognize a legally established nobility, the litterateurs among Gaul's powerful families certainly made the case for maintaining and strengthening aristocracies. Some authors appealed to the notion of a continued Roman aristocratic class by calling attention to distinguished lineage. One term offered by powerful landowners claiming ancestry back to the days of empire was *senator*. Obviously descendents of imperial officeholders such as Sidonius Apollinaris and his kin justifiably could call themselves *senatores*. But some were still using this term a full century after the disappearance of Western imperial rule. In the sixth century, the word *senator* came to represent a member of an "old" family that possessed large landholdings.[34] Although there is no evidence that any of Gregory of Tours' ancestors ever held imperial office, his kin certainly managed large estates for more than a century, and hence Gregory thought it fitting to identify his lineage as senatorial. Because they lacked institutional, and especially legal, recognition, aristocrats determined membership in their orders by demonstrating shared activities and adopting elitist attitudes. They proposed the principal attributes for nobility to be birth, high office, wealth, property, social affiliation, "good character," and a classical education.[35] They also utilized a vocabulary that asserted how members of their group

---

33. *PLS* 41.8. Another action that suggests the Merovingians were trying to curb the emergence of a legally recognized hereditary nobility was the practice among Frankish kings to eschew marriage to aristocratic women. Instead, they usually opted to wed either foreign royalty or slaves; Halsall, *Settlement and Social Organization*, 37.

34. Gilliard, "Senators of Sixth-Century Gaul," 684–97. An alternative to this definition is that the landowners had to claim that they were descendents of Roman senators; Brennan, "Senators and Social Mobility in Sixth-Century Gaul," 145–61.

35. Mathisen, *Roman Aristocrats in Barbarian Gaul*, 11.

were essentially superior to all others. Some terms by which aristocrats touted themselves above the rest of humanity emphasized possession of an inherent quality that made them worthy of their place atop society. Labels included *nobiles* (nobles), *optimi* (the best people), *boni* (the good people), *maiores* (the better people), *primores* (the first people), and *proceres* (the chief people). Other terms blatantly emphasized an aristocratic right to social domination such as *potentes* (powerful people) and *potentiores* (more powerful people).³⁶ Aristocrats used this vocabulary both to assure themselves, and remind others, that pursuing and maintaining *potentia* and *auctoritas* were actions reserved for members of their order alone. Furthermore, elitist authors proposed words to relegate others to the lower echelons of the population. Vocabulary emphasized "the others'" lack of noble essence for which low socioeconomic status rightly resulted. Words included *plebes*, *mediocres* (the common people), and *pauperes* (the poor people). Some derogatory terms stressed the non-noble being of commoners such as *minores* (the lesser people), *inferiores* (the inferior people), and worst of all, *mali* (the base people). Despite common use of these pejoratives, aristocrats occasionally recognized and even emphasized differences among non-elites, for example, by distinguishing people in terms of their freedom, or lack thereof, as by contrasting the terms *ingenui* (free people) and *servi*. Otherwise, our authors sometimes disregarded the variation among society's less privileged altogether and described others simply as *populus* (the people) or *multi* (the many).³⁷

Having established a vocabulary to distinguish their aristocratic selves from commoners, upper-class people next had to act the part; they had to live up to their own qualifications. Elite writers regarded birth as the most important determinant for consideration among their numbers.³⁸ Thus, when Sidonius commended a young nobleman to another aristocrat, his introduction stressed the subject's senatorial lineage first and foremost: "The *vir clarissimus*, Proiectus, a man of

---

36. Ibid., 9–12.
37. Ibid., 13. Some writers, however, Gregory of Tours among them, used the term *populus* to refer to all people, aristocrats included.
38. Ibid.

noble birth who can claim the distinction of having a father and an uncle among the *spectabiles* ... is very eager to be received into the bosom of your friendship, if you are not averse."[39] A century later, Gregory of Tours impressed upon readers of the *Historiae* the esteemed lineage of his own family members by depicting a king expressing awe at a relative's noble character: "The king remarked, 'This man [Gregory's great uncle Gundulf] is from one of the highest and greatest families.'"[40] Another criterion that aristocrats envisioned contributing to nobility was office-holding. During the last throws of the status-crazed late Roman era, highest office determined one's titulature. Thus, when Sidonius attained the position of *praefectus urbis Romae* in 468, he became a *vir inlustris*, which rank elevated him beyond the status of every senator bearing the lower grades of *spectabilis* and *clarissimus*.[41] While this senatorial pretense was one of the earliest victims of the disappearance of imperial rule in Gaul, emphasis on holding high office in royal administration provided a comparable substitute. Therefore when Gregory introduced readers to his aforementioned relation Gundulf as hailing *de genere senatorio*, he added a mention of how the king had elevated the man to the position of *dux*, as if this fact should enhance the audience's estimation of the fellow.[42] In addition to holding high secular posts, aristocrats imagined holding lofty ecclesiastical office, especially a bishopric, to enhance one's noble character. Thus, when Sidonius embellished the noble family of the aforementioned Proiectus, he called attention to the youth's grandfather, a *praestantissimus sacerdos*, after mentioning the two *spectabiles*.[43] Similarly, Venantius Fortunatus a century later indicated how ecclesiastical service ennobled Bishop Marcellus of Paris: "[Marcellus was a man] for whom the light of nobility (*nobilitatis lumen*) was to

39. Sid. Ap., *Ep.* 4.1.1 (Anderson ed. and trans., 1: 438–39): "Vir clarissimus Proiectus, domi nobilis et patre patruoque spectabilibus ... amicitiarum tuarum, nisi respuis, avidissime sinibus inferetur ... "
40. Greg. Tur., *Hist.* 4.15 (*MGH*, SRM 1.1, 147): "Respondit rex: 'Prima haec est et magna generatio.'"
41. *PLRE* 2: 117, s. v., "Gaius Sollius (Modestus?) Apollinaris Sidonius 6."
42. Greg. Tur., *Hist.* 6.11 (*MGH*, SRM 1.1, 281). Brennan, "Senators and Social Mobility in Sixth-Century Gaul," 159, contends that gaining royal patronage supplanted claiming senatorial status in establishing prestige.
43. Sid. Ap., *Ep.* 1.4.1 (Anderson, ed. and trans., 1: 438).

serve Christ gloriously without fault."[44] Ability itself, especially when coupled with high office, was another quality that aristocrats thought contributed to nobility. For example, Sidonius stressed the assiduity of one Gaudentius, a *novus homo* who attained the vicariate of *Septem Provinciae*.[45] Likewise, Venantius attributed the rise to prominence of Bishop Egidius of Reims to his merits: "By your distinguished deeds, Egidius, an honorable height [becomes you], from the merits of which your rank increased complimentarily."[46] Next to birth, perhaps the most important criterion for inclusion among Gallic aristocrats was one's acceptance by other aristocrats.[47] For example, in a letter to his friend Pelagius, Sidonius intimated that being numbered among elite people was a right that had to be earned and recognized by the already established *boni*: "Your friend Menstruanus ... has won the right to be counted amongst my dear and devoted friends. He is ... endowed with so excellent a character that when he is invited to share the friendship of any of the best people, he contributes no less benefit than he gains."[48]

In the sixth century, when military prowess was becoming more of a virtue, and when maintenance of a neighborhood's social order required a willingness among locals to pursue and mete justice, an increasingly significant criterion for nobility entailed an ability to project forcefulness and to defend one's honor, violently if need be.[49] For example, Venantius Fortunatus sang about how warfare ennobled King Sigibert,

---

44. Ven. Fort., *Vita Marcelli* 4 (*MGH*, AA 4.2, 50): " ... cui hoc fuit nobilitatis lumen insigne Christo sine culpa servire ..."
45. Sid. Ap., *Ep.* 1.4.1.
46. Ven. Fort., *Carm.* 3.15.1–2 (*MGH*, AA 4.1, 68): "Actibus egregiis venerabile culmen, Egidi, ex cuius meritis crevit honore gradus ... "
47. Mathisen, *Roman Aristocrats in Barbarian Gaul*, 12.
48. Sid. Ap., *Ep.* 2.6.1–2 (Anderson, ed. and trans., 1: 442–43): "Menstruanus amicus tuus ... meruit inter personas nobis quoque caras devinctasque censeri, ... et his morum dotibus praeditus ut, quotiens in boni cuiusque adscitur amicitias, non amplius consequatur beneficii ipse quam tribuat."
49. See Liebeschuetz, "Violence in the Barbarian Successor Kingdoms," 43, who writes: "In Merovingian society, honor affected not only a man's self-respect but also his standing in society and therefore his ability to protect his family, dependents, and allies." Nira Pancer, *Sans peur et sans vergogne*, 81–101, differentiates between a fifth-century, genteel male "Gallo-Roman" honor displayed in Sidonius Apollinaris's pages, and a Merovingian male honor found in Venantius Fortunatus's poems, the latter combining "Gallo-Roman" virtues with "Germanic" bravado. Furthermore, for early Merovingian female honor, see ibid., 211–57.

although his intent was supposedly peaceable: "Conqueror, whose fame carries him from the setting to the rising of the sun and makes him a noble and eminent ruler, who could do you justice? ... Your wars have granted peace with new-found prosperity, and your sword has brought forth true joy."[50] Presumably the poet anticipated that the courtly audience before whom this piece would be sung would have concurred that martial ability makes a king "noble and eminent." Similarly, Gregory of Tours depicted King Guntram expressing an obligation to defend his family's honor after the murder of his brother, Chilperic, by stating: "I should not be counted among men, if I fail to avenge his murder within the year."[51] Gregory similarly portrayed a Frank aristocrat at Tours named Chramnesind, whose sense of honor was compelling him to avenge slain kinsmen, uttering a like expression: "Unless I avenge the murder of my relatives, I ought to lose the label of man and I should be called a weak woman."[52] Gregory was in general an outspoken critic of violence in the forms of local feuds and the wars waged among Merovingians. Furthermore, the bishop certainly opposed the particular methods with which Guntram and Chramnesind reacted to the perceived slights to their families' honor. The king accused a bishop (wrongly in Gregory's estimation) as an instigator in his brother's death, and then he dispatched soldiers who slew another suspect in Chilperic's assassination, but not without defiling sanctuary at Saint Martin's basilica.[53] Meanwhile, Chramnesind retaliated after his family's loss by murdering his antagonist, Sichar, thereby threatening to extend what was already a protracted episode of local violence in the Touraine.[54] Still, while Gregory abhorred the resulting violence, perhaps he harbored

---

50. Ven. Fort., *Carm.*, 6.1a.1–3, 15–16 (*MGH*, SRM, 4.1, 129): "Victor, ab occasu quem laus extendit in ortum / et facit egregium principis esse caput, / quis tibi digna ferat? ... prosperitate nova pacem tua bella dederunt / et peperit gladius gaudia certa tuus ..."; George, trans., *Venantius Fortunatus: Personal and Political Poems*, 31–32; Pancer, *Sans peur et sans vergogne*, 98.

51. Greg. Tur., *Hist.* 8.5 (*MGH*, SRM 1.1, 374): "Denique nec nos pro viris haberi debemur, si eius necem ulciscere non valemus hoc anno."

52. Greg. Tur., *Hist.* 9.19 (*MGH*, SRM 1.1, 433): "Nisi ulciscar interitum parentum meorum, amittere nomen viri debeo et mulier infirma vocare."

53. Greg. Tur., *Hist.* 7.21, 29, 8.5.

54. Greg. Tur., *Hist.* 7.47, 9.19. For more on Sichar, Chramnesind, and new terminology for their "feud," see Halsall, "Violence and Society in the Early Medieval West," 1–2, 19–29.

an appreciation for the underlying honor code.[55] For example, after describing the murder of his own brother Peter, Gregory rather smugly related how the culprit met his end by being sliced into pieces.[56] The bishop thought this last instance of vengeance acceptable because it was divinely meted, but nevertheless his telling of the story reflects a concern and recourse not unlike those of Guntram and Chramnesind to publicly emphasize and restore family honor after a violent attack. As for his thoughts on martial prowess, Gregory, whom we recall was peacock-proud of his great uncle the *dux*, did not hesitate to laud a warrior, so long as his cause was just. For example, about the victor of the Catalaunian Plains, he wrote: "[Aetius'] intelligence was keen, he was full of energy, a superb horseman, a fine shot with an arrow and tireless with the lance. He was extremely able as a soldier and he was skilled in the art of peace."[57] While clerics might qualify an appreciation of martial spirit by insisting in writings that it should serve a peaceful purpose, nevertheless, violence had become a recognizably legitimate indicator of nobility for many, if not most, Gallic elites.[58]

Another attribute that sixth-century aristocrats likely regarded as an indicator of human quality more than did earlier nobles whose numbers had been better delineated was wealth.[59] This is not to say that wealth had not contributed at least in a *de facto* sense to people's nobility well back into the Roman era. Salvian of Marseilles in the early fifth century wrote somewhat sarcastically, but tellingly, that he could not distinguish between affluent and noble people, "for such is the misery of this time that no one is considered nobler than he who has great wealth."[60] Contrast Salvian's negativity with Gregory of Tours' mention of wealth

55. Pancer, *Sans peur et sans vergogne*, 98–99.
56. Greg. Tur., *Hist.* 5.5.
57. Greg. Tur., *Hist.* 2.8 (*MGH*, SRM 1.1, 51): "... animo alacer, membris vegitus, equis promptissimus, saggitarum iactu peritus, contu inpiger, bellis aptissimus, pacis artibus celebris ..." Trans. by Lewis Thorpe, *Gregory of Tours, History of the Franks* (Harmondsworth: Penguin, 1974), 119. Here Gregory was quoting from the otherwise lost history of Renatus Profuturus Frigeridus. For Gregory's conception of just warfare, see Wynn, "Wars and Warriors in Gregory of Tours' *Histories*," 6–8.
58. For violence as a legitimate feature of early medieval local dispute settlement, see Innes, *State and Society in the Early Middle Ages*, 129–39.
59. Gilliard, "Senators of Sixth-Century Gaul," 693.
60. Salvian of Marseilles, *De gubernatione dei* 3.10.53 (*CSEL* 8, 60): "... quia tanta est miseria huius temporis, ut nullus habeatur magnis nobilis quam qui est plurimum dives."

to impress upon readers the social significance of a family mentioned in the *Historiae*. When Gregory described the deaths and confiscation of property of a certain Severus and his sons, he concluded the anecdote by noting that they were very rich.[61] The author can only have tacked on this final mention of riches because he expected it to augment the reader's appreciation of the tragedy. Elsewhere, Gregory put words into the mouth of Queen Fredegund to reveal how lucre could launch people into aristocratic ranks. The queen remarked, "... remember that rather often soldiers die in war, whereby their relatives, affected by huge wealth, rise high above all nobles, and they surpass all."[62] Here, Gregory's words betray an air of elitist disgust at the thought of commoners surpassing aristocrats. Like Salvian's whining, Gregory's words also contain an element of obvious exaggeration, but there is truth in jest. Fredegund herself, a person whom Gregory loathed, had risen from slave to queen, and her meteoric rise to high status in a court setting was hardly an isolated incident. What needs be emphasized here is that Gregory, like Sidonius and Salvian before him, thought that Gallic society rightly had a hierarchy of humanity, and aristocratic echelons were too sacrosanct for gauche people merely to be able to purchase membership. Of course, for every elitist declaration of a need for aristocratic exclusion, the same authors offered an anecdote revealing how they were willing to make exceptions for certain individuals trying to join their ranks.

Neither the image derived from secular legislation nor ecclesiastics' literature reflects exactly how Gallic society was arranged. Each kind of source projects a different vision for the same world. This is not to say, however, that the sources do not reveal features of the processes whereby aristocrats actually attempted to structure a society in which they principally would benefit. One aspect of the "making" of Gallic society plainly visible in our evidence is patronage. Kings and aristocrats regarded *patrocinium* as a rightful and effective means by which to formulate a hierarchical world to their advantage. A reason Gallic magnates

---

61. Greg. Tur., *Hist.* 5.25 (*MGH*, SRM 1.1, 232): "Erant enim eis magni thesauri."
62. Greg. Tur., *Hist.*, 8.29 (*MGH*, SRM 1.1, 392): "... considerate saepius fortes viros in bello conruere, unde nunc parentes eorum nobilis effecti opibus inmensis cunctis supereminent cunctisque praecellent."

relied on patronage was that it was an inherited practice that was to their minds, like slavery, essential to the proper structuring of the world. Late Romans especially could no more have conceived of a society without patrons and clients than one without masters and slaves. Ancient patronage was "a reciprocal exchange relationship between people of unequal status and resources."[63] Patrons initiated the exchange process by granting services called *beneficia*. While recipients of services whose rank was the same as their patrons might more appropriately be termed protégés, beneficiaries whose social and economic position differed considerably from patrons were called clients. The term *cliens* was demeaning, and although a polite patron might not use it to characterize a protégé, the latter might use it ingratiatingly to describe his situation in relation to a patron.[64] In Gaul, both secular and ecclesiastical leaders relied on *patrocinium*, especially the distribution of largesse, to impress betters and equals, to foster dependency of inferiors, and to build social authority.[65] During the Barbarian era, kings replaced governors and emperors as the chief source for institutional patronage, which included distribution of offices, privileges, gifts, and land in return for political loyalty. Kings replenished their treasuries primarily by conducting successful wars and gathering booty, but also by preserving the imperial tax system and by repossessing fiscal estates from deceased magnates lest their families become overly powerful.[66] Patronage on a local level frequently took the form of ecclesiastical leaders encouraging the faithful to recognize dead saints as patrons, who would in turn reward properly reverent

---

63. Peter Garnsey and Richard Saller, *The Roman Empire: Economy, Society and Culture* (Berkeley and Los Angeles: University of California Press, 1987), 152–53.

64. Ibid., 153.

65. On gift-giving as an essential component for early medieval power-brokering, see Smith, *Europe after Rome*, 198–214.

66. On Merovingian techniques for building and maintaining power, see Van Dam, "Merovingian Gaul and the Frankish Conquests," 209–13. Wickham, *Framing the Early Middle Ages*, 56, characterizes the Merovingian polity as a "weak state" possessing "a landed army but also a strong sense of public power acting as a focus for political legitimation, inherited from the Roman world." In contrast, the Byzantine and Arab states with their tax systems and paid armies were "strong." Wickham, ibid., 105–15, explains that Merovingian power derived from control of land, not taxes, although the kings were able to maintain revenues from the declining tax apparatus. For the Merovingians using patronage as a check against the growth of aristocratic power, see Halsall, *Settlement and Social Organization*, 33–39.

clients by healing infirmities, fending off demons, assuring fertile crops and spouses, and defending town and countryside.[67] Episcopal patrons expected the faithful to give alms and pay tithes, and in turn they redistributed part of this wealth back to "the poor." Clients, both wealthy and poor, had better conform to orthodox beliefs and demonstrate that conformity by attending church, especially on important holy days.[68] Bishops reminded clients, peasants especially, that those who angered the holy patrons by insisting on working on Sundays or saints' days might face chastisement in the form of excommunication or perhaps via some heaven-sent infirmity.[69] For both prominent ecclesiastics and kings, then, part and parcel of the ideal hierarchical society involved people of every station "following the rules" by minding their social superiors, obeying the laws, and going to church.

ARISTOCRATS AND ARISTOCRACIES

Literary sources portray the powerful in Gaul upholding criteria such as family ties, education, forcefulness, *patrocinium*, and office holding to show that they were literally the best (*optimi*) society had to offer. By the end of the sixth century, Gallic magnates had yet to secure institutional recognition for persons of aristocratic rank. Not only did a legally established nobility fail to materialize; neither did aristocrats ever constitute a cultural or political monolith. There was no Gallic aristocracy; rather,

---

67. John H. Corbett, "*Praesentium signorum munera*: The Cult of the Saints in the World of Gregory of Tours," *Florilegium* 5 (1983), 44–61. Paul Anthony Hayward, "Demystifying the Role of Sanctity in Western Christendom," in *The Cult of Saints in Late Antiquity and the Middle Ages: Essays on the Contribution of Peter Brown*, ed. James Howard-Johnston and Paul Anthony Hayward (Oxford and New York: Oxford University Press, 1999), 127, doubts the extent to which "Gregory's culture of tomb centered veneration" was acceptable to non-aristocrats. Epigraphy is a medium independent of literature that illuminates devotion to saints among non-elites and in parts of Gaul where certain cults previously were unknown through hagiography; Handley, *Death, Society and Culture*, 140. Epitaphs and graffiti confirm a strong Gallic devotion to episcopal saints such as those usually promoted in Gregory's pages. To show that this kind of source constitutes a reliable indicator of the kind of sanctity practiced in a region, Spanish epigraphy, in contrast to that from Gaul, confirms other evidence and attests to a preference in that region for martyr cults; ibid., 142–54. Bailey Young, "Sacred Topography: The Impact of the Funerary Basilica," 180, refers to extra-mural cemeteries as "the greatest repositories of Christian memories," and he characterizes reverence for saints as "anchored in funerary monuments built in their honor and now linked in a liturgical network."

68. Wood, *Merovingian Kingdoms*, 72.

69. Ibid.

there were aristocracies.[70] In the Barbarian era, the different power sets to which aristocrats might belong differed by activity and by region. Three principal actions that identified prominent Gauls as belonging to an aristocracy were possessing large landholdings, participating prominently at court, and acquiring high church office. These aristocracies were not exclusive; for example, many ecclesiastical aristocrats also were large landowners. During the sixth century, regional aristocracies materialized around fixed centers, royal courts, each of which had its own king and a "secretary of state," the *maior domus*. After the death of King Charibert in 567, three court-centered aristocracies became relatively permanent – Burgundy, Neustria, and Austrasia. Previous to these, there already existed regional aristocracies in Aquitaine and arguably Provence.[71] Frankish kings living to the north allotted Aquitanian and Provençal cities to one another and taxed their residents from a distance. Gallic aristocrats were therefore able to identify their family interests by behavior (land ownership, government or church involvement), by region, or by any combination.

One difficulty encountered by aristocratic writers who envisioned establishing solidarity among fellow social elites was that invariably

70. John Matthews, *Western Aristocracies and Imperial Court*, 146–72, 329–51, identified in late fourth- and early fifth-century Gaul multiple aristocracies including propertied upper-class provincials, some of whom occasionally joined or replaced governing aristocrats ennobled by imperial service. Wickham, *Framing the Early Middle Ages*, 168–203, stresses the regional nature – from his empire wide perspective, "sub-regional" – of Gallic aristocracies. Despite local variations, late ancient aristocracies kept some semblance of a shared cultural milieu; Michele R. Salzman, "Elite Realities and Mentalités: The Making of a Western Christian Aristocracy," in *Élites in Late Antiquity, Arethusa* 33.3, ed. Michele R. Salzman and Claudia Rapp (Baltimore: Johns Hopkins University Press, 2000), 347–62.

71. Wood, *Merovingian Kingdoms*, 55–58. Guy Halsall, *Settlement and Social Organization*, 249–61, interprets evidence including burial items in northern Gallic cemeteries to conclude that the Gallic north experienced pronounced social disruption in the fifth century, from which aristocrats would be recovering through the sixth. He contrasts stable aristocracies to the south with non-existent to emerging ones in the north, where elites initially reliant upon royal patronage became a landed aristocracy around 600. Matthew Innes, *State and Society in the Early Middle Ages*, 173, also using cemetery evidence, asserts that the Middle Rhenish aristocracy coalesced from "local landowners and incoming barbarian leaders" to constitute "a new elite in a new society." Chris Wickham, *Framing the Early Middle Ages*, 171–78, acknowledges the particular strength of the birth and land based Aquitanian aristocracy, but he rejects theories touting marked differences between northern and southern aristocratic experiences. He asserts that a northern landed aristocracy did not have to be made anew, and that Merovingians from Clovis and beyond cooperated with what was a continuous body of landowning elites, whose membership included figures such as Remigius of Reims and Lupus of Champagne; ibid., 178–97.

the nobles themselves organized into competing factions. A common trend in the formation of Gallic factions was a willingness on the part of individual aristocrats to secure immediate benefits by joining with an alternative royal patron. The promise of quick and easy influence in the form of office and treasure enticed some aristocrats to support young Merovingians. Together, an aspiring king and a cabal of landed aristocrats might hope to convert the landowners' region into the next great center for royal power. For example, in 555, Chramn, a son of King Chlothar I whom the ruler had stationed at Clermont, began calling himself king. He conferred the title count of Clermont upon the senatorial aristocrat Salustius. While Salustius enjoyed his new position, two militants named Imnachar and Scapthar, perhaps hopeful of becoming generals for the new regime, confiscated the wealth of the city's previous *comes*, Firminus.[72] At Poitiers, people whom Gregory termed "evil men" (i.e., more ambitious aristocrats) then persuaded Chramn to offer allegiance to his uncle Childebert I. A year of successful campaigning in the Limousin, around Chalon-sur-Saône, and toward Tours helped convince Childebert to join the seemingly capable upstart against Chlothar, who conveniently was occupied in a war against the Saxons.[73] Chramn and his allies' position suddenly deteriorated, however, with Childebert's death in 558, which left Chlothar I the sole legitimate Frankish monarch. In 560, Chramn fled to Brittany, but there Chlothar's troops apprehended and slaughtered the fugitive along with his wife and daughters.[74] Presumably it was at this juncture that Salustius lost his office, or his life. A year later, reportedly on the very anniversary of his son's demise, Chlohtar died. With the succession of the king's four surviving sons, aristocrats across Gaul would enjoy four centers of institutional patronage from which to seek privileges.[75]

Factionalism and periodic violent upheaval must have confused the process of determining social rank, even according to the most broadly defined categories. Nevertheless, hopeful makers of nobility intended

---

72. Greg. Tur., *Hist.* 4.13.
73. Greg. Tur., *Hist.* 4.16–18; Mar. Avent., *Chron.*, s. a. 556.
74. Greg. Tur., *Hist.* 4.20; Mar. Avent., *Chron.*, s. a. 560.
75. Greg. Tur., *Hist.* 4.21.

their rhetoric of "shared experiences" to continue into the future. Thus, Sidonius wrote to his friend Aquilinus, "… let us be … two souls of a single mind, and let us teach our children to live in mutual affection desiring or rejecting, seeking or avoiding the same things."[76] These sentiments, however, were merely an aspect of an ideal of noble solidarity that did not match reality. In fact, the very sources in which the powerful proposed unity reveal how aristocrats could not live up to their own rhetoric. One problem was that aristocrats were ever at odds to determine whom to exclude from noble circles. For example, when the parvenu Gaudentius obtained the office of *vicarius Septem Provinciarum*, Sidonius readily admitted him to friendship, but the young noblemen whom Gaudentius passed over were not as accepting; instead, they stewed about their "trampled on nobility."[77] Another difference of opinion over noble qualifications involved a debate between Gregory of Tours and Bishop Sagittarius of Gap. When the latter publicly remarked that the sons of King Guntram could not ascend the throne because their mother was of servile origin, Gregory contradicted the assessment, noting that Sagittarius was "ignoring the fact that, irrespective of their mother's birth, all children born to a king count as a king's sons."[78] Apparently, even qualification to membership within Gaul's first family was subject to deliberation.[79]

If factionalism ultimately nullified the possibility for widespread aristocratic identity, so too did an inability to agree on who counted among noble echelons occasion the chance for people of lower status to enter higher ranks. Thus far, the voices of several authors have testified to a Gallic society that was recognizably hierarchical, built one social layer upon another. But these levels were separated by ill-defined borders, and the tiers themselves consisted of living, breathing, potentially

---

76. Sid. Ap., *Ep.* 5.9.4 (Anderson, ed. and trans., 2: 202): "… simus … animae duae, amimus unus, imbuamusque liberos invicem diligentes idem velle nolle, refugere sectari."

77. Sid. Ap., *Ep.* 1.3 (Anderson, ed. and trans., 1: 346): "calcata generositas."

78. Greg. Tur., *Hist.*, 5.20 (*MGH*, SRM 1.1, 228): "… ignorans, quod, praetermissis nunc generibus feminarum, regis vocitantur liberi, qui de regibus fuerant procreati."

79. Speculation on what makes a Merovingian continues. Ian Wood, "Deconstructing the Merovingian Family," 164, recently has offered: "The Merovingian family was not … an unquestionably biological unit, it was rather a political construct."

socially mobile individuals. At this point, we shall begin an examination of participants in several of Gaul's aristocracies as separated by behavior: landholders, courtiers, and ecclesiastical aristocrats. Because this study ultimately pertains to non-elites, we shall frequently turn to examples of protégés as they tried to advance into the highest ranks. The first aristocracy on which we shall focus is that which consisted of prominent persons combining resources, especially land, through marriage.

LANDED ARISTOCRATS

The basis of power for most Gallic noble families was landholding.[80] With the disappearance of empire, large landowners to the south distinguished themselves as *nobiles* by continued use of the term *senator*.[81] The *senatores*' principal strategy for preserving social preeminence was to marry offspring into families with like pedigree, and combine resources.[82] Gregory of Tours' family exemplifies the process. Gregory was the product of several generations of multiple large landowning clans, his father's relatives originating from the Auvergne and his mother's from Burgundy. The historian identified three of four of his maternal great grandparents as having senatorial status, meaning they were large landowners. The parents of his mother's father were Gregorius, *ex senatoribus primis*, and Armentaria, who was *ex senatoribus*.[83] Gregory's mother Armentaria took her name from this grandmother. The younger Armentaria's mother's father was Florentinus, a native of Geneva who was *ex senatoribus*.[84] He married Artemia, whose family background

---

80. Power did not result simply from possessing land. Innes, *State and Society in the Early Middle Ages*, 93, writes: "... control of land was necessary to fund a lifestyle and to enter the social spheres in which one could create the personal contacts which allowed one to exercise power."

81. For Gregory of Tours' synonymous use of *nobilis* and *senator*, see Gilliard, "Senators of Sixth-Century Gaul," 692.

82. In what follows, I privilege the notion of a traditional Roman concept of "marriage," which implies partners of theoretically equal rank and parental consent for, if not parental instigation of, the union. There was great diversity in early medieval sexual partnerships including marriage, concubinage, and other arrangements, for which see Smith, *Europe after Rome*, 125–35. Likewise, there was considerable variation for early medieval inheritance strategies; ibid., 135–47. Regarding transmission of resources, I am less interested in stratagems to preserve patrimony than efforts to preserve or augment status. On the centrality of these goals for families passing along property to the next generation, see ibid., 143.

83. Greg. Tur., *VP* 7.1 (*MGH*, SRM 1.2, 237).

84. Greg. Tur., *VP* 8.1 (*MGH*, SRM 1.2, 241).

Gregory did not provide. Gregory's most poignant evidence for the importance of intermarriage in the designs of large landed families comes from anecdotes about his paternal kin. When remarking about his uncle Gallus, future Bishop of Clermont, Gregory blended the usual ecclesiastical rhetoric of distain for wealth with a description intended to impress readers with the subject's social prominence: "Such was St Gallus, a man of the Auvergne, whom neither the greatness of his birth nor the elevation of the senatorial order nor his immense riches were able to turn away from the riches of God."[85] Gallus's parents, Gregory's paternal grandparents Georgius and Leucadia, were "from the principal senatorial families, and there were none better born nor more noble in Gaul."[86] This landed aristocratic couple apparently intended to pair both of their sons with equally socially affluent mates. Georgius wanted Gallus to wed "the daughter of a certain senator" (*cuiusdam senatoris filiam*), but the pious young man reportedly fled to a monastery outside Clermont.[87] When the abbot realized that the eager youth was a product of the city's "first family" (*de prima proginie*), he sent messengers to obtain the father's permission before ordaining Gallus.[88] Although Georgius begrudgingly relented, the father obviously had hoped to maintain or augment his family's fortunes by combining resources with another large landowning clan. Given that Gallus's betrothal amounted to an episode of local power brokering, the abbot's precaution of communicating with the senatorial patriarch was understandable and wise. Fortunately for Georgius, despite the "loss" of Gallus to the church, a younger son, Florentius (Gregory's father), proved more obedient to his parents' design for securing continued family prosperity. It might have been something of a coup that Georgius was able to arrange Florentius's betrothal to the very senatorial Armentaria.

---

85. Greg. Tur., *VP* 6, *praef.* (*MGH*, SRM 1.2, 230): "... sicut sanctus Gallus incola Arvernae urbis, quem a Dei cultu abstrahere non potuit nec splendor generis nec celsitudo senatorii ordinis nec opulentia facultatis ..." Trans. by Edward James, *Gregory of Tours, Life of the Fathers*, 2d ed., TTH1 (Liverpool: Liverpool University Press, 1991), 32.

86. Greg. Tur., *VP* 6.1 (*MGH*, SRM 1.2, 230): "Qui ita de primoribus senatoribus fuerunt, ut in Galliis nihil inveniatur esse generosius atque nobilius." Trans., by James, *Gregory of Tours, Life of the Fathers*, 33.

87. Greg. Tur., *VP* 6.1 (*MGH*, SRM 1.2, 230).

88. Greg. Tur., *VP* 6.1 (*MGH*, SRM 1.2, 230).

An example of the high stock landed aristocrats placed in reserving offspring for mates of appropriate rank involves Gregory's account of an attempted abduction. In 590, an agent of King Chilperic's named Cuppa conducted a night raid on an estate of the late Bishop Badegisel of Le Mans with the intention of stealing away with, and marrying, the prelate's daughter. Cuppa, however, neglected to take account of the bishop's widow: "The girl's mother, the materfamilias Magnatrude, recognized the man and his trick. With her slaves she sallied out against him, and repelled him by force. Several of Cuppa's men were slain, and so it was not without shame that he escaped."[89] Magnatrude was a woman intent upon maintaining her wealth and noble status. Immediately after the death of her husband in 586, she had caused a stir at Le Mans by refusing to relinquish control of properties Badegisel apparently had bequeathed to the church. Four years later, her spirited resistance of Cuppa's amorous advances toward the daughter reflects the lengths to which a prominent matron might go to preserve offspring for a more affluent suitor.

One powerful family that Gallic landed aristocrats had little hope of marrying into was the Merovingians. Frankish kings apparently early established a policy of marrying either foreign princesses or women of servile rank from royal properties.[90] Famous examples of each were the longtime antagonists, Brunhild the Visigothic princess and spouse of King Sigibert, and Fredegund, the slave turned queen wedded to Chilperic.[91] One propertied noblewoman whose ambition overcame the usual Merovingian predilection for spouses was Deuteria. In the 530s, as Clovis's sons were beginning to retake southernmost Gaul from the Ostrogoths, Prince Theudebert marched on behalf of his father Theuderic toward Béziers, and sent troops to demand the surrender of a stronghold called Cabrières.[92] Deuteria's husband was absent when

---

89. Greg. Tur., *Hist.* 10.5 (*MGH*, SRM 1.1, 487): "… praesensit eum dolumque eius Magnatrudis matrisfamilias genetrix scilicet puellae; egressaque cum famulis contra eum, vi reppulit, caesis plerisque ex illis, unde non sine pudore discessum est."

90. Halsall, *Settlement and Social Organization*, 37.

91. In a survey of the wives and concubines of Chlothar I's heirs, Guntram, Charibert, Sigibert, and Chilperic, Gregory evinced an elitist disdain for kings marrying women of servile origin; Greg. Tur., *Hist.* 4.25–28.

92. Greg. Tur., *Hist.* 3.21.

envoys arrived, and so not only did the magnate's wife readily hand over the fort, but she also visited the prince, and they fell in love.[93] Deuteria gave birth to a daughter with whom she was residing at Clermont in 534 when King Theuderic died. Theudebert all the while had been betrothed to a Lombard princess, Wisigard. But emboldened by his father's demise, the new king immediately called Deuteria from Clermont and married her.[94] Politically astute advisors to the king, however, bristled at the loss of political advantage caused by Theudebert's refusal to marry the Lombard princess.[95] Perhaps it was pressure from the advisors' unceasing criticisms that contributed to a mounting paranoia on Deuteria's part. Despite giving birth to a second child, a son named Theudebald, Deuteria reportedly began to imagine that her spouse coveted the daughter, and so the mother ordered that the girl be murdered.[96] In the end, Theudebert bowed to his advisors' will and abandoned Deuteria for Wisigard. When the latter died prematurely, Theudebert again rebuffed Deuteria by marrying another woman.[97] Here Deuteria disappears from Gregory's pages. Like more conventional Frankish queens and other Gallic noblewomen, she perhaps spent her twilight years strategizing to secure her offspring's future and thereby protect her own continued existence.[98] In Barbarian Gaul, not only did "family planning" enable continued prosperity; to not engage in it was to risk social dislocation and even premature death.[99]

While managing the combined resources of two families was a long term advantage derived from marriage, the occasion of a wedding itself afforded aristocrats an immediate benefit in that it enabled kin to display their wealth and assert their honor and social prominence before an assemblage. Perhaps even more than the ceremony itself, a bridal procession could communicate a family's reputation before an

---

93. Greg. Tur., *Hist.* 3.22.
94. Greg. Tur., *Hist.* 3.23.
95. Greg. Tur., *Hist.* 3.27.
96. Greg. Tur., *Hist.* 3.26.
97. Greg. Tur., *Hist.* 3.27.
98. See Wood, *Merovingian Kingdoms*, 120–29, for the survival strategies of Merovingian queens.
99. Furthermore on late ancient aristocratic marriages, see Mathisen, *People, Personal Expression, and Social Relations*, 1: 92–103, 107–12.

even greater audience of peers and inferiors. Such would have been the boon that Chilperic and Fredegund expected in 584 when they hosted an engagement party for their daughter, Rigunth, who was betrothed to the Visigothic Prince Reccared. After this ceremony, the princess joined a bridal train, which included an armed escort, hundreds of horse, some 50 carts filled with precious treasures, and 4,000 uprooted and disgruntled servants and commoners.[100] The massive entourage had managed to creep from Paris to Toulouse when news of Chilperic's assassination brought the march to an end.[101] Rigunth was despoiled of her treasure; she temporarily sheltered at a church in Toulouse and eventually found her way back to Paris under escort of the aforementioned Cuppa.[102] Prior to the princess's homecoming, Queen Fredegund attempted to recoup a measure of her family's tarnished prestige by despoiling, and even mutilating, many of the procession's participants as they returned from the ill-fated expedition.[103] More quotidian efforts for aristocrats to showcase family honor through weddings would have involved hosting an elaborate banquet and displaying the bride in a jewel-bedecked bridal gown.[104]

Just as Gallic aristocrats organized lavish weddings to symbolize the combination of familial resources and preservation of power, so too did they conduct elaborate funeral ceremonies to achieve the passage of family status and prestige, and to transmit power, to the next generation.[105] Two kinds of ostentatious burial customs, one concentrated in the north and the other to the south but neither restricted to one half of Gaul, were the prominent display of grave goods and burial within or near funerary churches.[106] The display of distinctive and even valuable items before

100. Greg. Tur., *Hist.* 6.45.
101. Greg. Tur., *Hist.* 7.9.
102. Greg. Tur., *Hist.* 7.39.
103. Greg. Tur., *Hist.* 7.15; Gradowicz-Pancer, "De-Gendering Female Violence," 10, 12–13.
104. Evidence for Gallic marriage rituals is very rare. Gregory mentioned a wedding dress when writing about the nuptials of the legendary "two lovers" of Clermont; however, he depicted the bride opining that the gown brought her shame, for she would rather have become a nun; Greg. Tur., *Hist.* 1.47.
105. Innes, *State and Society in the Early Middle Ages*, 173.
106. Display of grave goods, common to northern Gaul from the late fifth into the seventh centuries, is generally thought to have been an effective means of ritualized competitive display in a socially unstable environment; Halsall, *Settlement and Social Organization*, 247–263; Effros, *Merovingian Mortuary Archaeology*, 118; idem, *Caring for Body and Soul*, 19; Handley, *Death, Society and*

interment, a practice particularly conducted for burials in northern row grave cemeteries, enabled a family to exhibit its social significance for as long as the goods were visible to the living. Quantity and quality of burial items varied widely by region and also within individual cemeteries.[107] Typical grave goods included clothes, swords, other weapons, brooches, belts, buckles, jewelry, crosses and other religious indicators, coins, and eating and drinking vessels.[108] An opportunity to showcase the deceased with the soon-to-be-interred goods before more members of the public and for an extended period was a funeral procession. A body would be transported on a bier or litter from home to cemetery or funerary basilica.[109] At the gravesite, outward burial markers, especially epitaphs, which might include a mention of the deceased's status or their prominent title or occupation, would offer more enduring indicators of social worth. Most Gallic epitaphs come from south of the Loire, but Trier has the third largest number of funerary inscriptions among late ancient Western cities, second only to Rome and Carthage.[110] Family members usually raised epitaphs, for it was they who had the most to gain from sustaining the memory of a prominent ancestor.[111] Epitaphs that include a mention of status or occupation overwhelmingly commemorate secular and ecclesiastical elites.[112] Surviving epitaphs commonly accompany burials at or near churches. Although Gaul's elites would not adopt the practice of interment at churches and monasteries en masse until the seventh century, burials near churches had become a distinct social phenomenon in the fourth century, and burials near

Culture, 14. For a survey of trends in funerary topography from the fourth to the seventh century, see Effros, *Merovingian Mortuary Archaeology*, 188–200.

107. Effros, *Merovingian Mortuary Archaeology*, 130. For analysis of the variety among grave goods discovered at several Merovingian cemeteries, and how scholars over more than a century have interpreted these findings, see ibid., 127–63.

108. Ibid.

109. Effros, *Caring for Body and Soul*, 180. After Bishop Gallus of Clermont's body was displayed for three days, the corpse was processed from a cathedral to the basilica of Saint Lawrence; Greg. Tur., *VP* 6.7. See further, e.g., Greg. Tur., *VP* 7.3, 8.5; *Hist.* 3.18.

110. Effros, *Caring for Body and Soul*, 81. The latest count of epitaphs and graffiti from Trier by Mark Handley, *Death, Society and Culture*, 5, stands at 958, nearly a third of the number for all Gaul.

111. Effros, *Caring for Body and Soul*, 87, 91.

112. Handley, *Death, Society and Culture*, 39–40.

saints' tombs and relics (burial *ad sanctos*) soon followed.[113] For example, at Trier in the late fourth and early fifth centuries, some of the faithful were burying relations at a southern extra-mural cemetery devoted to Saint Eucherius, the city's first bishop, while others were interring kin in a northern cemetery associated with the cults of Saints Paulinus and Maximinus.[114] Bishop Cyrillus of Trier (d. 475), a devotee of Saints Eucherius and Valerius, had himself buried *ad sanctos* beneath the altar in the church of Saint Eucherius.[115] Likewise, Bishop Nicetius of Trier (d. 566), whom Gregory depicted in a miniature *Vita* principally identifying with the cult of Saint Maximinus, was buried *ad sanctos* in Maximinus's church in the northern cemetery.[116] By choosing a church affiliated cemetery, a person was selecting the saint who presumably would assist in securing the salvation of his soul.[117] As for the motivation for the surviving kin to bury relatives at churches, this practice benefited their efforts at ostentation, because churches "attracted larger, more diverse audiences and thus constituted an effective location for competitive display."[118]

If "marrying up" and amassing resources were central to most aristocratic designs for maintaining social prominence, persons on the edge of aristocracy might employ the same stratagems as an element of their schemes to secure noble recognition. One socially ambitious person situated at the cusp of the Barbarian era who actually used the aristocratic rhetoric of inclusion to instigate entry into an aristocratic circle was Amantius, a merchant and native of Clermont.[119] According to Sidonius

113. Handley, "Beyond Hagiography: Epigraphic Commemoration," 197–98; Effros, *Merovingian Mortuary Archaeology*, 211.

114. Handley, "Beyond Hagiography: Epigraphic Commemoration," 189. This epigraphic evidence reveals how Eucherius's cult was active a full two centuries before Gregory of Tours offered the earliest literary attestation of the cult in the *Life of the Fathers*; Greg. Tur., *VP* 17.4; Handley, ibid., 190, 198.

115. Handley, ibid., 196. Handley's comparison of the number of epitaphs from Trier's cemeteries, ibid., 198, suggests that the cult of Eucherius was more popular than those of Paulinus and Maximinus through the early fifth century, but the holy patrons of the northern cemetery became more popular thereafter.

116. Greg. Tur., *VP* 17.4, 6.

117. Handley, *Death, Society and Culture*, 155.

118. Effros, *Merovingian Mortuary Archaeology*, 213. Around 600, the quantity and diversity of grave goods decreased in both north and south, while use of epigraphs dropped off precipitously; ibid., 130; Handley, *Death, Society and Culture*, 182–83. Also seventh-century elites in large numbers opted for church burials over row graves, and they began to regard Christian liturgies as the most effective means to communicate status; Effros, *Merovingian Mortuary Archaeology*, 173.

119. See Mathisen, *People, Personal Expression, and Social Relations*, 1: 47–52, 54, 56–57.

Apollinaris, Amantius relocated from the Auvergne to Marseilles in order to escape a modestly wealthy yet miserly father. Upon arrival at the coast, the merchant used his church affiliation – he had been a lector – to acquire the ear of Bishop Eustachius of Marseilles from whom he secured a dwelling.[120] Once established as a client of the bishop's, Amantius next reconnoitered the community for aristocrats whom he might readily impress with appropriate manners and speech. Through the age-old practice of "saying whatever the right people want to hear," Amantius caused the aristocrats to desire his friendship:

> By watchfulness as well timed as it was frequent, he came to be recognized, then known, then admitted to intimacy by the magnates one after another and then by the count of the city, and so his assiduity gained him promotion to higher and higher circles every day: the best people vied in cherishing him; all supported him with their good wishes, many by their counsels, private persons by their gifts, officials by their favors; and thus his hopes and his resources increased by leaps and bounds.[121]

With a reputation established as protégé to a bishop and a count, Amantius now used this clout to procure a wife and her considerable wealth: "... this young man, alone and of modest resources, a stranger, a minor who left his native place ... sought, won, and married a girl of not inferior birth and of superior fortune, with the mediation of the bishop, because he was a Reader, and the sympathy of the Count, because he was a client. ..."[122] Amantius rightly counted on the fact that his prospective in-laws would be so bedazzled by the luster of his patrons that they would not think to examine his actual social circumstances. Not only

---

120. Sid. Ap., *Ep.* 7.2.3 (Anderson, ed. and trans., 2: 294).
121. Sid. Ap., *Ep.* 7.2.4–5 (Anderson, ed. and trans., 2: 296–97): "Agere cum singulis, prout aetatis ratio permitteret: grandaevos obsequiis, aequaevos officiis obligare. ...Summatibus deinceps et tunc comiti civitatis non minus opportunis quam frequentibus excubiis agnosci innotescere familiarescere, sicque eius in dies sedulitas maiorum sodalitatibus promoveri; fovere boni quique certatim, votis omnes plurimi consiliis, privati donis cincti beneficiis adiuvare; perque haec spes opesque istius raptim saluatimque cumulari."
122. Sid. Ap., *Ep.* 7.2.7 (Anderson, ed. and trans., 2: 298–99): "Adulescens, solus tenuis peregrinus, filius familias et e patria ... discedens, puellam non inferiorem natalibus, facultatibus superiorem, medio episcopo, quia lector, solacio comitis, qui cliens ... uxorem petit, impetrat, ducit."

did he exaggerate the extent of his possessions in the distant Auvergne, but Amantius also duped the bride's parents into transferring a large part of their fortune to the young couple's control.[123] Subsequently the mother-in-law learned of the deceit and threatened a suit against the merchant, but according to Sidonius, she dismissed this idea when grandchildren started to arrive.[124] Still Amantius hoped to appease the prominent matron. Because Eustachius had died, he next plotted to give himself over to the patronage of the bishop's successor, Graecus. To this end, the wily Amantius presented – or more properly, misrepresented – himself to Sidonius Apollinaris as an impoverished trader and newly ordained lector. Sidonius afforded the new client a letter of recommendation to present to Graecus.[125] Amantius then used the epistle to convince the new bishop to heal the breach with the mother-in-law. Afterward, Amantius continued to trade and carry letters back and forth between Sidonius and Graecus, and simultaneously he continued to augment his fortune.[126] Regarding his letter carrier, Sidonius wrote to Graecus: "Here is Amantius again, the bearer of my trifles; he is returning again to his well-loved Marseilles in order to carry home, as usual, his pickings from the city's spoils. …"[127] By the time he wrote the previous sentence, Sidonius had learned of Amantius's deceptions, but he in no way thought to rebuke his client; rather, Sidonius had a good laugh over the matter. After all, the old Amantius who had abandoned Clermont might have been a "wily traveler" (*callidus viator*),[128] but the new Amantius was assiduous and wealthy, a "splendid young man" (*iuvenis eximius*).[129] By virtue of his wealth and acceptance within an elite circle, he had become for all intents and purposes a Gallic aristocrat. As far as Sidonius was concerned, that the merchant had infiltrated the lower ranks of aristocracy mattered less than the fact that Amantius

123. Sid. Ap., *Ep.* 7.2.8.
124. Sid. Ap., *Ep.* 7.2.8.
125. Sid. Ap., *Ep.* 6.8.
126. Cf., Sid. Ap., *Ep.* 7.7, 7.10, 9.4.
127. Sid. Ap., *Ep.* 7.7.1 (Anderson, ed. and trans., 2: 324–25): "Ecce iterum Amantius, nugigerulus noster, Massiliam suam repetit, aliquid, ut moris est, de manubiis civitatis domum reportaturus …"
128. Sid. Ap., *Ep.* 7.2.1 (Anderson, ed. and trans., 2: 292–93).
129. Sid. Ap., *Ep.* 7.2.9 (Anderson, ed. and trans., 2: 300–01).

proved to be a worthy client. Amantius was not merely a shrewd schemer; by the bonds of *patrocinium*, he was Sidonius's shrewd schemer!

The case of Amantius reveals how the "rhetoric of inclusion" was not entirely the reserve of aristocrats. Others could learn the skill and play it to their own socio-economic advantage. Ambitious persons such as Amantius likely realized that if they had something to offer social betters, the latter in turn might welcome them into their numbers. Presumably the invitation of a *novus homo* to a distinguished circle generally came attached with a limiting provision, such as continued service as protégé to one's patron. Note that although Amantius had become filthy rich, he remained a merchant. Furthermore, cunning social climbers must have recognized that the "collective acceptance as an aristocrat by other aristocrats" could only be so collective.[130] In the first place, a would-be parvenu could not possibly achieve the endorsement of every noble, because every aristocrat was not of like opinion. Secondly, contrary to aristocratic rhetoric, one need not gain the support of all nobles; rather, one only had to obtain the approval of a few aristocrats whose opinion would cause others to follow suit in offering friendship. If sustaining and amassing wealth and land was a basic means of generating noble recognition, a less common but more colorful entree to another kind of aristocracy was participation at a king's court.

COURTLY ARISTOCRATS

Like Gaul's great landowners, powerful members at royal courts advanced rhetoric proclaiming themselves as aristocrats. Kings and courtiers welcomed panegyrics that extolled their inherent nobility. Prominent Gauls gravitated to courts in search of privileges such as fiscal lands and prestigious offices and titles to supplement their landed wealth. Kings had replaced emperors as distributors of institutionalized patronage, the benefits of which included loans of fiscal property and tax exemptions. For their part, landed aristocrats, now deprived of advancement through the imperial *cursus honorum*, readily sought positions in royal courts to achieve distinction and augment fortunes. One landed

---

130. Mathisen, *Roman Aristocrats in Barbarian Gaul*, 12.

aristocrat who followed this course of action was Lupus.[131] Venantius Fortunatus described him as hailing from "Roman stock" (*Romanae stirpis*), which "ethnic" description identifies Lupus's family as traditionally relying on landholding, not warfare, to secure status.[132] Lupus augmented his nobility through participation at the Austrasian court, where he served in a military, judicial, and diplomatic capacity. He led the Franks on an undated successful assault versus a band of Saxons and Danes, and he also participated on an embassy to Marseilles.[133] In 567, he attended the wedding of Sigibert and Brunhild at Metz, where he befriended Venantius and became an early patron of the poet. Lupus merited receiving the office of *dux* under King Sigibert, and apparently he kept this title under Childebert II. Venantius's first poem for Lupus was an encomium that lauded his courtly and military contributions, but perhaps more befitting were the poet's verses that stressed the duke's eloquence and appreciation for literature.[134] Venantius called attention to Lupus's regard for the classics by comparing his officiousness to that of Roman Republican consuls and noting his familiarity with Homer and Virgil, not to mention the Psalmist.[135] By emphasizing Lupus's literary interests at a public reading of these poems, Venantius would have helped the duke garner a favorable impression among Austrasian aristocrats admiring of that attribute. One such fellow was Gregory of Tours, whose writings confirm and laud Lupus's literary proclivities. From Gregory one reads that the duke extended his patronage to another literarily adept upstart named Andarchius, about whom there will be more to say later. Gregory's material about Lupus also attests to the difficulties aristocrats could encounter when they became closely affiliated with royal courts. Like Gregory, Duke Lupus extended an almost unqualified level of support for Queen Brunhild. In 581, an Austrasian faction hostile to the queen forced the duke to flee the kingdom, and it plundered

---

131. *PLRE* 3: 798–99, s. v., "Lupus 1."
132. Ven. Fort., *Carm.* 7.7.45 (*MGH*, SRM 4.1, 160). Wickham, *Framing the Early Middle Ages*, 181, asserts that Lupus was a local landowner whose property "is most likely to have had a pre-Frankish core," but that he already was a "military aristocrat."
133. Ven. Fort., *Carm.* 7.7.49–58; Greg. Tur., *Hist.* 4.46.
134. George, *Venantius Fortunatus: A Latin Poet in Merovingian Gaul*, 79–82.
135. Ven. Fort., *Carm.* 7.8.25–28.

his property.[136] Lupus traveled to the court of King Guntram, where he remained six years until he was able to rejoin Childebert II and Brunhild in 587.[137] Having overcome this political setback, Lupus's family maintained the Austrasian court attachment, and ultimately they reaped the benefits of this connection. In 590, Lupus's son Romulfus succeeded the duke's former enemy Egidius as Bishop of Reims.[138] Lupus also procured an advantageous marriage for his anonymous daughter to Godegisel, another general in service to the Austrasian monarch.[139] Lupus's nuclear family exemplifies the interconnectedness of Gaul's landholding, courtly, and ecclesiastical aristocracies. The fates of Lupus's children, the one becoming a bishop and the other the wife of a general, also reflect the kinds of successful outcome aristocrats intended to achieve through their social strategizing.

One assumes that it was noblepersons such as Lupus and his brood that most often maintained and/or augmented power by securing courtly posts such as *comes* and *dux*; however, distinguishing oneself at court hardly was restricted to landed aristocrats. Just as kings frequently elevated servile concubines to royal wives, on a larger scale they also welcomed people of lesser rank into court aristocracies. If Frankish kings realized the advantage of emulating Roman emperors by availing written law codes and giving gifts to secure loyalty, presumably it was in imitation of their ruling predecessors that they also readily ushered *novi homines* into the noble ranks. Thus, another courtier who benefited from an encomium by Venantius was a "new man" named Conda.[140] Unlike Lupus, Conda was not of aristocratic origin. Unable to remark on his noble birth, Venantius instead praised the subject for being the initiator of his family's social prominence: "For if he who maintains the family's honour is esteemed, how much more praiseworthy is it to ennoble

---

136. Greg. Tur., *Hist.* 6.4.
137. Greg. Tur., *Hist.* 9.11.
138. Greg. Tur., *Hist.* 9.19. Egidius had been among those Austrasian nobles who turned on Brunhild and her supporters. In the end, Egidius's persistent court machinations brought about his own downfall. In 590, he was implicated in an assassination attempt on King Childebert II, exiled and deposed; *Hist.* 9.19.
139. Greg. Tur., *Hist.* 9.12.
140. Ven. Fort., *Carm.* 7.16; George, *Venantius Fortunatus: A Latin Poet in Merovingian Gaul*, 82–83; *PLRE* 3: 330–31.

a family?"[141] Conda's "ennobling" was a feat that entailed decades of service under six Merovingian rulers. As a young man, Conda found employ as *tribunus* under King Theuderic. Theuderic's son Theudebert promoted the agent to *comes* and also honored him with the *cingulum*, a decorated belt that symbolized royal favor and conferred high rank.[142] Theudebert next elevated Conda to *domesticus* and made him tutor for Prince Theudebald.[143] Although Venantius did not dwell upon this courtier's literary ability as he did Duke Lupus's, the job of tutor coupled with judicial obligations of his other posts indicates that Conda must have possessed a notable degree of literary competence. By evidencing a marked reliability, which Venantius cast as indispensability, Conda proved himself worthy to serve under his student Theudebald's successors, Chlothar I and Sigibert. The latter ruler made a final gesture certifying Conda's honor and nobility by declaring him a member of the king's table, the *conviva regis*.[144] Conda's steady advancement into and within the courtly aristocracy via a *cursus honorum* would have caused few nobles to complain. Publication of the poet's encomium for the *domesticus* indicates how Venantius anticipated other courtiers' appreciating the agent's abilities and deeds and regarding his social mobility as being well-deserved. But if Conda represents every aristocrat's version of the respectable parvenu, there were those *novi homines* whose infiltration of courtly ranks could wrinkle aristocratic noses.

One rags to riches tale involves a certain Andarchius, who was the personal slave of Felix, a man of senatorial family from Marseilles.[145] This master afforded Andarchius a tremendous opportunity by allowing him to join in literary studies, and so the slave became well versed in Virgil, Roman law, and arithmetic. According to Gregory of Tours, education gave Andarchius reason to despise his master, and it also provided him a chance to escape his detested social condition. A visit to Marseilles by

141. Ven. Fort., *Carm.* 7.16.11–12 (*MGH*, AA 4.1, 170–71): "Nam si praefertur generis qui servat honorem, quanta magis laus est nobilitare genus?" Trans. by George, *Venantius Fortunatus: Personal and Political Poems*, 65.

142. Ven. Fort., *Carm.* 7.16.17–20.

143. Ven. Fort., *Carm.* 7.16.23.

144. Ven. Fort., *Carm.* 7.16.41–42.

145. Greg. Tur., *Hist.* 4.46. Cf. Mathisen, *People, Personal Expression, and Social Relations*, 1: 58–60.

Duke Lupus occasioned the opportunity for Andarchius to demonstrate his talent before another potential patron. The Austrasian literary aficionado Lupus was duly impressed, and so he insisted that the slave join him at Sigibert's court. There the king placed Andarchius to work by sending him on missions. Andarchius now possessed two criteria by which aristocrats qualified themselves as such – literary talent and governmental employ. Some powerful figures must have thought these attributes enough to accept Andarchius as one of their own, for Gregory wrote: "On account of his [royal service] he was regarded as if an honorable man."[146] While Gregory held a personal disdain for the social upstart, his words betray how some imagined Andarchius's position at court to endow him with an air of respectability. Unfortunately for the former slave, ambition eventually got the better of him. While on a mission to Clermont, the agent attempted to marry into wealth and at the same time dupe and dispossess his prospective father-in-law, a certain Ursus. Andarchius's career was cut short when Ursus's slaves murdered the parvenu. It is interesting to compare the rise of Andarchius with that of Sidonius's client Amantius. While the conclusions of Andarchius's and Amantius's careers differed dramatically, there are notable similarities in their efforts to advance socially. First, both began their social ascent principally by securing patronage; Andarchius attached himself to Lupus, while Amantius became a client to the Bishop of Marseilles. Second, each tried to improve upon his initial boost to prominence by marrying into greater wealth, both doing so rather duplicitously. Finally, throughout their efforts at social climbing, neither parvenu enjoyed full aristocratic support, but the point is that neither really needed it. Each realized that contrary to the aristocratic rhetoric of solidarity, rather than gaining the respect of all, he actually needed only to impress a few powerful patrons who would extol their assiduity, or literary talent, and convince other nobles of their worth.

Another ambitious slave who displayed a different set of qualities to ascend into a court aristocracy was Leudast, the infamous rival of Gregory of Tours.[147] Because Leudast conspired to have Gregory

---

146. Greg. Tur., *Hist.* 4.46 (*MGH*, SRM 1.1, 181): "Ex hoc quasi honoratus habitus …"
147. *PLRE* 3: 786–88, s. v., "Leudastes."

removed as bishop, the latter was only too happy to include in the *Historiae* material providing full disclosure of Leudast's rise from ignominious origins:

> ... first I must tell you about [Leudast's] family, his place of origin and his character. ... He was the son of a certain Leucadius, a slave who looked after the vines on one of the estates. The time came for Leudast to go into service and he was given a job in the royal kitchens. His eyes were weak when he was a young man and the acrid smoke was harmful to him. He was therefore promoted from the kitchen pestle to the baker's basket. He pretended to enjoy himself amidst the fermenting dough, but eventually he abandoned his service and ran away. Two if not three times he was dragged back after escaping, but, since it was impossible to hold him, he was punished by having one of his ears slit. As there was no possibility of concealing this mark on his body, he fled to queen Marcovefa, whom King Charibert had married. ...[148]

Gregory undoubtedly delighted in slighting Leudast by recalling how he had been born a slave.[149] Reportedly, he was uncomfortable in the kitchen and bakery environment and so he fled to Queen Marcovefa. Because she herself was a slave turned queen, perhaps Marcovefa empathized with the ambitious Leudast's situation. Like Andarchius earlier, Leudast realized that the best hope for abandoning servile rank was to impress a patron. Just as the educated slave had ingratiated himself with Duke Lupus, so did Leudast exploit his relationship with Marcovefa:

> She received Leudast with great kindness, promoted him and put him in charge of the finest horses in her stable. In consequence, his

---

148. Greg. Tur., *Hist.*, 5.48 (*MGH*, SRM 1.1, 257): "... sed prius videtur genus ac patriam moresque ordiri. ...a fiscalis vinitoris servo Leuchadio nomine nascitur. Exinde ad servitium arcessitus, culinae regiae deputatur. Sed quia lippis erat in adolescentia oculis, quibus fumi acerbitas non congruebat, amotus a pistillo, promovitur ade cophinum. Sed dum inter firmentatas massas se delectari consimulat, servitium fugam iniens dereliquit. Cumque bis aut tertio reductus a fugae lapsu teneri non possit, auris unius incisione multatur. Dehinc cum notam inflictam corpori occulere nulla auctoritate valeret, ad Marcoveifam reginam, quam Chariberthus rex nimium diligens in loco sororis toro adsciverat, fugit." Trans. based on Thorpe, *Gregory of Tours, History of the Franks*, 314.

149. Gregory's criticisms of Leudast on paper also might have served a purpose of belittling whoever remained of the count's supporters at Tours after the latter had fallen from royal favor.

conceit and arrogance became so great that he applied for the post of master of stables. In this new appointment he looked down on and slighted everyone. He was proud and lived an extremely loose life and there was no limit to his covetousness. As the special favorite of his patron, he hurried here, there and everywhere to see to the queen's affairs. When she died, his purse was already well filled from his dishonest peculations and he was thus able to bribe King Charibert to allow him to retain his post.[150]

Here one notes similarities between Leudast and Sidonius's ambitious client Amantius. Both impressed their patrons by exhibiting a willingness to travel, Amantius carrying letters and Leudast performing errands. As much as Gregory would have wanted to deny it, Leudast must have possessed some admirable traits that caused the Parisian court to keep his services after the queen's demise. In 567, Charibert elevated Leudast from master of stables at Paris to *comes* at Tours. Unlike before, Gregory did not attribute this appointment to bribery. Unwilling to credit his enemy's promotion to ability or merit, the author instead blamed it on "the sins of the people" (*peccatis populi*) of Tours.[151] One stratagem that Leudast would have used to his advantage as a prominent royal agent was to effectively display a penchant for violence. The disapproving bishop wrote, "He exhibited himself as rapacious in plundering, enraged in brawling. ..."[152] Despite Gregory harboring resentment toward the *comes*, he likely was not misrepresenting Leudast's character by depicting him as pugnacious, for as has been mentioned, asserting a martial image had become a legitimate means for declaring authority and even nobleness. King Charibert might have regarded Leudast's bravado as an appropriate attribute for a count. Gregory, however, was not amused; the bishop complained, "He used to walk into the church-house in his cuirass and

---

150. Greg. Tur., *Hist.* 5.48 (*MGH*, SRM 1.1, 257–58): "Quae libenter eum colligens, provocat equorumque meliorum deputat esse custodem. Hinc iam obsessus vanitate ac superbiae deditus, comitatum ambit stabulorum; quo accepto, cunctos despicit ac postponit, inflatur vanitate, luxuria dissolvitur, cupiditate succenditur et in causis patronae alumnus proprius huc illucque defertur. Cuius post obitum refertus praedis, locum ipsum cum rege Charibertho, oblatis muneribus, tenere coepit." Trans. by Thorpe, *Gregory of Tours, History of the Franks*, 314.

151. Greg. Tur., *Hist.* 5.48 (*MGH*, SRM 1.1, 258).

152. Greg. Tur., *Hist.* 5.48 (*MGH*, SRM 1.1, 258): "... ibique se exhibet rapacem praedis, turgidum rixis. ..."

mail shirt, with his quiver hanging round him, his javelin in his hand and his helmet on his head."[153] Here, if Leudast was in fact attempting to "dress for success," it would have been logical that he do so at a church, for one could find no better urban venue for social theater than a crowded basilica. Fortunately for Leudast and so for other parvenus, gaining the confidence of every aristocrat did not matter when it came to infiltrating the highest social ranks. As had been the case for Amantius and Andarchius, another step toward securing social prominence likely involved Leudast's marrying a wealthy or noble woman. Gregory gives few details about Leudast's spouse, but he does mention that she and her father resided at Tours. Perhaps the wife hailed from the city; maybe she was even an aristocrat of the Tourangeaux.[154]

When Charibert died in 567, Leudast had to make one of those decisions that could make or break a courtier's career, deciding what successor to support. The Count chose wrongly; Tours was apportioned to King Sigibert, but Leudast had sided with Chilperic. Sigibert's troops therefore looted the count's possessions, and Leudast lost his post.[155] One wonders how Leudast made ends meet for the next seven years; Gregory did not say. Perhaps he quietly bided his time on his or his wife's properties. Suddenly in 574, Chilperic's son Theudebert seized Tours, and the prince restored Leudast as *comes*. At that time, Gregory had only recently arrived (November 573) at Tours himself. As a "foreigner" from the Auvergne, Gregory scarcely had begun to build his own authority locally. Even if he had wanted to do so, he was in no position to object to a royal decision to promote Leudast. But as Gregory recollected the situation, even then he was given a say in the count's reappointment:

> I had arrived at Tours around that time, and it was highly recommended to me by Theudebert that I give [Leudast] the countship, since he held it previously. Leudast acted toward me very humbly and modestly. He often swore on the tomb of the holy

153. Greg. Tur., *Hist.* 5.48 (*MGH*, SRM 1.1, 258): "... in domo ecclesiae cum toracibus atque loricis, praecinctus pharetra et contum manu gerens, capite galeato ingrederetur ..." Trans. by Thorpe, *Gregory of Tours, History of the Franks*, 315.
154. Greg. Tur., *Hist.* 6.32. Leudast's son died in 580; *Hist.* 5.49.
155. Greg. Tur., *Hist.* 5.48.

bishop [Martin] that he would never act against the cause of reason
and that he would remain faithful toward me regarding my business
and that of the church.[156]

Like any potentially successful social climber, Leudast knew the
importance of initially feigning support to all equals and superiors until
realizing who actually mattered, and who did not, in one's designs for
social ascension. If Gregory's position at Tours was not yet firm, neither was Leudast's. In that same year of 574, Sigibert recovered Tours
from Theudebert. The king sent Chilperic's rebellious son Merovech
to take whatever he could of Leudast's property, and so the count fled
to Brittany, where he hid out for about two years. But fortune's wheel
quickly turned again with the assassination of Sigibert in 575. Within
a year, Chilperic secured Tours and again restored Leudast as count.
With that king now in firm control of the city, Leudast would hold the
post for five more years.[157] No longer did he have to pretend to admire
Bishop Gregory or feign respect for the ostensible source of the bishop's
authority, Saint Martin. According to Gregory, the count's political
demise would result from his incessant assaults on the people of Tours,
the property of its churches, and its bishop. In 580, Leudast tried but
failed to convince King Chilperic that Gregory was engaged in a plot to
hand the diocese over to King Guntram.[158] When Chilperic was satisfied
that the allegation was untrue, he allowed the Tourangeux to choose
their count. They opted for a certain Eunomius. Leudast then added to
the treason charge a claim that Gregory had asserted Fredegund to be an
adulterer, but again he could not prove the charge. Thereafter, Leudast
himself became the target of a treason charge, and so he fled to Bourges
pursued by Chilperic's *regales pueri*.[159] Perhaps the latter agents harbored
their own hopes of dramatic social advancement akin to that which their

---

156. Greg. Tur., *Hist.* 5.48 (*MGH*, SRM 1.1, 258): "... cum iam ego Turonus advenissem, mihi a
Theodobertho strenue commendatur, ut scilicet comitatum, quem prius habuerat, potiretur.
Multum se nobis humilem subditumque reddebat, iurans saepius super sepulchrum sancti antestitis
[Martini], numquam se contra rationis ordinem esse venturum seque mihi tam in causis propriis
quam in ecclesiae necessitatibus in omnibus esse fidelem."

157. Greg. Tur., *Hist.* 5.48.

158. Greg. Tur., *Hist.* 5.47.

159. Greg. Tur., *Hist.* 5.49.

prey once had enjoyed. For a full three years, Leudast eluded capture, but more importantly, all the while he petitioned to regain the king's good graces, and not without some success. The ex-*comes* managed not only to lift an ecclesiastical censure but also to remove a secular condemnation as outlaw. Chilperic even decreed that Leudast could return to Tours, but Gregory, encouraged by Fredegund, refused to restore him to communion.[160] Then, in 584, Leudast made a bold move that truly proved his downfall; he traveled to Paris where he proposed to seek Fredegund's forgiveness for having raised the slanderous accusation. Here was one unforgiving slave turned queen; like Leudast, Fredegund too had a calculated stratagem for preserving honor and power that involved the use of threat and violence.[161] Oblivious to the danger he was in, Leudast was shopping in a Parisian market when the queen's men assaulted and captured him. After subjecting him to repeated torture, Fredegund had the throat that had accused the queen of adultery beaten until Leudast expired.[162] A self-righteous Gregory envisioned this enemy of Saint Martin as deserving of immediate damnation.[163]

It is impossible to assess how common instances of drastic social advancement such as those of Andarchius and Leudast were. Gregory included tales such as these in the *Historiae* not because of their subjects' incredible social mobility, but rather because he thought the stories' deadly conclusions befitted the greed and indifference toward the church that the actors had displayed while alive. Gregory also selected these stories because they pertained to the author's precious *patria* and diocese, the Auvergne and Touraine, respectively. Had Andarchius's intended father-in-law-*cum*-victim been a wealthy man from Arles instead of Clermont, or had Leudast been Count of Bourges instead of Tours, their tales likely would not have appeared in the *Historiae*. But these anecdotal examples, coupled with evidence from the legal sources, suggest that the Frankish kings generally were willing to privilege certain promising slaves, especially those with education or those

160. Greg. Tur., *Hist.* 6.32.
161. Gradowicz-Pancer, "De-Gendering Female Violence," 10–17.
162. Greg. Tur., *Hist.* 6.32.
163. Jones, "Death and Afterlife in the Pages of Gregory of Tours" (forthcoming).

living on royal estates. Therefore it is very likely that similar instances of advancement into court aristocracies happened, if only infrequently.

Several additional points might be made about these parvenus to courtly aristocracy. First, consider the role education played in Andarchius's rise. It is interesting to note how Lupus deemed the slave's enthusiasm for literature as a quality that trumped his low social position. Despite Andarchius's servile rank, Lupus apparently envisioned him as a credible ornament for the Austrasian court. Perhaps Lupus thought no differently about Andarchius than he did about the literarily talented Venantius Fortunatus. Apparently a display of literary talent before a Gallic courtier impressed by such ability could pay dividends in the form of social advancement regardless of a client's original rank. Otherwise, I find an interesting aspect of Leudast's career to be the lasting influence of the royal officeholder, despite his lowly social beginning. I am especially impressed by Leudast's ability to recover (almost) from his fall from grace in 580. Despite being declared an outlaw and excommunicated, Leudast was able to remove his possessions from Tours to Bourges. Twice he stayed alive by seeking sanctuary.[164] Once when some inhabitants of Bourges seized his property, he rounded up supporters, from Tours no less, and forcefully recovered it. While taking refuge in sanctuary at Poitiers, he reportedly used to exit the church from time to time and rob local houses. Regardless of the fact that Gregory's portrayal of the count as a ruffian was very biased, Leudast must actually have been a person who could be relied upon to effectively use violence to exercise power. While he was an outlaw, Leudast realized that he still could rely on an element from the Tourangeaux – perhaps some were trained soldiers; perhaps others were allied influential property owners with armed retainers – to join him and benefit in his belligerent exploits at Bourges and Poitiers. Because Leudast managed to have charges of both treason and excommunication lifted, this means that several bishops (unnamed by Gregory) and King Chilperic must have decided some time after 580 that Leudast, and perhaps his wife's family, was influential enough that it would be wise to compromise with him. This would then

164. Greg. Tur., *Hist.* 5.49.

suggest that Leudast had reason to be confident of his security when he sought his fatal audience with Fredegund in 584. Had the queen not harbored such personal resentment and brought about his unforeseen death, one can suspect that Chilperic would have restored him as count at Tours! A Merovingian king had use for a retainer who demanded such respect. And a proven ability to summon and lead violent men could take a person far in the courts of Barbarian Gaul, regardless of his social origin.

Ecclesiastical Aristocrats

A third kind of aristocracy, and in fact the one social sub-group for which the most evidence exists, consisted of prominent people at church. Even before imperial posts disappeared in Gaul, landed aristocrats had begun eyeing bishoprics as positions by which they might maintain and enhance local power. They found in high church office not simply an immediate benefit but also a lasting boon that their families ought to maintain. By the end of the fifth century, establishment of episcopal dynasties in Gaul had begun.[165] As has been mentioned, Avitus of Vienne succeeded his father as bishop around 494/96, and Caesarius succeeded a relation as Bishop of Arles in 502. The best evidence for a Gallic aristocratic family strategizing to control bishoprics is that pertaining to Gregory of Tours' kin. Gregory's maternal and paternal relatives vied with other aristocratic families to hold sees at Langres, Clermont, Lyons, and Tours. Of these cities, the family's firmest control seems to have been at Langres, which Venantius described as a "family see" (*patria sedes*).[166] In 506/07, Gregorius succeeded Armentarius, likely his father-in-law, as bishop of Langres.[167] Son Tetricus then succeeded his father Gregorius in 539/40. Tetricus's grandchildren included Eufronius, who became Bishop of Tours, and Armentaria, Gregory's mother. Gregory's older brother Peter was a

---

165. Mathisen, *Roman Aristocrats in Barbarian Gaul*, 91–93.
166. Ven. Fort., *Carm.* 4.3.2; Van Dam, *Saints and their Miracles*, 56.
167. Martin Heinzelmann, *Bischofsherrschaft in Gallien: Zur Continuität römischer Führungsschichten vom 4. bis zum 7. Jahrhundert: soziale, prosopographische und bildungs-geschichtliche Aspecte* (Zurich and Munich: Artemis, 1976), 213–14.

deacon at Langres, and the family likely anticipated his sitting on the cathedra after Tetricus. But as it turned out, a normal episcopal succession failed to transpire after Tetricus had a stroke, and so an interim bishop was assigned. When Tetricus died in 572/73, Peter proposed a relative, Silvester, to succeed, but the latter died before consecration. Peter then encountered unforeseen antagonism from within his own family; Silvester's son joined an opposition clerical party and accused the deacon of having used magic to kill the bishop-elect. Silvester's son even murdered Peter in 575 before being slain himself.[168] This regrettable struggle caused Gregory's family to lose the *patria sedes*. Silvester's successor was Pappolus (572/73–579/80), an archdeacon from Autun and no relation to Tetricus.[169] Gregory so reviled this interloper that he included in the *Historiae* a tale of how Saint Tetricus appeared to Pappolus in a dream and beat him with his staff, so that the unworthy bishop awoke in pain and three days later died while still spewing blood.[170]

A second possible "family see" for Gregory's kin was Lyons. There, Nicetius (Armentaria's uncle) succeeded his uncle Sacerdos as bishop around 552. Gregory was deacon at Lyons under Nicetius, and so perhaps he anticipated ascending this cathedra. But because Bishop Nicetius was notoriously outspoken, directing his abrasiveness against clerics, city officials and promiscuous Frankish kings, an anti-Nicetian faction developed within the clergy. When the bishop died in early 573, King Guntram interceded and elevated a member from his court, Priscus, as pontiff. Priscus actively demeaned the memory of Nicetius, and effected a purge of the supporters of Nicetius's family, supposedly even having some killed.[171] The deacon Gregory survived, however, and just as he had done with Pappolus of Langres, he later recalled how a family saint avenged his relatives' loss of a see. True to his belligerent character even in the afterlife, the vengeful Saint Nicetius reportedly caused clerics loyal to the new bishop to die various deaths, while the holy man

168. Greg. Tur., *Hist.* 5.5.
169. Greg. Tur., *Hist.* 5.5.
170. Greg. Tur., *Hist.* 5.5.
171. Greg. Tur., *Hist.* 4.36.

made Priscus's family members go insane, and Priscus himself become a dimwit.[172]

Although Gregory regarded the Auvergne as his *patria*, the bishopric of Clermont was not a "family see." In fact, if any aristocratic clan could lay claim to that cathedra it would have been the large landowning relatives of Sidonius Apollinaris and his senatorial wife's relations, the Aviti. Sidonius himself had succeeded an in-law, Eparchius, as Bishop of Clermont around 470, and at least four of his descendents would hold the post in the sixth and seventh centuries.[173] But because multiple Auvergnian aristocratic families spiritedly vied for the bishopric during each and every vacancy, the actual effective determinant for the office was appeal to whichever royal court controlled the city whenever a bishop died.[174] Thus, around 515, King Theuderic selected Apollinaris, Sidonius's son, after the latter requested the see at court.[175] When Apollinaris died after only a few months, Theuderic appointed Quintianus, former Bishop of Rodez, as Bishop of Clermont.[176] When the see fell vacant around 525, a clerical favorite attached to Theuderic's court announced that God wanted him upon the cathedra. King Theuderic concurred with God's will, and thereby Gallus, Gregory's father's brother, became bishop of Clermont.[177] Upon Gallus's demise in 551, the clergy at Clermont selected the priest Cato as bishop, but when Cato failed to take the necessary step of gaining royal approval, the very noble archdeacon Cautinus petitioned King Theudebald and acquired the see.[178] In 571, two candidates for the Auvergnian cathedra presented themselves before King Sigibert, and that ruler selected from between them the deacon Avitus to be the next bishop.[179] Avitus, who almost

---

172. Greg. Tur., *Hist.* 4.36.
173. Apollinaris, Avitus I, Avitus II, Bonitus. For possible Aviti as bishops of Clermont, see Ian Wood, "The Ecclesiastical Politics of Merovingian Clermont," in *Ideal and Reality in Frankish and Anglo-Saxon Society, Studies Presented to J. M. Wallace-Hadrill*, ed. Patrick Wormald (Oxford: Basil Blackwell, 1983), 34–53.
174. Ibid., 34.
175. Greg. Tur., *Hist.* 3.2.
176. Greg. Tur., *Hist.* 3.2.
177. Greg. Tur., *Hist.* 4.5, *VP* 6.3.
178. Greg. Tur., *Hist.* 4.7.
179. Greg. Tur., *Hist.* 4.35.

certainly was a descendent of Sidonius's, had contributed to Gregory's religious education. So although Gregory likely coveted the bishopric, he showed nothing but affection for the winner of the post. After later becoming Bishop of Tours, Gregory met with Avitus whenever he visited his paternal homeland, and he favored the ecclesiastical policies and opinions of his friend, the Bishop of Clermont.[180]

Between 571 and mid-573, Gregory of Tours had witnessed three cherished sees fall vacant and then become filled by persons other than himself. Thus, if ecclesiastical aristocratic families anticipated dominating certain bishoprics, the fact that multiple ecclesiastical aristocratic families harbored such expectations meant that it was possible for a hopeful nobleman to miss out on attaining the office. To acquire a see in Barbarian Gaul, an episcopal candidate needed to act quickly and decisively, as Gregory's uncle Gallus apparently had realized. In August 573, a fourth potential see in half as many years opened when Gregory's mother's cousin Eufronius died.[181] It now is commonly suspected that Eufronius anticipated his successor to be a subordinate from his own clergy, the archdeacon Riculf.[182] Riculf, however, did not act decisively, and this time Gregory did. Upon news of Eufronius's death Gregory did not piously attend his relative's funeral (as he had done the previous year when Nicetius died); rather, he raced to the court of King Sigibert. There he gained the support of Austrasian court luminaries, including Sigibert, Brunhild, Radegund, and Bishop Egidius of Reims. Sigibert selected Gregory to become the next bishop of Tours.[183] Thus, despite his family's ecclesiastical aristocratic background, Gregory's elevation was no foregone conclusion.

If an individual aristocrat had to act swiftly to gain a see, aristocrats on the whole held an edge over less socially privileged families when it came to acquiring bishoprics. One reason kings might favor members of large landed families for the position is that in exchange for granting the posts,

---

180. Gregory especially supported Avitus's decision to forcibly convert the Jewish community at Clermont in 576; Greg. Tur., *Hist.* 5.11.
181. For a reconstruction of the year's events, see McDermott, "Felix of Nantes: A Merovingian Bishop," 9–11.
182. Ibid., 16.
183. Ven. Fort., *Carm.* 5.3.

the rulers could expect aristocrats to offer in return their undivided loyalty and substantial resources in support of the throne. Rulers also might expect aristocratic pontiffs to provide effective services as administrators and diplomats. For their part, members of a diocese could anticipate that an aristocratic bishop would be able to draw from personal resources to provide for needs of the community in times of want. Otherwise, bishops from powerful families could use their resources to make it seem that they above all others deserved the exalted office, especially by building opulent churches, donating large tracts of lands, and fostering saints' cults. But despite potential advantages for nobles, persons of lesser social station sometimes became bishops.[184] If less affluent episcopal aspirants did not have the material means that members of large landowning families possessed going in, the office availed itself of church properties and resources with which candidates might thereafter tend to a community's needs and concurrently augment their social status.[185] For example, in 529, the freeman (*ingenuus*) Injuriosus, a native of Tours, succeeded Francilio, a man of senatorial family, as Bishop of Tours.[186] Although he lacked an aristocratic pedigree, Injuriosus nevertheless was able to accomplish several notable feats on his diocese's behalf. In addition to completing construction for Saint Mary's church inside the city walls, he also built a church of Saint Germanus and two villages.[187] Another apparent *ingenuus* turned bishop was Eusebius, a Syrian merchant who, judging by his previous profession, presumably was not of aristocratic rank. Being an international merchant, however, placed Eusebius in contact with royalty. Eusebius reportedly bribed a

---

184. Most Gallic bishoprics through the fourth and into the fifth century were held by men of "middle class" and curial rank; Rapp, *Holy Bishops in Late Antiquity*, 183–88. While aristocrats had begun dominating the position in Gaul from the fifth century, in Italy and the East, non-senatorial persons, mainly *curiales*, still held most sees into the sixth century; ibid., 188–92.

185. The behavior of Leudast's conspiratorial ally in 580, the archdeacon Riculf, although he was not a bishop, reveals how a non-noble prelate could utilize church resources to build clout. While Gregory was away for his trial at Berny, Riculf at Tours, assuming he soon would become bishop, distributed fields and vineyards belonging to the church among high-ranking clerics to secure their loyalty; Greg. Tur., *Hist*. 5.49.

186. Greg. Tur., *Hist*. 10.31.

187. Greg. Tur., *Hist*. 10.31. Given that the widowed Queen Clotild resided at Tours for all but the last two of Injuriosus's sixteen years as bishop, his famous building efforts likely owed considerable credit to the fact that they coincided with the powerful woman's own religious agenda.

king, presumably Guntram, in order to become Bishop of Paris in 591. Not only did the Syrian acquire the prestigious post, what is more amazing is that he did this despite one of his challengers' being the previous bishop's noble brother.[188] Eusebius thus disrupted a potential emerging aristocratic "family see." In 591, a more famous *ingenuus* who capped off an ecclesiastical *cursus honorum* was Plato, Gregory's faithful archdeacon at Tours.[189] Gregory repaid Plato's long years of loyalty by procuring for him the see at Poitiers in succession to Maroveus.[190] As had happened on the occasion of Gregory's episcopal advent, Plato entered Poitiers to the accompaniment of a laudatory *adventus* poem penned by Venantius, which verses emphasized the new pontiff's connection (as disciple) with the now powerful Bishop of Tours.[191] By elevating his own archdeacon to the neighboring see, Gregory gained a double benefit by replacing the problematic Maroveus with the obsequious Plato. The Bishop of Tours' support for Plato's elevation reveals that even for the somewhat elitist-minded Gregory, actual ties of friendship and *patrocinium* could trump his abstraction that bishoprics should be reserved for persons of senatorial lineage. Indeed, in an age when aristocratic rhetoric was increasingly flagrant in an assertion that bishoprics rightfully belonged to nobles, Gallic litterateurs still might admit to the contrary that episcopal office "ennobled" officeholders, and so original rank ultimately did not matter. This was the very message implied in Venantius's *Life* of the episcopal parvenu Marcellus of Paris, about whom the poet wrote: "Humble in the world, but lofty in heaven, mediocre by his parents but eminent by his merits; [Marcellus was a man] for whom *the light of nobility was to serve Christ* gloriously without fault. ..."[192] These words demonstrate how

---

188. Greg. Tur., *Hist.* 10.26.
189. In 580, Plato was implicated along with Gregory when Leudast and Riculf accused the bishop of treason. The count arrested the archdeacon and presented him before Chilperic, who ordered his execution. But the king rescinded his decision, and had Plato detained and guarded. Presumably the council that cleared Gregory acquitted Plato too; Greg. Tur., *Hist.* 5.49.
190. Ven. Fort., *Carm.* 10.14.
191. Ven. Fort., *Carm.* 10.14.9–12 (*MGH*, AA 4.1, 248): "Gaudia laeta paret praesentia sancta Gregori et geminas urbes adiuvet una fides. Qui modo discipulo Platone antestite summo sollemnem ecclesiae hic dedit esse diem."
192. Ven. Fort., *Vita Marcelli* 4 (*MGH*, AA 4.2, 50): "... in terris humilis, erectus in caelis, mediocris parentibus sed meritis celsus, cui hoc fuit *nobilitatis lumen* insigne *Christo* sine culpa *servire* ..." with my italics.

Venantius imagined God could predestine an individual for a bishopric regardless of the candidate's social origins. Likewise, for Gregory of Tours, although he was certain that bishops were central to the functioning of God's eschatological church in this world, in the final analysis he would have admitted that what mattered most was a bishop's proper conduct and other "proof" that God and the saints favored him (e. g., by granting the ability to perform miracles), and not a prelate's original rank.[193]

If the office of bishop "ennobled" its bearer, such a person still needed to display evidence of that nobility by living up to social expectations, primarily through acts of patronage. The most conspicuous ways ecclesiastical aristocrats promoted their families' probity and extended their authority was by bequeathing properties to churches and erecting lasting monuments to God and the saints in both city and countryside.[194] For example, Bishop Francilio of Tours was a Poitevin *ex senatoribus* who with his wife Clara was "very wealthy" (*divites valde*).[195] Because they had no son, this couple bequeathed most of their extensive tracts to the church of Saint Martin at Tours, leaving the remainder to relatives. Likewise, Bishop Ommatius of Tours, an Auvergnian *de senatoribus* and indeed a descendent of Sidonius Apollinaris's, left properties to churches located near the family's lands.[196] Within the walls of Tours, Ommatius restored the church of Saints Gervasius and Protadius and began construction of the basilica of Saint Mary. Similarly, Bishop Agricola of Chalon-sur-Saône, a man from *genere senatorio*, augmented his repute by erecting "many buildings in that city."[197] His construction projects included private residences and a cathedral ornamented with columns, marble, and mosaics. A conflagration at Tours occasioned the chance for the senatorial Bishop Eufronius to build the basilica of Saint Vincent within the city walls, while another fire at the church of Saint Martin enabled him to improve upon that edifice by topping it with a gleaming

193. For bishops and the eschatological church, see Heinzelmann, *Gregory of Tours: History and Society*, 161–66.
194. See Rapp, *Holy Bishops in Late Antiquity*, 220–23.
195. Greg. Tur., *Hist.* 10.31 (*MGH*, SRM 1.1, 532).
196. Greg. Tur., *Hist.* 10.31 (*MGH*, SRM 1.1, 532).
197. Greg. Tur., *Hist.* 5.45 (*MGH*, SRM 1.1, 256): "Multa in civitate illa aedificia …"

tin roof.[198] Eufronius enhanced his authority in the rural Touraine by building churches for several villages.[199]

An aristocrat need not be a cleric to participate in ostentatious ecclesiastical benefaction and benefit socially from it. King Sigismund has been mentioned for having initiated Burgundian royal promotion of Catholicism by founding the monastery of Saint-Maurice at Agaune, a project that also entailed the building of other houses and basilicas.[200] Similarly, the Catholic convert Clovis with his zealously pious bride Clotild initiated Frankish royal sponsorship of church-building programs by constructing a basilica of the Holy Apostles Peter and Paul at Paris.[201] It was by decree of King Chlothar I, presumably with accompanying funds, that Eufronius set the aforementioned roof atop Saint Martin's basilica at Tours.[202] Chlothar also promoted the cult of Saint Medard of Noyon (d. ca. 557) both by maximizing the pomp at that bishop's funeral and by beginning construction on the saint's basilica at Soissons, which project King Sigibert completed.[203] Among his ostentatious efforts of church promotion, King Guntram built the church of Saint Marcel at Chalon-sur-Saône.[204] Beyond royalty, other secular church builders intended to benefit socially from this activity, including a late fifth-century Auvergnian aristocrat named Victorius whom Euric had made *dux* of *Septem Provinciae*.[205] At Clermont, the magnate built underground chapels and secured columns for the church of Saint Julian, and also he erected the city's church of Saint Lawrence and a church of Saint Germanus at St-Germain-Lanbron. Victorius's building campaign undoubtedly constituted an element of a stratagem for members of the Visigothic regime to ingratiate itself with the Auvergnats, but this particular magnate's effort was in vain. The Clermontois came to

198. Greg. Tur., *Hist.* 10.31.
199. Greg. Tur., *Hist.* 10.31.
200. Greg. Tur., *Hist.* 3.5.
201. Greg. Tur., *Hist.* 2.43.
202. Greg. Tur., *Hist.* 4.20.
203. Greg. Tur., *Hist.* 4.19.
204. Oddly, Gregory only remarked about Guntram's charity and ecclesiastical support in general terms; Greg. Tur., *Hist.* 9.21. One only learns of the church at Chalon-sur-Saône from a seventh-century chronicle; Fredegar, *Chron.* 4.1.
205. Greg. Tur., *Hist.* 4.19.

perceive the *dux* as a habitual womanizer, and further suspected him in the murder of his predecessor. In his ninth year in office, Victorius had to flee the region to save his life.[206] Another magnate who expected a return for his church building investment was Duke Austrapius, a participant with Queen Radegund and Bishop Pientius in the construction of the women's monastery at Poitiers.[207] Austrapius apparently intended his public, pious contribution to help him appear to be a suitable episcopal candidate. Indeed, King Chlothar I subsequently rewarded him with a small bishopric adjacent to Poitiers. But Austrapius further anticipated the king's selecting him to succeed Pientius on the Poitevin cathedra. Unfortunately for the ambitious man, Chlothar died before Pientius, and King Charibert, who inherited control of Poitiers, frustrated Austrapius's designs by giving the bishopric to Pascentius.[208]

While women could not aspire to the ennobling office of bishop, nevertheless, like secular males they too could demand social distinction by erecting churches and founding monasteries, sometimes independently and other times with the accompaniment of husbands. Many Gallic men were married when they became priests or bishops, and rather than abandon their spouses, they promised to behave continently and treat their mates as "sisters." A canon from the Council of Tours (567), which cautions that a bishop and wife not dwell together, afforded bishops' spouses an unofficial but official-sounding title, *episcopa*.[209] This and other canons indicate that partnerships of priests and wives (*presbyterae*) continually raised clerical concerns about possible continued carnal behavior. Another potential problem with *episcopae* to some clerical eyes was that they might grow accustomed to the lucre derived from their spouses' position and try to keep church property. One possessive *episcopa* was the aforementioned pugnacious noblewoman Magnatrude, who fended off the assault on her estate by King Chilperic's agent Cuppa. Earlier, after her husband Bishop Badegisel's

---

206. Greg. Tur., *Hist.* 4.19.
207. Baudonivia, *Vita Radegundis* 5.
208. Greg. Tur., *Hist.* 4.18.
209. Council of Tours (567), c. 14; Brian Brennan, "'*Episcopae*': Bishops' Wives Viewed in Sixth-Century Gaul," *Church History* 54 (1985), 315.

death in 586, Magnatrude conducted a lengthy legal contest with the
episcopal successor for control of church goods, which she claimed to
be the personal belongings of her spouse.[210] Despite such problems, *episcopae* persisted throughout the sixth century no doubt in part because
of the valuable contribution they made toward promoting their powerful families' continued social influence. They especially used their position to augment their husbands' episcopal authority and publicize their
own roles as ecclesiastical patrons. For example, the anonymous wife
of Bishop Namatius of Clermont not only funded building an extra-
mural church of Saint Stephen, but also frequented the construction
site and personally directed painters applying frescoes to the walls.[211]
A more obviously ambitious bishop's wife was Placidina, the spouse
of Apollinaris of Clermont, Sidonius's son. She, with her sister-in-law
Alcima, had prompted Apollinaris to travel to King Theuderic's court
and petition to take the cathedra from the "people's choice," Bishop
Quintianus.[212] During Apollinaris's brief four-month tenure around 515,
Placidina and Alcima determined to build a funerary basilica for Saint
Antolianus on the site of an extant cemetery.[213] Workers had to unearth
many bodies to lay the building's foundation, and they disposed of the
corpses by unceremoniously heaping them into a mass grave. A vision
of Saint Antolianus then appeared to "a certain man" and expressed his
dismay over the sacrilege, which consternation undoubtedly reflected
popular sentiment. The saint also foretold that the building project
would never be completed. Indeed, a delicate tower built of columns
and arches suspended over the altar developed cracks, and it seemed
the structure would collapse. Some six decades later, Gregory's friend,
Bishop Avitus of Clermont, almost certainly a relation to these Aviti,
ordered repairs to the tower, at which time it came crashing down upon
the altar. Placidina and Alcima faired as badly as their church; when
the former's son Arcadius in 527 supported the wrong king in a contest
between two Merovingians, the women's possessions were confiscated

---

210. Greg. Tur., *Hist.* 8.39.
211. Greg. Tur., *Hist.* 2.17.
212. Greg. Tur., *Hist.* 3.2.
213. Greg. Tur., *GM* 64; *PLRE* 2, 54, s. v. "Alcima"; *PLRE* 2, 889–90, s. v., "Placidina."

and they were ordered into exile, never to receive mention again in Gregory's pages.[214]

Yet another distinguished *episcopa* was a second Placidina, a member of the Aviti and wife of the aristocratic Leontius, who succeeded his grandfather as bishop of Bordeaux. In a panegyric to Leontius, the poet Venantius enumerated Placidina's noble qualities, the most important being an imperial pedigree. Placidina was a great-great granddaughter of Emperor Eparchius Avitus (455).[215] Thus her very being added luster to her and Leontius's family reputation. But beyond merely affording a name, Placidina also operated in tandem with Leontius on projects of church building and cult promotion intended to foster their repute as ecclesiastical patrons. For example, after Leontius erected a church of Saint Martin at Bordeaux, Placidina, like the aforementioned *episcopa* of Clermont, oversaw the edifice's decoration. To commemorate the couple's benefaction, Venantius composed a poem that would have been painted on the church walls to remind the congregation of the clan to whom they should be grateful for the edifice.[216] Similarly, Placidina and Leontius together promoted the cults of Saints Bibianus and Eutropius at Saintes by ornamenting the holy men's tombs and donating expensive church plate. Again they relied on Venantius for laudatory verses inscribed on the church walls that commemorated their contributions.[217] Interestingly, behind the conspicuous efforts of church benefaction at Saintes was an obvious power play by which the couple was attempting to

214. Greg. Tur., *Hist.* 3.12. Cf. Mathisen, *People, Personal Expression, and Social Relations*, 184–88. Mathisen suggests that Placidina and Alcima may have known that they needed to work fast to complete the basilica, because Apollinaris was not going to last, and so the result "was a rather slipshod job of construction"; ibid., 187. Alternatively, given that the church lasted sixty years, and the tower only fell during Avitus's repairs, perhaps Gregory was simply exonerating his friend of the mishap and passing blame to several long dead Aviti for whom he held a special animus. After all, Apollinaris had taken the cathedra of Clermont from an Auvergnian saint whom Gregory admired, at the instigation of two covetous women, no less. Furthermore, Gregory singly blamed the ambition of Placidina's son Arcadius for precipitating the terrible destruction that King Theuderic's campaign wrought upon his Auvergnian *patria*. Just as he exonerated Avitus after the basilica's collapse, Gregory essentially pardoned the saintly Queen Clotild for notoriously ordering the deaths of two of her own grandchildren by insisting that Arcadius had frightened and befuddled her, and had not given the queen sufficient time to change her mind about the executions; Greg. Tur., *Hist.* 3.18.

215. Ven. Fort., *Carm.* 1.15; *PLRE* 2, stemma 14, p. 1317; *PLRE* 3, 1042, s. v. "Placidina."

216. Ven. Fort., *Carm.* 1.6.

217. Ven. Fort., *Carm.* 1.12–13. For other *episcopae*, see Greg. Tur., *Hist.* 1.41, 2.22, 4.36; *GC* 74, 75; Ven. Fort., *Carm.* 4.27.

reassert religious authority in the vicinity. Between 563 and 567, Leontius had run afoul of King Charibert when the former exercised his metropolitan rights by deposing Bishop Emerius of Saintes and replacing him with a priest from Bordeaux. Charibert interpreted this effort as a slight to royal prerogative, for it had been his father Chlothar who had given the cathedra to Emerius. In retaliation, Charibert rather heavy-handedly restored Emerius at Saintes and fined Leontius for his impertinence.[218] It was in the wake of this humiliation that Placidina and Leontius conducted their spirited restoration project. These efforts were designed to reestablish Leontius's metropolitan authority at Saintes and simultaneously upstage the newly restored Emerius. Thus, along these lines, the inscription for Bibianus's church effectively depicted Emerius as impotent to perform the rebuilding task without Leontius's assistance.[219] Because Placidina and Leontius's church-building programs carried an assertion that their family deserved control of Bordeaux's metropolitan see, perhaps it came as a shock for Placidina that a relative did not succeed her husband upon his demise around 573. Instead, the cathedra went to something of an ecclesiastical parvenu, a certain Bertram, about whom there will be more to say in the next chapter. Otherwise, another aristocratic, church-building husband and wife team was Duke Launebode of Toulouse and Beretrude, who erected a church of Saint Saturninus at Toulouse.[220] Their example again reflects that influential church patrons need not have been ecclesiastics. Furthermore, neither did a Gallic aristocratic woman need to have a spouse to secure social prominence through high-profile church affiliation.

As has been mentioned, Queen Radegund remained a politically influential figure despite having abandoned her husband Chlothar by founding the abbey of the Holy Cross at Poitiers, to which she bequeathed all possessions she had received from the king. Radegund also built an extra-mural basilica of Saint Mary intended for her interment and that

218. Greg. Tur., *Hist.* 4.26.
219. Ven. Fort., Carm. 1.12; Brian Brennan, "The Image of the Merovingian Bishop in the Poetry of Venantius Fortunatus," *Journal of Medieval History* 18 (1992), 125.
220. Ven Fort., *Carm.* 2.8.

of her nuns.[221] Otherwise, the queen also assured a continued family connection with the famous convent by welcoming Merovingian relatives – namely, Charibert's daughter Clotild and Chilperic's daughter Basina – into the fold. Furthermore, she asserted her authority in Merovingian family planning by stifling a momentary consideration on Chilperic's part to marry off Basina to the Visigothic prince, Reccared.[222] The example of Radegund reveals how a prominent religious matron, although cloistered, still could expect to function as an influential patron and concomitantly promote her aristocratic clan's future family interests. A century earlier, before Gallic churchmen forced prominent female ascetics into permanent sequestration, another model aristocratic religious matron who adopted an ascetic lifestyle and became her community's most prominent patron was Geneviève of Paris. According to her hagiographer, this daughter of two ecclesiastically involved parents declared at an early age that she would keep her virginity perpetually.[223] Reportedly Geneviève achieved her greatest miracle by organizing matrons at Paris to pray, thereby causing Attila the Hun to forego the city during his destructive 451 invasion of Gaul.[224] A more lasting act of patronage on Geneviève's part was presiding over construction of the church of Saint Denis.[225] Unlike the diversion of Attila's army, for which a similar miracle already had been credited to Saint Anianus of Orléans in an earlier *Vita*, Geneviève's church-building effort is not likely to have been a hagiographical fiction, for wall inscriptions at Saint Denis would have readily confirmed for the Parisian congregation the church's actual benefactor.[226] Besides this, church building was not beyond the purview of powerful Gallic women.[227] Late in life, Geneviève exerted

---

221. Greg. Tur., *Hist.* 9.42. For Radegund's funeral, see Greg. Tur., *GC* 104.
222. Greg. Tur., *Hist.* 6.34.
223. On Severus and Gerontia, see Jones, "The Family of Geneviève of Paris," 74–76.
224. *Vita Genovefae* 12–14.
225. *Vita Genovefae* 17–21.
226. Patrick Périn, "Settlements and Cemeteries in Merovingian Gaul," 73, has proposed a revision for the location of Geneviève's St-Denis. What was once thought to be Geneviève's church is actually a fourth-century structure, while what traditionally had been assigned to King Dagobert (d. 639) is actually Geneviève's building, complete with early Merovigian graves.
227. Gregory of Tours repeated a tradition derived from an anonymous *Passio* of Saint Julian that a late fourth-century laywoman from Spain fulfilled a vow by building the stone edifice for Saint Julian's shrine at Brioude; Greg. Tur., *VJ* 4; *Passio Iuliani* 5. Otherwise, Gregory mentioned that

her position as Paris's principal patron by negotiating with the Frank King Childeric for release of prisoners, and she apparently maintained an affable relationship with Clovis and Clotild as well.[228] The latter relationship is attested to by the royal couple's decision to inter Geneviève's corpse in their newly constructed church of the Apostles, where they also were to be buried.[229] It is suspected that Queen Clotild promoted Geneviève's sanctity from her ascetic abode at Tours by charging a cleric or monk from that city to write her *Vita*.[230] Once widowed, Clotild remained a prominent religious patron. She endowed lands to churches, monasteries, and shrines, and also she founded monasteries and built churches, including a suburban monastery of Saint Peter at Tours, a monastery of Saint Mary near Rouen, and a basilica of Saint Peter beyond the walls of Laon.[231] Thus, noblewomen whether married, single, or widowed, joined with all manner of aristocrats in maintaining and enhancing personal and familial prestige through conspicuous displays of religious patronage.

In conclusion, our sources offer evidence for three principal activities that confirmed nobility for those already established as aristocrats and ennobled others. The combination of resources via marriage among wealthy and large landowning families enabled aristocratic families to sustain their position atop society, as happened with Gregory of Tours' clan, and it enabled noble upstarts to augment their rank, as Amantius and Andarchius apparently realized it would. Likewise, court service and acquisition of secular titles added luster for propertied noble families, as it did for Duke Lupus, and courts also provided a venue where "new men" converted diligence into nobility, as happened for Conda and Leudast. Finally, high ecclesiastical office and ostentatious patronage of churches afforded a means for aristocrats such as Eufronius of Tours and Placidina of Bordeaux to assert why their communities should

---

an Aquitanian noblewoman named Victurina, likely a contemporary of Geneviève, constructed a church of Saint Julian on her own villa; *VJ* 47.

228. *Vita Genovefae* 26, 56.

229. Greg. Tur., *Hist.* 4.1.

230. Heinzelmann and Poulin, *Les vies anciennes*, 53; Ian Wood, "Forgery in Merovingian Hagiography," *Fälschungen im Mittelalter* 5, *MGH Schriften* 33 (Hanover: Hahn, 1988), 378.

231. Greg. Tur., *Hist.* 3.18; *Vita Clotildis* 11–13.

acknowledge them as their localities' best possible leaders of Christian society. The ennobling quality that possession of a bishopric conferred meant that persons of lesser rank such as Plato of Tours/Poitiers and Marcellus of Paris might fill such positions and fulfill their obligations. Indeed, the participation of parvenus in each of the three pursuits we have examined – marriage with wealthy landowners, acquisition of high secular office, and participation in high-profile church patronage – reveals how each of these ostensibly noble strategies actually were facets of more basic phenomena in which Gauls from every social station participated. Advantageous marriage, pursuit of secular office, and church affiliation were not behaviors distinctive to aristocrats; and as it turns out, Gallic aristocratic litterateurs actually had much to admit regarding the efforts of people from non-elite ranks to improve their social condition via these same stratagems.

The next chapter will focus upon the variety of free and servile people who tried to better their social predicament, and it will assess how members of different strata of *mediocres* could expect to fare.

SOCIAL STRUCTURE II: FREE AND SERVILE RANKS

CHAPTER FOUR

...the father said, "Why, dearest son, do you refuse my paternal will and wish not to marry, so that you can cause your seed to be a benefit for our family for ages to come? For our labor is all for naught, if there will be none to enjoy its fruits."

GREGORY OF TOURS, *De Vita Patrum* 20.1[1]

This chapter will continue laying out a model for society in Barbarian Gaul. The previous chapter focused on participants within Gaul's multiple aristocracies, large landowners, prominent courtiers, and ecclesiastical aristocrats. Gallic authors characterized people who succeeded in their strategies of marrying with landed elites, acquiring high secular office and prominently patronizing churches as society's "best" (*optimi*). But, as the hopeful expression of a non-aristocratic father for his son to continue the family line, presented in this chapter's introductory quote, indicates, schemes for social improvement in fact might differ between nobles and non-elites only by a matter of degrees. This chapter

1. Greg. Tur., *VP* 20.1 (*MGH*, SRM 1.2, 291): "... ait pater: 'Cur, dulcissime fili, voluntatem paternam respuis nec iungere vis conubio, ut semen excites nostro de genere saeculis sequentibus profuturum? Casso enim labore exercemur ad operandum, si possessor deerit ad fruendum.'"

concentrates on details of people from the lower social ranks as they sought social betterment through marriage, pursuit of secular office, and church affiliation. Analysis will progress according to descending rank, free to slave. Freepersons will be divided into two groups, *ingenui* and *pauperes*, according to terminology used by contemporary writers. But even this division cannot do justice to the variation, economic and otherwise, that existed within the large "middling" group of people that archaeologists and social historians are now realizing characterized late ancient societies.[2] Despite this variety of experience, however, many free people will have shared a general circumstance of dwelling in "shallow" poverty, situated above destitution, or "deep" poverty, into which condition many might plunge and resurface during their lifetime.[3]

INGENUI

Salic law equated *ingenui* with *franci* and hence identified them as people subject to military service. Gregory of Tours, however, used the term *ingenui* to indicate a broader group of freepersons, including those who according to the law were both *franci* and *romani*, the latter being non-combatants. While it is unclear whether Salic lawmakers intended to number nobles among the *ingenui*, Gregory certainly distinguished between *ingenui* and aristocrats. This and subsequent chapters will use the expression *ingenuus* as per Gregory's parameters. Most *ingenui* undoubtedly were rural farmers, but they also included townspeople. They were subject to taxation and military levy unless occupation dictated otherwise – for example, limited tax exemption for soldiers and military exemption for clerics. Variation in lifestyles among freepersons existed mainly according to differing levels of wealth and different occupations. Behavioral differences also will have resulted from some living in closer proximity than others to royal or ecclesiastical patronage

---

2. Brown, *Poverty and Leadership*, 47. For a reassessment of the traditional thesis of late ancient impoverishment focusing upon the Northern Gallic countryside, see Paul Van Ossel, "Rural Impoverishment in Northern Gaul at the End of Antiquity: The Contribution of Archaeology," in *Social and Political Life in Late Antiquity*, ed. W. Bowden, A. Gutteridge and C. Machado (Leiden and Boston: Brill, 2006), 533–65. For bibliography on late ancient "middle classes," see Schachner, "Social Life in Late Antiquity," 46–48.
3. Brown, *Poverty and Leadership*, 15.

centers that is, courts and towns, respectively. Regional social variation, such as the manner and extent to which local elites might routinely interfere in the lives of middling landowners, also will have contributed to lifestyle distinction among *ingenui*.[4] Still, this does not mean that the *mediocres* across Gaul, who shared many basic cultural principals, would not have found much familiar about the structuring of society from one end of Gaul to another. Therefore one must limit speculation on similarities and differences among freepersons according to what the evidence permits us to know about them. First, the sources indicate there was enough economic disparity among the free that litterateurs might divide them into distinct categories. Authors identified one group who had few or no resources according to their socio-economic deprivation (*pauperes*), while a second group possessed enough resources to merit being labeled by their free status (*ingenui*).[5] When writing about a person belonging to this latter, more well-to-do group, Gregory of Tours sometimes appended to an initial description the words "nevertheless he was a freeman" (*ingenuus tamen*), as if to inform readers that the non-aristocratic person in question were deserving of a modicum of respect despite lacking nobleness. Given that upper-level freepersons had some wealth, perhaps it is to be expected that the sources reveal them employing stratagems for social betterment that scarcely differed from aristocratic techniques. *Ingenui* tried to maintain and improve their social situation by marrying other landowners, by entering court circles, and through conspicuous church participation. Apparently, however, freepersons generally had a tougher time making social improvements than did aristocrats.

Litterateurs occasionally painted the *ingenui* as something of a "beleaguered middle class," neither aristocratic nor servile, having to counter the machinations of land-grabbing aristocrats, heavy-taxing government agents, and even unscrupulous ecclesiastics. An early voice whose social

---

4. Halsall, *Settlement and Social Organization*, 40, rightly cautions against accepting teleologically derived assessments that middling landowners of the Merovingian era must have experienced a condition that amounted to a mid-way point between Roman tenury and medieval serfdom.

5. On ecclesiastical authors' rhetorical usages of the term *pauperes*, see the section on *Pauperes* in the chapter.

criticisms mark what was the beginning of a centuries-long, sporadic but persistent aristocratic consolidation of Gallic lands was Salvian of Marseilles. Salvian was an early fifth-century nobleman and priest who fled from northern Gaul to Lérins on the south coast ostensibly to escape the barbarian incursions, but perhaps also because opportunities for imperial patronage had dried up in the north.[6] Regardless of his motives for relocating, from his monkish island oasis Salvian roundly criticized powerful Gauls for using heavy-handed tactics to force small landowners into debt and clientage. He even excused freepersons who attempted to retain a modicum of liberty by joining rebellious peasant bands and enlisting with barbarian armies.[7] A full century later, Caesarius of Arles indicated in his sermons how powerful people in his diocese were still conducting similar stratagems against lesser landowners. Specifically, Caesarius complained how a large landowner might collude with a government agent to raise taxes on a neighboring smallholder, so that the latter would seek a loan from the powerful figure, who in turn would pretend he could not grant it. Finally, the smallholder would agree to become a client of the supposedly sympathetic neighbor, never realizing that he had been the victim of the powerful man's deceit.[8] Subsequent evidence, most of it anecdotal, tends not to elaborate on such clinical calculations and collusions among the powerful but instead offers more action-packed episodes of land grabbing. For example, Gregory of Tours related how the aristocrat Cautinus of Clermont coveted the land of an

---

6. On the early fifth-century aristocratic influx at Lérins, see Mathisen, *Ecclesiastical Factionalism and Religious Controversy*, 81–83; Klingshirn, *Caesarius of Arles: The Making of a Christian Community*, 20–21.

7. E.g., Salvian of Marseilles, *De gubernatione Dei* 5.5. Salvian referred to beleaguered *curiales* and middling to small landowners rhetorically as *pauperes*; Cam Grey, "Salvian, the Ideal Christian Community and the Fate of the Poor in Fifth-Century Gaul," in *Poverty in the Roman World*, ed. Margaret Atkins and Robin Osborne (Cambridge: Cambridge University Press, 2006), 172–73. Contrary to the priest's rhetoric of the rich simply degrading the poor, Grey, ibid., 181, sees complexity of motivation in the novel relationships between *mediocres* and elites that Salvian depicted. For example, he, ibid., 177–80, describes how lesser landowners could have been strategizing for social advantage, e.g., by transferring a few lands to a more powerful person and thereby avoiding qualifying to have to pay harsh fiscal duties, or by becoming *coloni* and giving up some land in return for gaining the benefit of a patron.

8. Caes. Arel., *Serm.* 154.2; Klingshirn, *Caesarius of Arles: The Making of a Christian Community*, 205–06. Smith, *Europe after Rome*, 161–62, writes: "The transition from small freeholder to dependent peasant was rarely reversible; great estates expanded everywhere between the sixth and eleventh centuries, and small men lost out."

ingenuus named Anastasius.[9] An interesting twist to this tale is that the former was a bishop and the latter his priest. Cautinus demanded title deeds for a property that the late Queen Clotild had given the priest, but when Anastasius refused to relinquish them, the nobleman ordered his thugs to imprison the priest alive in a crypt. Anastasius escaped, however, and dashed to the court of Chlothar I, where he accused the prelate of attempted theft. Cautinus traveled to court, too, but the king judged in the freeman's favor and even demanded that new title deeds be drafted to assure that Anastasius's descendents would hold the property. According to Gregory, Cautinus's mistreatment of the priest was not a singular incident; rather, seizing adjacent properties was an oft-repeated element of the aristocrat's overall design to augment his local power. Gregory explained, "Cautinus took from the more powerful people with legal proceedings and accusations, but he simply pillaged the humbler people by force."[10]

This remark reveals how aristocrats might tailor their land-grabbing schemes according to the status of intended victims. Anastasius's successful appeal to Chlothar indicates how *ingenui* could expect to receive justice from a king's court, even in a property dispute against a landed aristocrat. Unfortunately for other freepersons, some covetous magnates were agents attached to the very royal courts to which they might hope to turn for protection. For example, Eberulf, treasurer to King Chilperic, reportedly used to treat properties of the Touraine's small landowners as if they were his own by grazing his horses and cattle on their fields and vineyards, and if anyone should remove the animals, the magnate sent armed men to cut them down.[11] Similarly, consider Chilperic's former count of the stables, Cuppa, who in the previous chapter we witnessed making an unsuccessful bid to forcibly acquire a noble bride, Magnatrude's daughter. In 590, Cuppa again tried to augment his social fortune, this time by raiding the environs of Tours

---

9. Greg. Tur., *Hist.* 4.12. Cf. Mathisen, *People, Personal Expression, and Social Relations*, 1: 54–56.
10. Greg. Tur., *Hist.* 4.12 (*MGH*, SRM 1.1, 142): "Et maioribus quidem cum rixa et scandalo auferebat, a minoribus autem violenter diripiebat."
11. Greg. Tur., *Hist.* 7.22.

to seize sheep and other movables.[12] But the Tourangeaux organized a force that chased down the culprit and recovered their possessions. Two of Cuppa's men were slain, while another pair was captured and taken to court at Metz. There, King Childebert II learned that Cuppa had evaded capture by negotiating with Animodius, an agent for the Count of Tours. Animodius and Cuppa were summoned to appear before a secular tribunal, but both bribed the presiding official, and so in the end neither paid a penalty for their conduct. Although it cannot be determined with what frequency freepersons had to contend with property coveting magnates, the evidence from this and similar episodes suggests that people who faced arrogant royal officials, active and former, were not averse to responding with stalwart military opposition, not unlike the manner in which the noble Magnatrude had tended to Cuppa. Perhaps many *ingenui*, like aristocrats, determined that violence was an effective means of recourse against well-connected persons. Presumably, Salvian would have approved of these underdogs' solutions.

Despite setbacks, individuals of free rank proved resilient and pressed on to enhance their lot in society. Like aristocrats, *ingenui* counted on combining resources through marriage of offspring to secure and even improve family fortunes. A prime piece of evidence for the importance that *ingenui* parents might place upon marriage comes from Gregory of Tours' imagined conversation between a father and son, the latter being a future saint. Leobardus was an Auvergnian freeman, and although his kin apparently were rural farmers, he managed to acquire an education by which he learned the psalms by heart.[13] Although Leobardus in his youth did not yet realize how God had destined him to enter the clergy, subtle pangs of religious sentiment caused him to resist his parents when they pressed him to find a bride:

> ...the father said, "Why, dearest son, do you refuse my paternal will and wish not to marry, so that you can cause your seed to be a benefit for our family for ages to come? For our labor is all for

12. Greg. Tur., *Hist.* 10.5.
13. Greg. Tur., *VP* 20.1.

naught, if there will be none to enjoy its fruits. Why should we have a house filled with treasures, if no one will arise from our family to use them? Why should we expend money to harness slaves on our estates, if it is to befall that they will be given over to another's dominions?"[14]

In writing this passage, Gregory, a dedicated celibate cleric, was attempting to represent an *ingenuus* father sharing with a son what the author imagined to be "common sense" secular advice. Gregory characterized the parental desire of wanting one's child to find a spouse as a "basic human habit" (*iuxta consuetudinem humanam*).[15] He further estimated the social stratagem of marrying and thereby amassing lands, movables, and slaves as an unquestionably normative course of action for *ingenui*, just as he thought it to be for aristocrats. Gregory's presentation of Leobardus's father's expectation compares with an episode from the previous chapter involving the senator Georgius, Gregory's grandfather, who had hoped his saintly son Gallus would wed a woman of suitably high social rank. In neither account did the author dwell upon the saint's having to overcome the obstacle of being pressured to marry. But whereas Georgius immediately allowed his son to join a monastery, Leobardus reportedly conceded to his parents' desires and presented traditional gifts – a ring and shoes – to his betrothed. It was only after the parents' sudden demise that Leobardus embarked upon a clerical career. According to these anecdotes, it would seem that parental expectations for sons to pursue a course of marital and familial bliss differed little between *ingenui* and aristocrats.[16] A further point to make about the plea of Leobardus's father concerns his mention of wealth. Judging by his words, wealthy *ingenui* must have been able to horde substantial

---

14. Greg. Tur., *VP* 20.1 (*MGH*, SRM 1.2, 291): "... ait pater: 'Cur, dulcissime fili, voluntatem paternam respuis nec iungere vis conubio, ut semen excites nostro de genere saeculis sequentibus profuturum? Casso enim labore exercemur ad operandum, si possessor deerit ad fruendum. Vel cur inplemus domum opibus, si de genere nostro non processerit qui utatur? Quid mancipia dato pretio nostris ditionibus subiugamus, si rursum alienis debent dominationibus subiacere?"

15. Greg. Tur., *VP* 20.1 (*MGH*, SRM 1.2, 291).

16. For an *ingenuus* widow pleading for her son to seek a beautiful *ingenuus* woman to marry, see Greg. Tur., *VP* 9.1. Church councils did not provide separate rules for people of different social rank regarding marriage; instead, all were forbidden to marry *contra parentum voluntatem*; e.g., Council of Tours (567), c. 21 (20).

movables in their houses and keep "many slaves" on multiple estates. Another individual whose example confirms freepersons in possession of sizeable amounts of property was one of Gregory's dearest friends, Aredius of Limoges. Aredius was "by origin a man from not mediocre parentage in his region, but very free."[17] He left home to pursue a secular career, but became a cleric instead. When his father and brother died, making him the only surviving son, Aredius dutifully returned to help his mother Pelagia manage the family property. But at home he took up an ascetic lifestyle, and requested that Pelagia manage the estates, which duties included overseeing the servants, fields, and vineyards. These properties find mention in an extant will of Aredius and Pelagia and a donation, which documents attest to the couple's holding around fifteen estates clustered in the southern Limousin.[18] Judging by the testament, it is possible that this family's wealth originated from wine production and export.[19] These resources were considerable enough that Aredius was able to embark on an ambitious church-building program, about which there will be more to say later. Thus, the examples of Leobardus, Aredius, and their kin suggest that well-to-do *ingenui* hardly differed from aristocrats in their hopes to advantageously marry off children and/or to secure property, servants, and wealth.[20]

Examples of saints having to overcome strong familial expectations for marriage appear so regularly in saints' lives that they certainly constitute a trope. Subtle differences in the presentation of male and female saints having to overcome family pressures to wed, however, suggest that the evidence betrays a semblance of actual social expectations and

17. Greg. Tur., *Hist.* 10.29 (*MGH*, SRM 1.1, 522): "... non mediocribus regionis suae ortu parentibus, sed valde ingenuus."

18. *Testamentum sancti Aredii*, ed. J.-P. Migne, *PL* 71 (Paris: J.-P. Migne, 1879), 1143–50; Wickham, *Framing the Early Middle Ages*, 173. Wickham, ibid., contends that Aredius likely typified the southern Gallic sub-regional aristocrat, and he assesses that his wealth would have been similar to that of the fourth-century noble upstart, Ausonius of Bordeaux.

19. See Wickham, ibid., 284–87.

20. Gregory's examples of Aredius and Leobardus scarcely would have fit into the traditional paradigm that depicted Gallic society divided into two groups, a few aristocratic landowners and a mass of impoverished persons. But it corroborates nicely with recent archaeological interpretations of Gallic society possessing a sizeable "middle class," which group "was not a monolithic entity, but rather a great spectrum of individuals who had varying statuses, wealth and technical capabilities"; Van Ossel, "Rural Impoverishment in Northern Gaul," 561.

conditions.[21] While mention of parental expectations for male saints to marry is common to Gallic saints' lives, either marriage posed no threat to a man's pursuit of holiness or else, if the saint did act counter to his parents' will, the threat rapidly dissipated, as was the case for both Gallus and Leobardus.[22] But according to the same sources, female saints faced a stiffer challenge in acting contrary to parental expectations for wedding. First, the evidence indicates that daughters generally obeyed their parents' will, for most female saints are portrayed as having been married or widowed and as having already produced children. One such person was the aforementioned Pelagia, who after the death of her husband and elder son emulated the younger Aredius and became an ascetic.[23] Second, unlike their depictions of male holy subjects, authors depicted would-be saintly women facing persistent opposition by parents and spouses. One person who faced a lasting dilemma was Monegund of Chartres, a female ascetic who abandoned a cell on her family estate and established a community of nuns elsewhere, only to be retrieved bodily by her husband.[24] Like Pelagia, Monegund was married and had produced children before she adopted the habit. Another married woman who pondered entering a convent after she had had children was Berthegund. Her mother and husband argued for decades about whether the woman should remain with the spouse or enter a nunnery.[25] The fact that most Gallic female saints were married with children not only attests to the significance of matrimony in family engineering; compared with the ease with which male saints such as Gallus and

---

21. Kitchen, *Rhetoric and Gender in Merovingian Saints' Lives*, 107–08.
22. The most common kind of holy man for whom marriage posed no threat was a bishop, whose wife became an *episcopa*. For example, although Gregorius of Langres was married and had children by Armentaria, this did not prevent Gregory of Tours from perceiving him as a devout practitioner of chastity. Reportedly the pair came together only for the purpose of procreating; Greg. Tur., *VP* 7.1. Another *ingenuus* male who initially obliged his parents by presenting betrothal gifts to a potential mate was a certain Venantius, whom Gregory depicted abandoning his betrothed to enter the church at Tours, with no interference from the parents; Greg. Tur., *VP* 16.1, and see the discussion in this chapter between pp. 148 and 149.
23. Like Aredius, Pelagia also would be regarded as a saint; Greg. Tur., *GC* 102.
24. Greg. Tur., *VP* 19; Kitchen, *Saints' Lives and the Rhetoric of Gender*, 111. On Monegund, see the discussion in this chapter between pp. 151 and 153.
25. Greg. Tur., *Hist.* 9.33. On Berthegund, who was no saint, see the discussion in this chapter between pp. 153 and 154.

Leobardus entered the church, their example also suggests that expectations for daughters to obey parents and wed were more forcefully upheld than they were for sons.

We would know next to nothing about the marital strategies of Gallic freepersons if most of the subjects for whom evidence survives had not eventually eschewed matrimony for a religious lifestyle. Similarly, another stratagem by which *ingenui* improved their social lot for which the evidence is slim entails participation in secular pursuits, either in the army or at court. Legal sources indicate that rank and file *franci* were *de facto* freemen. The laws also reveal how royal courts appreciated both free young men with a will to fight and the free young women who could produce more. Unfortunately, there survives no ode to the common Gallic soldier. As one can with marriage, however, one can tease out some evidence from tales about saints who began secular careers before they entered the church. One such person was the aforementioned Aredius. According to Gregory, Aredius in his youth was invited to King Theudebert's court and placed with the "royal courtiers" (*aulitis palatinis*).[26] If this anecdote constitutes a glimpse at how the Merovingians gathered pools of potential officers and agents, then Aredius's selection would suggest that royal operatives thought wealthy *ingenui* to be acceptable along with aristocratic recruits.[27] It cannot be known what Theudebert had in mind for Aredius, for Gregory did not elucidate on his stay at court.[28] Instead, the author recorded how Bishop Nicetius of Trier espied the youth and carried him back to his diocese, where Aredius became a cleric. But Gregory provided a bit more detail about another *ingenuus* who entered a court, Patroclus, an inhabitant of Berry and son of Aetherius.[29] About Patroclus's

---

26. Greg. Tur., Hist. 10.29 (*MGH*, SRM 1.1, 522).
27. Bernard Bachrach, "The Education of the 'Officer Corps' in the Fifth and Sixth Centuries," in *La noblesse romaine et les chefs barbares du IIIe au VIIe siècle*, ed., Françoise Vallet and Michel Kazanski (Paris: Association Française d'Archéologie Mérovingienne et Musée des Antiquités Nationales, 1995), 9, in describing the education of the Merovingian "officer corps" seems to assert that all candidates were "young aristocrats."
28. The analysis by Bachrach, ibid., 10–11, of the campaigns of Germanus of Auxerre and the patrician Eunius Mummolus indicates that fifth- and sixth-century Gallic maneuvers closely corresponded with late Roman military tactical strategizing.
29. The notion that whenever Gregory provided a person's father's name it was tantamount to his declaring the family's nobility is incorrect, as this example plainly reveals.

family, Gregory wrote that they were "not of the highest nobility, but free nevertheless."[30] Like Leobardus's family, Patroclus's clan appears to have been rural landowners with some appreciation for the value of education. As the story goes, young Patrolcus was sent to the fields to tend sheep while his brother Antonius attended school. Antonius soon belittled his brother, commenting that his pursuit of letters made him "nobler" (*nobiliter*) than Patroclus.[31] Gregory did not intend the haughty remark to indicate an overweening pride on Antonius's part. Rather the statement was to be read as a sign from God that Patroclus too should pursue an education. Rightly interpreting his sibling's boast, Patroclus attended school and soon bested Antonius in knowledge and wit. By virtue of his learning, Patroclus was recommended to Nunnio, an agent for King Childebert I, and soon entered the Parisian court. As with Aredius, Gregory revealed nothing of Patroclus's function at court, but here it is telling that it was the freeman's education that enabled him to stand out before the courtier. Nunnio's eye for a schooled person recalls Lupus's recognition of the literarily adept Andarchius, whom the duke whisked away to Metz.[32] Otherwise, as with Aredius, Patroclus's stay at court did not last. Upon his father's demise, he returned home to manage the family property, where his mother asserted the usual parental pressure for him to join with an appropriate mate, in this case a "beautiful freeborn girl" (*puellam pulchram ingenuamque*).[33] As with the saintly Leobardus, Gregory did not dwell upon Patroclus's marital dilemma. Soundly determined to pursue a clerical career, Patroclus simply rebuffed his mother. His situation differed from Aredius's in that the latter's widowed mother Pelagia apparently exerted no pressure for her son to marry. Instead she wholeheartedly embraced Aredius's ascetic lifestyle, and joined him. Indeed, Pelagia's ardent support for her son's clerical career and her pious behavior compare closely to that of another mother and son, the doting Armentaria and Gregory of Tours. Never mind that one

30. Greg. Tur., *VP.* 9.1 (*MGH*, SRM 1.2, 252): "... non quidem nobilitate sublimi, ingenui tamen."
31. Greg. Tur., *VP.* 9.1.
32. For vignettes of late ancient parents and children, several involving adults arranging youngsters' education, see Mathisen, *People, Personal Expression, and Social Relations*, 1: 77–91.
33. Greg. Tur., *VP.* 9.1 (*MGH*, SRM 1.2, 253).

pair was aristocratic and the other *ingenui*. As with nobles so for wealthy freepersons, the church afforded many opportunities for illustrious and socially advantageous career moves. Fortunately, here is one strategy for social enhancement for which Gallic sources provide ample evidence.

As was mentioned in Chapter Three, some freemen even at the end of the sixth century still could acquire bishoprics.[34] Ecclesiastical aristocrats justified welcoming such parvenus to their ranks by rationalizing that holding the cathedra ennobled a person. But bishoprics in Gaul were of a limited number, and aristocrats horded most of them. Two other respectable clerical positions, however, to which male *ingenui* could aspire in great numbers were priest and abbot.[35] Throughout the sixth century, sacerdotal positions proliferated for the multiple churches that were being constructed in every Gallic urban space.[36] Priestly posts easily numbered in the many thousands.[37] Furthermore, many more priesthoods were appearing in the countryside.[38] For example, Caesarius of Arles contributed to the growth of sacerdotal positions by taking his urban ascetic brand of Christianity to the *pagus* by legislating establishment of parishes.[39] In cities where ecclesiastical institutions were well

34. On the modest social origins of late ancient bishops through the fifth century, most hailing from curial ranks, see Rapp, *Holy Bishops in Late Antiquity*, 173–78, 183–88.

35. For principal recruitment of late ancient clerics from men of "middling" status, see Brown, *Poverty and Leadership*, 48, who writes: "... the Christian Church stood squarely in the middle of Roman society. It occupied the extensive middle ground between the very rich and the very poor. 'Middling' persons formed its principal constituency."

36. On the sixth-century Gallic townscape with emphasis on an increase in ecclesiastical structures, see Nancy Gauthier, "Le paysage urbaine en Gaule au VIe siècle," in *Grégoire de Tours et l'espace gaulois*, ed. Nancy Gauthier and Henri Galinié (Tours: Association Grégoire 94, 1997), 49–63; and idem, "From the Ancient City to the Medieval Town: Continuity and Change in the Early Middle Ages," in *The World of Gregory of Tours*, ed. Kathleen Mitchell and Ian Wood (Leiden, Boston, and Cologne; Brill, 2002), 47–66.

37. Based on Gregory of Tours' mention of thirty-eight places within the Touraine having one or more churches – the city of Tours itself had at least thirteen – James, *The Franks*, 150, estimated that across Gaul there would have been "a minimum of 4000 places with churches around the year 600." Robert Godding, *Prêtres en Gaule mérovingienne* (Brussels: Société des Bollandistes, 2001), 465–527, offers a prosopography of 386 Merovingian priests.

38. See Claude Lorren and Patrick Périn, "Images de la Gaule rurale au VIe siècle," in *Grégoire de Tours et l'espace gaulois*, ed. Nancy Gauthier and Henri Galinié (Tours: Association Grégoire 94, 1997), 93–109; Patrick Périn, "Settlements and Cemeteries in Merovingian Gaul," in *The World of Gregory of Tours*, ed. Kathleen Mitchell and Ian Wood (Leiden, Boston, and Cologne: Brill, 2002), 85–89.

39. On the establishment of rural parishes about the diocese of Arles, see Klingshirn, *Caesarius of Arles: The Making of a Christian Community*, 63–65. Evidence from canons attests to a sixth-century increase

established, urban priests primarily originated from bishops' retinues and climbed a clerical *cursus honorum* to attain the position.[40] For the burgeoning rural churches and parishes, however, many married, secular *ingenui* directly entered the priesthood late in life. These country priests commonly kept their wives, contrary to the bishops' repeated canonical censures.[41] Other free people desirous of Christian leadership roles became founders of ascetic communities, both urban and rural. For an *ingenuus* seeking entrée to the clergy, becoming an ascetic and gathering several monks around himself would have been an easier process than acquiring a bishopric, and many would have found it a distinctive, fulfilling, and influential lifestyle choice, too. Of course, the model Gallic ascetic was Saint Martin, who famously founded the monastery of Marmoutiers across the Loire River from Tours. Those who read about Martin in the pages of Sulpicius Severus would have learned of the latter's emulation of his spiritual master. By 400, the provincial aristocrat had converted an estate into an ascetic retreat. Subsequent emulators of these paradigmatic figures varied their ascetic program between the outlandish thaumaturgy of Martin and the more cerebrally oriented pursuits of Sulpicius's circle.[42] One early Gallic attempt to establish a remote ascetic retreat was that of two brothers who settled in the Jura Mountains in the mid-fifth century, Romanus and Lupicinus. Neither an anonymous *Vita* produced around 520, nor Gregory of Tours' subsequent writings about the two, allude specifically to the brothers'

in parishes beyond Arles; however, by 600, "a regular subdivision of dioceses into parishes still did not exist" for Gaul; Georg Scheibelreiter, "Church Structure and Organisation," in *The New Cambridge Medieval History*, volume I, *c. 500–c. 700*, ed. Paul Fouracre (Cambridge: Cambridge University Press, 2005) 686–87. Archaeological analysis for the origins of parishes is still in its infancy; see Périn, "Settlements and Cemeteries in Merovingian Gaul," 85–86.

40. On city priests, see Godding, *Prêtres en Gaule mérovingienne*, 212–39.

41. See ibid., 240–60. On the celibate urban priest and rural married priest, see ibid., 111–54, especially at 135.

42. Van Dam, *Leadership and Community*, 135, comments that Sulpicius's monastery "resembled most of all an aristocratic spa, in which 'learned men' spent their time in discussions similar to those they had once enjoyed on their estates." Another Aquitanian provincial aristocrat, and a contemporary of Sulpicius's, was Paulinus of Nola, whose grand ascetic retreat in southern Italy was made known to the Gauls through circulation of his popular literary works; see Dennis E. Trout, *Paulinus of Nola: Life, Letters, and Poems* (Berkeley, Los Angeles and London: University of California Press, 1999), 200–02. Gregory was familiar with Paulinus of Nola's writings, but he attributed Paulinus of Périgueux's work to the other Paulinus; e.g., Greg. Tur., *Hist.* 2.13.

social rank. But the earlier account records that the pair hailed from a "not insignificant family" (*non adeo exiguae familae*).[43] That comment coupled with a mention that Romanus abandoned a *villa* suggests that the family were prominent albeit non-aristocratic landowners.[44] Both brothers founded a monastery, each apparently built of wood. Romanus resided at Condadisco, while Lupicinus controlled Lauconnus.[45] The pair also established an abbey for women at Balma, where they installed their sister (traditionally named Yole) as abbess.[46] Despite the supposed remoteness of their location and theoretical isolation of their vocation, the family's ascetic venture brought followers, repute and social distinction to the Jura siblings. By the time of Romanus's death, 150 monks were dwelling at Lauconnus alone.[47]

With hundreds of people now looking upon Lupicinus as a patron, he was able to exercise his newfound authority by demanding justice in the Burgundian kingdom. For example, when a courtier of King Chilperic's (not the Frankish one) reduced some freemen to slavery, Lupicinus marched to Geneva and petitioned the ruler for their release. An opponent accused the abbot of treason, but Lupicinus fended off the charge. Not only did the king rule in the cleric's favor, but he also freed the captives and loaded Lupicinus with gifts for his monasteries.[48] The case of Lupicinus shows that in the early years of Barbarian Gaul, an abbot could amass not just ecclesiastical authority but also a degree of political dominion, even if he were merely *ingenuus* in origin.[49] In the next century, more freepersons would distinguish themselves by "fleeing the world." Sixth-century *ingenui* ascetics, like their aristocratic brethren, participated in a variety of ostentatious pious activities to advertise and

---

43. *Vita Iurensium patrum* 4 (*SC* 142, 242).
44. *Vita Iurensium patrum* 5 (*SC* 142, 244).
45. *Vita Iurensium patrum* 6, 24.
46. *Vita Iurensium patrum* 25, 60.
47. *Vita Iurensium patrum* 24.
48. *Vita Iurensium patrum* 92–95.
49. The example of Lupicinus's saving freepersons from the brink of servitude typifies what Brown, *Poverty and Leadership*, 61–63, reveals to have been one of the essential functions of the late ancient Christian leader, although here an abbot now appropriates what had been the traditional function of a bishop. The bishops of the fourth and fifth centuries who were protecting "middling" people from destitution were primarily of "middling" rank themselves.

augment spiritual and social authority, including building churches, founding monasteries, acting the visionary, presiding over rituals, promoting saints' cults, and practicing thaumaturgy.[50]

As mentioned earlier, one *ingenuus* who possessed the resources to build churches and found monasteries was Abbot Aredius of Limoges. About his friend, Gregory wrote: "He built churches in honor of God's saints and procured their relics. He tonsured men from his own household as monks and established a monastery [Saint Yrieix] ... The blessed woman [Pelagia] supplied them with food and clothes."[51] This passage reveals how a well-to-do *ingenuus* turned ascetic could find a ready supply of monks, and perhaps lesser clerics also, in the person of his many servants. Among the edifices Aredius erected in the Limousin was an oratory near his monastery in which he placed relics of Saint Martin.[52] Several miles distant from this he constructed a church of Saint Julian filled with that martyr's relics, and also built a shrine intended to house a single canister in which Julian had caused water to be transformed into balsam.[53] Aredius acquired relics such as jars of holy water and oil during frequent pilgrimages to sites such as Tours.[54] The fact that Aredius was able to persist in building projects indicates that he must have maintained a large measure of his wealth, despite having renounced the world. This behavior would have been consistent with the example of the pioneering elite ascetic-*cum*-church builder, Paulinus of Nola, an early fifth-century Gaul who established a retreat in southern Italy, where he lavishly decorated church buildings. Paulinus's eloquent poems and letters, some of which provided descriptions of the splendor and minutia

---

50. Given that persons of "middling" status traditionally participated in Christian leadership roles, having begun to do so in Gaul in the second century, and despite the dominance of aristocrats as bishops in Gaul from the fifth century, I see no reason to join Paul Hayward, "Demystifying the Role of Sanctity," 127, in harboring "considerable doubt" about "the population as a whole" embracing beliefs in saints and miracles.

51. Greg. Tur., *Hist.* 10.29 (*MGH*, SRM 1.1, 523): "Construxit templa Dei in honore sanctorum, expediitque eorum pignera ac ex familia propria tonsorata instituit monachos cenobiumque fundavit ... beata mulier victum atque vestitum singulis ministrante."

52. Greg. Tur., *GC* 9.

53. Greg. Tur., *VJ* 41.

54. Even before Gregory became bishop of Tours, Aredius had become a regular visitor to the church of Saint Martin; Greg. Tur., *GC* 9, *VM* 2.39, 3.24, 4.6, *Hist.* 10.29.

of his decorations, were popular among socially prominent Gauls.[55] The celebrated ascetic did not emphasize material renunciation so much as "the importance of intellectual and spiritual detachment from wealth."[56] What mattered most was how the well-to-do ascetic should use his wealth. For Paulinus, and probably for Aredius, too, building and decorating "beautiful ecclesiastical buildings could stand as a model for interior transformation."[57] Such efforts also would outwardly verify one's spiritual virtue and social significance.[58]

Another freeborn person turned ascetic and church builder was a Lombard named Vulfolaic.[59] After learning of Martin's example and then teaching himself to read, Vulfolaic became a monk at Aredius's monastery. In the manner of his mentor, Vulfolaic ventured to Tours to procure a relic of holy oil from Martin's church. Later he relocated, and built a large church outside the town of Carignan near Trier, where he gathered monks around him. Famously, Vulfolaic subsequently attempted to discourage some locals from revering a statue of Diana by mounting a nearby column and becoming a stylite. His feat of endurance convinced the peasants to help him rid of the large statue of the goddess, but Vulfolaic did not leave his column.[60] Certain bishops then arrived to dissuade him from continuing in this manner, arguing: "This path you are following is not proper. It is not possible to compare your ignoble self with Symeon of Antioch who sat on the column. ... Come

55. Lucy Grig, "Throwing Parties for the Poor: Poverty and Splendour in the Late Antique Church," in *Poverty in the Roman World*, ed. Margaret Atkins and Robin Osborne (Cambridge: Cambridge University Press, 2006), 150–51.

56. Ibid., 154, where Grig shows Augustine holding a like viewpoint.

57. Ibid., 160; and see further, Trout, *Paulinus of Nola*, 145–59.

58. One rural church-builder who is not depicted practicing asceticism was a priest named Nanninus. At the Auvergnian village of Vibriacensis, he built an oratory dedicated to Saint Julian. He acquired relics from the nearby church of Saint Ferreolus, apparently at the behest of Bishop Avitus of Clermont; Greg. Tur., *VJ* 48, 49. Gregory did not mention that Nanninus was of noble birth, and I suspect that he would have been an *ingenuus*.

59. Greg. Tur., *Hist.* 8.15.

60. Trier is on the periphery of the very Christianized Barbarian Gaul for which this study takes account, and so while these peasants might have been pagans, it is perhaps more likely that they were not. See note 62. At the least, the place with Diana's statue was not an active pagan site. Yitzhak Hen, *Culture and Religion in Merovingian Gaul*, 174, insightfully points out how the temple was long neglected when Vulfolaic arrived there. The anecdote makes no mention of priests and sacrifices; furthermore, the fact that Vulfolaic was able to sit on one of the temple's columns, which perhaps had been a support for the roof or a large statue, suggests that the site already was a ruin.

down and instead live with the brothers whom you assembled about yourself.”[61] Although Vulfolaic readily obeyed his superiors' demands, a bishop subsequently duped the ascetic into visiting a distant manor and sent men to destroy the column so that he could not repeat his behavior.[62] The case of Vulfolaic has become a *cause célèbre* primarily because Gregory included it in the *Historiae*, not in his *Miracula*. While the tale reveals how powerful Gallic ecclesiastics would not tolerate blatantly unconventional and potentially influential challenges to their authority, it should not be interpreted as evidence for a struggle between clerics of separate social rank. There was no Gallic noble conspiracy to prevent freepersons from distinguishing themselves through pious behavior. Established ecclesiastics were willing to permit clerical upstarts to help “Christianize” the *pagus*, so long as the latter acted in a proper, disciplined manner (best practiced in a communal environment), and more importantly so long as they remembered their obligation to defer to superiors within the clerical hierarchy.[63] Along those lines, Gregory twice toward the conclusion of this anecdote placed into the mouth of Vulfolaic words to the effect that it was sinful not to obey one's bishop. Presumably it was the Bishop of Trier who had subtly reminded Vulfolaic

---

61. Greg. Tur., *Hist.* 8.15 (*MGH*, SRM 1.1, 382–83): “Non est aequa haec via, quam sequeris, nec tu ignobilis Symeoni Antiochino, qui columnae insedit, poteris conparare. ...Discende potius et cum fratribus, quos adgregasti tecum, inhabita.”

62. *Pace* Hen, his initially insightful analysis of the stylite at the temple devolves into an unlikely scenario when he imagines that Vulfolaic was “a disturbed person” who having settled at the abandoned temple, battled “imaginary pagans,” and shouted at passersby to abandon their pagan ways. Hen suggests that the locals wanted to rid of the menace, and so they called in the bishop, who carried him away. The locals are attributed with destroying the column, lest Vulfolaic should return; Hen, *Culture and Religion in Merovingian Gaul*, 174. Here it seems Hen is trying to defend his thesis that Gaul is almost fully Christianized, and he is right to make that claim. But rather than paint Vulfolaic as a lunatic and reduce the rustics into figments of the recluse's imagination, I think it more plausible to simply accept most of Vulfolaic and Gregory's story at face value. A sane Vulfolaic found a community of peasants, perhaps pagan but likely Christian, unwilling to abandon its reverence for a traditional sacred space, and likely fearful of what would become of them if they did. So the abbot Vulfolaic became a stylite, and he so impressed the locals that they joined him, their new patron, in completing the destruction of the temple's pagan imagery. Therefore these Christian client-peasants would have been rightly upset when the bishop insisted that Vulfolaic leave them and return to his monastery. As for Gregory, he certainly could distinguish between a sane ascetic and an insane one. An example of the latter was Winnoch, who reportedly took to heavy drinking, chased passersby with a knife, and had to be locked in a cell, where ultimately he died a raving lunatic; Greg. Tur., *Hist.* 8.34.

63. Greg. Tur., *Hist.* 8.15.

of his proper place in the clerical pecking order by assigning to him the office of deacon, not priest.

Two other *ingenui* ascetics distinguished for their construction efforts were Ursus and the aforementioned Patroclus, both of whom hailed from the region of Berry. Gregory described Ursus as an "inhabitant of the city of Cahors" (*Cadurcinae urbis incola*); hence, presumably he was a *cives*.[64] Gregory offered nothing in the way of highlighting Ursus's personality, for the latter was active in the early sixth century. Instead, the author concentrated on the freeman's building program. In the region of Berry, Ursus established three monasteries, each of which he placed under the direction of a prior. He then located to the Touraine, where he built an oratory and established a monastery placed under the direction of a saintly prior named Leobatius. Ursus built a fifth monastery called Loches along the Indre River, where he finally settled as abbot and gathered monks around him.[65] A final project involved Ursus's construction of a mill along the Indre, which a courtier of King Alaric II coveted but failed to acquire.[66] A figure more contemporaneous with Gregory whose construction efforts were not quite as robust as Ursus's was Patroclus. When last we saw this very educated freeman, he had abandoned Childebert's court and returned home to Berry. Ignoring his mother's plea that he wed, he entered the clergy and became a deacon at Bourges. But a desire to practice a rigorous asceticism caused Patroclus to abandon the clerics for a more rural locale.[67] At the village of Néris, he built an oratory where among his contributions to the locals he taught children how to read. But being desirous of even greater solitude, Patroclus relocated to the forested region of Mediocanthus, where, he built a cell.[68] As seems to have been the case for many upstart ascetics, Patroclus could not help but attract followers. He managed to maintain his hermit's lifestyle, however, by building five miles from his cell a monastery called Columbier, to which he ushered his monks

---

64. Greg. Tur., *VP* 18.1 (*MGH*, SRM 1.2, 284).
65. Greg. Tur., *VP* 18.1.
66. Greg. Tur., *VP* 18.2.
67. Greg. Tur., *VP* 9.1.
68. Greg. Tur., *VP* 9.2.

and an abbot.[69] The construction efforts of Ursus and Patroclus attest that *ingenui* shared a desire with aristocrats to Christianize the Gallic countryside, and they also betray how *ingenui* were able to amass and manage whatever resources were necessary to accomplish their pious goals. Furthermore, the examples of Patroclus and Vulfolaic testify to the internal tensions with which prominent recluses might have to wrestle. Patroclus struggled between a personal desire to live a life of solitude and a compulsion to use his financial resources to build an edifice that would bring more of the rural population to play an active role in the faith. Meanwhile, Vulfolaic wavered between an early commitment to a monastery he had established and a newer desire to practice a more distinctive brand of asceticism and provide patronage for a rural community that appreciated his presence.

As was so among aristocrats, *ingenui* need not be clerics to establish churches. One such person was Litomeris, who constructed a church of Saint Julian at Pernay, a village located west of Tours along the Loire.[70] Presumably Litomeris built this church on his own estate. His effort will have benefited from the support of the aristocratic Bishop of Tours, who presided over the edifice's dedication and provided the church with relics of Saints Julian and Nicetius of Lyons.[71] Another layperson intent upon establishing a sacred space was Eufronius, a wealthy Syrian merchant at Bordeaux. Unfortunately for Eufronius, his own bishop, Bertram, schemed to take his wealth. To this end, in one instance the bishop forcibly tonsured the freeman to make him a priest.[72] Eufronius countered the affront merely by leaving town and returning after his hair grew back. While he had no interest in holding priestly office, Eufronius did distinguish himself by piously converting his house into a shrine in which he placed relics of the Syrian martyr Sergius. But this exotic

---

69. Greg. Tur., *VP* 9.3.

70. Greg. Tur., *VJ* 50. Gregory identified Litomeris neither as noble nor a cleric, and so I take him to have been a freeman. I believe he is identical to the Litomeris, styled an *indigena* from Tours, whom Gregory depicted being healed of a fever at the tomb of Saint Sollemnis; *CG* 21 (*MGH*, SRM 1.2, p. 311). Sollemnis's church was located at Luynes, which is north northwest of Pernay. The home whence Litomeris departed upon becoming ill could have been his presumed estate at Pernay, another estate perhaps near Luynes, or a townhouse at Tours.

71. Greg. Tur., *VJ* 50, *VP* 8.8.

72. Greg. Tur., *Hist.* 7.31.

saint brought more unwanted attention; the pretender Gundovald imagined that Sergius's finger bone could make him invincible in battle, and so the magnate's allies, Bishop Bertram and Duke Mummolus, entered the edifice and demanded a fragment. Eufronius offered 200 gold pieces if they would leave, but to no avail. A tussle ensued and the pair left with a shard of the relic. Eufronius's sizeable offer of coinage indicates the financial wherewithal an *ingenuus* merchant could possess and put toward establishing a public pious venture. The offering also reveals the lengths to which a freeperson might go to protect his spiritual investment.[73]

Besides building churches, another conspicuous way that *ingenui* displayed spiritual authority was by proclaiming visions. Another freeperson who became an abbot was a citizen of Bourges named Venantius.[74] As a youth he reportedly was content to wed, until he chanced to visit a monastery at Tours, and immediately decided to become a monk. There is no mention that Venantius's parents objected to the son's sudden decision to eschew life's usual secular course. The abbot readily welcomed the *ingenuus* into the community. Having distinguished himself over the years by a sincere humility and charity, Venantius became his brothers' choice to succeed as abbot. Because the monastery he had entered was a long-established site situated near the basilica of Saint Martin, Venantius had no cause to engage in building projects.[75] Nevertheless, he was able to demand attention by taking on the role of a visionary. For example, one Sunday during mass he reportedly witnessed an aged cleric

73. A more frequent and less spectacular, but still ostentatious, way that late antique *ingenui*, like aristocrats, could use their riches to help their souls would have been to donate to churches decorations and vessels all inscribed with the donors' names and intended for public display; Brown, *Poverty and Leadership*, 55, 96; and Grig, "Throwing Parties for the Poor," 157. All the while they could maintain their wealth, and follow a viewpoint espoused by the likes of Augustine and Paulinus of Nola "that it was the *use* rather than possession of riches that was significant"; Grig, ibid., 154. By holding onto their wealth, free people also could remain regular almsgivers. Brown, *Poverty and Leadership*, 55, writes: "It was lay persons of the 'middling' class who made the regular, weekly offerings for the poor and the clergy. It was they who provided the silver vessels and the silken hangings for the altar. It was they who would cover the floor with mosaics, each contributing the relatively small sums needed for so many square feet of mosaic work, proudly marking the patches with their names and even, on occasions, with their portraits …"

74. Greg. Tur., *VP* 16.1. Venantius was active during the fifth century; James, *Gregory of Tours, Life of the Fathers*, 103, n. 3.

75. On this monastery, see Pietri, *La ville de Tours*, 407–09.

(Saint Martin) near the top of the apse making the sign of the cross over the host. Venantius alone espied this sight and declared his vision before his monks. Gregory interpreted Venantius's ability to witness the sign as proof that he was the Lord's "faithful servant, to whom it was worthy to reveal the secrets of heavenly mysteries."[76] This description attests how an abbot could expect subordinates to accept a vision as proof that the prelate possessed sufficient authority to deserve to understand celestial secrets.[77] On a second occasion, Venantius claimed to hear angels celebrating mass in heaven, so he ordered the monks immediately to do likewise, and on a third, the abbot professed to hearing Saint Martin singing the Lord's Prayer from his tomb. In like fashion, Venantius claimed he once communicated with a deceased priest named Passivus at his tomb and learned thereby that the dead man's soul was in heaven.[78] Venantius's visions brought him great repute. Humble people visited his monastery in search of healing and liberation from demons, and Venantius in turn marked them with the sign of the cross. Like most of his visions, whatever cures the holy man brought about would have benefited the reputation of Saint Martin. The actual ministrations of the living Venantius thus provided a tangibility that, when combined with the repute of the invisible saint (Martin), would have helped encourage pilgrims to continue to come to Tours.

While some freepersons declared visions, other *ingenui* ascetics distributed largesse to establish spiritual authority. Senoch was a free inhabitant of Poitou whom Gregory identified as a Taifal (*genere Theifalus*).[79] Senoch located to the Touraine, where he became a cleric and adopted the life of a recluse. He constructed a cell by refurbishing a ruin of old walls, and he allowed other pious persons to gather around him. It is unclear whether Senoch's simple renovation resulted because he lacked resources to build a new edifice or because the cell lay near

---

76. Greg. Tur., *VP* 16.2 (*MGH*, SRM 1.2, p. 275): "… fideli famulo … cui etiam dignatus est arcanorum secreta caelestium revelare."

77. Moreira, *Dreams, Visions and Spiritual Authority in Merovingian Gaul*, 15–16.

78. Greg. Tur., *VP* 16.2.

79. Greg. Tur., *VP* 15.1 (*MGH*, SRM 1.2, 271). The residents of Theifalia presumably imagined themselves the descendents of the nomadic Taifali, who settled in Poitou in the third or fourth century; James, *Gregory of Tours, Life of the Fathers*, p. 95, n. 1.

a ruined oratory, also refurbished, where, according to Senoch, Saint Martin once had prayed. Bishop Eufronius presided over installation of Martin's relics in the oratory, and at the same ceremony he elevated Senoch to deacon, thus assuring that the entire enterprise would operate under episcopal sanction.[80] Like other ascetics, Senoch offered the sign of the cross to heal locals' disabilities. Also like others, Senoch received from pious almsgivers and grateful healed persons much wealth, which he in turn redistributed to the poor. Standing out among the recipients of Senoch's largesse were more than 200 slaves and debtors whom the recluse liberated from masters and prisons.[81] Thus Senoch became a patron to hundreds of rural people of low rank. In that capacity, he further aided rural clients by building bridges at locations along rivers that were prone to flooding.[82] Upon the recluse's death, a multitude of grateful clients, including those he had ransomed, attended the funeral and wondered how they would get by without their *pater sanctus*.[83] Notably, in Senoch's latter years, his presiding bishop, Gregory, did not seem the least bit bothered by the ascetic's popularity. Indeed, on one occasion when Senoch apparently considered abandoning his regimen, Gregory rebuked him for behaving vainly and caused him to renew his vocation.[84] Afterward, Gregory had to temper Senoch's restored zeal by cautioning him against closing himself off within his cell for too long a period. Gregory did not feel threatened by the *ingenuus* abbot's sizeable pool of humble clients. Nor did the bishop ever act heavy handedly toward Senoch the way that Vulfolaic's superiors had behaved, for Gregory saw in the recluse a worthy accomplice who aided in the promotion of Martin's cult. Indeed, for his troubles, Gregory ordained Senoch as a priest.[85] Thus, like the visionary Venantius, the client-amassing thaumaturge Senoch was able to prosper as a locally distinguished cleric, all ultimately to the benefit of the clergy at Tours, with whom together they proclaimed the *virtutes* of Saint Martin.

80. Greg. Tur., *VP* 15.1.
81. Greg. Tur., *VP* 15.1.
82. Greg. Tur., *VP* 15.3.
83. Greg. Tur., *VP* 15.4 (*MGH*, SRM 1.2, 274).
84. Greg. Tur., *VP* 15.2.
85. Greg. Tur., *VP* 15.3, *Hist.* 5.7.

According to Gregory, all of the aforementioned ascetics performed miracles of healing. Of course, crediting saints with healing abilities is the most common hagiographical trope. But as has been mentioned, many such accounts in Gallic sources do more than constitute mere literary devices; they also attest to actual behavior. *Ingenui* ascetics were no less determined than many aristocratic bishops to augment spiritual authority by attempting to heal the afflicted. Through thaumaturgic efforts they also aspired to enable people to cope in a world too intimate with disease and death.[86] One ascetic who tried to overcome a terrible loss by aiding others was Monegund of Chartres. Because Gregory did not attribute nobility to Monegund, referring to her only as "indigenous to the city of Chartres" (*Carnotenae urbis indigena*), she presumably was an *ingenua*.[87] Monegund's early life typified that of free Gallic women in that she married "according to the will of her parents" (*parentum ad votum*) and bore children, two daughters.[88] After the girls' untimely demise, the mother became inconsolable until finally she abandoned her mourning clothes for a habit and confined herself to a single-windowed cell on her family's property. Gregory wrote, "There, despising the vanities of the world and having nothing more to do with her husband, she devoted herself entirely to God, in whom she confided, praying for her sins and for the sins of the people."[89] Besides prayer, Monegund's regimen included fasting and baking bread for the poor. Her reputation increased after being credited with healing a blind woman and a deaf man.[90] Monegund's husband did not attempt to frustrate his wife in her new vocation. Perhaps he anticipated benefiting socially from having a prestigious ascetic in the family, as King Chlothar perhaps had intended to do with his former wife Radegund. Not only could a live-in saint on the estate enhance a family's prestige, but as a gatherer of alms she also

---

86. On difficulties maintaining early medieval populations, including declining temperatures and periodic epidemics up to ca. 700, and on the common recourse of seeking Christian healers, see Smith, *Europe after Rome*, 51–80.
87. Greg. Tur., *VP* 19.1 (*MGH*, SRM 1.2, 286).
88. Greg. Tur., *VP* 19.1 (*MGH*, SRM 1.2, 286).
89. Greg. Tur., *VP* 19.1 (*MGH*, SRM 1.2, 286): "… ibique contemptu mundi ambitu, spreto viri consortio, soli Deo, in quo erat confisa, vacabat, fundens orationem pro suis populisque." Trans. by James, *Gregory of Tours, Life of the Fathers*, 119.
90. Greg. Tur., *VP* 19.1.

might prove a source of wealth.[91] At some point, however, a conflict of interest arose between Monegund and her relations. If the breach did not involve finances, it at least pertained to a matter of pride. For while the relatives, presumably the husband included, were enjoying their new status, the sincere religious was becoming disenchanted. Gregory explained, "lest she incur a lapse through vainglory, Monegund left her husband, family, and everyone from her house, and desired to go faithfully to the church of the blessed bishop Saint Martin [at Tours]."[92] Like Abbot Venantius, Monegund took up residence in a cell at Martin's basilica, where she renewed her prayers, fasting, and healing efforts. Hearing of his wife's restored reputation, the husband brought friends to Tours and carted Monegund back to Chartres. There she prayed to Saint Martin for strength, slipped out of her cell, and returned to Tours. Afterward her spouse apparently troubled her no more.[93] Gregory provided no details as to why the husband desisted in trying to retrieve his wife. Perhaps he realized the futility in fighting on two fronts – Monegund's obvious conviction and the determination of the clergy at Tours who shared the ascetic's affection for Martin. Perhaps after the first abduction the clerics at Tours doubled their guard at the church to assure that Monegund could not be seized again. Martin's basilica certainly had the resources to protect one of its own from molestation.[94] The church also facilitated the thaumaturge in conducting her spirituality at a more prominent level. Upon her return, Monegund founded a small convent and handpicked her nuns.[95] In return for receiving a secure location to practice her craft, she used her healing proficiency to bring prestige to the basilica. When ill people came to the living Monegund, she, like Abbot Venantius before her, credited any healing to the *virtus* of the deceased saintly patron Martin. Monegund and her nuns also produced mats of interwoven twigs that the church distributed, perhaps as tokens

91. See Greg. Tur., *GM* 105, for a cloistered woman who amassed a sizeable fortune by performing pious actions and then hoarding the money that she was expected to use to redeem captives.
92. Greg. Tur., *VP* 19.2 (*MGH*, SRM 1.2, 287): "... ne vanae gloriae lapsum incurreret, sancti Martini antestis basilicam, relicto coniuge cum familia vel omni domo sua, fideliter expetivit."
93. Greg. Tur., *VP* 19.2.
94. On guardians of Gallic churches, see the discussion in Chapter Six.
95. On Monegund's convent, see Pietri, *La ville de Tours*, 411–13.

with which pilgrims could further promote the ascetic's reputation, or perhaps to serve as physical reminders for the faithful to return to the basilica for their healing needs.[96]

Unlike Monegund, another influential female ascetic at Tours who apparently had every intention of advancing her family's fortunes through church affiliation was Ingitrude. I locate the case of Ingitrude and her kin here among a discussion of *ingenui* because her clan's social status rather defies estimation. Ingitrude was a relation of the sisters Ingund and Aregund, two slaves who were consecutive wives of King Chlothar I.[97] Perhaps Ingitrude, like the sisters, originated from servile rank, but this is not entirely certain. It probably was by virtue of her ties with a court that Ingitrude was able to marry a man of means. Here again it is unclear whether the spouse was a landed aristocrat, a well-to-do *ingenuus*, or a courtier who had made a fortune through royal service. At any rate, Ingitrude and husband had three children: two sons, one named Bertram and the other anonymous, and a daughter called Berthegund. At an unknown date presumably after the demise of her spouse, Ingitrude made a decisive career choice by founding an abbey in the forecourt of Saint Martin's basilica at Tours.[98] Ingitrude apparently intended to affect her nuclear family's rise to social prominence through high-profile church participation. First, her son Bertram became Bishop of Bordeaux around 573, thereby interrupting the Leontian dynasty. While King Guntram likely instigated Bertram's elevation, it cannot be known what role, if any, Ingitrude played in campaigning for her son. But the mother certainly interfered in her daughter's life. Although Berthegund was married with children, Ingitrude twice convinced her to leave her spouse and estates to become abbess at the nunnery at Tours. Bishop Gregory was deeply appalled by the mother's suggestion that Berthegund, a wife of more than twenty years, leave her husband without his say. On each occasion, Berthegund initially obeyed her mother but stayed at the convent only briefly. In the first instance,

---

96. Greg. Tur., *VP* 19.2.
97. Greg. Tur., *Hist.* 4.3. According to Gregory, it was at Ingund's instigation that Chlothar set about seeking out a suitable mate for Aregund. In the end he found one, himself.
98. Greg. Tur., *Hist.* 9.33.

she left after Gregory threatened excommunication for abandoning her spouse, and in the second, she departed Tours to join her brother at Bordeaux. Berthegund's husband several times petitioned Bertram to hand over his wife, but the bishop refused, arguing that his sister's marriage was not legitimate because it never had parental approval. When the spouse acquired from Guntram a royal decree that she return home, Berthegund responded by fleeing for sanctuary at Saint Martin's basilica.[99] After Bertram died in 585/86, Ingitrude appealed a third time for Berthegund to become her abbess, but amicability between mother and daughter soon deteriorated when the two began to quarrel over the family's wealth.[100] Neither episcopal mediation on Gregory's part, nor royal decree by Childebert II, could end the bitter feud. Ingitrude disinherited her daughter and secured another relation (perhaps a granddaughter through her anonymous son) as abbess. But when Ingitrude died in 590, Berthegund successfully petitioned Childebert for all possessions including those that her mother had bequeathed to the convent at Tours, which really irked Gregory. Berthegund retired to estates near Poitiers and apparently eschewed the religious lifestyle for good. The example of Ingitrude compares with that of Radegund in revealing how being cloistered need not prevent a prominent female ascetic from controlling sizeable finances and concurrently wielding the clout that came with that ability. Furthermore, Ingitrude's persistent behavior toward Berthegund again indicates the real pressures a parent could bring to bear on a daughter to submit to parental will. The indecisive Berthegund seems to have been genuinely torn by the contrary harangues of Gregory and her mother. Despite the bishop's threatening removal from the church for leaving a husband without his consent, Ingitrude had managed to convince her daughter, temporarily at least, that "a married person will never see the Kingdom of God."[101]

---

99. Bertram fell from Guntram's favor in 585 after supporting the pretender Gundovald; Greg. Tur., *Hist.* 8.2.

100. Greg. Tur., *Hist.* 9.33.

101. Greg. Tur., *Hist.* 9.33 (*MGH*, SRM 1.1, 452): "Non enim videbit regnum Dei coniugio copulatus." Similarly, in his telling of the legend of the "two lovers" of Clermont, Gregory had the reluctant bride declare: "Infelix ego, quae debui sorte mereri polos, hodie demergor in abyssos"; Greg. Tur., *Hist.* 1.47 (*MGH*, SRM 1.1, 30). In this instance, however, the woman's fear of damnation apparently

The church of Saint Martin figured prominently in the efforts of Monegund and Berthegund to abandon their spouses. Other women who desired to disassociate themselves from a husband might more often do so by acquiring lower profile positions among the expanding throng of female ascetics.[102] For example, a woman named Gunthetrude used the occasion of sudden blindness to leave her home in Saint-Quentin by seeking a cure at Martin's basilica at Tours.[103] After remaining there many days, she was able to see with one eye. This miracle afforded her the excuse that she now was indebted to the saint as a patron. Gunthetrude foreswore a husband and children, donned a habit, and remained at the church. Stories such as those of Gunthetrude and Berthegund rarely offer details of the family situation that such women hoped to elude. While some undoubtedly intended to escape emotional and/or physical abuse, others sought out a church environment to overcome psychological trauma associated with the departure of loved ones, as happened with Monegund. The examples of Monegund, Ingitrude, and Gunthetrude indicate that the social pressures brought to bear upon women of *ingenuus* rank hardly differed from those of aristocrats. Like the latter, freewomen who became ascetics usually did so only after fulfilling their social obligation to birth legitimate heirs for spouses. Those few who managed to survive years of procreation and then find a niche where they could practice asceticism must have been truly resourceful indeed.

If, as the literary evidence suggests, *ingenui* men and women were able to perform ostentatious pious activities such as building churches as aristocrats did, one may wonder whether freepersons would have ranked among the "elites" to whom scholars generally attribute elaborate burial practices such as securing the dead in stone sarcophagi and erecting epitaphs.[104] I suspect that wealthy *ingenui* shared with aristocrats a compulsion to make shows of status at weddings and funerals in order to

---

arose not from a belief that marriage led to perdition, but from a concern that by marrying she was reneging on an earlier vow to become a nun.

102. On women using the cult of saints to leave husbands, see Van Dam, *Saints and their Miracles*, 101–02.

103. Greg. Tur., *VM* 2.9.

104. E. g., Handley, *Death, Society and Culture*, 41; Périn, "Settlements and Cemeteries in Merovingian Gaul," 74–75, 86–87.

declare family prestige and confer it on the next generation. The best evidence for finding freepersons engaging in competitive display comes from inscriptions. The vast majority of Gallic epitaphs bearing the status or occupation of the deceased pertain to persons from the highest echelons of secular and ecclesiastical aristocracy; however, several epitaphs do mention people with jobs uncharacteristic of aristocrats.[105] For the years 300 to 750, examples include three merchants, three physicians, a midwife, six soldiers, two veterans, and two teachers.[106] These epitaphs strongly suggest that members of "middling" families did commission funerary inscriptions. Furthermore, most epitaphs make no mention of status or occupation. About these, Mark Handley surmises: "[T]here is room for thinking that this group of commemorands were of a social standing broadly similar to, but perhaps slightly lower than, those with a recorded status or occupation."[107] I would interpret this to mean that freepersons participated in the "epigraphic habit." Couple this with the fact that it was exorbitantly expensive to raise an epitaph, and most Gauls simply could not have afforded to do so.[108] This would indicate that raising epitaphs was an activity likely common to the upper echelons of Gaul's free population. In contrast to aristocrats and well-to-do *ingenui* making competitive displays with funerary inscriptions, poorer persons and slaves generally had no epitaphs to mark their dirt burials.[109] More problematic is any attempt to assess the social condition of individuals who displayed grave goods during funerals, a practice common to inhabitants of northern Gaul during the Barbarian era. First, buried items are no mirror for a person's life; the presence of a sword in a grave does not mean that the deceased was a warrior, nor does jewelry necessarily identify a woman.[110] Second, quantity, quality, and even absence of burial goods do not necessarily correspond to social standing,

---

105. Handley, *Death, Society and Culture*, 41.
106. Ibid., 40. For the period 450–600, these include one each of merchant, soldier, veteran, and teacher; ibid., 54. Compare further Handley's tables for epitaphs indicating status and occupation for Carthage, Salona, and regions of Gaul and Spain; ibid., 37–38, 43, 47, 51, 53, 55, 57–60.
107. Ibid., 64.
108. Ibid., 39.
109. Effros, *Caring for Body and Soul*, 89. Two Gallic slave boys received commemorations on epitaphs from masters, not relatives; Handley, *Death, Society and Culture*, 40–41.
110. Effros, *Merovingian Mortuary Archaeology*, 147–48, 161.

or a lack thereof.[111] Still, the presence of certain expensive grave goods and elaborate burials obviously would have been beyond the economic means of most. Furthermore, an increasingly elaborate gradation of burial accommodations existed from the plain earthen grave in which most were interred, to wooden coffin, to stone, to stone above ground.[112] If only the most affluent Gauls could have afforded burials in stone sarcophagi, there were less expensive alternatives, likely achievable for wealthy *ingenui*, such as a variety of plaster sarcophagi which were mass-produced in the Seine and Marne for a time.[113] In all likelihood, the wide array of free families probably did what they could to express honor and prestige through burial customs.[114] For those freepersons with the means of an Aredius and Pelagia, that likely meant burial inside a fine sarcophagus located in a cemetery associated with a saint. For others, it amounted to burying the dead with a single bronze coin or a distinctive, colorful snail shell, and for many more, not even that.[115]

PAUPERES

While the upper range of *ingenui* schemed to amass either estates and servants or spiritual authority, other free people scarcely subsisted. Gallic authors denoted the lowest among the free as *pauperes*, "the poor." We shall concentrate on particular elements from the poor as per their relations with secular and church authorities in greater detail in the next two chapters. For now, let us consider in general terms the variation within this social sub-group and the pitfalls and possibilities they faced in trying to improve their social lot. Late ancient ecclesiastical writers often used a broad brush when applying poverty to their representations of society, especially those contained in theological tracts and sermons. For example, Augustine in the *Enarrationes* labeled smallholders among *pauperes*, a category whose

---

111. Ibid., 124.
112. Ibid., 182–87.
113. Ibid., 187; Périn, "Settlements and Cemeteries in Merovingian Gaul," 76–77.
114. Effros, *Merovingian Mortuary Archaeology*, 116, writes that Gallic burial practices cannot be characterized in terms of popular versus elite.
115. Ibid., 145–46, 167.

members he usually mentioned in vague terms.[116] Similarly, Salvian of Marseilles and Caesarius of Arles, in their aforementioned complaints about local Gallic elites wresting lands from social inferiors, rhetorically identified as *pauperes* some who actually would have been *curiales*.[117] Otherwise, ecclesiastics sometimes emphasized the poverty of destitute persons, especially in saints' lives.[118] Aristocratic authors identified some poor people with a vocabulary that indicated explicitly economic hardship and poverty (e.g., *aegens*, *aegenus*, *indigens*, *inops*, *mendicus*, and, most commonly, *pauper*). Otherwise, they offered words to denote the pauper's pitiable condition (e.g., *miser* and *miserabilis*), although the latter terms might be used to describe ill and disabled people of any economic background. Like other Gallic authors, Gregory of Tours could be flexible about whom he labeled *pauper*. But analysis of his usage of the term reveals that he perceived of a group with relatively well-defined parameters. While he ranked *pauperes* below the *minores*, a term synonymous with the somewhat affluent *ingenui*, he consistently distinguished them from unfree *servi* and *mancipia*.[119] Three distinct sub-groups among Gregory's *pauperes* were rural middle to small land-owners and peasants, urban workers, and beggars. In modern scholarly parlance, the able-bodied among Gregory's rural and urban paupers, subject as they were to falling into destitution and perhaps rebounding

---

116. Richard Finn, "Portraying the Poor: Descriptions of Poverty in Christian Texts from the Late Roman Empire," in *Poverty in the Roman World*, ed. Margaret Atkins and Robin Osborne (Cambridge: Cambridge University Press, 2006), 135–36. Finn, ibid., 136, explains that portrayals of the "poor" in Augustine's sermons needed to be vague, because to offer graphic depictions of the destitute would risk "triggering that conventional response of contempt" for the poorest and beggars, which would endanger the preacher's effort to cajole the wealthy to give alms.

117. Grey, "Salvian, the Ideal Christian Community," 172–73; Klingshirn, *Caesarius of Arles: The Making of a Christian Community*, 205–06.

118. Finn, "Portraying the Poor," 140; and see Brown, *Poverty and Leadership*, 46.

119. Johannes Schneider, "Die Darstellung der Pauperes in den *Historiae* Gregors von Tours: Ein Beitrag zur sozialökonomischen Struktur Galliens im 6. Jahrhundert," *Jahrbuch für Wirtschaftsgeschichte* (1966, teil 4), 66, 69, 73. Sara Hansell MacGonagle, *The Poor in Gregory of Tours: A Study of the Attitude of Merovingian Society toward the Poor, as Reflected in the Literature of the Time* (Ph.D. diss., New York: Columbia University, 1936), 100–102, broadly defined Gregory's "poor" as "all those who did not belong to the class of the rich." Specifically she identified *matricularii*, other beggars, small holders, slaves, prisoners, captives of war, and lepers. Here MacGonagle erred only in her estimation that Gregory included slaves as *pauperes*.

from it, are deemed the "conjunctural poor," while the author's beggars, having been "trapped by the structure of economic system," become the "structural poor."[120] Regarding the conjunctural poor of the country-side, Gregory's miracle stories often incidentally allude to peasants own-ing some property such as oxen, horses, gardens, and cottages.[121] Because they had property, royal officials could anticipate exacting payments from rustic *pauperes*. In 578, King Chilperic insisted that "the poor" of the Touraine pay ban money after they failed to join his army on an expedi-tion against the Bretons.[122] This and other evidence from Gregory attests that peasants were susceptible to recruitment as rank and file soldiers for impromptu Merovingian campaigns.[123] Indeed, for the Frankish king-doms, as for other barbarian realms, farmer-soldiers amounted to "the pre-ponderant element in Rome's successor states' armies." [124] The resources possessed by the rural poor varied markedly.[125] Gregory mentioned one *pauper* from Reims who was affluent enough to be able to donate a fertile field to a church.[126] By and large, however, the poor farmers Gregory described were recognizably economically disadvantaged, such as a *pauper* "whom necessity forced to cart wood from the forests" and

120. Robin Osborne, "Introduction: Roman Poverty in Context," in *Poverty in the Roman World*, ed. Margaret Atkins and Robin Osborne (Cambridge: Cambridge University Press, 2006), 1. For bibli-ography on the poor and peasants in Late Antiquity, see Schachner, "Social Life in Late Antiquity," 48–55, 52–55.

121. Oxen: Greg. Tur., *GM* 66, 103; *VM* 2.47; *GC* 30; horse: Greg. Tur., *VJ* 21; garden: Greg. Tur., *GM* 46; *VM* 2.40; cottage: Greg. Tur., *Hist.* 4.20; *GM* 10, 47, 60, 89, 103; *GC* 30. For property owning *pauperes*, see František Graus, *Volk, Herrscher und Heiliger im Reich der Merowinger: Studien zur Hagiographie der Merowingerzeit* (Prague: Nakladatelství Československé akademie věd, 1965), 137; Schneider, "Die Darstellung der Pauperes," 69.

122. Greg. Tur., *Hist.* 5.26. Schneider, "Die Darstellung der Pauperes," 70, also commented that plunder-ing soldiers recognized rural paupers' property as a source of profit.

123. See also Greg. Tur., *Hist.* 6.31, 7.42; Bernard S. Bachrach, "Grand Strategy in the Germanic Kingdoms: Recruitment of the Rank and File," in *L'armée romaine et les barbares du IIIe au VIIe siècle*, ed., Françoise Vallet et Michel Kazanski (Paris: Association Française d'Archéologie Mérovingienne et Musée des Antiquités Nationales, 1993), 62.

124. Ibid., 57.

125. Schneider, "Die Darstellung der Pauperes," 69. On various aspects of Gallic peasant society, see Wickham, *Framing the Early Middle Ages*: 393–406, for aristocrat-peasant relations in the middle Rhine and Seine-Oise; 473–81, for abandonment of Roman villas particularly in Gaul; 504–14, for northern Gallic villages; 535–70, for post-Roman peasant societies when "aristocracies were at their weakest, and peasantries at their most autonomous" (ibid.,519).

126. Greg. Tur., *GC* 78.

another who "possessed nothing except what he was able to work with his oxen by cutting the ground with a plow."[127] Many of the impoverished rustics depicted by Gregory were fortunate among the rural poor in that they were proximate or mobile enough to have access to the poor relief available at churches.[128] For inhabitants of sections of countryside where the establishment of churches and monasteries was slow to keep pace with a Gallic population making a noticeable rural shift, the bouts of "deep poverty" they experienced would have been the worst.[129] A second group among Gaul's conjunctural poor was city dwellers. Gregory differentiated between socially distinguished urban *cives* and *pauperes*. He imagined the latter to consist of people with a wide array of means, from modest to few.[130] For Gregory, an urban setting did not hide people from the eyes of revenue-seeking kings and royal retainers.[131] For example, when Princess Rigunth's bridal train was leaving for Spain in 584, King Chilperic ordered that agents stockpile goods taken "from the cities along the way" (*de civititatibus in itinere*), and Childebert II warned Chilperic against requisitioning anything "from his cities" (*de civitatibus*).[132] So what city residents paid for this venture? Gregory complained, "The king ordered that nothing be given from the fisc, but that all be gathered from the poor."[133] Urban laborers were an important element of the audience to whom Caesarius of Arles directed his sermons. Indeed, Caesarius sometimes cut his preaching short on behalf of the "poor who had to rush to work."[134] These gainfully employed Arlésien paupers might have included both urban and nearby rural workers. If the inhabitants of Arles, and also Marseilles, were able to enjoy the benefits of continued high levels of economic traffic, residents of most Gallic

---

127. Greg. Tur., *GC* 30 (*MGH*, SRM 1.2, 316): "… quem necessitas conpellebat lignum ex silvis evehere"; Greg. Tur., *GM* 103 (*MGH*, SRM 1.2, 108): "… nec ei erat alia possessio, nisi quod ab his potuisset tellurem scindens vomere laborare."
128. Brown, *Poverty and Leadership*, 51.
129. Ibid.
130. On Gallic cities, see Wickham, *Framing the Early Middle Ages*, 665–68, 674–81.
131. Schneider, "Die Darstellung der Pauperes," 70–71.
132. Greg. Tur., *Hist.* 6.45 (*MGH*, SRM 1.1, 317–18).
133. Greg. Tur., *Hist.* 6.45 (*MGH*, SRM 1.1, 318): "… nihil de fisco suo rex dari praecepit, nisi omnia de pauperum coniectures."
134. Caes. Arel., *Sermo* 91.8 (*CCL* 103, 378): "… pauperes, qui ad opera sua festinant."

towns could not share their euphoria.[135] They would have been feeling periodic pangs brought on by an intermittent but extended late ancient retraction from urban life. Thus, to call most urban people "poor" as litterateurs often did would not have been inappropriate.[136]

While some *pauperes* sustained themselves independently and paid taxes, others had nearly nothing of their own. Gregory identified beggars (*mendici* or *aegenes*) as a sub-group of *pauperes*. For example, he described a beggar (*aegens*) calling another his "fellow pauper" (*conpauper*), and elsewhere he labeled a man seeking alms as a *pauper*.[137] For some Gallic *mendici*, begging amounted to a profession, whereas for others it served as a momentary expedient during a period of economic duress. Thus, certain beggars endured "structural poverty," particularly the chronically infirm, while others amounted to the "conjunctural poor" enduring their worst moments. An example of the latter involves a girl named Palatina who was afflicted with paralysis so that her knees bent to her thighs. Her father brought her to the tomb of Saint Martin, where she begged for alms. The girl lay in the church three months until she fully recovered her health during the saint's July festival.[138] One of

135. Simon Loseby, "Marseille and the Pirenne Thesis, I," 203–29, uses archaeological evidence with Gregory's text to show how Marseilles remained the most prosperous Gallic port through the sixth century. Several other Gallic cities that enjoyed uncommon prosperity in the early Merovingian era were those fortunate enough to become royal "capitals." For archaeological corroboration of a marked economic revival at Metz, coinciding with its establishment as the Austrasian court's primary urban center, see Guy Halsall, "Town, Societies and Ideas: The Not-So-Strange Case of Late Roman and Early Merovingian Metz," in *Towns in Transition: Urban Evolution in Late Antiquity and the Early Middle Ages*, ed. Neil Christi and Simon T. Loseby (Aldershot: Scolar, 1996), 235–61. Loseby, "Gregory's Cities: Urban Functions," 239–70, explains that while most Gallic cities underwent considerable urban decay, they still retained relevance in Gregory's day as centers for Merovingian tax gathering, local administration, defense, formation of religious identity, and continued economics.

136. Brown, *Poverty and Leadership*, 51, writes, "… by 400 there was no doubt that the inhabitants of the average town were a distinctly shabby lot." For a strong critique of current archaeologists' efforts to bring "the urban poor" into the light, see Steve Roskams, "The Urban Poor: Finding the Marginalised," in *Social and Political Life in Late Antiquity*, ed. William Bowden, Adam Gutteridge, and Carlos Machado (Leiden and Boston: Brill, 2006), 487–531.

137. Greg. Tur., *GM* 44, *GC* 109 (*MGH*, SRM 1.2, 68, 368). This evidence counters the views of Bosl, Graus, and Schneider, who all contended that Gregory viewed *pauperes* as poor but socially higher than *aegenes*; Karl Bosl, "*Potens* und *pauper*: Begriffsgeschichtliche Studien zur gesellschaftlichen Differenzierung im frühen Mittelalter und zum 'Pauperismus' des Hochmittelalters," in *Alteuropa und die moderne Gesellschaft, Festschrift für Otto Brunner* (Göttingen: Vandenhoeck & Ruprecht, 1963), 72; Graus, *Volk, Herrscher und Heiliger*, 247; Schneider, "Die Darstellung der Pauperes," 68–69.

138. Greg. Tur., *VM* 2.14.

the "structural poor" for whom mendicancy was an only option was Maurusa, a woman who suffered gout in one hand, two twisted legs, and blindness. About her, Gregory wrote, "while living she was regarded as being dead and there was no hope of nourishment for her except when someone held out a pitying hand. She daily would watch for the care of the faithful and she used to request necessities for her livelihood."[139] After six years, Saint Martin restored to Maurusa the use of her hands and feet, and she regained her sight two years after that. While some beggars like Maurusa had homes to return to, other "professionals" roamed from town to town. Traveling troops of supplicants apparently were not uncommon in Gaul. Some ecclesiastics considered them such a threat to the social fabric that they legislated for clerics to dissuade the bands from passing through their dioceses.[140] Perhaps clerics feared that the troops would constitute a challenge to their churches' poor boxes. Indeed, traveling beggars could be resourceful. They probably relied on their newness to a community to generate significant amounts of alms. When contributions died down along with their loss of novelty, they moved to the next town. Gregory attested that wandering *mendici* were astute enough to showcase certain of their members with the worst deformities to garner sympathy and augment income. For example, about one unfortunate lad, he wrote:

> At Bourges there was a woman who conceived and gave birth to a son whose knees were bent up to his stomach and his heels back to his legs, whose hands hugged his chest, and whose eyes were closed. This boy resembled more closely some monster than the appearance of a man, and many laughed when they saw him. ...After he was grown, she gave him to beggars who took him, put him on a wagon, hauled him about, and displayed him to the people; the beggars received much charity because of him. This went on for a long time. When he was eleven years old, the boy came to the festival of the blessed Martin. He was thrown inside [the church] and lay in misery

---

139. Greg. Tur., *VM* 2.3 (*MGH*, SRM 1.2, 160): "... tamquam mortua putabatur superstis, nec erat ei spes alimonii, nisi qui manum misericordiae porrexisset. Cotidie autem respectum intuens devotorum, victus necessaria deposcebat."
140. E.g., Council of Tours (567), c. 5.

before the tomb. At the conclusion of the festival he recovered his sight and his hearing. Then he returned to his usual occupation and requested alms.[141]

Here, Gregory admitted that Saint Martin only afforded the youth a partial recovery. Of course, Gregory and others would have interpreted the persistence of a malady not as evidence of a saint's inability to heal but as an indication of a sinner's need for more faith. Given that this boy was a steady source of *multum stipendii* for his begging brethren, one may wonder whether his fellows wanted him fully restored to health anyway. For traveling mendicants, saints' festivals likely mattered as much as occasions to lighten the load of pilgrims and almsgivers than to find cures.

Coupled with the harsh realities of illness, disability, and hunger, all sub-groups among Gaul's poor periodically incurred some of the harshest treatment the powerful had to offer.[142] As just mentioned, the passage of Princess Rigunth's bridal train was no reason for the poor to celebrate. When the cities failed to procure sufficient provisions for that troop, the magnates simply took resources from the rural populace: "They despoiled the paupers' cottages and devastated their vineyards, cutting the branches and taking the grapes. They stole the cattle along with anything they could find, leaving behind nothing along the path they trod."[143] Transitory secular leaders were not the only travelers who might impose on peasants; so might religious figures. For example, monks

141. Greg. Tur., *VM* 2.24 (*MGH*, SRM 1.2, 167); "In Biturgo quoque fuit quaedam mulier, quae concipiens peperit filium, cuius poplites ad stomachum, calcanei ad crura contraxerant; manus enim adhaerentes percori, sed et oculi clausi erant. Qui magis monstrum aliquod quam hominis speciem similabat. Qui cum non sine dirisione multorum aspiceretur …Adumtumque tradidit mendicis, qui accipientes posuerunt eum in carrucam et trahentes ostendebant populis, multum per eum stipendii accipientes. Dum haec per longa tempora gererentur, anno aetatis suae undecimo advenit ad festivitatem beati Martini, proiectusque a foris ante sepulchrum miserabiliter decubabat. Transacta autem festivitate, visum auditumque recepit. Inde reductus ad solitam consuetudinem, postulabat stipem." Trans. by Van Dam, *Saints and their Miracles*, 239–40.

142. On the tribulations endured by the poor in Merovingian Gaul, see Michel Mollat, *The Poor in the Middle Ages: An Essay in Social History*, trans. by Arthur Goldhammer (New Haven, CT: Yale University Press, 1986), 24–32.

143. Greg. Tur., *Hist.* 6.45 (*MGH*, SRM 1.1, 319): "Nam hospiciola pauperum spoiliabant, vineas devastabant, ita ut incisis codicibus cum uvis auferrent, levantes pecora vel quicquid invenire potuissent, nihil per viam quam gradiebantur relinquentes …"

carrying relics of Saint Saturninus through the vicinity of Brioude simply expected to receive lodging at the cottage of a pauper.[144] As the institutional church completed its mastery of Gallic society, no group seems to have been more forcefully manhandled than peasants. City-dwelling ecclesiastics such as Caesarius preached for them to conform to urban Christian modes of behavior, with little apparent concern for the anxieties country folk might experience if made to abandon traditional survival habits.[145] Clerics passed a steady stream of legislation forbidding peasants and slaves from tending to their agricultural duties on Sundays and saints' days.[146] In 585, King Guntram supported his kingdom's bishops by issuing an edict that forbade Sunday labor by force of secular law.[147] Hagiographers, Venantius Fortunatus and Gregory included, sought to convince agricultural laborers to believe that working during saints' festivals would result in disabilities.[148] For example, Gregory wrote how a peasant named Leodulfus from Bourges feared his newly mowed hay would get wet in a storm, so on Sunday morning he hitched his oxen and gathered the hay on a wagon.[149] Immediately Leodulfus's feet felt as if on fire, but he misunderstood the divine warning sign. Then, after mass, which presumably the pauper attended, Leodulfus returned to his task and was struck blind. After an entire year, he traveled to the festival of Saint Martin and regained his sight and the saint's forgiveness.

In addition to using literary scare tactics to make peasants revere God and the saints on ecclesiastical terms, clerics also pressured the rural poor to abandon loyalties to traditional sacred spaces. The case of Vulfolaic's convincing peasants to replace reverence for an abandoned pagan holy site with respect for the stylite has been mentioned. Similarly, but on a less imposing scale, a pauper from Embrun was making a huge profit

144. Greg. Tur., *GM* 47, and see also Greg. Tur., *GC* 30.
145. Klingshirn, *Caesarius of Arles: The Making of a Christian Community*, 209–10.
146. Ian Wood, "Early Merovingian Devotion in Town and Country," in *The Church in Town and Countryside*, ed., Derek Baker (Oxford: Clarendon, 1979), 61–65.
147. *Capitularia Merowingica* 5.
148. Wood, *Merovingian Kingdoms*, 72, comments: "It is not difficult to depict the early medieval Church as a power-house of psychological oppression."
149. Greg. Tur., *VM* 4.45. Jacques Le Goff, *Time, Work and Culture in the Middle Ages*, 94, claimed he could find no name for a peasant in any early medieval literature.

by selling from his garden magical pears that could heal any illness.[150] Upon learning about this, local ecclesiastics "realized" that the martyrs Nazarius and Celsus had been buried beneath that very arbor. When the pauper refused to allow clerics to cut down the pear tree, they waited until the owner was absent, felled the tree, and then erected a church on the spot. This episode parallels Vulfolaic's story in that the would-be recluse, like the magic pear salesman, was a victim of a clerical deception that resulted in the negation of the victim's ability to act in a personally fulfilling and socially advantageous way. Just as deacon Vulfolaic obeyed his bishop and returned to his monastery, similarly did the pauper subsequently enter the church. Gregory explained, "The poor man was distinguished by such faith that eventually he deserved to become a cleric for this cathedral."[151] Here it is interesting that the offending clergy apparently felt compelled to compensate, or placate, the pauper by ushering him into a conventional clerical position. Indeed, however uncommon, it was not impossible for a *pauper* to achieve a position of distinction in the church. One poor man who attained the priesthood was Riculf of Tours, about whom Gregory wrote: "For this man was called forth from the paupers under Bishop Eufronius and was ordained archdeacon."[152] Many more humble Gauls would have gained entrée to the church not through the clergy but by becoming monks.

---

150. Greg. Tur., *GM* 46.

151. Greg. Tur., *GM* 46 (*MGH*, SRM 1.2, 70): "Tantaque pauper ille fide praelatus est, ut sacerdotium in hac ecclesia deinceps promereretur." Trans. by Raymond Van Dam, *Gregory of Tours, Glory of the Martyrs*, TTH 4 (Liverpool: Liverpool University Press, 1988), 70. This anecdote is fraught with problems, not the least of which is the fact that Nazarius and Celsus were martyred and buried at Milan in Italy, not Embrun in Gaul; idem, 70, n. 54. If as May Vieillard-Troiekouroff, *Les monuments religieux de la Gaule d'après les oeuvres de Grégoire de Tours* (Paris: Librairie Honoré Champion, 1976), 117–18, suspected, Gregory has misread a *passio* of Nazarius and Celsus and the church in question actually was at Milan, this still would not negate the impression that Gregory leaves that it was not rare for a pauper to become a cleric.

152. Greg. Tur., *Hist.* 5.49 (*MGH*, SRM 1.1, 262): "Nam hic sub Eufronio episcopo de pauperibus provocatus, archidiaconus ordinatus est." As Gregory intimated, an advantage that likely facilitated Riculf's rise into the high clergy was the fact that he and Chilperic's son Clovis were fast friends. Fredegar provides the tale of another poor man turned high cleric. He explains how a pauper aided Queen Brunhild when she had to flee the Austrasian court in 599. Once the queen was secure with her grandson Theuderic II in Burgundy, she presented the pauper with the bishopric of Auxerre; Fredegar, *Chron.* 4.19. While this episode is unlikely, it cannot be entirely discounted.

A peasant from Brittany who rose to prominence as an ascetic was Friardus of Besné.[153] Gregory depicted young Friardus behaving piously while tending to his agricultural duties, including bundling hay with other harvesters. Friardus began to ponder becoming an ascetic after he succeeded in performing such miracles as avoiding stinging wasps while harvesting and falling from a tree and managing to land totally unscathed. Leaving behind his family, homeland, and "little shack" (*hospitiola*), Friardus joined Abbot Sabaudus on an island near Nantes called Vindunitta, where he established a cell.[154] There Friardus distinguished himself by performing miracles such as causing dead wood from sticks he replanted to revive, and delaying his own death until Bishop Felix of Nantes could find the time to attend his deathbed.[155] Unlike with other upstart ascetics, Gregory did not record that Friardus attracted followers, although he did mention other monks living on the island. Nor did Gregory report that Friardus engaged in construction projects, but perhaps he did not have to because Vindunitta already was an established retreat.

One person of humble origin who did build an oratory was Caluppa.[156] This Auvergnian was from childhood raised a monk at Méallat. As with Patroclus, his pursuit of a harsh ascetic regimen precipitated a break with the brothers, and so Caluppa relocated to a nearby but hard to reach ravine, where he constructed some semblance of an oratory (*oratoriolum parvulum*) that was continually beset by snakes.[157] Bishop Avitus of Clermont established episcopal authority over the recluse by ordaining

153. Jacques Le Goff, *Time, Work and Culture in the Middle Ages*, 92, and František Graus as well were wrong to assert that there were no medieval peasant saints before the thirteenth century. Le Goff's attempt, ibid., 89–92, to explain a supposed disappearance of the peasant in fifth- and sixth-century literature is unconvincing.

154. Greg. Tur., *VP* 10.2 (*MGH*, SRM 1.2, 257).

155. Greg. Tur., *VP* 10.3–4. About Gregory's reasons for including the tale of this bumpkin saint, Edward James, *Gregory of Tours, Life of the Fathers*, 75, n. 6, offers: "One wonders if this slightly odd, if not comic, life of Friardus, the only Nantais saint in Gregory's works, and the most rustic of them all, was not influenced by Gregory's own antipathy towards his episcopal colleague Felix …"

156. Gregory did not mention Caluppa's social rank, but one may surmise that the recluse was of low birth from the fact that Caluppa's *Life* follows that of Friardus, and here Gregory continued a theme of poverty leading to salvation; Greg. Tur., *VP* 11, *praef.*

157. Greg. Tur., *VP* 11.1 (*MGH*, SRM 1.2, 259).

him deacon and priest.[158] Another pauper who built a church edifice was the aforementioned peasant of Brioude forced to host clerics carrying relics of Saint Saturninus. On the night after his guests departed, this poor man dreamed that an old man (Saturninus) warned him to abandon the cottage, but the peasant forgot about the admonition.[159] Gregory attributed the man's dismissal of the vision to his *rusticitas*. Within the year, the peasant fell into such a destitute state he could not feed his household. Finally it dawned on him that the family's despair was the result of his having offended the saint by remaining in the house, and so he acted accordingly. Gregory wrote, "After he tore down the cottage he built an oratory out of the wooden planks. Every day he prayed in this oratory and requested the assistance of the blessed martyr. Finally his misfortunes ceased. As he put his hands to work there were such good results as a consequence that in a short time he regained more than he had lost."[160] On the one hand, this anecdote causes one to wonder whether the dream in which Saint Saturninus threatened the pauper reflected a desire, or even pressure, on the part of the clerics to establish an oratory on the peasant's lands. For elsewhere in his text, Gregory certainly portrayed the designs of the clergy at Tours as the will of Saint Martin. On the other hand, perhaps there was no clerical pressure. Perhaps the pauper expected the vision to authorize his own intention to participate in, and benefit from, a saint's cult. Since Gregory's senatorial family controlled the region where this peasant lived, perhaps the pauper was one of their clients.[161] Gregory's inclusion of this tale in the *Miracula* certainly indicates that the author approved of the poor man's action, but it also may suggest his endorsement of the foundation of this particular oratory. If indeed the peasant was a client, building the oratory would only complement the ecclesiastical aristocratic family's strategy

158. Greg. Tur., *VP* 11.3.

159. Greg. Tur., *GM* 47.

160. Greg. Tur., *GM* 47 (*MGH*, SRM 1.2, 71): "Tunc amoto turgio, oratorium ex ligneis formatum tabulis collocavit; in quo cotidie orationem fundens, opem beati martyris flagitabat. Tandem cessantibus plagis, aptanti manus ad operam tanta fructuum consequentia fuit, ut in modici temporis spatio amplius quam perdiderat repararet." Trans. by Van Dam, *Gregory of Tours, Glory of the Martyrs*, 71–72.

161. Gregory recorded that the event occurred "in our territory"; Greg. Tur., *GM* 47 (*MGH*, SRM 1.2, 71): "infra nostro territorio."

to further spread saints' cults and thereby consolidate control over a part of the Auvergnian *pagus*. Meanwhile, the peasant would have benefited by recouping *amplius quam perdiderat*.

Another pauper for whom a vision perhaps occasioned entry into the church was Sisulfus. When he awoke from a nap with his fingers bent into his palm, Sisulfus wondered what sin he had committed to cause the deformity. But Saint Martin appeared to him in a vision and explained that the disability had happened for an instructive purpose:

> [Martin] said: "Your disability reveals the anguish that awaits sinful people. Therefore go now through the villages and the fortresses, travel as far as the city, and proclaim that everyone is to abstain from perjury and usury and that on Sundays no one is to do any work contrary to the mystical rites [of the liturgy]. ...For the wrath of the Lord is causing the hatreds and illnesses and other evils that the people endure. And therefore be prompt in announcing that people are to reform, lest they die a cruel death as a result of their own crimes. After you have done what I have ordered, then hurry to the church at Tours; I will visit you there, and I will beg the Lord that you might be healed."[162]

While a cleric such as Gregory of Tours generally would have assessed an injury such as Sisulfus's as a sign of a person's sinfulness, the pauper interpreted his handicap as a reason to begin a new vocation as a preacher. The vision not only attested that the usual explanation for disability did not apply in his case, but also it legitimized his preaching. Because Sisulfus's discouragement of perjury and Sunday work coincided with two main elements of the bishop's agenda, Gregory and Saint Martin would have approved. The *pauper* arrived at Martin's basilica in September 577, and after kneeling at the tomb for three days, he recovered the use of his hand on the fourth. But was Sisulfus permitted to continue preaching,

---

162. Greg. Tur., *VM* 2.40 (*MGH*, SRM 1.2, 173–74): "... ait: 'Debilitas tua tormentum indicat populi delinquentis. Vade ergo nunc per vicos et castella et ad civitatem usque pertende et praedica, ut se omnis homo a periuriis et usuris absteneat et in die dominico nullum opus absque solemnitatibus misticis agat. ...Nam hostilitates et infirmitates et alia mala, quae perfert populus, indignatio Domini commovet. Et ideo adnuntia velociter, ut emendent, ne crudeliter in scelere suo dereperant. Tu vero, his peractis quae imperavi, Turonus ad basilicam propera; ibique te visitans, obteneo apud Dominum, ut saneris'." Trans. by Van Dam, *Saints and their Miracles*, 249–50.

or did he become a cleric? Gregory's account certainly was not intended to encourage all persons of low rank to become preachers, for self-aggrandizing, popular ministers might threaten the established clergy's monopoly on local spiritual authority. But Sisulfus appears to have been well on his way to becoming part of the clerical establishment, not only because he voiced the bishop's socio-spiritual program, but also because he had become a client of the church's at Tours by virtue of having been the recipient of Martin's healing *virtus*. While Gregory was not forthcoming about Sisulfus's future, becoming a cleric was a plausible aspiration for *pauperes*.

Not only peasants but even beggars could hope to improve their lot through church affiliation. One pauper who achieved renown was a native of Gregory's Auvergne, Lupicinus, who as a youth begged for alms at the houses of the pious.[163] Lupicinus was so successful that he shared his bounty with others. As an adult, the pious man adopted the life of a recluse. At Lipidiacum, he discovered some ruined walls in which he cloistered himself, withdrawing entirely from view of others. A source of Lupicinus's nourishment was a "woman of rank" (*matrona*) who provided wheat and barley, so that he could both eat and dole out the remainder to others in need.[164] Because the hermit distributed bread to the locals, the lady also would have been a source for his popularity, too. The hermit's repute caused sick people to seek him out for cures, and other monks gathered around his cell. Lupicinus's personal regimen included wearing a large stone about his neck and "resting" his head on a staff with two thorns that stuck into his chin. He would spit blood on the wall of his cell, and after his death the locals gathered these drops as relics.[165] When Lupicinus died, there ensued an argument for possession of the holy corpse between peasants living in the vicinity of the cell and the *matrona* who had nurtured the saint. The latter wanted to bury the body on a distant estate at Trézelle. When the locals tried preemptively to settle the matter by conducting a hasty burial, the powerful woman summoned her "helpers" (*solatiis*), presumably a polite word

163. Greg. Tur., *VP* 13.1.
164. Greg. Tur., *VP* 13.3.
165. Greg. Tur., *VP* 13.2.

for armed servants, who chased off the peasants (*fugatis paginsibus*).[166] Afterward, the rustics repented and the lady permitted them to join in an elaborate funeral procession for the saint.[167] The tale of Lupicinus attests that even freemen of the least means might manage to secure socially fulfilling lives as leaders of bands of monks. Like other *ingenui* who lacked the resources to construct a fitting monastery, they might establish a cadre of simple cells among local ruins. Of particular interest for this story, however, is the recluse's anonymous patron. The *matrona's* forceful treatment of the peasants betrays her determination to continue benefiting from the memory of a saint whose holiness she had cultivated. Tellingly, the peasants of Lipidiacum had hoped they would control the saint's tomb and cult, but they were no match for the propertied woman. Her involvement with Lupicinus was so pervasive that one wonders whether the very opportunity for him to become a recluse had been contingent upon the patron's permission, or even her design.

Perhaps more typical of the level of social improvement that beggars might aspire to are the examples of Piolus and Theodomund. Piolus was a youth born with hands so twisted that he could not perform manual labor.[168] By the age of ten years, the pain had become so great that he went to the church of Saint Martin. There he remained as a beggar for many days until his fingers straightened. At age fifteen, Piolus was struck by a high fever and became a mute. Although Martin healed the fever, the boy's speech was lost. Thereafter he communicated by clicking together boards tied to his hands. As a direct result of this miracle, Piolus became employed under vinedressers as a living scarecrow. Afterward, during Epiphany in 576, Piolus again visited the basilica, and he became a cleric at Martin's shrine at Candes. Again Piolus's promotion was accompanied by a restoration of health. After keeping vigils at the saint's tomb, he recovered his speech and hearing. Piolus's healings and repeated associations with Saint Martin netted him an advance from indigent beggar, to hobbled but employed *pauper*, to healthy cleric. His miraculous

---

166. Greg. Tur., *VP* 13.3.
167. Gregory heard the story from a very old priest named Deodatus. He also knew people who had recovered from illness by use of the holy spit; Greg. Tur., *VP* 13.2, 3.
168. Greg. Tur., *VM* 2.26.

improvements visibly confirmed the saint's approval of him in his new positions, just as Martin's cures for Bishop Gregory's many ailments often publicly affirmed the saint's acknowledgement of the bishop's spiritual authority at Tours.[169] Similarly, years before Piolus and Gregory arrived at Tours, there was a mute man named Theodomund who used to beg for alms for himself and others at Saint Martin's basilica.[170] After three years, he miraculously recovered his hearing and speech. Upon learning of this miracle, Queen Clotild sponsored the man's education (memorizing the Psalter), and he became a cleric. Perhaps it was successful episodes such as those of Piolus and Theodomund that inspired the *pauper* Sisulfus to react as ardently and optimistically as he did to Saint Martin's summons to preach. Again, if Sisulfus did become a cleric at Tours, he would have owed his elevation to his patron Gregory, just as Piolus did Gregory, and Theodomundus Clotild, and Lupicinus the anonymous *matrona*. The evidence regarding the roles of all these actors seems to suggest that in regards to the social advancement of *pauperes*, possessing a modicum of resources mattered less than enjoying the willingness of a patron.

SERVI

There was a thin line that separated pauperism and servitude in Gaul. Just one season of famine, or plague, could force thousands of *pauperes* to sell themselves or their children into slavery in exchange for food.[171] The raid of a modest band of brigands could ensnare many dozens of members of a community, and if a nearby bishop did not ransom the captives, the lot could lose its freedom.[172] Contrary to a once traditional concept, slavery did not pass into insignificance during Late Antiquity as a result of an end to Roman conquests and/or a steady rise of the colonate.[173] A continued meaningful presence of slaves, both

169. On the interconnectedness of illness, healing and social promotion, see Van Dam, *Saints and their Miracles*, 91–92.
170. Greg. Tur., *VM* 1.7.
171. Greg. Tur., *Hist.* 7.45.
172. For Breton raids in the late sixth century, see Greg. Tur., *Hist.* 5.29, 31, 9.18, 24, 10.9.
173. See Garnsey and Humfress, *Evolution of the Late Antique World*, 85–88; Wickham, *Framing the Early Middle Ages*, 259–60. For bibliography on slaves, see Schachner, "Social Life in Late Antiquity," 50–52.

agricultural and domestic, readily visible in writings of the Barbarian era, endured.[174] So too did a warranted fear of falling into servitude persist among the many freepersons who already lived on the edge of impoverishment. Prevention of the free becoming unfree – for example, by ransoming captives abducted in raids – was a tremendously important component of late ancient Christian charity.[175] These fears and remedies were justified, for if most poor people were to some extent beholden to patrons, the wills of slave-masters proved even more restricting for people of servile rank. Regarding slaves themselves, secular lawmakers provided penalties to discourage doing them physical harm; however, they fully acknowledged the right for some humans to own others. Likewise, aristocratic litterateurs often were sympathetic to the plight of individual servants who chafed under the brutality of the worst masters, but they did not oppose the institution of slavery.[176] Saints appear in *Vitae* as slave owners as often as they do as redeemers of the unfree.[177] Gallic writers offered a frank, unfeeling vocabulary to identify members of the class; demeaning terms included *servus, famulus* (slave), *puer* (literally boy), and *mancipium* (literally property). Ranking just above slaves both legally and socially were half-free people (*liberti*), whose numbers included manumitted slaves. While a slave was subject to his master *de facto* and *de iure*, half-free people remained dependant upon patrons *de facto*. In both cases, the place of the inferior party within society was defined by service and dependency.

Like rural *pauperes*, agricultural slaves received pressure from church leaders who forbade them to work on Sundays and holy days.[178] But

---

174. On the persistence of slavery in Gaul, see Ross Samson, "Slavery, the Roman Legacy," in *Fifth-Century Gaul: A Crisis of Identity?* ed. John Drinkwater and Hugh Elton (Cambridge: Cambridge University Press, 1992), 218–27; and Heike Grieser, *Sklaverie im spätantiken und frühmittelalterlichen Gallien (5.-7. Jh.): Das Zeugnis der christlichen Quellen* (Stuttgart: Franz Steiner, 1997). Wickham, *Framing the Middle Ages*, 281–82, emphasizes the general lack of a (plantation) slave system in Late Antiquity, Gaul included. Without dismissing the impact of legal condition between slave and free, he stresses the similitude of economic relationships between free and unfree tenants to their lords; ibid. 262. In general, see ibid., 259–65, 558–66. For consideration of the slaves who worked the vineyards of Aredius of Limoges; see ibid., 284–87.

175. Brown, *Poverty and Leadership*, 62–63; Rapp, *Holy Bishops in Late Antiquity*, 228–32.

176. Brown, *Poverty and Leadership*, 61, writes: "Slave owners were urged by Christian preachers, as they had been urged in pagan times by philosophers, to control themselves and to abstain from cruelty and from sexual abuse of their slaves."

177. Kitchen, *Saints' Lives and the Rhetoric of Gender*, 39.

178. E. g., Greg. Tur., *VM* 2.13, 2.57, 3.29.

unlike the free poor, slaves were not recognized as humans before the law, and this legal subterfuge translated into the worst indifference the powerful could mete upon social inferiors. Thus, Duke Rauching, the most callous abuser of slaves to appear in Gregory's pages, was said to have "acted towards his own servants as if he did not think them to possess any humanity."[179] Rauching reportedly delighted in torturing his servants by making them hold candles between their thighs until dripping wax scalded their legs. But the duke's most notorious exploit involved a young slave couple who married without his permission.[180] After the ceremony, a wary priest caused the master to swear an oath that the two would not be parted. Rauching swore, and true to his word after the priest released the pair to his custody, the duke ordered them to be buried alive together. The cleric learned of the abuse and rushed to the burial site, arriving in time to save the man but not the woman. Despite random episodes of abuse and a general verbal categorization as non-human, individual slaves attempted to rise beyond their detestable condition. Although the evidence is slim, one finds a few episodes involving persons of servile status pursuing a path of improving their lot through marriage. One virtual slave, in fact a "bound cottager," who was anxious to marry was the dependent of a southern Gallic aristocrat named Pudens.[181] After the youth eloped with a female client of Sidonius Apollinaris's, Pudens petitioned Sidonius to allow the arrangement. The latter responded with a curt letter insisting that Pudens elevate the status of the servant in order to keep his friendship and to enable the woman to maintain her reputation. Sidonius wrote: "The woman is already free. The only thing that will cause her to be regarded as taken in lawful marriage, not made over as a plaything, will be that our culprit, on whose behalf you plead, should promptly be made a client instead of a tributary payer and so begin to have the standing of a plebian rather than a *colonus*."[182] Sidonius published this letter not to show that he

---

179. Greg. Tur., *Hist.* 5.3 (*MGH*, SRM 1.1, 197): "... se ita cum subiectis agebat, ut non congosceret in se aliquid humanitatis habere ..."
180. Greg. Tur., *Hist.* 5.3.
181. Sid. Ap., *Ep.* 5.19; and see Mathisen, *People, Personal Expression, and Social Relations*, 1: 64–65.
182. Sid. Ap. *Ep.* 5.19 (Anderson, ed. and trans., 2: 238–39): "Mulier autem illa iam libera est; quae tum demum videbitur non ludibrio addicta sed assumpta coniugio, si reus noster, pro quo precaris, mox cliens factus e tributario plebeiam potius incipiat habere personam quam colonariam."

cared about his lowly client but rather to upstage, in a friendly sort of way, a fellow aristocrat of slightly lower status. The suggested change in the groom's status likely would not have made much difference for the cottager's economic circumstance.[183] Whatever the actual outcome of Sidonius and Pudens' arrangement, their negotiation reveals the extent to which Gallic aristocrats controlled the destinies of servants, even free clients. But the couple's elopement, like the marriage of the impertinent slaves of Rauching who acted without that lord's leave, reveals how socially low persons were determined to go about living despite the imposition of artificial hurdles such as minute social criteria. Regarding the motivations for Pudens and Sidonius's dependents and for Rauching's slaves, unfortunately, it cannot be known whether the mates joined together for economic benefit or love, although the latter seems likely in both instances. Another tale, however, that may suggest how matrimony could hold social significance even for servile persons involves an Auvergnian slave turned monk named Brachio.[184] According to Gregory, for several years this youth studied letters under the tutelage of Abbot Aemilianus, who manumitted the boy after securing him from another master, a duke no less. While Brachio had been conspiring to take up the ascetic lifestyle, his brother contemplated murdering him "because he did not want to marry."[185] Gregory offered no reason why the brother despised Brachio to the point of wanting him to die, but the resentment might have stemmed from the latter's failing to take full advantage of his social situation. Even when he had been the duke's slave, Brachio had been privileged to act as the master's huntsman and to wear fine clothes. Once he was free, the brother likely expected him to use his court connection to secure a socially advantageous marriage and improve the family's situation. The fact that Brachio eschewed this "logical" path to become a monk at Aemilianus's tiny and remote retreat, which itself had scarcely been established, befuddled and infuriated the sibling, who, although he was of servile status, nevertheless thought "according to the custom of the world" like the father of

183. Mathisen, *People, Personal Expression, and Social Relations*, 1: 65, n. 80.
184. Greg. Tur., *VP* 12.1.
185. Greg. Tur., *VP* 12.2 (*MGH*, SRM, 1.2, 263): "… cur non nollet matrimonio copulari."

Saint Patroclus. Unlike Brachio, other slaves who grew up in proximity to a court took advantage of the opportunities that that rare environment brought by impressing patrons and rising up the secular ranks. We already have seen in the examples of Leudast and Andarchius how a former slave with a court connection might use displays of bravado or literary ability to benefit socially. Additionally, we saw how the ambitious Leudast successfully augmented his status by marrying a wealthy (and probably noble) woman, and Andarchius tried to do the same. Much to the chagrin of Brachio's brother, that former slave did not pursue this course of action. Of course, most slaves could never have come close to such opportunities. To appreciate more fully that which enabled social improvement for servile persons, and also to witness the kind of advancement that slaves more commonly could aspire to, let us return to the evidence for promotion within the church.

Servitude did not preclude Gauls from pursuing a meaningful lifestyle through church involvement. Evidence from the canons indicates that it was not unknown for slaves to be ordained as priests.[186] One slave turned renowned churchman with whom Gregory was familiar through a *Life* (now lost) was Mitrias of Aix.[187] It is uncertain that Saint Mitrias actually existed, however, and if he did, it is unknown whether he had been a cleric or a monk. A saintly *servus* whom Gregory knew personally and who achieved acclaim as an ascetic was the aforementioned Brachio, the well-attired slave of Duke Sigivald, who himself was an infamous courtier stationed by Theuderic in the Auvergne.[188] According to Gregory, Brachio chanced upon Aemilianus's sylvan retreat while hunting a boar. Gregory did not record Aemilianus's social station, but because it is written that he owned some property before entering the forest of Pionsat, the hermit might have been either an *ingenuus* or pauper.[189] Aemilianus immediately encouraged Brachio to abandon Sigivald, and without his master's knowledge Brachio prepared to join the monk. He learned to read by requesting young clerics to help him decipher *tituli*

---

186. Godding, *Prêtres en Gaule mérovingienne*, 85–90.
187. Greg. Tur., *GC* 70.
188. Greg. Tur., *VP* 12.2, and see *GC* 38 for Brachio often telling Gregory stories.
189. Greg. Tur., *VP* 12.1.

painted alongside images in a local oratory. It was only upon Sigivald's death, however, that Brachio finally was able to join Aemilianus, this despite the objections of the monk's angry brother.[190] Aemilianus and Brachio gathered other monks about them, and when the aged hermit died, the former slave succeeded him as abbot. When Brachio decided to found a monastery, he sought woodland property from Sigivald's daughter, Ranichild.[191] Now a renowned abbot, Brachio established two more monasteries and built an oratory at Tours. Brachio's experiences compare with those of several slaves considered previously. As it was for Andarchius, it seems that a necessary prerequisite to Brachio's beginning his new vocation involved the prompting of a potential new patron. Abbot Aemilianus was to Brachio what Duke Lupus had been for Andarchius. Also noteworthy is the role of literacy, which obviously was necessary if Brachio were to become an abbot. Andarchius's literary talent, which itself was made possible by the encouragement of the senator Felix, attracted Duke Lupus. Similarly, Brachio's rise to prominence transpired because the slave displayed an eagerness to learn. Also relevant to Brachio's tale is the fact that despite his religious conviction, he was unable to join Aemilianus until his former master died, and even then Sigivald's daughter apparently remained a patron. This may lead one to wonder whether the very reason Aemilianus was intent on associating with Brachio was to benefit from the latter's connection with Sigivald's family. Apparently it was only after Ranichild's client joined Aemilianus that the latter had the resources to build a monastery.[192] Thus Brachio's career as an ascetic appears to have been every bit as beholden to Sigivald's family as the pauper-recluse Lupicinus's hermit lifestyle had been to the anonymous *matrona*. Brachio's continued building projects as abbot also might have resulted as much from Ranichild's social and religious ambitions as his own.

Yet another slave who desired the life of an ascetic was Portianus. Gregory labeled Portianus's master a "barbarian," by which he probably

190. Greg. Tur., *VP* 12.2.
191. Greg. Tur., *VP* 12.3.
192. Before Brachio's arrival, Amilianus's retreat amounted to little more than a tiny garden the hermit had cleared among the trees; Greg. Tur., *VP* 12.1.

meant in this instance an Arian, perhaps a Visigoth.[193] Portianus frequently fled to a monastery, and the abbot repeatedly had to request a pardon so that the master would not punish the slave upon his return. Eventually the owner accused the abbot of inciting the slave to flee. It was on the occasion of yet another return journey that the master happened to become blind. He asked the abbot to accept the slave into his service, hoping that the good deed would make him deserving of regaining his sight. The abbot pleaded for Portianus to make the sign of the cross over the man's eyes, and after some delay the slave healed the former master. Thereafter, Portianus became a cleric, and by virtue of his fame he succeeded the abbot.[194] In that capacity, Portianus once pleaded on behalf of Auvergnian farmers when King Theuderic's army camped in the fields of Artonne. Interestingly, the man before whom the abbot protested the soldiers' behavior was Brachio's old master, Duke Sigivald.[195] Portianus reportedly saved the duke and his retainers from drinking poisoned wine (the cup contained a snake), after which Sigivald released many captives to the saint. In the tale of Portianus, Gregory depicted the slave as acting far more aggressively toward his secular master than Brachio had behaved. Rather than awaiting his master's demise, Portianus obstinately and continually fled to a local monastery. The slave-owner's suspicion that the abbot was encouraging the flight might have been well founded, for Gallic hagiography includes many examples of clerics persistently petitioning masters to transfer particular slaves to a church's service. Thus it is likely that the abbot's will was instrumental in freeing Portianus, just as Aemilianus's was in procuring Brachio for his retreat, and Duke Lupus's in acquiring Andarchius for the Austrasian court. In general it seems social mobility was similar for slaves as for *pauperes*; advancement necessitated a willingness to act on the slave's part and also the aid or prompting of a patron. Along these lines, it probably was common for servile people to advance into the church whenever a master

193. Greg. Tur., *VP* 5.1.
194. Greg. Tur., *VP* 5.1.
195. Greg. Tur., *VP* 5.2.

bent upon becoming an ascetic caused his household to become monks, as happened with the servants of Aredius of Limoges.[196]

Beyond becoming an ascetic, a kind of advancement many more slaves could hope to achieve through church affiliation was simple liberation, as the example of a slave named Veranus attests.[197] When gout overwhelmed Veranus so that he became completely lame, his master, the Priest Symon, placed him before Saint Martin's tomb and vowed that if the saint healed the slave he would be liberated, tonsured, and handed over to the holy man's service. After a week, Veranus received his health and his freedom, and in accodance with Symon's words he became a client for the saint. Another person whom Martin liberated was a freedwoman enslaved a second time by her patron's sons and sold to barbarians.[198] The woman became crippled (which ailment Gregory attributed to Martin because it ultimately benefited her) and so her masters abandoned her. Afterward at Martin's church she recovered her health and freedom. Similarly, the sons of a patron that long before had liberated a couple seized their free daughter and reduced her to slavery. When she refused to work, her masters bound her with chains. Then, during Martin's festival, the stocks that bound her feet split, and the woman raced to the basilica, where she received her freedom.[199] As with Veranus, the latter woman's liberation would have entailed becoming a client for the saint's church. The results of the last two anecdotes typify what servile persons liberated by clerics usually could expect in terms of freedom; freed slaves would remain beholden to patrons.

CONCLUSION

Analysis of evidence according to our model for Gallic society reveals how people of every rank were able to use similar social strategies, which differed only by a matter of degrees. Common to all manner of people were efforts to maintain or augment family resources by marrying a spouse within one's rank or above it. Gregory's family's

196. Greg. Tur., *Hist.* 10.29.
197. Greg. Tur., *VM* 2.4.
198. Greg. Tur., *VM* 2.59.
199. Greg. Tur., *VM* 4.41.

actions, Patroclus's father's words to his son, and the consternation of Brachio's brother attest to the significance of this stratagem for aristocrats, freepersons, and servile people. Rarer opportunities for social improvement were to be had at royal courts. The examples of Aredius, Andarchius, and Leudast show how kings and courtiers did not rule out talented *ingenui* and *servi* for consideration as military and government agents. The best evidence for social strategizing for Gauls of every social rank pertains to involvement in the church. One witnesses well-to-do freepersons, paupers, and slaves achieving social success by performing conspicuous activities similar to those used by ecclesiastical aristocrats, including constructing church buildings, founding monasteries, and claiming visions and healings to legitimize and proclaim spiritual authority. In comparing this biographical data, it would seem that the most significant divide among participants in the various endeavors under analysis was not that between aristocrats and *ingenui* but rather the one between *ingenui* and *pauperes*. For whereas wealthy free people appear to have acted usually of their own accord like aristocrats, paupers and slaves often remained utterly dependent upon patrons even after social advancement.

Having completed a general analysis of participants in Gallic society acting according to a set of socially advantageous behaviors, we shall in the next four chapters investigate in greater detail the social constraints and opportunities presented to specific groups of people who were more or less socially privileged. Each group that we shall consider came into contact with saints' cults, and so they are rather well-represented in the sources, especially hagiography. First we shall look in greater detail at two groups of people of lower social station – incarcerated persons and the "poor" who were intimately affiliated with churches. Then we shall examine two potential challengers for saintly healers – physicians and enchanters.

THE PASSIVE POOR: PRISONERS

CHAPTER FIVE

One night in the jail at Clermont, the chains holding the prisoners
came undone by the intervention of God, the gates were unfastened,
and they all rushed out to seek sanctuary in a church. Count
Eulalius had them loaded with fresh chains, but no sooner had these
been placed in position than they snapped asunder like brittle glass.
Bishop Avitus pleaded for the prisoners to be released, and they were
given their liberty and sent home.

GREGORY OF TOURS, *Historiae* 10.6 [1]

Violence and crime were endemic in Barbarian Gaul. [2] Gregory of Tours'
Historiae include many episodes in which the powerful benefited from

---

1. Greg. Tur., *Hist.* 10.6 (*MGH*, SRM 1.1, 488): "Apud Arvernus vero vincti carceris nocte, nutu Dei disruptis vinculis reseratisque aditibus custodiae, egressi, ecclesiam ingressi sunt. Quibus cum Eulalius
comes onera catenarum addi iussissit, ut super eos posita, extemplo ceu vitrum fragile comminuta
sunt; et sic, obtenente Avito pontifice, eruti, propriae sunt redditi libertati." Trans. by Thorpe, *Gregory
of Tours, History of the Franks*, 553.
2. Ross Samson, "The Merovingian Nobleman's Home: Castle or Villa?" *Journal of Medieval History* 13
(1987), 288–89, uses evidence from Gregory's *Historiae* and estimates, supposedly in a manner that
overcomes the author's bias for depicting slaughters, that one-third of Gallic aristocrats died violently, most of these succumbing to feud, or vendetta, rather than dying in battle. Wolf Liebeschuetz,
"Violence in the Barbarian Successor Kingdoms," 37–46, combines Gregory's testimony with evidence

forceful, illicit activities. For example, in 584 after Count Innocentius
of Javols failed to indict Abbot Lupentius for treason against Queen
Brunhild, the count attacked as the abbot returned home and lopped
off his head.[3] Despite this callous action, Innocentius suffered no punishment; to the contrary, Brunhild helped him secure the bishopric of
Rodez.[4] It seems Innocentius presumed that because he was in good
stead with the queen he needed not fear any reprisal such as imprisonment. Indeed, aristocrats likely assumed they would not be cast into
prison, for sources suggest that lockups were reserved not for them but
for the socially disadvantaged.[5] In a society that already was sufficiently
hostile, the downtrodden suffered one of the most horrid of possible
environments in the *carcer*. The misery that traditionally accompanied
imprisonment came to the attention of early Christian leaders, and so
tending to inmates became an early hallmark of the religion. Besides
providing food and comfort for the incarcerated, Christians attempted
to right the injustice of people being wrongfully jailed.[6] Fifth-century
Roman laws facilitated bishops and clerics in conducting these ministrations.[7] With the rise in social significance of saints' cults in the fifth
and sixth centuries, clerical intervention for prisoners would take on a
distinctive character. This chapter will examine inmates as a distinct
group among Gaul's less privileged. A consideration of the social situation of incarcerated persons precedes analysis of the conditions they
endured and the jurisdictions under which they fell. The chapter will
focus on how ecclesiastics justified their intervention and determined
some prisoners' fates. Through an invitation to participate in a ritual

---

from law codes that implies that kin was responsible for seeking either compensation or vengeance
after an assault to argue that Gallic society was indeed violent.
3. Greg. Tur., *Hist.* 6.37.
4. Greg. Tur., *Hist.* 6.38.
5. *Contra* František Graus, "Die Gewalt bei Anfängen des Feudalismus und die 'Gefangenenbefreiungen' der merowingischen Hagiographie," *Jahrbuch für Wirtschaftsgeschichte* (1961, teil 1), 99;
and Kitchen, *Saints' Lives and the Rhetoric of Gender*, 39–40, who both contend that Gallic hagiography reflects an ecclesiastical desire for complete eradication of imprisonment. One needs to distinguish between bishops releasing prisoners and ransoming *captivi* taken during war. Ecclesiastics had
separate techniques and motives for addressing each of these problems; see Rapp, *Holy Bishops in Late
Antiquity*, 226–32.
6. See Rapp, *Holy Bishops in Late Antiquity*, 229.
7. *CTh* 9.3.7 (a. 409); *Sirm. Const.* 13 (a. 419); Rapp, *Holy Bishops in Late Antiquity*, 229.

of "miraculous release," certain inmates could reintegrate with their communities, but only at a cost of future social dependency.

PRISONERS AND SOCIAL STATUS

Status traditionally played a large role in determining whether or not a person would be confined in a *carcer*. Immunity to imprisonment, both before and after trial, had been a freeperson's theoretical right in the late imperial era. According to the letter of Roman law, accused people were entitled to a month's grace without incarceration before being taken to a provincial capital for trial.[8] But this privilege probably pertained only to the powerful, not the socially disadvantaged. Accused persons who lacked influence might be incarcerated as a matter of form.[9] Thus the fourth-century orator Libanius complained about an expectation among the powerful that a mere accusation on their part should result in imprisonment for people of lesser station: "This is the normal treatment of the weaker at the hands of the influential, of the penniless at the hands of the wealthy, of the masses at the hands of the élite who expect any charge they make to count for more than proof."[10] Sources for Barbarian Gaul reveal conditions similar to those of the previous age. The status-conscious Bishop of Tours, for example, was forthcoming and consistent about the kinds of detention subjects in his text encountered. Although Gregory commonly remarked that aristocrats were loaded with chains when arrested, he usually depicted them being placed under some form of house arrest, even when suspected of serious offenses such as high treason. Gregory used the term *in custodia* or the dative *custodiae* in reference to this kind of detention. For example, he wrote that in 577, King Chilperic summoned to court Bishop Praetextatus of Rouen to answer a charge of treason before an assembly of bishops. But neither before nor after the proceeding did the author depict Praetextatus being imprisoned; instead, one reads that after being found guilty and sentenced to exile, the bishop was detained temporarily *in custodia*, not *in*

---

8. See *CTh* 9.2.3 (a. 380), 9.2.6 (a. 409).
9. A. H. M. Jones, *The Later Roman Empire, 284–602: A Social, Economic, and Administrative Survey* (Norman, OK: University of Oklahoma Press, 1964), 1: 521.
10. Libanius, *Orationes* 45.3–4 (Jones, ed. and trans., 2: 163).

carcere.[11] Throughout the hearing, it does not appear that the prelate was unduly put upon, for Gregory certainly would have complained about any rough treatment had the king meted it upon one of God's bishops, especially one whom the author admired like a saint.[12]

Gregory sometimes provided details about the manner of detention for magnates. He wrote that in 582, when Duke Guntram Boso arrested Bishop Theodore of Marseilles on a charge of supporting the pretender Gundovald, the duke held him *in custodia* in a "small cell" (*cellula*) and did not permit him to approach the cathedral.[13] By *cellula*, Gregory almost certainly meant a room in a church complex, not a prison.[14] If the latter had been the case, it would have been superfluous to mention that the bishop was not permitted to venture to the cathedral. In fact, church edifices appear to have been the usual location to detain ecclesiastics awaiting trial. In 579, when Bishops Salonius of Embrun and Sagittarius of Gap were accused of crimes, they were lodged *in basilica beati Marcelli sub custodia*.[15] Similarly, when Abbess Rusticula of Arles was accused of treason around 613, captors held her *in cella monasterii* ...

11. Greg. Tur., *Hist.* 5.18 (*MGH*, SRM 1.1, 223).
12. The bishop of Rouen undoubtedly had acted treasonously by marrying Chilperic's rebellious son Merovech to Sigibert's widow, Queen Brunhild. Gregory was the most outspoken supporter for Praetextatus at his trial. Praetextatus was punished by being exiled to an island beyond the city of Countances, but after Chilperic's demise in 584, the prelate recovered his bishopric; Greg. Tur., *Hist.* 7.16. Two years later, an assassin murdered him in his cathedral, and as was often the case for such an occurrence, Gregory blamed Queen Fredegund; Greg. Tur., *Hist.* 8.31. Fredegund rightly perceived stepsons such as Merovech as threats to her political survival, and she would have felt the same about any bishop that supported their cause. Many Gauls would have perceived the queen's premeditated, violent retaliation against Praetextatus as a proper defense of personal honor, but not Gregory, of course; see Nira Gradowicz-Pancer, "Femmes royales et violences anti-épiscopales à l'époque mérovingienne: Frédégonde et le meurtre de l'évêque Prétextat," in *Bischofsmord im Mittelalter: Murder of Bishops,* ed. Natalie Fryde and Dirk Reitz (Göttingen: Vandenhoeck and Ruprecht, 2003), 37–50. In the *Historiae,* Gregory depicted Praetextatus as a martyr, issuing a prophetic deathbed utterance by which readers were to understand the author's opinion that Fredegund's soul was doomed; Jones, "Death and Afterlife in the Pages of Gregory of Tours" (forthcoming).
13. Greg. Tur., *Hist.* 6.24 (*MGH*, SRM 1.1, 291–92).
14. *Contra* Thorpe, *Gregory of Tours, History of the Franks,* 352, who translated: "Count (sic) Guntram Boso arrested Bishop Theodore and threw him into prison for doing this ... "
15. Greg. Tur., *Hist.* 5.27 (*MGH*, SRM 1.1, 233). For other powerful characters held *in custodia:* Bishop Theodore of Marseilles (again) and Epiphanius of Fréjus (in 582): Greg. Tur., *Hist.* 6.24; Bishop Theodore (yet again, in 585): *Hist.* 8.12; Bishop Egidius of Reims: *Hist.* 10.19; an abbot of Cahors: *Hist.* 7.30; Merovech, son of Chilperic: *Hist.* 5.14; Clovis, son of Chilperic: *Hist.* 5.39; Swabian envoys: *Hist.* 5.41; Hermangild, son of King Leuvigild: *Hist.* 6.40; Gundovald, pretender: *Hist.* 7.30; Priscus, a wealthy Jew: *Hist.* 6.17.

sub custodia.[16] Only rarely does one witness a powerful figure being incarcerated; Gregory's entire corpus includes only four instances, and only one happened as recently as his episcopacy. The only case involving imprisonment of a high ecclesiastic is that of the archdeacon Vigilius of Marseilles, whom the Governor of Provence Albinus accused of theft around 572. Albinus heavy-handedly dragged Vigilius from church during mass on Christmas day, pummeled him, and placed him in what Gregory referred to as *custodia carcerali*.[17] This strange terminology seems to indicate confinement in a prison. Of course, there was nothing at all normative about Albinus's treatment of the archdeacon. Perhaps the author expected readers to be offended as much by mention of the cleric's incarceration as by his beating and forced dismissal during performance of the holy office. Not only did Gregory depict the entire city populace in a state of dismay, but he concluded the anecdote by describing how King Sigibert, too, expressed contempt for his own agent's behavior and ordered that Albinus pay fourfold what he had fined the cleric. One secular magnate whom Gregory depicted going to jail was none other than the bishop's personal foe, the *comes* Leudast. In 580, the count with rebellious clerics at Tours failed to convince King Chilperic that Gregory had slandered Queen Fredegund, and eventually that same charge fell back upon him. Chilperic dismissed Leudast from office and had him punched, kicked, loaded with chains, and tossed *in carcerem*.[18] Leudast left the jail after pinning the rumor's origin on a sub-deacon named Riculf. The king then had this man chained, brutally tortured, and *custodiae deputatur*.[19] Here there is no mention of imprisonment for the cleric, even though he had conspired to remove a bishop from his see. Perhaps Gregory, who saw to it that Riculf's life was spared, also was able to determine he be detained in a church instead of a prison. If he did do this, it probably owed less to any pity for the offending

16. *Vita Rusticulae* 11 (*MGH*, SRM 4, 345).
17. Greg. Tur., *Hist.* 4.43 (*MGH*, SRM 1.1, 178).
18. Greg. Tur., *Hist.* 5.47 (*MGH*, SRM 1.1, 257). Gregory was so enamored with the notion of Leudast's being imprisoned that he repeated the tale elsewhere; *Hist.* 5.49.
19. Greg. Tur., *Hist.* 5.49 (*MGH*, SRM 1.1, 259): "Ad ille iterum vinctus, relaxato Leudaste, custodiae deputatur ..." Thorpe, *Gregory of Tours, History of the Franks*, 317, again misleadingly translates "... Riculf the subdeacon was loaded with chains and thrown into prison in [Leudast's] place."

sub-deacon than to the bishop's general disdain for any cleric's having to endure detention in the secular judicial system.[20] Otherwise, the only other secular magnates whom Gregory depicted in jail were two prisoners of war awaiting execution.[21] But these figures are more rightly termed *captivi*, not inmates. Thus, while incarceration of influential secular figures probably happened more frequently than did imprisonment of clerics, instances of both likely were exceptional.

The *carceres* of Gaul were not intended to hold powerful persons, but rather non-elites. Whenever Gregory mentioned prisons, he usually did not remark about the social station of the people held within. Instead he addressed most *incarcerati* in the same generally nondescript manner that he used to refer to other people of low rank. Thus the bishop gave no further details about the *quattuor vincti in carcere* at Tours in 577,[22] or the *culpabiles quosdam urbis Turonicae* confined in a *carcerali ergastulo* in 592,[23] or the *homines qui carceris vinculis tenebantur* arrested in the same year.[24] Whenever Gregory did include specifics about a lowly prisoner, it usually involved a character with a personal connection to the author. For example, he related that during his trial in 580, a loyal client, the carpenter Modestus, was apprehended, tortured, beaten, and loaded in chains.[25] He then was jailed *inter duos custodes catenis et cippo teneretur vinctus*.[26] Also attesting to the low social status of prisoners was

20. Gregory did show pity for the principal cleric involved in the conspiracy, the archdeacon and priest Riculf, by seeing that that culprit was punished by being placed into a monastery, rather than allowing him to fall under secular jurisdiction. The archdeacon Riculf is not to be confused with the sub-deacon Riculf. It is the senior Riculf who apparently expected to succeed Eufronius as bishop of Tours in 573. His willingness to participate in Leudast's plot reveals how he still anticipated becoming bishop a full seven years later. After Gregory returned from his trial at Berny and relegated the senior Riculf to becoming a mere monk, the latter fled his detention and joined Bishop Felix at Nantes; Greg. Tur., *Hist.* 5.49.

21. King Chlodomer in 523 imprisoned the Burgundian ruler Sigismund before executing the king and his family; Greg. Tur., *Hist.* 3.6, 5.18. Count Chanao of Brittany killed three brothers and captured a fourth, Count Macliaw. The latter was placed in prison to await execution, but Bishop Felix of Nantes secured his release; Greg. Tur., *Hist.* 4.4.

22. Greg. Tur., *VM* 2.35 (*MGH*, SRM 1.2, 172).

23. Greg. Tur., *VM* 4.39 (*MGH*, SRM 1.2, 209).

24. Greg. Tur., *VM* 4.41 (*MGH*, SRM 1.2, 210).

25. This arrest also resulted from an accusation by Leudast. Gregory's loyal archdeacon Plato also was arrested on this occasion and personally taken by the *comes* to Chilperic's court.

26. Greg. Tur., *Hist.* 5.49 (*MGH*, SRM 1.1, 260). A slave arrested by Count Becco and *vinctum in carcere* was a client of Saint Julian's church at Brioude, which Gregory's family controlled; Greg. Tur., *VJ* 16 (*MGH*, SRM 1.2, 121).

the continued interchangeability in the sources of the word *carcer* with *ergastulum* (slave-prison).[27]

If social status were a principal criterion that determined whether a person could be subject to incarceration, there were several reasons why one might end up in jail in the first place. Prisons provided for detention of accused and convicted people, and they served as a *de facto* brand of punishment. Arrest and imprisonment of accused people was the purview of both secular officials and private accusers.[28] Traditionally, a plaintiff could appeal to a local municipal authority, who could arrest an accused person.[29] King Chilperic in 580 sent agents whom Gregory termed *regales pueri* to apprehend the alleged slanderer Leudast.[30] But in Barbarian Gaul, it likely more commonly fell upon an offended person's kin to round up suspects.[31] For example, rural inhabitants of the Touraine in 591 who had been robbed bound a suspect with a rope and personally dragged him to Tours for incarceration.[32] Alongside accused persons, convicted felons also were detained in prisons to await punishment. Gregory imagined that Saint Martin himself once endured a stay in prison so that he might free people who were awaiting execution.[33]

Another category of inmates was people being held in prison as a form of punishment. Traditionally, Roman law opposed the use of jails for this purpose.[34] The jurist Ulpian had stated succinctly, *carcer enim ad continendos homines, non ad puniendos haberi debet.*[35] Among later legal compendiums, neither the Theodosian Code, nor *Liber Constitutionum*, nor *Pactus legis Salicae* prescribed imprisonment as punishment. Indeed, the Salic code and Merovingian capitularies do not even mention prisoners or prisons as a feature of criminal justice. Nevertheless, narrative sources reveal that incarceration remained a viable means to penalize

27. Greg. Tur., *VM* 4.39; Ven. Fort., *VG* 30, 67.
28. For prisons as detention centers, see *CTh* 9.2.1–6 and 9.3.1–7.
29. Arrest by local officials: *CTh* 9.2.5 (a. 409); and see Jones, *Later Roman Empire*, 1: 521.
30. Greg. Tur., *Hist.* 5.49.
31. See Liebeschuetz, "Violence in the Barbarian Successor Kingdoms," 39.
32. Greg. Tur., *VM* 4.35.
33. Greg. Tur., *Hist.* 5.18. See also Greg. Tur., *VP* 8.7.
34. Norman, ed. and trans., *Libanius, Orationes*, 2: 157.
35. *Digesta* 48.19.8.9 (Mommsen et al., 4: 847).

in Gaul. According to Gregory, Count Leudast once instigated the wrongful imprisonment of a freeborn Parisian visiting Tours by accusing him of being a fugitive slave. Rather than holding the boy in a *carcer*, the count kept him chained and guarded at his own domicile.[36] Gregory did not explain Leudast's motives for seizing this young man, who was by occupation a tailor. Perhaps the arrest of the pauper represents a strategy on the part of the bellicose count to threaten imprisonment and thereby acquire clients from the ranks of the socially disadvantaged. One ruse among the powerful for which Gregory did attest was the use of incarceration to bleed money from impoverished victims. For example, a creditor at Tours forced a man unable to pay off a debt to be confined in prison. He apparently intended to keep the debtor jailed until he paid him back or, the more likely scenario, until he died: "When the creditor realized that he would be able to extort nothing further … he tightened the man's chains even more and offered him neither food or drink, saying: 'I shall starve you making of your countenance a lesson for everyone, until all is returned to me.'"[37] This creditor's expectation that the victim's public humiliation would prove a frightening deterrent for other delinquent debtors coincides with the sources' consistent depictions of the harsh environment of prisons. Inmates endured insufferable conditions including perpetual darkness, filth, and harsh bodily restraint in the form of stocks, chains, and fetters that were applied to hands, legs, and even necks.[38] Thus, debtors, slaves, and paupers – almost uniformly originating from the more humble social ranks, confined and encumbered with chains and manacles; for a multiplicity of reasons prisoners recognizably counted among the lowliest disadvantaged persons of Barbarian Gaul.

A modern sociologist might characterize Gaul's inmates as including elements of both the conjunctural poor (e.g., an able-bodied pauper nabbed while attempting to steal a precious ornament from a

---

36. Greg. Tur., *VM* 2.59. For other arrests Gregory thought wrongful, see *VM* 3.53, *VJ* 16.
37. Greg. Tur., *VM* 3.47 (*MGH*, SRM 1.2, 193): "Denique, cum videret creditor, quod ei nihil extorqueri possit … artius eum in vincula constringit, negatoque cibo potuque, dicebat: 'Ego te faciam ad omnium documentum fame tabescere, donec omnia reddas'."
38. Darkness: Greg. Tur., *Hist.* 7.15; filth: Greg. Tur., *Hist.* 6.36; restraints: Greg. Tur., *VM* 2.35, 3.41, 4.16, *VP* 7.3, 8.6, 8.7, 8.10, *GC* 65, 86.

church) and the structural poor (e.g., a beggar caught taking from the poor box). From the perspective of elite Gallic ecclesiastical authors, however, prisoners should be defined by their miseries and associated with other unfortunates such as the destitute and chronically ill. An inscription from the walls of the church of Saint Martin at Tours penned by Paulinus of Périgueux thus reads: "[Many] rejoice in [Saint Martin's] gift: the blind, the lame, the poor, the possessed, the distressed, the sick, the disabled, the oppressed, *the imprisoned*, the grieving, the needy."[39] In a similar vein, writers interchanged the words *culpabiles* and *miseri*. Thus, on the one hand, Gregory alluded to the fetters and chains "of criminals" (*culpabilum*)" at Lyons, while, on the other, he mentioned the binding accoutrements "of the wretched" (*miserorum*) at Châlons-sur-Marne and Soissons.[40] Prisoners not only endured miserable conditions, but they were counted among other *miserabiles*. By advancing this discourse of wretchedness and encouraging a perception of inmates as *miseri*, ecclesiastics intended their communities to think of prisoners' torments in the same way that they viewed the sufferings of ill and disabled persons – as salient symptoms of sinfulness.

CRIME AND SIN

According to a Gallic ecclesiastical mindset, misfortunes were to be perceived as manifestations of sin.[41] People should view imprisonment, like death and illness, as a visible result of some misdeed. Hagiographers especially promoted such notions. In Gregory's world, crime (*scelus*) and sin (*peccatum*) could be interchangeable. For example, Gregory surmised that a man with a "wicked mind" (*iniqua mente*) attempted to steal a jeweled cross from the church of Saint Julian of Brioude because "he was being compelled by a Satanic agent" (*a satellite Satanan inpellebatur*).[42]

---

39. Edmond Le Blant, ed., *Inscriptions chrétiennes de la Gaule antérieures au VIIIe siècle* (Paris: L'imprimerie imperiale, 1856), v. 1, no. 176; "... quo munere gaudent; caecus, clodus, inops, furiosus, anxius, aeger; debilis, oppressus, captivus, maestus, egenus." Trans. by Van Dam, *Saints and their Miracles*, 314, with my italics.

40. Greg. Tur., *VP* 8.6, *GC* 65, *GC* 93 (*MGH*, SRM 1.2, 247, 336, 357).

41. Van Dam, *Saints and their Miracles*, 87.

42. Greg. Tur., *VJ* 20 (*MGH*, SRM 1.2, 123).

Furthermore, the thief fell asleep because he was "weighed down by sin" (*conpraessus peccati sopore*).[43] Similarly, when Sisulfus, the pauper-turned-preacher of the previous chapter, awoke from a nap to find his hands painfully disabled, he informed Saint Martin that he did not know "what crime" (*quid sceleris* instead of *quid peccati*) he had committed to cause the injury.[44] According to this mode of thinking in which sin and crime were nearly synonymous, two possible results that wrongdoers might expect after committing a misdeed were illness and even death. Thus Gregory wrote that a chronic drinker from Bayeux who continued "to sin" (*peccatis facientibus*) by getting drunk on wine died.[45] Likewise, Sisulfus told Gregory that Saint Martin had admonished him to "swiftly announce that people reform, lest they cruelly *perish* as a result of their own *crime*" (*in scelere suo*).[46] Gregory and others also believed sinful, criminal activity could result in illness. As has been seen, one kind of illicit activity that clerics insisted was a cause of physical duress was offending sacred time by performing agricultural chores on Sundays and other holy days. Desperate laborers who acted against canon and secular laws forbidding this behavior could become convinced that they were committing sin and that they might deserve punishment. Thus, according to Gregory, when a farmer from Bourges named Leodulfus loaded hay on a Sunday, his eyes suddenly shut and he became blind.[47] Similarly, the face of a woman became swollen and blistered because she insisted on hoeing weeds during the festival of Saint John the Baptist.[48]

Ecclesiastics also linked notions of imprisonment and illness. Metaphorical language, then as now, sometimes connected physical affliction with binding and incarceration.[49] For example, Gregory related that Leudard, the slave of a deacon at Nantes, "had been bound

---

43. Greg. Tur., *VJ* 20 (*MGH*, SRM 1.2, 123).

44. Greg. Tur., *VM* 2.40 (*MGH*, SRM 1.2, 173).

45. Greg. Tur., *VM* 2.53 (*MGH*, SRM 1.2, 177).

46. Greg. Tur., *VM* 2.40 (*MGH*, SRM 1.2, 173–74): "Et ideo adnuntia velociter, ut emendent, ne crudeliter in scelere suo depereant.

47. Greg. Tur., *VM* 4.45.

48. Greg. Tur., *VM* 2.57. On illnesses caused by infringement of Christian liturgical time, see Van Dam, *Saints and their Miracles*, 87–88.

49. Van Dam, *Saints and their Miracles*, 99.

by the chain of blindness" (*caecitatis fuisset catena constrictus*).[50] This verbal connectivity allowed people to perceive imprisonment, like illness, as a possible right result of some misdeed. Thus, after King Guntram's hunting horn was stolen, many men were placed in chains.[51] After a man took the law in his own hands by killing his brother's murderer, a judge imprisoned him.[52] After someone stole a hawk belonging to Count Becco, the count imprisoned a servant attached to the church of Saint Julian.[53] Of course, regarding crime and arrest, the causal relationship is egregiously obvious; when a crime occurred, suspects would be rounded up and imprisoned. But for Gregory, other hagiographers, and presumably many listeners and readers, imprisonment of malefactors confirmed their own theory of causation: that crime, equaling sin, necessarily resulted in a person's being reduced to some wretched state. The direct result of a misdeed could be imprisonment, but could just as easily be illness or death. Furthermore, incarceration, like illness and death, could result from a sin caused not by the actual culprit, or sinner, but by another. For example, about a child from Bourges born blind and terribly crippled, Gregory suspected that the boy's condition resulted not from his own wrongdoing, but because, as his mother confessed, the parents had offended sacred time by conceiving the youth on the night before a Sunday.[54] Similarly, a man brought to Tours for imprisonment was incarcerated, not because he had committed an offense but rather "through the calumny of evil [accusers]."[55] For Gregory and other ecclesiastics, along with whomever they could convince, sin caused misfortune regardless of who was responsible. Furthermore, regardless of whether one was at fault or not, belief that sin caused one's wretched condition could instill in ill, disabled, and incarcerated persons some sense of culpability. For example, recall again how Sisulfus, when he incurred his disability, initially felt guilty, wondering *quid sceleris* he

50. Greg. Tur., *VM* 4.20 (*MGH*, SRM 1.2, 204–05).
51. Greg. Tur., *GC* 86.
52. Greg. Tur., *VP* 8.7.
53. Greg. Tur., *VJ* 16.
54. Greg. Tur., *VM* 2.24.
55. Greg. Tur., *VM* 4.35 (*MGH*, SRM 1.2, 208): "per calumnias malorum."

had committed to cause the condition. Similarly, when a merchant standing before the altar of Saint Hilary of Poitiers saw that his gift was miraculously rejected, he became ridden with guilt because he realized his sin – or as Venantius Fortunatus tellingly referred to it, *crimen* – was that he secretly had not wanted to make the offering.[56] Such guilt could be compounded by a perception that persons enduring adverse situations were burdens, sometimes literally, upon their community.[57] For example, Gregory and Venantius often pointed out how blind, paralyzed, and other disabled persons had to be led about or carried by others.[58] People might perceive these "sinners" as transgressors against their community. Of course, in the case of prisoners, the transgressions in question were as obvious as the crimes for which they had been arrested. Feelings of culpability would have been more intense for those who actually committed misdeeds. Given this overwhelming sense of guilt, any solution to the dilemmas of ill or imprisoned *miserabiles* would not simply disappear with a mere remission of disease or, in the case of prisoners, release from jail. Rather, resolution needed to entail "confession, judgment, forgiveness and reconciliation."[59] What inmates needed along with other *miserabiles* was forgiveness from, and reintegration within, their communities.

There were, of course, important differences between illness and imprisonment, one being the nature of the sin that caused them. While illness usually was thought to be the "public manifestation" of a "hidden or private" misdeed, imprisonment was the result of a public sin – that is, a crime.[60] Furthermore, whereas illness demanded the attention of a healer, an injurious criminal action necessitated the regard of a judicial authority. Complementing the medical needs of ill people, local ecclesiastics proclaimed that saints were physicians.[61] Likewise, corresponding to the needs of prisoners, clerics insisted that saints were judicially

---

56. Ven. Fort., *Vita Hilarii* 11 (*MGH*, AA 4.2, 10): "inmensi pudoris reatu perculsus."
57. Van Dam, *Saints and their Miracles*, 89.
58. E.g., Greg. Tur., *VM* 1.39, 2.5, 2.11, 3.6, 3.39; Ven. Fort., *Vita Germani* 37, 38, *Vita Hilarii* 10.
59. Van Dam, *Saints and their Miracles*, 89.
60. Ibid.
61. Ibid., 95; and see the section on Physicians, Bishops, and Saints in Chapter Seven.

competent. Prisoners in Gaul fell under the jurisdiction of counts and their subordinates, or "judges" (*iudices*), as hagiographers often ambiguously identified them. Therefore, if saints were going to have jurisdiction over prisoners, then they too would have to be judges, or at least mediators like their living counterparts, the bishops.[62] Thus, Fortunatus described Saint Hilary of Poitiers as an "incorruptible mediator" (*incorruptibilis arbiter*) capable of conducting a "judicial examination" (*examinatio iudicii*).[63] Likewise, Gregory depicted a priest threatening that if a thief stole from the shrine of Saint Nazarius, the martyr would become "a judge following his trail" (*de vestigio iudex*).[64] Similarly, Gregory portrayed Saint Julian of Brioude acting tantamount to a secular judicial official by applying torture, forcing confession, and passing sentence upon a thieving deacon. Gregory wrote: "... when the flames of judgment were applied to his soul [the deacon] confessed his crimes."[65] Gregory concluded that Julian's supernatural *iudicium* sentenced the deacon to hell. One quasi-judicial function that hagiographers commonly ascribed to saints was punishing perjurers.[66] Another was liberating incarcerated persons from bondage. For example, Gregory promoted the judicial competency of Saint Martin by publishing the following brief episode: "A judge determined to lock up some guilty men in the prison in the city of Tours. The prisoners were lamenting, when the blessed confessor's power manifested breaking the captives' chains asunder and permitting them freely to enter the basilica."[67]

Miraculous release of prisoners is a hagiographical *topos* traceable back to biblical and apocryphal works.[68] A biblical example from the *Book of Acts* famously relates how an angel liberated the Apostle Peter from a

62. Edward James, "*Beati pacifici*: Bishops and the Law in Sixth-Century Gaul," in *Disputes and Settlements: Law and Human Relations in the West*, ed. J. A. Bossy (Cambridge: Cambridge University Press, 1983), 25–32; Mitchell, "Saints and Public Christianity," 80–81.

63. Ven. Fort., *Vita Hilarii* 11 (*MGH*, AA 4.2, 10).

64. Greg. Tur., *GM* 60 (*MGH*, SRM 1.2, 79).

65. Greg. Tur., *VJ* 17 (*MGH*, SRM 1.2, 122): "... admotis animae iudicii facibus, crimina confitetur."

66. Greg. Tur., *VJ* 19, 40; *GM* 20, 53, 58; *GC* 93; *VP* 8.9; *Hist.* 8.16, 8.40.

67. Greg. Tur., *VM* 4.39 (*MGH*, SRM 1.2, 209): "... culpabiles quosdam urbis Turonicae iudicis sententia carcerali ergastulo conclusisset, lamentantibus vinctis, virtus beati confessoris apparuit, quae, disruptis vinculis compeditorum, liberos in basilicam abire permisit."

68. For extensive lists of miraculous prison releases and related miracles in Merovingian sources, see Graus, "Die Gewalt bei Anfängen des Feudalismus," 106–56. On Venantius's propagandistic intent

jail cell.[69] Similarly, the apocryphal *Acts of Pilate* contain the story of an angel who lifted the walls of a prison to rescue Joseph of Arimathea.[70] The impact that these ancient tales made upon Gallic hagiographers is attested by Gregory's inclusion of the latter story as an early anecdote of the *Historiae*.[71] Authors of Gallic *Lives* early attributed to their holy heroes the ability to free prisoners. Sulpicius Severus wrote that Saint Martin, while alive, once lay outside the house of a count and by force of will caused him to release many inmates.[72] Similarly, Constantius of Lyons related how Saint Germanus of Auxerre miraculously caused the gate of a jail at Ravenna to open and the chains and fetters of prisoners to fall away, resulting in their liberation.[73] Gregory and Venantius would have been well aware of this trope when they depicted saintly prison releases in their texts. But the accounts of miraculous liberation that Gregory described during his episcopacy, particularly those attributed to Saints Julian and Martin, which the author very likely lifted from miracle registers at these saints' shrines, should not be dismissed as mere literary fabrications of activities the author imagined holy people would have performed.[74] Rather, one should consider how Gregory's stories might communicate in a stylized fashion a ritualized behavior being performed by people in his community attempting to manage their difficult circumstances. By agreeing to accept their bishop's explanation that incarceration was the result of sinfulness, prisoners dared to hope for the intervention of a holy mediator. Meanwhile, ecclesiastics intent upon promoting saints as powerful patrons obliged them. Let us now examine in detail the ritual of miraculous release whereby some prisoners might be liberated from bondage and reintegrated into communities.

for writing tales of miraculous release of prisoners, see Collins, "Observations on the Form, Language, and Public of the Prose Biographies of Venantius," 116–18.

69. Acts 12: 6–11. See also Acts 16: 25–34.
70. *Gesta Piloti* 12–13.
71. Greg. Tur., *Hist.* 1.21.
72. Sulp. Sev., *Dialogi* 3.4 (*CSEL* 1, 201–02).
73. Constantius of Lyons, *Vita Germani* 36 (*MGH*, SRM 7, 277).
74. On miracle registers at the churches of Saints Julian and Martin, see Wood, *Gregory of Tours*, 29; and Shanzer, "So Many Saints – So Little Time," 25–27.

THE RITUAL OF MIRACULOUS RELEASE OF PRISONERS

Since crime and imprisonment affected an entire community, prisoners and convicts needed not only to be released but reunited with neighbors. Reintegration required the participation of other members of the community besides inmates, including cooperative patrons and a welcoming public. Because crimes and resultant incarceration were public, the process by which prisoners were to be released should be a public ritual.[75] The ritual of miraculous release as it played out in Gaul involved up to three stages: the liberation itself, sanctuary, and pardon. The actual release of prisoners and liberation of convicts involved specific places and times. The stage of sanctuary usually routed incarcerated persons to saints' tombs. The final stage of the process secured pardon from secular judges.

The first stage of ritual release logically occurred where confined and convicted people were situated, most often at prisons but sometimes at a gallows or church. A *carcer* was the usual site where, authors asserted, saints affected miraculous liberation. For example, Gregory described at length how Saint Nicetius of Lyons (d. 573) once rescued a man who avenged the death of a brother who had been killed during a riot, only to be imprisoned by a judge:

> The prisoner invoked the names of several saints to excite their compassion, and then turned as it were to his own man of God, and said "I have heard tell of you, holy Nicetius, that you are powerful in works of mercy and generous in the freeing of piteous captives. I beg you now to deign to visit me with that excellent kindness by which you have so often shone in the deliverance of others who are in chains." Shortly afterwards, as he slept, the blessed man appeared to him, and said, "Who are you, who call the name of Nicetius? And how do you know who he was, since you do not cease to pray to him?" Then the man told him all about his case, and added, "Have pity on me, I beg you, if you are the man of God whom I invoke."

75. See Van Dam, *Saints and their Miracles*, 89.

The saint said to him, "Rise up, in the name of Christ, and walk free: you will not be restrained by anyone." He woke up, and was full of astonishment at seeing his chains shattered and the beam broken, and immediately, without being stopped by anyone, he went undaunted to the tomb of the saint.[76]

This anecdote evidences how the ritual of miraculous release might begin with a vocal appeal on the part of prisoners for a saint to aid their cause, a practice that has been characterized as a mix between "name-magic" and prayer.[77] If one considers this action beyond its prayerful component, an astute inmate cognizant of a local ecclesiastical administration's effort to promote a particular saint could know to what entity one should appeal. Indeed, at the time when this release occurred, between Nicetius's death in 573 and Gregory's writing about it, an effort was underway to establish that saint's cult.[78] In fact, as has been mentioned, the effort of Gregory's family to promote Nicetius's sanctity was being undermined by that bishop's successor, Priscus, and this factionalism reportedly involved bloodshed.[79] I suspect that the unrest that precipitated this man's arrest pertained to the feud between Lyons' ecclesiastical factions. Gregory wrote that the prisoner slew the murderer of his brother three days after the riot. He also wrote that the inmate appealed to "as it were his own man of God" (*quasi ad sanctum Dei propriae*), Nicetius. Was this prisoner a loyal supporter of Nicetius's faction,

76. Greg. Tur., *VP* 8.7 (*MGH*, SRM 1.2, 247): "... multorum sanctorum nominibus invocatis, misericordiam precaretur, quasi ad sanctum Dei propriae conversus, ait: 'Audivi de te, sancte Niceti, quod sis potens in opere misericordiae ac pius in conpeditorum flentium absolutione. Deprecor nunc, ut me illa supereminenti pietate visitare digneris, quae in reliquorum absolutione vinctorum saepius claruisti.' Et post paululum obdormiens, apparuit ei vir beatus, dicens: 'Quis es tu, qui nomen Niceti invocas? Aut unde nosti, quis fuerit, quod eum obsecrare non desinis?' At ille causam delicti ex ordine reserans, adiecit: 'Miserere, quaeso, mihi, si tu es vir Dei quem invoco.' Cui sanctus ait: 'Surge in nomine Christi et ambula liber; a nullo enim conpraehenderis.' At ille in hac expergefactus voce, se absolutum, catenis comminutis confractaque trabe, miratur. Nec mortaus, nemine retenente, usque ad eius sepulchrum perrixit intrepidus." Trans. by James, *Gregory of Tours, Life of the Fathers*, 58.
77. Giselle de Nie, *Views from a Many-Windowed Tower: Studies of Imagination in the Works of Gregory of Tours* (Amsterdam: Rodopi, 1987), 259. Other invocations by prisoners and convicts: Greg. Tur., *VM* 1.11, 21, 23, 2.35; 3.47, 53, 4.16; *VP* 7.3, 4; *Hist*. 5.49; *GC* 99.
78. In addition to Gregory's brief *Vita Nicetii* in the *De Vita Patrum*, there already was published an anonymous *Vita S. Nicetii* with which Gregory was familiar; Greg. Tur., *VP* 8, *praef.*
79. On Priscus's murderous ways, and his jealousy toward those who remained loyal to Saint Nicetius, see Greg. Tur., *Hist*. 4.36.

perhaps even a cleric? If so, while the judge understandably would have made the arrest in an effort to reestablish public order, besides kin it would have been Nicetius's heirs and clerics loyal to the bishop's memory who would have most wanted the prisoner to be liberated.[80] Perhaps the prisoner's release somehow enabled both factions to agree to suspend the local disturbance for the time being.

Beyond invoking a saint's name and expressing a desire to flee the *carcer*, prisoners played an essentially passive role in the ritual of miraculous release. The actual liberation with all that it encompassed – for example, in hagiographical terms, bursting gates and shattering chains and fetters – necessarily involved clerical intervention. Thus it is ecclesiastics who would have been the operative agents in 591 when Saint Martin freed several people from a seemingly impregnable prison at Reims. Gregory explained:

> I had occasion to visit the presence of King Childebert. During my journey I approached on a road through a district [in the territory] of Rheims and [there] met a man. In his own account he [told] me that the prison in Rheims in which this man's slave was being held with other captives had been opened by Martin's power, and that the captives had been released from prison and departed as free men. ...But the bishop's power moved these stones, as the man claimed in his account. He demolished the platform, broke the chains, and opened the stocks that held the captives' feet; since the door had not been opened he then lifted the men in the air, and brought them outside through the open roof. He said: "I am Martin, a soldier of Christ and your liberator. Depart in peace and leave with your freedom!"[81]

80. Furthermore on Nicetius's reputation for releasing prisoners, see Greg. Tur., *VP* 8.10.
81. Greg. Tur., *VM* 4.26 (*MGH*, SRM 1.2, 205–06): "Fuerat nobis causa quaedam Childeberthi regis adire praesentiam. Pergentibus quoque nobis, iter per pagum Remensem adgressi sumus, repperimusque hominem quendam, qui nobis relatu suo, patefactum carcerem huius urbis, in quo inter reliquos vinctos huius famulus tenebatur, Martini virtute fuisse, vinctosque ab ergastulo absolutos liberos abscessisse. ... sed virtus antistitis, ut ipse relator asseruit, lapides dimovet, disicit pulpita, catenas confregit et trabem, quae vinctorum coartabat pedes, aperuit ac, nec reserato ostio, homines per aera sublevatos foris tecto patente produxit, dicens: 'Ego sum Martinus, miles Christi, absolutor vester. Abscedite cum pace et abite securi!'" Trans. by Van Dam, *Saints and their Miracles*, 295.

Gregory concluded this anecdote by relating how some of these prisoners afterward appeared before King Childebert II, who in turn relieved them of the judicial arbitration fee. It has been suggested regarding this incident that friends of the inmates likely opened up the prison's roof, but this could hardly have been so.[82] First, such a scenario implies that the king would have permitted a flagrant affront to royal justice – a prison break – to go unpunished, and then he would have rewarded it by dismissing the culprits' fees. But Merovingian rulers were neither that naïve nor forgiving. Second, this theory does not account for any role played by the prison release's principal beneficiaries, ecclesiastics promoting the cult of Saint Martin. According to Gregory, this release happened as the 4 July festival of Saint Martin was approaching. Furthermore, the very person who was most interested in propagating Martin's cult and who ultimately determined whether an event should be interpreted as a miracle performed by that holy person – Gregory himself – was in the vicinity. Therefore, in this instance, as in other cases of miraculous release, one must realize the instigation of prominent clerics. Most of Saint Martin's miraculous releases happened at Tours, where Gregory would have condoned, and occasionally personally supervised, such efforts. Because this liberation happened near Reims during one of Gregory's visits to the Austrasian court, it likely involved the instigation of that city's pontiff. Bishop Romulfus of Reims, the son of Venantius's patron and friend Duke Lupus, had ascended the cathedra a year prior to this miracle. Presumably Romulfus shared his father and Gregory's partisan support for Childebert II and Brunhild. Romulfus's order to liberate prisoners in the name of Saint Martin would have constituted a fitting welcome for a visiting Austrasian ally, the Bishop of Tours. As for the manual aspect of the prison release, one should suspect the involvement of the bishop's retinue. Lesser clerics such as doorkeepers (*ostiarii*) and gravediggers (*fossores*), and the registered poor (*matricularii*), about whom there will be much to say in the next chapter, were ever at the ready to act in the interests of their bishop and patron saint. Thus, ecclesiastics

---

82. De Nie, *Views from a Many-Windowed Tower*, 258–59.

who were promoting a saint, not prisoners' friends, caused the ritual of miraculous release from Gaul's *carceres*.[83]

Beyond jail, another venue where ritual liberation might occur was at a gallows.[84] For example, Gregory wrote that a priest once prayed to the martyr Quintinus to forgive a horse thief: "While the priest offered this prayer with tears, the chains of the gallows were broken, and the accused man fell to the ground."[85] The presence of the priest in this passage again reminds us that it was concerned local clerics who were most capable of securing criminals' release. Another of Gregory's tales of a person's being freed from a noose seems scarcely miraculous. As the criminal was hanging, an abbot traveled about three miles there and back to gain the permission of a count to remove the fellow from the gallows. The miracle lay in the criminal's surviving for the duration.[86] Otherwise, prisoners sometimes were liberated near the church of the very saint to whom credit for the miracle was intended. For example, Gregory reported that in 584, a girl who had been wrongfully enslaved refused to work, and so she was chained and fettered. When she appealed to Saint Martin, the stocks that held her feet broke, and she ran to the saint's basilica still draped in chains: "But just as her feet touched the holy threshold, immediately the chains broke and fell from her neck. Thus she was provided with both safety and liberty."[87] Similarly, in 591/92, while men were directing a captive toward a *carcer* at Tours, the bonds allegedly loosened before the church of Saint Peter, but the guards made them tighter. Then, as soon as the prisoner saw the church of Saint Martin, the

---

83. Other miraculous liberations of inmates: Greg. Tur., *VM* 1.11, 2.35, 3.47, 4.39, 4.41; *VP* 7.3, 8.7; *Hist.* 5.8, 5.49, 8.33, 10.6; Ven. Fort., *Vita Albini* 16; *Vita Radegundis* 11; *Vita Germani* 30, 61, 66, 67.

84. See Graus, "Die Gewalt bei Anfängen des Feudalismus," 125–34, who does not entertain the possibility of actual events underlying some of these tales.

85. Greg. Tur., *GM* 72 (*MGH*, SRM 1.2, 87): "Haec sacerdote cum lacrimis deprecante, disruptis vinculis patibuli, reus ad terram ruit." Other releases of convicts from gallows: Greg. Tur., *VM* 1.11, 3.53 (two incidents); *Hist.* 6.8; *CG* 99.

86. Greg. Tur., *VM* 3.53. Gregory explained, however, that this liberation was a second attempt. In the previous effort to hang the criminal, the rope broke, but the men simply suspended him again. For more ascetics releasing criminals from gallows: Greg. Tur., *VM* 1.11 (nun); *Hist.* 6.8 (recluse and monk); *CG* 99 (abbot and monk).

87. Greg. Tur., *VM* 3.41 (*MGH*, SRM 1.2, 192): "Verum ubi primum pedes eius sacra limina contigerunt, statim confractae catenae caeciderunt a collo eius, et sic incolomitate pariter libertateque donata est."

chains fell completely from his hands.[88] Gregory wrote that he himself witnessed this miracle. His presence at the scene again enables one to appreciate the bishop's involvement.

As with the occurrence of other *virtutes*, the miraculous release of prisoners often happened at holy times, especially during saints' festivals. Gregory detailed several instances when prisoners enjoyed liberation during annual festivities in honor of Martin, one on 4 July and the other on 11 November (the saint's death day). For example, he recorded that a girl prevented from attending the saint's festival on 11 November 584 escaped her bonds, [89] while the aforementioned rescue of prisoners at Reims occurred four days before the 4 July festival.[90] Sometimes prisoners were liberated a few days after Martin's festival. Examples include a release three days after 4 July 577,[91] one a few days after 4 July 592,[92] and another a few days after 11 November of the same year.[93] In none of the last three anecdotes did Gregory indicate why the inmates had been imprisoned. Perhaps they were rambunctious people who had imbibed overly much during celebrations of the saint, or maybe they were petty thieves. These malefactors could have been released, ritually and publicly, toward the conclusion of festivities.[94] Gregory credited Martin with liberating prisoners on other holy days, too, including Easter.[95] The frequency of miraculous release on these significant dates further substantiates the notion that this activity was occasioned according to the expectations of local ecclesiastics, not as the result of contrivance by prisoners and accomplices, and certainly not by virtue of extemporaneous shattering of faulty chains.

88. Greg. Tur., *VM* 4.35.
89. Greg. Tur., *VM* 3.41.
90. Greg. Tur., *VM* 4.26. (*MGH*, SRM 1.2, 206): "Hoc autem factum est ante quattuor festivitatis dies in anno memorati regis [Childebert II] sexto et decimo." The date was June 30, 591.
91. Greg. Tur., *VM* 2.35.
92. Greg. Tur., *VM* 4.39.
93. Greg. Tur., *VM* 4.41.
94. Nearly all criminals rescued from gallows in Gregory's pages were convicted thieves; Greg. Tur., *VM* 1.21, 3.53; *Hist.* 6.8; *GC* 99; *GM* 72. Gregory related several miracles involving thefts during saints' festivals; e. g., theft of a horse: *VJ* 18; a jeweled cross: *VJ* 20. For drunkards at saints' festivals, see e. g., Caes. Arel. *Serm.* 225.2, 5; Hen, *Culture and Religion in Merovingian Gaul*, 245.
95. Greg. Tur., *VM* 4.16.

Other special occasions during which prominent ecclesiastics might orchestrate the ritual release of prisoners were during a saint's funeral and while transferring saints' relics. For example, the newly deceased Bishop Germanus of Paris displayed his judicial *virtus* in 576 as pallbearers carried his body past the city's *carcer*. Gregory wrote: "For as the prisoners called [the name of Saint Germanus] the body [being transferred] along the street became heavy, and when they were released, it was able to be lifted again with no sweat. Then those who had been released, now free men, followed the funeral procession all the way to the church in which [Germanus] was buried."[96] Another incident occurred after King Chararic of Galicia sent messengers to obtain relics of Martin intended for a church being built in that saint's honor. While clerics were processing and displaying these relics amid applause and the singing of Psalms, some prisoners heard the noise and called upon Saint Martin to free them. Then the guards fled, the locks of the fetters broke, and the prisoners were liberated.[97]

The last two anecdotes reveal how ecclesiastics could adapt and employ the ritual of miraculous release to promote a newly formed cult or to implant a well-established one in a new region.[98] Introduction of a novel cult necessitated memorable activities such as processions and singing, events in which the community at large would be encouraged to participate. Promoters of cults must have appreciated the impact a ritual release of prisoners could add to the pomp, and the impression it might make. Passionate invocations from inmates would intermingle with the singing. Suddenly the prisoners would rush from the lockup and join the throng. They would vociferously tout the efficacy of the saint's powers and thereby attest to the presence, or arrival, of the community's holy patron. Along these lines, one release of prisoners that Gregory would have been too

96. Greg. Tur., *Hist.* 5.8 (*MGH*, SRM 1.1, 204): "Nam carceraris adclamantibus, corpus in platea adgravatum est, solutisque eisdem, rursum sine labore levatur. Ipsi quoque, qui soluti fuerant, in obsequium funeris usque basilicam, in qua sepultus est, liberi pervenerunt."

97. Greg. Tur., *VM* 1.11. See also *VM* 3.47.

98. Popularity for Saint Martin's cult did not rest on promotion by Gregory alone. Epigraphic evidence offers a medium beyond Sulpicius's, Venantius's, and Gregory's writings, which attest to an early, widespread fondness for Martin in south-western and south-eastern Gaul, where previously it was thought the cult was unknown, and also in Spain and Italy; Handley, *Death, Society and Culture*, 139–42.

young to recollect, but which his maternal relations will have remembered because of its social significance for the family happened during the funeral of Bishop Gregorius of Langres (d. 539/40).[99] Gregorius's body was transported on a bier from Langres to Dijon, near which town the family likely owned estates and wielded considerable influence.[100] The porters reportedly made a brief stop just north of Dijon before carrying the bier through the walls to an intramural church, where the corpse was displayed several days while neighboring bishops arrived.[101] Relatives likely made the pontiff to appear in his finest episcopal apparel as his body lay publicly in the church, and perhaps even for the procession, which image would have publicized before many in the region the social significance of the aristocratic man's surviving relations, particularly his son and episcopal successor Tetricus.[102] Finally, on day five the body was processed a second time to the basilica of Saint John for burial, but not without further spectacle, as Gregory explained:

> And behold, men in prison began to cry out, addressing the body of the saint, "Have pity on us, most pious lord, so that those whom you did not free while you were on this earth, may obtain their liberty from you now that you are dead and possess the heavenly kingdom. Come to us, we implore you, and have mercy upon us." As they said these words and others like them, the body grew heavy so that it could no longer be held up, and the bearers put the bier to the ground and waited to see what the power of the holy bishop would bring about. As they waited, suddenly the doors of the prison opened, the beam which held the feet of the prisoners broke in the middle, their bonds were loosened and the chains shattered, and they came to the body of the saint with nobody to stop them.[103]

99. Greg. Tur., *VP* 7.3.
100. Wood, *Gregory of Tours*, 43; Loseby, "Gregory's Cities: Urban Functions," 243.
101. I wonder whether Gregory's rather offhanded mention of the bier's resting briefly just north of Dijon might indicate the location of a family estate.
102. On funeral processions as opportune moments for ostentatious and competitive display, see Effros, *Caring for Body and Soul*, 180–81. On literary representations of clothing the deceased, see ibid., 32–39. Effros, ibid., 33, cautions that authors were not seeking "to provide a faithful description of early medieval mortuary customs."
103. Greg. Tur., *VP* 7.3 (*MGH*, SRM 1.2, 238–39): "... et ecce vincti carceris ad beatum corpus clamare coeperunt, dicentes: 'Miserere nostril, piissime domne, ut, quos vivens in saeculo non absolvisti, vel defunctus caeleste regnum possedens digneris absolvere; visita nos, quaesumus, et Miserere nostri'.

Here, in the wake of the death of a powerful local patriarch, an aristocratic family needed to show itself as capable of continuing to act as patrons. It opted to assert its social wherewithal by enabling a group of inmates to reintegrate with the community. In addition to providing the funeral itself, Tetricus chose to produce a ritual miraculous release of prisoners to initiate the prolonged theatrics that would entail the making of Saint Gregorius of Langres.[104] Perhaps in the event of a prison release during a funeral procession, wonderment was not to be had in watching junior clerics loosen prisoners so much as in witnessing the production of the pallbearers and corpse coming to a halt before a jail, or listening to the mingling of the inmates' shouts, and perhaps the joyous shrieks of their relatives, with the clerics' chanting.

Whatever part of the initial stage of miraculous release the public might see, the ritual must have had a dramatic impact. Indeed, hagiographers indicate the intensity of the moment by relating how the spectacle intimidated any who might oppose the prisoners' release, particularly secular judicial officials and prison guards. For example, Gregory wrote that when Saint Quintinus freed a condemned person, "the judge, terrified with fear and admiring of Quintinus' divine power, did not presume to harm the man further."[105] Similarly, when prisoners at Tours appealed for Saint Martin to save them, they were freed "with the guards being terrified and turned in flight."[106] Likewise, Saint

---

Haec et alia illis clamantibus, adgravatum est corpus ita, ut eum penitus sustenere non possent. Tunc ponentes feretrum super terram, virtutem beati antestitis praestolabant. His ergo expectantibus, subito reseratis carceris ostiis, trabis illa qua vinctorum pedes coartabantur, repulsis obicibus, scinditur media, confractisque catenis, omnes pariter dissolvuntur et ad beatum corpus, nemine retenente, perveniunt." Trans. by James, *Gregory of Tours, Life of the Fathers*, 46.

104. Some time after the funeral, yet another prisoner, this one being escorted by guards along the northern approach to Dijon, called the name of Gregorius, and at the very extramural spot where the bier earlier had rested (on a family estate?) he was liberated from his bonds. After this, Bishop Tetricus enlarged the funerary basilica of Saint John by adding on an apse, and after vigils and amid singing he presided over a ceremonial translation of his father Saint Gregorius's remains to the new location. Gregory, in describing how the sarcophagus lid fell off and revealed the saint looking pristine, also mentioned here that he had been buried with his bishop's vestments; Greg. Tur., *VP* 7.4. A similar instance of theater on the occasion of a funeral happened during the procession of Nicetius of Lyons' corpse, when a blind man stopped the parade and climbed under the bier, where he miraculously regained his vision; Greg. Tur., *VP* 8.5.

105. Greg. Tur., *GM* 72 (*MGH*, SRM 1.2, 87): "Quod audiens iudex, perterritus et divinam admirans virtutem, nihil illi ultra nocere praesumpsit."

106. Greg. Tur., *VM* 1.11 (*MGH*, SRM 1.2, 212): "... exterritisque custodibus et in fugam versis."

Martin in 577 rescued four prisoners who then fled to the cathedral: "The guards were so stupefied that they did not dare reproach these men even with words; instead, following the others, they hid themselves with the prisoners in the church!"[107] The last anecdote exemplifies how clerics and prisoners transitioned to the second stage of the ritual of miraculous release – sanctuary.

Like the extension of clerical charity towards prisoners, the practice of sanctuary originated well before the sixth century. A canon of the Council of Serdica (343) insisted that a condemned person at a church should not be molested while a bishop traveled to appeal to the emperor.[108] In Gaul, sanctuary became a means whereby ecclesiastics asserted the holiness of churches and promoted saints as patrons.[109] Bishops secured the integrity of sanctuary by legislating against those who would infringe upon it.[110] Gregory's *Historiae* contain descriptions of several instances where powerful magnates used subversive and violent means to try and oust other powerful figures claiming political asylum at churches.[111] Despite such high-profile cases, most Gauls likely respected the right of sanctuary.[112] Clerics intended sanctuary to protect socio-economically disadvantaged people, and in this capacity it probably involved fewer instances of violation, although these were not

---

107. Greg. Tur., *VM* 2.35 (*MGH*, SRM 1.2, 172): "Custodes autem in tantum obstupefacti fuerunt, ut nec verbis quidem eos increpare praesumerent; qui etiam sequentes eos, cum eisdem se in eclesia addiderunt." For intimidation of a count, see Greg. Tur., *VP* 8.10. Similarly, Gregory related that King Guntram ordered that three men seeking sanctuary be bound in chains. But when he heard that Saint Sequanus of Langres had miraculously liberated them from their bonds, the king himself became terrified; Greg. Tur., *GC* 86.
108. Rapp, *Holy Bishops in Late Antiquity*, 254. On the late ancient development of Christian sanctuary considered in the context of the bishop's charge to aid the poor, see ibid., 253–60.
109. James, "*Beati pacifici*: Bishops and the Law," 36–40; Walter Ullmann, "Public Welfare and Social Legislation in the Early Merovingian Councils," in *Councils and Assemblies*, ed., G. J. Cuming and L. G. Baker (Cambridge: Cambridge University Press, 1971), 13–16; Rob Meens, "The Sanctity of the Basilica of Saint Martin. Gregory of Tours and the Practice of Sanctuary in the Merovingian Period," in *Texts and Identities in the Early Middle Ages*, ed., R. Corradini, R. Meens, C. Pössel, and P. Shaw (Vienna: Österreichische Akademie der Wissenschaften, 2006), 278–80.
110. See, e. g., the Council of Orléans (511), c. 1, 3; Council of Épaon (517), c. 39; Council of Orléans (541), c. 22; Council of Mâcon (585), c. 8.
111. See, e. g., Greg. Tur., *Hist.* 4.13, 4.18, 5.2, 5.4, 6.12, 9.38.
112. James, "*Beati pacifici*: Bishops and the Law," 37; Meens, "The Sanctity of the Basilica of Saint Martin," 283. Even the otherwise *iniquus* Duke Roccolen, whom Chilperic sent to retrieve Guntram Boso from Saint Martin's church, refused to violate sanctuary; Greg. Tur., *Hist.* 5.4.

unheard of.[113] But whoever transgressed against a saint in this manner might have hell to pay, at least according to hagiographers. For example, Gregory attested that when a man blind in one eye tried to remove someone from the church of Saint Julian of Brioude, the offender lost sight in his other eye.[114] Similarly, when a certain Maurus attempted to retrieve a fugitive slave from the church of Saint Lupus at Troyes, the transgressor immediately was reduced to making animal noises, and three days later he died.[115]

Sanctuary as a second stage in the process of miraculous release, because it entailed a ritualized production, probably encountered little opposition. Indeed, hagiographers were quick to indicate that people present during miraculous liberations were too intimidated by saintly powers to prevent prisoners from obtaining asylum. Thus, Gregory wrote that when Saint Martin loosed the chains of an imprisoned debtor, the man "entered the holy church with no one stopping him" (*nullo retenente*).[116] Similarly, after Saint Nicetius of Lyons liberated an inmate, the latter "fearlessly marched all the way to the saint's tomb with no one stopping him" (*nemine retenente*).[117] Upon arrival at church, miraculously released prisoners could expect the protection of a holy liberator, which translated practically into the aid of an ecclesiastic. Gregory described how he, as the earthly representative for Saint Martin, defended released prisoners.[118] For example, in 577, he interceded with authorities on behalf of four men whom Martin had released and who had sought sanctuary at the cathedral at Tours. Gregory wrote that these men thanked

113. James, "*Beati pacifici*: Bishops and the Law," 40. Baxo, a client or slave of Ruricius of Limoges who sought sanctuary at a small church in Userca, patiently waited there while his master interceded with a prominent landowner in the region; Ruricius of Limoges, *Ep.* 2.20; Mathisen, *Ruricius of Limoges and Friends*, 173–74. Avitus of Vienne transferred an anonymous slave under armed guard from a basilica at Vienne to one at Lyons. The slave seems to have been a witness in an important trial that Gundobad was investigating; Avitus of Vienne, *Ep.* 44; Shanzer and Wood, *Avitus of Vienne*, 216–19.
114. Greg. Tur., *VJ* 10.
115. Greg. Tur., *GC* 66.
116. Greg. Tur., *VM* 3.47 (*MGH*, SRM 1.2, 193).
117. Greg. Tur., *VP* 8.7 (*MGH*, SRM 1.2, 247): "… usque ad eius sepulchrum perrexit intrepidus." See also Greg. Tur., *VM* 2.35; *VP* 7.3.
118. Since he was Martin's representative, Gregory also was a source for healings. Therefore he carried with him relics of Saint Martin, which he dispensed to ill people during his travels. See Van Dam, *Saints and their Miracles*, 93.

God "because He had deigned to liberate them by the intercession of the bishop" (*obtentu pontificis*).[119] But by *pontifex*, did he mean Saint Martin or himself? According to the story, both bishops played a role in the release. Here it appears Gregory was intentionally employing the word *pontifex* in an ambiguous manner to associate his own will with that of Martin.[120] Miraculously released prisoners would have realized that a bishop shared the protective essence of the community's saintly patron. For example, in 580, when Gregory's client, Modestus the carpenter, was arrested, tortured, and cast into a prison, Saints Martin and Medard broke his stocks and fetters and liberated him.[121] Modestus then immediately ran to the church of Saint Medard, where he found Gregory, the worldly representative for Saint Martin, keeping vigils. Thus the liberated carpenter was guaranteed the protection of two holy arbiters, Medard and Martin, the latter by proxy. Similarly, in 591/92, when a bound man was miraculously liberated directly in front of the church of Saint Martin at Tours, he did not rush to the tomb; rather, he went to the nearer, equivalent source of divine authority. Gregory related: "[The prisoner], leaping from the horse on which he was sitting, grabbed my feet, explaining that he was being condemned unjustly."[122] Likewise, according to Venantius Fortunatus, when prisoners at Radegund's royal villa at Péronne miraculously escaped a *carcer*, they immediately dashed to the saintly queen.[123] In this last instance, the holy person to whom the inmates rushed was still alive. More often than not, however, Latin hagiographers credited miraculous release to deceased saints, and so sanctuary was to be had at buildings attached to the suburban tombs of the holy, or at the cathedrals that housed the saints' living representatives, bishops.[124] In keeping with episcopal promotion of such cults,

119. Greg. Tur., *VM* 2.35 (*MGH*, SRM 1.2, 172): "... quod eos obtentu pontificis dignatus fuerit libare."
120. On Gregory's use of this tactic, see Van Dam, *Saints and their Miracles*, 93.
121. Greg. Tur., *Hist.* 5.49.
122. Greg. Tur., *VM* 4.35 (*MGH*, SRM 1.2, 208): "... exiliensque de caballo in quo sedebat, pedes nostros arripuit, exponens, se iniuste damnari."
123. Ven. Fort., *Vita Radegundis* 11. See also Ven. Fort., *Vita Germani* 30, 66, in which freed prisoners bolted for the living Bishop Germanus.
124. Sanctuary at a saint's basilica: Greg. Tur., *VM* 3.41, 4.39, 4.41; *VP* 8.7; *Hist.* 5.49, 8.33; Ven. Fort., *Vita Albini* 16; *Vita Germani* 67; at a cathedral: Greg. Tur., *VM* 1.21, 2.35.

the ritual of miraculous release of prisoners would have been largely an urban phenomenon.[125]

Western promoters of saints' cults generally intended the tomb to be the focal point where a holy being's reputation was to be enhanced. Thus, ecclesiastics at Tours permitted ill, disabled, and possessed people to congregate and lie about Saint Martin's sepulcher for months and years awaiting miraculous recovery. Because the processes of exorcism and healing involved reintegration, it was necessary that these miracles happen "with the people watching."[126] But unlike with healing and exorcisms, the wondrous stage in the ritual of release, usually the actual liberation of prisoners from jail, could not happen at a tomb; nor was it likely to be public. Therefore, the stage of sanctuary moved the focus of the ritual of miraculous release to the saint's residence. It also enabled incarcerated persons to confront the public before whom they would be expected to attest to the divine power of the holy liberator. Prisoners might even bring with them tangible evidence as proof of their contact with the holy – specifically broken accoutrements from prison. Clerics allowed the shattered chains and fetters of successive miraculously released prisoners to pile up at tombs as mounting testimonies to a local saint's divine judicial authority. For example, Gregory wrote about the tomb of Saint Nicetius of Lyons: "If one wishes to know how many prisoners were freed by the saint and how many chains and fetters he has broken, one has only to look at the mass of irons which are today in the church, gathered together for such occasions."[127] Gregory offered similar descriptions for the sepulchers of Saints Medard at Soissons and Memmius at Châlons-sur-Marne.[128] Finally, sanctuary provided the

---

125. Like other late ancient ecclesiastically sponsored charitable activities, the people most likely to benefit from prison release were those proximate to a bishop's urban "safety net"; Brown, *Poverty and Leadership*, 50.

126. People could witness healings at the tombs since they often occurred during services, sometimes even as clerics were reading the saints' lives. See Van Dam, *Saints and their Miracles*, 89–91.

127. Greg. Tur., *VP* 8.10 (*MGH*, SRM 1.2, 250): "Quanti per hunc sanctum carcerali ergastulo revincti absoluti sunt, quantorum conpeditorum catenae sive conpedes sint confracti, testis est hodie moles illa ferri, quae in basilica eius aspicitur, de supradictis suppliciis adgregata." Trans. by James, *Gregory of Tours, Life of the Fathers*, 61. Gregory's priest John saw these chains and fetters when he stopped to pray at Nicetius's tomb; Greg. Tur., *VP* 8.6.

128. Medard: Greg. Tur., *Hist.* 4.19; *GM* 93. Memmius: Greg. Tur., *GM* 65.

appropriate setting for the final stage of the ritual of miraculous release, reconciliation between the community and those thought to have trespassed against it.

The ritual of miraculous release was equivalent to atonement for public sin, and so it required one final stage, pardon. Because arrest and conviction fell under the jurisdiction of secular judicial officials, liberation traditionally was their prerogative. In the imperial age, emperors sporadically had enacted general pardons for criminals. Christian emperors eventually established Easter as an appropriate time for pardoning.[129] In Barbarian Gaul, secular figures maintained this prerogative, even for prisoners who participated in the ritual of miraculous release. Thus, Gregory related that the man who avenged his brother's murder without consent of a secular official, after Saint Nicetius of Lyons miraculously liberated him, still needed to be pardoned by an *iudex* to be excused from the death penalty.[130] Similarly, prisoners rescued by Saint Martin in 592 entered his church where they "were excused from condemnation by the judge."[131] The granting of formal pardon by secular *iudices* assured counts and their subordinates that they maintained jurisdiction despite ecclesiastical intervention. Furthermore, public recognition of pardon by secular officials provided confirmation that the ritual of miraculous release should be acknowledged as a legitimate exercise. If this were not the case, hagiographers would not have pointed out as frequently as they did how judges gave pardons. Mundane grants alone would not fully exonerate prisoners. As an ancient constitution addressed to the Roman senate had attested, "A pardon, conscript fathers, brands the very persons whom it liberates; it does not remove the infamy of crime."[132] Therefore, a secular judge's pardon was not essential to the process of miraculous release in and of itself; rather, its importance lay in what it symbolized,

---

129. *CTh* 3.38.1 (a. 322), 9.38.3 (a. 367). Easter Day: *CTh* 9.38.4 (a. 370), 9.38.6 (a. 381), 9.38.7 (a. 384), 9.38.8 (a. 385), *Sirm. Const.* 8 (a. 386).

130. Greg. Tur., *VP* 8.7 (*MGH*, SRM 1.2, 247): "Tunc a iudice noxialis culpae damnatione concessa, laxatus abscessit ad propria."

131. Greg. Tur., *VM* 4.41 (*MGH*, SRM 1.2, 210): "… per iudicem immunes a damno laxati sunt." Other pardons: Greg. Tur., *VM* 1.11, 1.23, 4.16, 4.26, 4.35, 4.39; *VP* 7.3; *GC* 86, 99; Ven. Fort., *Vita Germani* 66.

132. *CTh* 9.38.5 (a. 371) (Mommsen, ed., 496): "Indulgentia, patres conscripti, quos liberat notat nec infamiam criminis tollis, sed poenae gratiam facit."

secular acceptance of the holy arbiter's lenient judicial decision. A similar lesson was to be gained from Gregory's telling of a legend about an *iudex* who discovered a thief nosing about the tomb of the recently buried Bishop Helius of Lyons, and determined that the perpetrator must die. When the corpse of the saint grabbed hold of the thief and refused to let go, "the judge understood the wish of the dead man and made a guarantee about the man's life. Then the man was pardoned and restored unharmed."[133] As he often did, Gregory appended a note that this incident happened "with the people watching" (*populis expectantibus*).[134] By granting a pardon, the judge provided a public example, which everyone else in the community was to follow; they should consent to the saint's decision and forgive the offending party.

Of course, counts and judges were not obligated to accept the judicial decisions of their cities' saints and bishops. Count Armentarius of Lyons, for example, regularly reopened cases that the cantankerous Bishop Nicetius of Lyons had declared closed.[135] Gregory regarded such disagreement with ecclesiastical and holy mediators as obstinacy, and he sometimes criticized it by verbally belittling secular judicial authority in comparison with saintly *iudicium*. Thus, writing about the altar of Saint Julian of Brioude, he commented, "… however often the judges' power has been meaninglessly enacted in this place, it has been confounded."[136] For the most part, however, ecclesiastics and counts cooperated, and so clerics likely usually instigated the miraculous release of prisoners when they knew local secular judges would prove amenable. For example, most of the prison releases that Saint Martin caused at Tours happened late in

---

133. Greg. Tur., *GC* 61 (*MGH*, SRM 1.2, 334): "Tunc intellegens voluntatem defuncti, facta iudex de vita promissione, laxatur et sic incolomis redditur." Trans. based on Raymond Van Dam, *Gregory of Tours, Glory of the Confessors*, TTH 5 (Liverpool: Liverpool University Press: 1988), 68.

134. Greg. Tur., *GC* 61 (*MGH*, SRM 1.2, 334).

135. Greg. Tur., *VP* 8.3.

136. Greg. Tur., *VJ* 43 (*MGH*, SRM 1.2, 131): "… et potestas iudicium, quotienscumque in eo loco superflue egit, confusa discessit." Venantius commonly depicted saintly bishops petitioning judges to free prisoners and then miraculously liberating them only after the judges refused the initial request; Ven. Fort., *Vita Albini* 16, *Vita Germani* 30, 61, 66. Venantius depicted Albinus causing an obstinate prison guard to die after he opposed the saint in freeing prisoners; Ven. Fort., *Vita Albini* 12.

Gregory's episcopacy at a time when the bishop's friend, Gallienus, was count.[137] Thus, the judges who obligingly conferred pardons to Martin's freed prisoners probably are to be identified with Gallienus and/or his subordinates.

After local judicial officials formally exculpated miraculously released prisoners, the latter then were able to reconcile with others in their community. This reconciliation is evidenced through former inmates returning to mundane affairs and participating in significant social events. For example, prisoners released during Saint Gregorius of Langres' funeral joined their neighbors in the procession and even helped pallbearers carry the bier.[138] Furthermore, like other community members in good standing, miraculously released prisoners were able to return to their abodes. Thus, convicts freed by Martin in 592 and pardoned by a judge "left for their own homes" (*ad propria abscesserunt*).[139] Because most prisoners were of low social rank, some miraculously released persons might receive financial assistance with their new lease on life. Venantius Fortunatus related that after Bishop Germanus of Paris delivered prisoners from a jail, he additionally secured their possessions, which had been confiscated by the fisc.[140] Relieved of this burden, the former inmates could more easily resume a normal life.

---

137. According to John Corbett, "*Praesentium signorum munera*," 61, five of nine prison releases effected by Martin and recorded in the *Libri quattuor de virtutibus beati Martini episcopi* occurred between 588 and 594. Gallienus was count of Tours by July 589; Greg. Tur., *Hist.* 5.49. Martindale, *PLRE* 3: 501, conservatively suggested Gallienus was "probably a *comes* at Tours in 589." For a bolder, yet likely, estimation that Gallienus held the post from late 587/early 588 to beyond Gregory's death, see Timothy Bratton, *Tours: From Roman "Civitas" to Merovingian Episcopal Center, c. 275–650 A.D.* (Ph.D. diss., Philadelphia: Bryn Mawr College, 1979), 151–52. Two other releases date between 581 and 587. The count during these miracles could have been Leudast's successor in 580, Eunomius, but he was rather hostile toward Gregory; Greg. Tur., *Hist.* 5.49. He was no longer count by 584; *PLRE* 3: 462. Otherwise, the *comes* could have been Eborinus, with whom Gregory likely was amicable, for he recorded how Saint Martin healed the count's wife; Greg. Tur., *VM* 3.34; *PLRE* 3: 432, s. v., "Eborinus 1."

138. Greg. Tur., *VP* 7.3. Likewise, for healed people resuming participation in events such as celebrating the liturgy and mass alongside neighbors, see Van Dam, *Saints and their Miracles*, 90–91.

139. Greg. Tur., *VM* 4.39 (*MGH*, SRM 1.2, 209). See also Greg. Tur., *VP* 8.7; *Hist.* 10.6. Beneficiaries of the process of illness and healing also returned to their homes; e.g., Greg. Tur., *VM* 2.22.

140. Ven. Fort., *Vita Germani* 30.

CONCLUSION

The ritual of miraculous release had profound implications for ecclesiastics, participant prisoners, and others in Gallic communities. For clerics, the process was but one of several methods whereby they increased spiritual authority and amassed clients. Judging by the frequency of particular kinds of miracle depicted in hagiography, bishops and holy persons gathered clients from the humbler social echelons mostly by ritual healing.[141] But people freed from jails, whether this was done ritually or through more mundane mediation, constituted a not insignificant part of the *miseri* whom clerics aided. For example, as witnessed in the previous chapter, Abbot Senoch of the Touraine liberated more than 200 people from servitude and debt.[142] Like captive prisoners of war whom Gallic ecclesiastics often redeemed and turned into clients, Senoch's liberated debtors would have become bound by similar obligations to their deliverer.[143] Another saint noted for liberating prisoners and amassing clients was Eparchius, a recluse of Angoulême who, while living, often sought pardons for convicts from judges.[144] As happened with Abbot Senoch, when Eparchius died in 581, his clients gathered to mourn: "He was carried from his cell and given to his tomb. Then a great crowd of those whom he had redeemed, as I have said, walked in his funeral procession."[145] As dependents of a living ascetic, released prisoners would have honored their debts by providing loyalty to their patron and his church. But they might also enjoy benefits. Primarily, of course, the ritual of miraculous release afforded participant inmates an opportunity to overcome their unfortunate condition and escape its sinful stigma. Once freed from jail and forgiven by neighbors, prisoners no longer would be perceived as burdens to the community. Furthermore,

---

141. Van Dam, *Saints and their Miracles*, 101–03.
142. Greg. Tur., *VP* 15.1.
143. For released prisoners of war becoming clients of their liberating bishop, see William E. Klingshirn, "Charity and Power: Caesarius of Arles and the Ransoming of Captives in Sub-Roman Gaul," *Journal of Roman Studies* 75 (1985), 201–02.
144. Greg. Tur., *Hist.* 6.8.
145. Greg. Tur., *Hist.* 6.8 (*MGH*, SRM 1.1, 278): "... protractusque a cellula, sepulturae mandatus est. Magnus autem conventus, ut diximus, de redemptis in eius processit exsequiis."

as with the process of illness and healing, participating in miraculous release might contribute a small amount of prestige to freed persons by enabling them to assert how they enjoyed the favor of the community's holy patron. Claiming a relationship with a saint could benefit a person regardless of social status. Whether powerful ecclesiastics, influential citizens, or repentant socially downtrodden thieves, people involved in miracles might become living testimonies to the *virtutes* of holy beings. Some maintained this special status by continually reminding others how a saint had favored them. For example, Gregory's uncle Gallus used to show off a large scar on his foot, the wound of which Saint Julian had healed.[146] Similarly, about a thief who prayed to Saint Martin while hanging from a gallows and survived for two days until retrieved alive by a nun, Gregory remarked: "He who was kept in this world still lives today as a testimony to the power of the holy man [Martin]."[147] Perhaps this former thief was able to milk admiration for his association with the community's holy patron by showing others the rope marks on his neck, just as Bishop Gallus proudly did with his scar.

Finally, the ritual of miraculous release of prisoners, like that of healing, provided a lenient means to heal social breaches between community members at large and people suspected of having transgressed against them. For example, a count of Angoulême informed Gregory that when he once ordered a habitual criminal to hang, the holy recluse Eparchius, who habitually freed inmates, as usual sent a monk to petition for the man's release.[148] But on this occasion, a mob appeared and argued that the count would lose his authority if he allowed this to happen. Bowing to this pressure, the official tortured the culprit and condemned him to the gallows. Undaunted however, Eparchius prayed, reportedly thereby causing the convict's chains to snap and the gibbet to collapse. Afterward, the count appeared before Eparchius to explain why he had ignored his request to spare the criminal. To the agent's amazement, the recluse presented the convict before him, still alive.

---

146. Greg. Tur., *VJ* 23.
147. Greg. Tur., *VM* 1.21 (*MGH*, SRM 1.2, 149): "Qui usque hodie ad testamonium virtutis beati viri vivus habetur in saeculo."
148. Greg. Tur., *Hist.* 6.8.

In this instance, Eparchius secured through the ritual of miraculous release what he could not through any ordinary petition, the count's pardon. Here, Eparchius and his monks, and even the count, expected the ostensible wondrous occurrence to cause a change of heart among those community members who previously had nearly rioted when they thought the culprit might be liberated. Like so many other hagiographical accounts of miraculous release of prisoners, this episode attests to the essential roles played by a willful ecclesiastic and an agreeable secular official in an inmate's liberation. For their part, prisoners of low social rank who were fortunate enough to be freed by a saint could only respond with gratitude and loyal service. In exchange for torment and death, they would become lifelong clients for socially prominent ecclesiastics.

THE ACTIVE POOR: *PAUPERES* AT CHURCH

CHAPTER SIX

And the Lord Himself in the Gospel said "The first will be last and the last shall be first" (Matthew 20:16). May divine mercy then shine with its love upon the poor, so that the small shall become great and the weak shall become coheirs with the One Son. For He has appointed the poverty of this world to heaven, where the empire of this world cannot reach, so that the poor peasant can go there when he that is dressed in purple cannot.

GREGORY OF TOURS, *De Vita Patrum* 5, *praef.*[1]

The sixth century witnessed virtually complete assimilation of Gallic bishoprics by socially prominent persons. A few zealous, reform-minded prelates – for example, Caesarius of Arles – tried to curtail other bishops' overt worldly aristocratic behavior such as overindulging at banquets and hunting. Others, among them Gregory of Tours, eschewed the familial survival strategy of producing progeny. But none touted sweeping

---

1. Greg. Tur., *VP* 5, *praef.* (*MGH*, SRM 1.2, 227): "Sic et ipse Dominus in evangelio ait: Erunt primi novissimi et novissimi primi. Inlicet ergo amore suo divina misericordia corda inopum, ut de parvis magnos statuat ac de infimis Unigeniti sui faciat coheredes. Praefecit enim de hac mundana aegestate in caelo, quo scandere non potuit terrenum imperium; ut accedat illuc rusticus, quo accedere non meruit purpuratus." Trans. by James, *Gregory of Tours, Life of the Fathers*, 28.

social changes such as leveling society or eradicating the institutions of imprisonment and slavery. Instead, high ecclesiastics defended hierarchical principles and used clerical resources such as the cult of saints to perpetuate hierarchy. The previous chapter revealed how prisoners constituted a group of passive *miserabiles* for whom ecclesiastics were willing to secure liberation in exchange for loyalty. By inviting them to participate in the ritual of miraculous release, clerics reintegrated inmates into community life at the cost of indebtedness to a church establishment. Judging by the small number of hagiographical anecdotes pertaining to liberation, the ritual of miraculous release was but a sideshow in the overall production of the cult of saints. Far more common were ecclesiastical appeals for people of low rank to seek out churches for healing and exorcisms. Chapter Four briefly considered how some *pauperes* and even slaves improved their social situation through church affiliation. Tellingly, advancement usually happened either after the death of a master or with the support of a patron in the client's religious enterprise. The present chapter proposes to extend the examination of people of low rank associated with churches. It will address the extent to which the poor could reasonably hope to advance through church office, and it will elaborate upon the role of low-level clerics and church affiliated *pauperes* in the operation of saints' cults. The chapter will reveal the activity of a determined group of *miseri* who, unlike prisoners, were anything but passive when it came to improving their lot.

PAUPERES AND CHURCHES

"Blessed are the poor, for yours is the Kingdom of God" (Luke 6:20). Gallic ecclesiastics could not escape the fact theirs was a religion originally intended to benefit the poor, nor did they try. Gregory of Tours imagined that when the church arrived at Bourges during the reign of Emperor Decius (249–251), most "senators and other better people of the place were still obligated to their pagan religions, while those who believed were from the poor."[2] But high ecclesiastics need not

---

2. Greg. Tur., *Hist.* 1.31 (*MGH*, SRM 1.1, 24): "Senatores vero vel reliqui meliores loci fantasticis erant tunc cultibus obligati; qui vero crediderant ex pauperibus erant ..."

have imagined that early Christians had depended upon aristocratic leadership any less than they thought contemporary believers ought to. For example, Gregory remarked that the first church in Bourges was a house belonging to "a certain Leocadius, a leading senator of Gaul, who was from the family of Vettius Epagatus."[3] Epagatus had been one of forty-eight martyrs of Lyons reportedly slaughtered in the arena in 177 and remembered in the pages of the church historian, Eusebius.[4] According to Gregory's paternal family tradition, both Epagatus and Leocadius were ancestors.[5] By declaring these senatorial saints as kin, not only was Gregory yet again publicizing the illustrious lineage of his clan; more generally, he was intimating that persons of aristocratic rank were the rightful leaders of the Gallic church. But elitist attitudes among prominent ecclesiastics never precluded consideration for the poor. Scriptural passages remained a source of clerical inspiration for literary material and behavioral emulation. For example, when Gregory portrayed Emperor Tiberius II (578–582) as a model "cheerful" almsgiver, he depicted the ruler quoting the Gospels to legitimize his charitable actions in the face of a notable critic, the emperor's own wife.[6] Neither did ecclesiastical aristocrats abandon the notion that generosity toward the poor was a duty essential to church leaders.[7] For example, in the *Historiae*, Gregory portrayed Sidonius Apollinaris piously removing silverware from his own house to give to the poor, again despite a chiding wife.[8] Biblical references even helped high ecclesiastics recognize sanctity effusing from individuals of low social station. Thus, as recorded in the introductory quotation for this chapter, Gregory quoted Matthew 20:16 to support his opinion that the slave turned abbot Portianus was worthy of being regarded a saint, "for truly [God] ennobled him with

---

3. Greg. Tur., *Hist.* 1.31 (*MGH*, SRM 1.1, 31): "Leocadium quendam et primum Galliarum senatorem, qui de stirpe Vecti Epagati fuit …"
4. Eusebius of Caesarea, *Ecclesiastical History* 5.1.
5. Greg. Tur., *VP* 6.1.
6. Greg. Tur., *Hist.* 5.19, with Tiberius quoting Matthew 6:20. Johannes Schneider, "Die Darstellung der Pauperes," 61, suggested Paul's "cheerful giver" of 2 Corinthians 9:7 as Gregory's inspiration to remark about Tiberius's *hilarus*.
7. Kathleen Mitchell, "Saints and Public Christianity," 77, asserts that Gregory portrayed saints in his *Historiae* more than those in the *Miracula* as "spokesmen for principles of Christian charity."
8. Greg. Tur., *Hist.* 2.22.

great powers."[9] But how could ecclesiastics reconcile aristocratic control of churches with New Testament insistence that beatitude belonged to the poor? To do so, clerics had to equate the church with the poor.

Verbal affiliation of church and poor was part of a traditional, albeit evolving, strategy by which ecclesiastics defended their interests. In the pre-Constantinian church, Christian leaders of modest means, occupied with time-consuming clerical responsibilities, came to expect financial support through taking a share of the offerings of almsgivers.[10] Thus, Christians early recognized two sets of Christian poor: the socio-economic poor, "impoverished fellow believers – orphans, widows, the sick, the imprisoned, refugees and the destitute," and a metaphorical band of poor: "The bishop and the clergy [who] were supported by a share of the offerings of the faithful."[11] In the fourth century, bishops and clerics became recipients of Constantine's generous distribution of tax exemptions. Subsequently, Christian leaders faced with less giving emperors and scrutinizing imperial officials had to justify their maintenance of such privileges by sufficiently displaying their churches' commitment to the poor.[12] Therefore, Christian charity in the fourth century expanded from the traditional variety aimed at succoring the community of believers to "a more general 'care of the poor' performed in return for pubic services."[13] Between the fourth and sixth centuries, as the social prominence of Christian leaders increased exponentially, especially in Gaul where ecclesiastical aristocracies materialized earlier than elsewhere in the West, episcopal "lovers of the poor" now asserted themselves as "governors of the poor."[14] While late ancient preachers continued to emphasize the destitution of *pauperes*, simultaneously they expanded the parameters of "the poor" to include a much larger group consisting of low to "middling" persons.[15] As Peter Brown asserts, "Christian rhetoric

---

9. Greg. Tur., *VP* 5, *praef.* (*MGH*, SRM 1.2, 227): "… verum etiam magnis virtutibus sublimavit."
10. Brown, *Poverty and Leadership*, 20–26.
11. Ibid., 24. Brown, ibid., 26, explains: "Thus, when Constantine decided to patronize the Christian church in 312 he found a body committed to a double charge: a duty to give to the poor and a duty to support the clergy."
12. Ibid., 29–31.
13. Ibid., 31.
14. Ibid., 45.
15. Ibid., 46.

'had the conceptual effect of pauperizing the poor by first creating the most distinctive, dramatic image of the lowest class, and then imposing that image upon the lower classes as a whole.'[16] Furthermore, as prominent Christians, intent upon publicly displaying their piety, poured more and more wealth into churches, bishops defended their control of this substantial lucre all the more by associating its management with performance of their traditional charge to aid the poor. Thus, Gregory of Tours recorded how a demon once advised Bishop Magneric of Trier: "All that is required of you is to look after the property of your church with diligence, lest any resource for the support of the poor be diminished."[17] Indeed, as generous bequeathals were becoming regular, in Gaul it was not uncommon for relatives to try to recoup losses by taking back donations to churches.[18] Clerics tried to counter such efforts through recourse to metaphor; because the church was guardian to the poor, those who attempted to retrieve donations must be "murderers of the poor" (*necatores pauperum*).[19] The means for recovering resources from churches, like the properties themselves, were varied, and so to further secure church possessions, clerics expanded the list of those who fit the metaphor. Ecclesiastics attending the Council of Agde (506) castigated clergy and laity, relatives and regretful donors, for taking items bequeathed to churches and monasteries.[20] Prelates at the Council of Orléans (549) censured as *necatores pauperum* people who diverted property donated to churches and took property from the xenodochium at Lyons, and those who tried to recover bequeathals from priests, churches, and other holy places.[21] Ecclesiastics attending the Council of Arles (554) adjudged

---

16. Ibid., where Brown adopts for late ancient ecclesiastics Gertrude Himmelfarb's explanation of Victorian techniques for representing the "poor."

17. Greg. Tur., *Hist.* 8.12 (*MGH*, SRM 1.1, 379): "Satius enim tibi erat, res ecclesiae tuae diligenter inquirere, ne pauperibus aliquid deperiret …" Trans. by Brown, *Poverty and Leadership*, 45.

18. E. g., Greg. Tur., *Hist.* 8.39.

19. Mac Gonagle, *The Poor in Gregory of Tours*, 24–25.

20. Council of Agde (506), c. 4 (*CCL* 148, 194): "Clerici etiam vel saeculares, qui oblationes parentum aut donatas aut testamentis relictas retinere perstiterint, aut id quod ipsi donaverint ecclesiis vel monasteriis crediderint auferendum, sicut synodus sancta constituit, velut necatores pauperum, quousque reddant, ab ecclesiis excludantur."

21. Council of Orléans (549), c. 13, 15, 16. Radegund used similar metaphorical language, calling those who tried to take property or otherwise meddled in the affairs of her convent at Poitiers "robbers and despoilers of the poor"; Greg. Tur., *Hist.* 9.42 (*MGH*, SRM 1.1, 472): "praedones et spoiliatores

senior clerics who failed to properly maintain church property entrusted to their care as *necatores pauperum*.[22]

Prelates' concerns for protecting church property were justified. Gregory's pages include numerous examples of people attacking shrines and otherwise absconding with church possessions. For example, around 524, Abbot Brachio's former master, Duke Sigivald, who also was a relation of King Theuderic, grabbed a villa that Bishop Tetradius of Bourges had bequeathed to the church of St. Julian at Brioude.[23] Fortunately for the church, on this occasion Sigivald restored the estate after he contracted a debilitating fever, and the bishop convinced the duke's wife that her spouse would die unless he gave back the land.[24] Perhaps the reprimand included reading the relevant canon about *necatores pauperum* from the Council of Agde, which Tetradius had attended. Not only did ecclesiastics cry foul against unlawful seizures of property, but they also directed their rhetoric against governmental efforts to gather revenue. Thus, when King Chlothar I tried to tax the churches throughout Gaul, Bishop Injuriosus of Tours leveled against him a charge tantamount to stealing from the poor, saying: "If you insist on taking God's property, the Lord will swiftly take away your kingdom, for it is a wicked thing to be filling your storehouses with the alms of the poor, whom you ought to be feeding from your granaries."[25] This passage essentially implicated Chlothar as a "thief of the poor" (*fer pauperum*). In the end, the king bowed to the will of Bishop Injuriosus and Saint Martin and allowed the church at Tours to keep its tax-exempt status.

Beyond land-grabbing magnates, a far more common kind of *necator pauperum* that worried Gallic ecclesiastics was the grave robber. Stealing

---

pauperum," which preserves Radegund's letter to several bishops on the foundation of her nunnery. On use of the metaphor *necatores pauperum* in relation to episcopal exemption for monasteries, see Rosenwein, "Inaccessible Cloisters," 184–85.

22. Council of Arles (554), c. 6 (*CCL* 148A, 172): "Ut clericis non liceat facultates, quas ab episcopo in usu accipiunt, deteriorare. Quod si fecerint, si iunior fuerit, disciplina corrigatur, si vero senior, ut necator pauperum habeatur."

23. Greg. Tur., *VJ* 14.

24. Greg. Tur., *VJ* 14.

25. Greg. Tur., *Hist.*, 4.2 (*MGH*, SRM 1.1, 136): "'Si volueris res Dei tollere, Dominus regnum tuum velociter aufert, quia iniquum est, ut pauperes, quos tuo debes alere horreo, ab eorum stipe tua horrea repleantur.'"

grave goods gradually increased throughout the sixth century and into the seventh, reaching epidemic levels.[26] Not unlike certain among those "murderers of the poor" who attempted to recover properties that family members had bequeathed to churches, many grave robbers would have been relatives looking to recoup expensive or meaningful goods interred with kin.[27] One such person apparently was Duke Guntram Boso, who coveted precious items left with a female in-law buried in a basilica near Metz.[28] Soon after the funeral, much of the town joined its bishop and local dignitaries, the duke included, in celebrating Saint Remigius's festival at the saint's extra mural church. Presumably choosing this occasion when the city's populace would be preoccupied with revelry, Guntram Boso's retainers broke into the church where the woman had been interred and stole from her tomb much gold and jewelry. Several monks espied the robbers, however, and informed the bishop and duke. Initially the thieves fled the crime scene, but knowing that their deed had been witnessed, and being fearful of capture and punishment, they returned to Metz and restored the goods at the church's altar. Subsequently, the entire matter was brought before a tribunal with King Childebert II presiding. Duke Guntram Boso was able to offer no defense for his sacrilegious behavior, and so he went into hiding. Clerical use of metaphors associating church and poor may have proved somewhat effective, perhaps especially when coupled with threats of corporal punishment, excommunication, or divine retribution. If ecclesiastics intended verbal linkage of *ecclesiae* and *pauperes* to help churches keep their possessions, then the metaphorical vocabulary needed to bear some semblance to fact. To this end, clerics encouraged the conspicuous

---

26. Effros, *Caring for Body and Soul*, 57. Effros, ibid., 57–58, cites evidence from two northern Gallic, early medieval cemeteries that 30 percent and 39 percent of the graves were robbed soon after interment. She notes that while these figures are not completely reliable, the trending increase is certain. Grave robbery decreased only around the mid-seventh century as the practice of interring burial items waned; ibid., 58.

27. Effros, ibid., 59, explains that many thieves would have known the deceased person's sex, for they efficiently "tended to excavate female graves only in the area near the head and neck, while they explored the length of male burials for armament." Furthermore, seemingly conscientious robbers commonly left behind burial items bearing Christian imagery, which they might have thought would protect corpses until Judgment Day; ibid., 59–60.

28. Greg. Tur., *Hist.* 8.21.

display of *pauperes* about their churches and property. Not only did they welcome visiting beggars to join other *miserabiles* about the saints' tombs, but some churches also maintained a fixed number of permanent *mendici* on the grounds.

The relationship between clerics and some *pauperes* living near or at Gallic churches was reciprocal. Ecclesiastical invitations for the poor to settle at churches enabled clerics to claim preservation of a traditional program of defending the poor, and it also allowed them to augment their client pool. Meanwhile, for *pauperes*, churches became viable avenues through which they might fulfill personal needs, achieve prestige, and even advance socially. The kinds of success a pauper could achieve at church depended somewhat on individual initiative. Most poor people came to church simply to share the experience of community with neighbors. To the dismay of some preachers, church attendees often used the occasion of assembling to catch up on gossip. Caesarius of Arles composed several sermons criticizing members of his congregation who persisted in disrupting his locution with casual conversation.[29] Of course, the preacher regarded it his business to remind people to be attentive to their prospects for salvation, an important part of which was being charitable toward the poor. But Gallic sermons along with wall paintings and church inscriptions also served as reminders that the poor, too, must be almsgivers.[30] For example, *pauperes* entering the west doors of Saint Martin's church at Tours faced the following admonition:

> *Let whoever comes to renew his vows to the highest God learn to confess*
> *Christ according to the account in the Gospel.*
> *Although he trembles in his heart and prays as a suppliant stooping*
> *on his knees, if he ceases his good works, his faith certainly is meaningless.*
> *Rich and poor alike are subject to this law; he who lacks wealth will*
> *demonstrate his good works by his intentions.*
> *Nor do meager and limited resources excuse anyone; the merit is*
> *determined by the intent, not by the value.*

29. Caes. Arel., *Serm.* 76.2, 77.6–7, 78.2.
30. Anne-Marie Abel, "La pauvreté dans la pensée et la pastorale de Saint Césaire d'Arles," in *Études sur l'Histoire de la Pauvreté (Moyen Age-XVIe siècle)*, ed. Michel Mollat (Paris: Publications de la Sorbonne, 1974), 1: 117–18, suggested that Caesarius especially directed his sermons to the poor.

He who has bestowed whatever is necessary presents very much; although
he will have given little, he wishes [to present] all the greatest gifts.[31]

Apparently, some whom ecclesiastics labeled *pauperes* and depicted
needing defense from tax-collectors were not so destitute that they could
not give to the church.[32] *Pauperes* would have reacted to such messages
out of a mixture of compliance and sincere religiosity. In addition to
encouraging the faithful poor to give alms, clerics also pressured them
to entrust a part of their possessions to churches so that the patron saint
could protect the goods from "evil men." One poor woman (*exigua*),
for example, "entrusted" (*subdiderat*) several chickens to Saint Sergius
and brought them to a basilica "whenever necessity demanded" (*cum*
necessitas flagitasset).[33] While Gregory asserted that this woman's behavior resulted from a level of devotion akin to that of the poor woman
with two mites from Luke 21: 1–2, nevertheless the anecdote betrays an
element of clerical coercion in the form of assurance, for it records that
the pauper was acting "according to a vow" (*ex voto*).[34] Presumably the
woman gave this promise to keep supplying chickens before the altar of
the saint's church. Such a public ritual would have added pressure for
her to maintain the pious behavior.

While most *pauperes* offered up alms, others came to church to receive
succor especially in forms of sustenance and improved health. Because
illness and disability often hindered the conjunctural poor from working and drove them to become beggars, many sought both simultaneously. Clerics facilitated the visitation of pilgrims and accommodation
of the sickly and destitute by establishing hostels, *xenodochia*, which frequently were located alongside roads leading up to urban ecclesiastical

31. LeBlant, *Inscriptions chrétiennes*, 1: no. 173: "Discat evangelico Christum sermone fateri, / quisque
venit summo vota referre Deo. / Quamvis corde tremens, supplex genu, cernuus oret, / si cesset opere,
nempe fides vacua est. / Lege sub haec pariter locuples pauperque tenetur: / cui census desit, mente
probabit opus. / Nec quemquam excusat tenuis atque arta facultas: / affectu constat gloria, non pretio. /
Qui tribuit quaecumque opus est, is plurima confert: / parva licet dederit, maxima quaeque cupit ..."
Trans. by Van Dam, *Saints and their Miracles*, 313.
32. This reference to "the poor" may have been directed toward the broad group of "middling" persons
living near the edge of poverty that preachers rhetorically referred to as *pauperes* and who perceived
themselves as paupers; Brown, *Poverty and Leadership*, 49.
33. Greg. Tur., *GM* 96 (*MGH*, SRM 1.2, 103).
34. Greg. Tur., *GM* 96 (*MGH*, SRM 1.2, 103).

centers.[35] While many people likely found some form of comfort at these buildings, clerical writers concentrated upon the benefits that the poor might find at saints' basilicas. One newly disabled pauper permitted to beg for nourishment at the shrine of Saint Julian at Brioude was Anagild, a mute, deaf, and blind paralytic left by his family. Gregory reported that he lay "at the holy entrances" (*ad limina sacrosancta*) for a whole year, when finally the martyr cured him of all disabilities.[36] In the meantime, the prominent positioning of Anagild in the doorway presented visitors to the shrine an unavoidable reminder of the association of church and poor. When he received his healing Anagild would have become a client to the patron Saint Julian. To best advertise the saints' *virtutes* before the entire community, clerics hoped the holy would perform their healing miracles on the poor while many were present at the churches, preferably during services on Sundays and at saints' festivals. Indeed, the saints, and *pauperes*, were able to oblige.[37] For example, one poor woman who was ever ready to support the cause of Saint Martin at Tours was Maurusa, who despite being both blind and crippled apparently made a living by begging from her homestead. Gregory recorded that Maurusa's condition eventually worsened so that she lost control of her limbs, and so she directed believers to set her at Saint Martin's tomb. There she cried for the blessed man's help and prayed for mercy until the saint responded:

> Finally that piety that was not of a habit to send off the poor with nothing regarded her. At the festival the fibers of her thirsty nerves were relaxed. With the right hand that she had been unable to use

35. Brown, *Poverty and Leadership*, 33–34, comments on the novelty of the "Christian poorhouse-cum-hospital" for ancient society and for Christianity, too. Brown, ibid., 34–35, attributes innovation of the *xenodochium* to the fourth-century East. For the story of Saint Basil of Caesarea's employing his establishment of a *xenodochium* to prove that he was the proper successor as the city's next bishop, and to show that the Cappadocian churches deserved their tax-exempt status, see ibid., 35–44. The first known Gallic *xenodochium*, attached to Saint-Maurice d'Agaune, is attested to the mid-fifth century. These hostels became common across Gaul in the sixth century; Thomas Sternberg, *Orientalium More Secutus: Räume und Institutionen der Caritas des 5. bis 7. Jahrhunderts in Gallien* (Münster: Aschendorffsche, 1991), 147–307. At least fifteen of thirty-four locales where one or more *xenodochia* have been identified for the Merovingian era were operating such a building by the end of the sixth century; Sternberg, ibid., 288–90.

36. Greg. Tur., *VJ* 12 (*MGH*, SRM 1.2, 119).

37. Van Dam, *Saints and their Miracles*, 90–91.

for six years she made the sign of the blessed cross over the bone. She then got to her feet so that she was able to go back to her little home with no one supporting her.[38]

By pointing out that Maurusa was able to return home without assistance, not only did Gregory intimate that the poor woman could resume something of a normal life, but also he stressed how she became less of a hindrance for her neighbors. Thus, in addition to healing her limbs, Saint Martin also relieved her of the guilt that would have been associated with her disability.[39] Of course, one might recall that it was ecclesiastics like Gregory in the first place who were trying to convince believers that people should feel guilty for having disabilities. Unfortunately for Maurusa, Martin initially left her blind. But the pauper next used her blindness to occasion yet another opportunity to testify before others to the *virtutes* of the community's invisible patron. Gregory continued: "After two years passed the woman again approached the blessed patron's tomb where she started to pray even more intensely, as was proper. And soon with eyes open she arose into the light that had been restored to her."[40] Gregory concluded the anecdote by commenting that Maurusa recovered her sight soon after his arrival at Tours. It has been proposed that this occasion was Saint Martin's festival on 11 November 573, the first celebration over which Gregory presided as the city's bishop.[41] This timing suggests that Maurusa's recovery corresponded with the new bishop's determination to cause the Tourangeaux to realize that their holy patron Martin had accepted him as the community's legitimate ecclesiastical leader. To that end, Gregory concurrently was claiming that Saint Martin had healed him of a deadly bout of dysentery.[42]

---

38. Greg. Tur., *VM* 2.3 (*MGH*, SRM 1.2, 160): "Tandem pietas illa respiciens, quae pauperes dimittere numquam consuevit inanes, in festivitate sua laxata sunt fila nervorum arentium, et sic de dextra, quam per sex annos non iudicaverat, signum beatae cricis ad os faciens, in pedibus restituta est, ita ut ad hospitiolum suum nullius usu adiutorio remearet ..."

39. Van Dam, *Saints and their Miracles*, 91.

40. Greg. Tur., VM 2.3 (MGH, SRM 1.2, 160): "Post annos autem duos iterum veniens ad beati patronis tumulum, coepit adtentius, sicut erat opportunum, orare; mox apertis oculis, in rediviva luce surrexit."

41. Corbett, *"Praesentium signorum munera,"* 55.

42. Greg. Tur., *VM* 2.1.

That Maurusa two years previously had been the beneficiary of a public miracle at Martin's tomb suggests that the pauper might have been well attuned to conspicuously miraculously recovering to the benefit of her clerical patrons and their ecclesiastical program.[43]

Another structurally impoverished woman determined to maintain the prestige that could come with receiving a cure from a saint was a paralytic named Foedamia. According to Gregory, relatives abandoned this girl at the church of Saint Julian at Brioude, where she could be "displayed" (*exhibita est*) and beg for alms.[44] Having endured this condition for eighteen years, one evening while the faithful were celebrating vigils, the martyr appeared in a dream and provided Foedamia a cure. Gregory wrote: "As she offered a prayer while sleeping, it seemed like many chains dropped off of her limbs onto the floor. Awakened by the clanking noise, she then felt as if she had fully recovered her health in every limb. All were amazed [to witness] her rising immediately from her cot, and she was yelling thanks as she proceeded into the holy basilica."[45] Not only did Foedamia impress the crowd by her mobility; furthermore, she assured the assembly that the martyr had been responsible for the miracle by recounting a dream in which Julian rebuked her for not attending the ceremony before compassionately bearing her to the tomb. In a society accustomed to accepting the authorizing agency of dreams, Foedamia's declaration of this vision would have lent legitimacy to her experience. But it also conferred a degree of prestige upon the beggar: for one night, Foedamia was the center of attention, an obvious friend of God's friend, Saint Julian. The attention one such as she received when healed at a saint's tomb must have been gratifying especially for a person with little to no social clout. Although hagiographers added to their descriptions of ritual healing the phrase "with the people watching" (*spectante populo*) in order to assure readers that miracles actually happened (for how could they not happen if the people saw them), still, the visibility of Foedamia's

---

43. I am not suggesting that such conspicuous recoveries need be conscious or deceitful efforts.
44. Greg. Tur., *VJ* 9 (*MGH*, SRM 1.2, 118).
45. Greg. Tur., *VJ* 9 (*MGH*, SRM 1.2, 118): "... dum in sopore fundit orationem, visum est ei, quasi multitudo catenarum ab eius membris solo decidere. A quo etiam sonitu expergefacta, sensit omnium artuum recepisse plenissimam sanitatem. Protinus surrexit a lectulo, et stupentibus cunctis, cum gratiarum actione vociferans, sancta est ingressa basilicam."

healing also attests to the modicum of repute a pauper might enjoy as recipient of a saint's benefaction.[46] Foedamia was not about to allow her notoriety to expire precipitously; instead, she repeatedly informed others how the holy patron of Brioude had appeared to her. Gregory concluded the anecdote:

> Moreover it is said that it was the habit of this woman to report the appearance of that man who had spoken to her. She used to say that he was tall in stature, refined in dress, exceptional in elegance, with a merry face and golden hair that was graying. He had a fluid gait, a free voice, and a most agreeable allocution. The whiteness of that man's skin shown beyond the brilliance of a lily, so that among the many thousands of men she often saw, there was none like he. And so to many it did not seem absurd [to think] that the blessed martyr had indeed appeared before her.[47]

Foedamia thus found meaningfulness by becoming a living advertisement for the cult of Saint Julian. Importantly, her impressions of Julian as an elegant and erudite man were remarkably similar to contemporary visions of Saint Martin; not, however, the unkempt historical Martin, but rather the elegant image derived from the contemporary aristocratic ideal. Foedamia's description of Julian conformed to the desired image of the pauper's ecclesiastical patrons. The *multi* who thought it "quite reasonable" that the saint presented himself to the pauper likely included the church's clerics, and perhaps even Gregory's relatives, since it is they who principally promoted Julian's cult. Foedamia's remembrance of Julian was a welcomed service on the part of a loyal client who helped confirm and transmit an aristocratic image of a patron saint among lower-class inhabitants of the Auvergne. By committing her story to paper, Gregory in turn ensured that Foedamia's desired association with

---

46. See also Greg. Tur., *VM* 1.11, 2.55.

47. Greg. Tur., *VJ* 9 (*MGH*, SRM 1.2, 118–19): "Ferunt etiam quidam, solitam fuisse eam referre habitum viri qui eam fuerat adlocutus. Dicebat, eum statura esse procerum, veste nitidum, elegantia eximium, vultu hilarem, flava caesariae, inmixtis canis, incessu expeditum, voce liberum, allocutione blandissimum, candoremque cutis illius ultra lilii nitorem fulgere, ita ut de multis milibus hominum, quae saepe vidisset, nullum similem conspicaret. Unde multis non absurde videtur, ei beatum martyrem apparuisse."

Julian would endure to the end of days.[48] If long lasting albeit durational visitations of paupers helped clerics to remind others of the essential link between church and poor, attaching a permanent corps of *pauperes* to churches could do this even more. Furthermore, a band of resident poor could provide services to high ecclesiastics far beyond what temporary and visiting paupers would be able to contribute.

THE REGISTERED POOR

Matricularii ostensibly were beggars whom ecclesiastics invited to make permanent residence at late ancient churches or otherwise regularly subsidized. Their names were maintained on a register called a *matricula*.[49] Although clerics regarded them as *pauperes*, some registered poor hardly appear to have lived in a state of ruin.[50] Rather, they enjoyed a privileged

---

48. One may compare Foedamia's effort to be remembered in association with a saint to like efforts by Gregory's senatorial relations; e.g., Greg. Tur., *VJ* 23, *VP* 8.1. Another self-promoting pauper was a boy who after being healed of a crippling disability hunted down Bishop Gregory to inform him of the miracle. Gregory rewarded the boy's zeal by making his story one of the longest, most detailed accounts in his books on Martin's miracles; *VM* 2.24.

49. Émile Lesne, *Histoire de la propriété ecclésiastique en France aux époques romaine et mérovingienne* (Lille and Paris: R. Giard and H. Champion, 1910), 1: 381–84, errantly attributed the origin of the poor register to early Merovingian Gaul. Judith Herrin, "Ideals of Charity, Realities of Welfare: The Philanthropic Activity of the Byzantine Church," in *Church and People in Byzantium*, ed. R. Morris (Birmingham: Center for Byzantine, Ottoman and Modern Greek Studies, University of Birmingham, 1986), 153, identified John Chrysostom as organizing a poor register in the fourth century. Michel Rouche, "La matricule des pauvres: Évolution d'une inscription de charité du Bas Empire jusqu'à la fin du Haut Moyen Age," in *Études sur l'Histoire de la Pauvreté (Moyen Age-XVIe siècle)*, ed. Michel Mollat (Paris: Publications de la Sorbonne, 1974), 1: 91, rather optimistically contended that *matriculae* existed in all Gallic cities and large towns. M. de Waha, "À propos d'un article recent, quelques reflections sur la matricule des pauvres," *Byzantion* 46 (1976), 357, countered with a low estimate, judging poor registers to exist only in large cities. This is wrong, as evident by the presence of a *matricula* at rural Brioude; Greg. Tur., *VJ* 38. On scholarly debate surrounding the Gallic *matricula*, see Sternberg, *Orientalium More Secutus*, 107–113. The first Gallic *matricula* attested by a contemporary source is that at Reims around 535; ibid., 123–26. Of twenty locales identified with a *matricula* in the sixth and seventh centuries, nine apparently had such a register in the sixth century: Auxerre, Reims, Tours, Candes, Lyons, Limoges, Saix, Trier, and Angoulême; ibid., 144. A comparison of literary references for *matriculae* and *xenodochia* suggests that the latter were almost twice as common to Gaul as the former. These samples are too small to regard this as a completely reliable way to gauge the popularity of these institutions.

50. One category of listed poor that in some locales seem to have constituted an influential special interest group with a "fierce sense of entitlement" is the "order of widows"; Brown, *Poverty and Leadership*, 59. John Chrysostom was critical of the amount of money that churches spent on widows who were not economically downtrodden. Less scrupulous was Pope Gregory, who subsidized his own aunt and two other widows from socially prominent families with enough funds that they would have been able to maintain their elite households; ibid., 59–60. Of course, loyal, affluent widows would have been major contributors to churches upon their demise. For the example of the affluent Erminethrudis

position *vis-à-vis* those beggars who received only temporary assistance from churches. First, some *matricularii* enjoyed living quarters called "houses of the poor" (*domi pauperum*).[51] These buildings comprised part of the increasingly expansive urban church complexes. Second, *matricularii* received regular gifts in money and kind from almsgivers. Gregory wrote that those on the register at Saint Martin's church at Tours received daily contributions from donations by the faithful.[52] Specifically, Gregory recorded that when one pious woman suffered a disabled arm, she traveled to Saint Martin's cell, where she provided nourishment for people listed on the *matricula*. Within the day, her arm healed and she returned home, but she showed her gratitude to the saint by thereafter annually providing "sufficient food to the aforementioned brothers" (*antedictis fratribus alimentum sufficientem*).[53] Another regular source of sustenance for the resident poor was produce taken from fields earmarked for the poor listed on the *matricula*.[54] *Matricularii* also received irregular supplements to their income through inheritances. Some high ecclesiastics remembered the registered poor in their wills. Bishop Bennadius of Reims (d. 459), for example, included *matricularii* among his beneficiaries,[55] while his successor Remigius (died ca. 532) bequeathed gifts to the registered poor at both Reims and Laon.[56] Bishop Bertram of Le Mans (d. 616) donated a year's supply of food along with his clothes to the poor on the *matricula* at the basilica of Saint Martin de Pontlieu.[57] Adalgisel-Grimo, a deacon of Verdun, guaranteed in his testament (634) food and housing for lepers attached to the town's

---

(late sixth to seventh century) bequeathing clothes, jewels and lands to multiple churches, see Effros, *Caring for Body and Soul*, 27, 200–01.

51. Greg. Tur., *VM* 2.27.

52. Greg. Tur., *VM* 1.31. On the *matricula* at Tours, see Pietri, *La ville de Tours*, 714–24.

53. Greg. Tur., *VM* 2.22 (*MGH*, SRM 1.2, 166). See also Greg. Tur., *VM* 2.23, *VJ* 38.

54. Greg. Tur., *VM* 3.14. Bishops attending a council at Clermont prescribed excommunication for any one who seized church property and property belonging to beggars; Council of Clermont (535), c. 5 (*CCL* 148A, 106). Presumably the bishops had in mind beggars attached to the churches.

55. Flodoard, *Historia Remensis Ecclesiae* 1.9 (*MGH*, Scriptores 13, 421): "viduis in matricula positis." Because the source is late (tenth-century), this earliest attestation for a *matricula* in Gaul has been called into question; Sternberg, *Orientalium More Secutus*, 118.

56. Remigius of Reims, *Testamentum* (*MGH*, SRM 3, 337, 339).

57. Bertram of Le Mans, *Testamentum*, in *Actus Pontificum Cenomannis in urbe degentium*, ed. G. Busson and A. Ledru (Le Mans: Au siège de la Société, 1901), 108.

basilica of Saint Peter, and for paupers living on a villa who perhaps were listed on a *matricula*.[58] Resourceful *matricularii* utilized their proximity to churches to achieve other means for profit. For example, the registered poor at the church of Saint Martin at Tours once discovered a child, and after inquiring about its parents for three days without luck, they finally sold the infant and divided the spoils among themselves.[59] The fact that this incident was preserved in a *formula* suggests that finding homes for orphans abandoned at churches might have become a regular function for local *matricularii*.

The perquisites of guaranteed food, shelter, and revenue came at a price for the registered poor. More than other *pauperes*, they would have been beholden to ecclesiastics through the bonds of *patrocinium*. As clients, they owed particular services such as guard duty and protection for bishops, priests, and saints. Fulfillment of these responsibilities, however, afforded them more opportunities to achieve a prominence akin to that enjoyed by other *pauperes* through church affiliation. The most obvious service that *matricularii* performed was to be conspicuous on church property. High ecclesiastics likely relied upon them more than other paupers to substantiate accusations against *necatores pauperum*. Perhaps a reason that clerics posted *matricularii* in certain *villae* belonging to churches was to dissuade malefactors from absconding with the church's belongings. Thus, in what seems a somewhat defensive posture, Gregory offered one tale intended to caution his congregation against trespassing on property belonging to *matricularii*. He wrote that in 582, a man was walking through a villa belonging to the *matricula* when a demon assaulted him, so that the man became so bent forward he could not walk upright without crutches.[60] Fortunately, Saint Martin miraculously healed the fellow during the next festival. This episode may represent a not uncommon instance in which Gallic writers remembered physical assaults as

58. Wilhelm Levison, "Das Testament des Diakons Adalgisel-Grimo vom Jahre 634," in *Aus rheinischer und fränkischer Frühzeit: Ausgewählte Aufsätze von Wilhelm Levison* (Düsseldorf: L. Schwann, 1948), 129–30; Effros, *Caring for Body and Soul*, 195.
59. *Formulae Turonenses* 11 (*MGH*, LL sectio 5, *Formulae*, 141).
60. Greg. Tur., *VM* 3.14.

supernatural encounters.[61] If this is so, perhaps it was not a demon but rather a *matricularius* who treated the man to his impaired condition. After all, as will be seen shortly, violence was not beyond the purview of the registered poor. A second duty of the *matricularii* was to fill the poor box and guard it. About those on the register for Saint Martin's basilica Gregory wrote: "Because the faithful daily bring necessities for the *matricula* ... the blessed paupers make it a habit that while many others are elsewhere, they leave behind a guard who takes up the offerings."[62] Just as in the previous tale, Gregory included in this anecdote the story of a man who filched a gold coin from the poor box, and then died. Given the charge of the *matricularii* to guard the church's money and property alongside the happenstance that those who attempted to take from them regularly incurred injury, one may suspect that some among the registered poor might have been prone to intimidation. Along these lines, a third duty that *matricularii* performed was to assist ecclesiastics in their personal ambitions. One powerful cleric who enjoyed an extraordinary degree of loyalty from his church's *pauperes* was the priest Cato from Clermont, whom Gregory described as "a priest of great humanity devoted to the poor."[63] The author contrasted this pious priest with the notorious Bishop Cautinus, whom we earlier witnessed trying to steal property from another priest, Anastasius. In 571, Cato remained in the city during a vicious plague, burying the dead and conducting mass, while Cautinus fled from town to town to avoid the pestilence. Commenting on the priest's heroic, and ultimately fatal, behavior, Gregory wrote, "I believe that although [Cato] possessed vainglory this event was a cure

---

61. See Greg. Tur., *VM* 3.37, for a woman at the loom who claimed to be assailed by a demon but who likely was a rape victim. On this interpretation, see Suzanne Wemple, *Women in Frankish Society*, 41, who perceived a negative impact upon early medieval young women being instilled with a false sense of modesty: "A sexual assault had such a devastating psychological effect on a victim's self-esteem that normally she preferred to conceal her shame than take her case to court. Those unfortunate enough to be raped blamed their assaults on demons, and it was not unusual for women who had been defiled to kill themselves."

62. Greg. Tur., *VM* 1.31 (*MGH*, SRM 1.2, 153): "Cum ad matriculam illam ... cotidie a fidelibus necessaria tribuantur, consuetudinem benedicti pauperes habent, ut, cum multi ex his per loca siscesserint, custodem inibi derelinquant, qui quod fuerit oblatum accipiat."

63. Greg. Tur., *Hist.* 4.31 (*MGH*, SRM 1.1, 166): "... presbiter multae humanitatis et satis dilectur pauperum."

for him.["64] Indeed, Gregory elsewhere had criticized Cato for possessing an overweening pride, but in so doing he also revealed how an influential ecclesiastic could rely on his *pauperes*. In 555, Bishop Guntharius of Tours died, and so Bishop Cautinus, seeing the vacancy as an opportunity to rid himself of Cato, proposed the priest for the post. But the "prideful" Cato coveted the cathedra at Clermont. Therefore, when King Chlothar I sent a deputation of clerics to offer him the bishopric, Cato relied upon the *pauperes* to provide an excuse to reject the royal decision. Gregory wrote:

> But [Cato], because he was desirous of vainglory, gathered a crowd of paupers and ordered them to call out these words: "Why, good father, are you leaving your sons, whom up to now you have cared for? Who will give us food and drink, if you leave? We beg you not to abandon us, whom you are accustomed to feed!" Then Cato turned to the clergy from Tours, and said, "You see, dearest brothers, how much this crowd of paupers loves me. I cannot leave them and go with you."[65]

These *pauperes* whom Cato called upon likely were, or at the least included, *matricularii*. It even has been suggested, based on this passage, that Cato was the priest assigned to the *matricula* at Clermont.[66] Regardless of this possibility, Cautinus's discomfiture toward the ambitious priest certainly must have been exacerbated by the fact that the city's *pauperes* regarded Cato more than him as their patron. This could be a perilous predicament for a Gallic bishop, because *matricularii* were known to act physically on behalf of their patrons.

A final function of *matricularii* was to provide muscle for ecclesiastics. Gregory illustrated how violently resident *pauperes* could act on behalf of their patrons in his telling of what must have been the most egregious

---

64. Greg. Tur., *Hist.* 4.31 (*MGH*, SRM 1.1, 166): "… et credo, haec causa ei, si quid superbiae habuit, medicamentum fuit."

65. Greg. Tur., *Hist.* 4.11 (*MGH*, SRM 1.1, 142): "At ille, ut erat vanae gloriae cupidus, adunata pauperum caterva, clamorem dari praecepit his verbis: 'Cur nos deseris, bone pater, filios, quos usque nunc edocasti? Quis nos cibo potuque reficiet, si tu abieris? Rogamus, ne nos relinquas, quos alere consuesti.' Tunc ille concersus ad clerum Turonicum, ait: 'Videtis nunc, fratres dilectissimi, qualiter me haec multitudo pauperum diligit; non possum eos relinquere et ire vobiscum.'"

66. Rouche, "La matricule des pauvres," 93.

abuse of sanctuary in his personal experience. In 585, King Guntram and Queen Fredegund encouraged a Frank named Claudius to retrieve an asylum seeker blamed for Chilperic's assassination.[67] The accused, Duke Eberulf, with some of his men, was claiming sanctuary at the basilica of Saint Martin at Tours. Claudius arrived at the church, and under a pretense he exchanged oaths of friendship with his intended victim and proposed that they share a meal. When Eberulf's servants left the premises in search of fine wine, Claudius and his soldiers attacked and slew Eberulf in the church vestibule. To protect themselves from the duke's vengeful servants, the attackers fled to an abbot's cell, where the violence resumed. Eberulf's men hurled spears through windows and transfixed Claudius with a blow. Claudius's retainers hid behind doors and under beds. Two clerics attempted to usher the abbot out of harm's way by dragging him through a line of swordsmen, but when they opened the doors, Eberulf's armed retainers filed into the cell. The defilement of sanctuary and continued naked violence were clear affronts to the honor of Saint Martin, whom Claudius reportedly had never respected.[68] As of 585, Bishop Gregory for nearly twelve years had been going to extraordinary lengths to promote this saint as the foremost patron in the Touraine and beyond. Unfortunately, the bishop happened to be visiting (or was he hiding?) at a manor some thirty miles away when this situation came to a head. [69] But although their corporeal patron was absent, the church's

---

67. Greg. Tur., *Hist.* 7.29. On the Eberulf affair and its political consequences, see Meens, "The Sanctity of the Basilica of Saint Martin," 281–87.

68. Although the slaughter did not happen at the altar of Martin's basilica, it still counted as defilement, for late Roman and Gallic prelates had legislated canons to greatly extend the saint's area of protection to include other church buildings and courtyards. Such extensions enabled sanctuary seekers to be located away from the altar, thereby protecting that sacred space from disturbance, as it did in this case. See Meens, "The Sanctity of the Basilica of Saint Martin," 278–80.

69. After a priest barred Eberulf's direct access to Saint Martin's tomb, the duke railed at Gregory for not protecting him. Gregory afterward shared with the duke a dream he had in which King Guntram entered the basilica, and while Eberulf only feebly grasped the altar cloth, twice letting go, Gregory went chest to chest with the king to defend his charge. An unimpressed Eberulf responded by threatening to murder Gregory and as many clerics as possible; Greg. Tur., *Hist.* 7.22. Rob Meens, ibid., 281–82, points out that this exchange reveals how the duke was in possession of a sword, which would have been contrary to the rules of sanctuary. Despite the bishop's expression of personal bravado, perhaps it was due to this threat that he abandoned Tours. Another theory, which I strongly doubt, but is intriguing nevertheless, is that Gregory intentionally absented himself so that Claudius would have been free to strike his intended victim. Meens, ibid., 285, offers the possibility "that Gregory had been instrumental for the king [Guntram] in the killing of Eberulf and that it was this that brought

dependents knew how to respond to the indignity being heaped upon their spiritual guardian. Gregory recorded:

> Some of the *matricularii* and other *pauperers* were so incensed at the crime that they tried to pull the roof off the cell. Then possessed people and a number of beggars seized sticks and stones and rushed to avenge the violence done to their church, bearing it ill that such atrocities as had never been witnessed before should now have been perpetrated there. What more [can I say?] Those who had taken refuge were dragged from their hiding places and cruelly put to death. The floor of the abbot's cell reeked with blood. The dead bodies were pulled out and left to lie naked on the ground. The killers seized what loot they could and disappeared into the darkness, which had now fallen.[70]

Tellingly, as the *pauperes* of Tours meted vengeance upon the defilers of Martin's shrine, the *matricularii* led the charge. If in fact they had only rocks and clubs to wield against soldiers bearing spears and swords, then their onslaught could have succeeded only by force of numbers. Thus the registered poor at individual churches could include large numbers of potentially violent persons.[71] By virtue of their proximity to powerful ecclesiastics and because of the extraordinary services rendered, they earned food, housing, and more. Because their functions resembled

---

him royal favour at Orléans." Meens, ibid., adds that whether or not Gregory had a hand in Eberulf's demise, the culprit's death helped facilitate the rapprochement between king and bishop. This event would have influenced Gregory's admiration for Guntram, which in turn will have had an affect on the compositional structure of the *Historiae*.

70. Greg. Tur., *Hist.* 7.29 (*MGH*, SRM 1.1, 349): "Nonnulli etiam matriculariorum et reliquorum pauperum pro scelere commisso tectum cellolae conantur evertere. Sed et inergumini ac diversi egeni cum petris et fustibus ad ulciscendam basilicae vilentiam profiscuntur, indigne ferentes, quur talia, quae numquam facta fuerant, essent ibidem perpetrata. Quid plura? Extrahuntur fugaces ex abditis et crudeliter trucidantur; pavimentum cellolae tabo maculatur. Postquam vero interempti sunt, extrahuntur foris et nudi super humum frigidam relinquuntur. Percussores vero nocte sequenti, adpraehensis spoliis, fuga dilabuntur." Trans. based on Thorpe, *Gregory of Tours, History of the Franks*, 412.

71. As epilogue, Gregory reported that Guntram confiscated Eberulf's ancestral properties about Tours, thereby ironically leaving the duke's wife destitute at Saint Martin's basilica; Greg. Tur., *Hist.* 7.29. Gregory was godfather to Eberulf's son, having held him at the baptismal font; Greg. Tur., *Hist.* 7.22. But given the bishop's animus toward the family, one wonders whether he would have been willing to subsidize the widow anywhere near the extent to which Pope Gregory financially supported widows of socially prominent Roman families.

those of the lower clergy, their best chance for social advancement likely was to be had by entering those ranks, to which we now turn.

Clerics of the Lower Orders and Church Custodians

The functions of *matricularii* were similar to those of clerics of the lower orders. By the sixth century, lesser clerical posts had yet to be established definitively. For example, two fifth-century religious tracts, the *Statuta ecclesiae antiqua* and *De septem ordinibus ecclesiae*, both of Gallic provenance, offer discordant rankings of low-level clerics.[72] *De septem ordinibus* lists the bottom three positions as lectors (*lectores*), doorkeepers (*ostiarii*), and gravediggers (*fossarii*),[73] while the lengthier *Statuta ecclesiae antiqua* lists the lowest orders as acolytes (*acolythi*), exorcists (*exorcistae*), lectors (*lectores*), doorkeepers (*ostiarii*), and cantors (*psalmistae* or *cantores*).[74] Among the lower clerical posts for which the narrative sources provide evidence, that which differed most from the others was *lector*. According to both *De septem ordinibus* and the *Statuta ecclesiae antiqua*, *lectores* were more prestigious than doorkeepers.[75] The principal function of *lectores* was to conduct readings of Scripture before the congregation, and therefore the post necessitated that one be literate.[76] This qualification did not exclude people of lower rank from the post, for the literarily competent slave Andarchius was a lector before Duke Lupus wrested him from his master, Felix.[77] However, the office of lector commonly would have gone to young, socially prominent upstarts, especially at urban churches, where lifelong clerics ventured to climb an

---

72. From the early Middle Ages, scholars wrongly attributed *De septem ordinibus ecclesiae* to Saint Jerome; Migne, ed., *PL* 30, 162–63. Similarly, the origin of the *Statuta ecclesiae antiqua* was misdated to fourth-century Africa. Only in the nineteenth century was it identified as a work of late fifth-century Gaul. See Charles Munier, ed., *Les Statuta Ecclesiae Antiqua: Édition – Études critiques* (Paris: Presses Universitaires de France, 1960), 101. Both works concur on the four highest ecclesiastical orders: bishop, priest, deacon, and sub-deacon; *De septem ordinibus ecclesiae*, c. 4–7; *Statuta ecclesiae antiqua*, c. 90–93.
73. *De septem ordinibus ecclesiae*, c. 1–3.
74. *Statuta ecclesiae antiqua*, c. 94–98. The final canons of the *recapitulatio ordinationis officialium ecclesiae* of the *Statuta ecclesiae* address nuns (*sanctimoniales virgines*) and widows (*viduae*); c. 99–100.
75. *De septem ordinibus ecclesiae*, c. 3; *Statuta ecclesiae antiqua*, c. 96–97.
76. *Statuta ecclesiae antiqua*, c. 96.
77. Greg. Tur., *Hist.* 4.46.

ecclesiastical *cursus honorum*.[78] This then was a position through which upper-class ecclesiastics were expected to cut their teeth. Closer to the functions of *matricularii* were the duties of other low-level clerics such as gravediggers and doorkeepers.

Ranking among the bottommost clerics were gravediggers (*fossores* or *fossarii*). *De septem ordinibus* ranked the *order fossariorum* as the first and lowest grade of the church.[79] Beyond the obvious responsibility of burying the dead, another duty for *fossores* apparently was to defend the interests of churches, forcefully if necessary. A famous fourth-century episode from Italy in which gravediggers joined pallbearers (*lecticarii*) as ecclesiastical muscle involved these low-level clerics using deadly force to secure the Roman cathedra for Pope Damasus.[80] Turning the tables, Sidonius Apollinaris related that he once chanced upon several grave diggers – he called them "coffin-carriers with burial rakes" (*baiuli rastris funebribus*) – as they inadvertently were unearthing the tomb of his grandfather, and so without petitioning the Bishop of Lyons for permission, he gave the toughs a lashing then and there.[81] Although Gregory of Tours did not refer to an order of gravediggers, his pages include examples of what might have been *fossores* engaged in the church's heavy business. One candidate was a church custodian (*aedituus templi*) whose responsibility was "to keep impure people from the tombs" (*inmundi ab his arcerentur*) at the basilica of Saints Agricola and Vitalis at Bologna. When an audacious man reached into a tomb at this shrine to take an item from the ashes, "the lid crushed his head," and the man barely escaped alive.[82] Given the *fossores'* charge to guard church assets, and their propensity to use force, one wonders whether the *aedituus templi* weighed on the thief's conscience by lending his mass to the stone lid atop the culprit's noggin. Another episode potentially involving

---

78. E. g., Cato at Clermont: Greg. Tur., *Hist.* 4.6; Marcellus of Paris: Ven. Fort., *Vita Marcelli* 4. On the Gallic ecclesiastical *cursus honorum*, see Godding, *Prêtres en Gaule mérovingienne*, 32–49; Scheibelreiter, "Church Structure and Organisation," 689–90.

79. *De septem ordinibus ecclesiae*, c. 1.

80. Brown, *Power and Persuasion in Late Antiquity*, 103. Damasus's *fossores* were instrumental in ridding of a rival episcopal candidate's persistent supporters.

81. Sid. Ap., *Ep.* 3.12 (Anderson, ed. and trans., 2: 40–41).

82. Greg. Tur., *GM* 43 (*MGH*, SRM 1.2, 67): "... missoque introrsum capite, obpraessus ab eo."

fossores pertains to the nefarious activity of the aforementioned Bishop Cautinus, who buried the priest Anastasius alive and stationed *custodes* to watch over him.[83] Because these guards employed a sarcophagus to detain their prey, perhaps they were *fossores*. Or maybe they were not; perhaps Gregory, like the author of the *Statuta ecclesiae antiqua*, did not regard *fossores* as a separate clerical order. Perhaps he deemed grave digging and tomb watching to be jobs appropriate for *ostiarii*, or perhaps *matricularii*. Regardless, the lowest group of clerics universally considered as an order, and singled out in Gregory's text was doorkeepers (*ostiarii*).

According to *De septem ordinibus*, *ostiarii* ranked only above *fossores*,[84] while the *Statuta ecclesiae antiqua* listed *ostiarii* only higher than cantors, who were not ordained.[85] The principal duties of *ostiarii* were to attend church doors and manage the congregation during services.[86] *De septem ordinibus* charges that *ostiarii* "will guard all things that are inside and outside," which may mean that they also were responsible for protecting or overseeing cemeteries, too.[87] As a sign of their responsibilities they were entrusted with keys either for a church or its altar. Narrative sources depict *ostiarii*, like *matricularii*, guarding. For example, Gregory wrote that a wayward bird once flittered about a church at Clermont, dousing oil lamps until the *ostiarii* managed to kill it.[88] Gregory interpreted the bird's conduct as a presage for a plague that struck the Auvergne in 571. While readers might have imagined the bird's behavior to be unusual, they likely would have thought nothing extraordinary about *ostiarii* dutifully restoring order inside a church, in which setting people frequently became rambunctious, as Caesarius of Arles often complained. A third duty of doorkeepers was to protect

---

83. Greg. Tur., *Hist.* 4.12 (*MGH*, SRM 1.1, 143).
84. *De septem ordinibus ecclesiae*, c. 2.
85. *Statuta ecclesiae antiqua*, c. 97–98.
86. According to Scheibelreiter, "Church Structure and Organisation," 690, members of the order were no longer clerics in the sixth century. Given that Gregory referred to them frequently, perhaps this demoting trend, presumably spreading from Rome, did not happen in Gaul until the seventh century.
87. *De septem ordinibus ecclesiae*, c. 2 (Migne, ed., *PL* 30, 52): "… omnia quae intus sunt extraque custidant …"; Handley, "Beyond Hagiography: Epigraphic Commemoration," 194.
88. Greg. Tur., *Hist.* 4.31.

the interests of their patrons with force if necessary. For example, in 581 a faction of clerics at Marseilles plotted with Governor Dynamius of Provence to oust Bishop Theodore.[89] The root cause of this factionalism was King Childebert II and Guntram's dispute over division of the city's revenues. When Guntram gave orders that Dynamius detain Theodore, rebellious clerics seized the opportunity to loot the coffers and pillage church property. Childebert then sent Duke Gundulf, Gregory's relation, to aid Theodore. When Dynamius and the rebel clerics prevented the bishop and duke from entering the city gates, the latter pair responded with a ruse. They invited Dynamius to meet them inside the extramural church of Saint Stephen. But as soon as the governor entered the edifice, the *ostiarii* slammed the doors shut, thereby separating Dynamius from his armed soldiers. Next the two parties fruitlessly debated their differences at the altar, and then Dynamius retreated as far as the sacristy, but lacking the protection of his retainers he was "rebuked terribly" (*terribiliter increpant*).[90] Outside the church, the governor's soldiers brandished their weapons, but they were driven off. Duke Gundulf then secured the support of the city's leading citizens, so that later he and Bishop Theodore triumphantly reentered Marseilles, reportedly to the delight of a cheering multitude.[91] In this episode, one witnesses yet again the forceful role of church guardians – in this instance, *ostiarii*. In actuality, the actions of church custodians, be they *matricularii*, *ostiarii* or *fossores*, must have appeared virtually indistinguishable. Perhaps their unanimity of conduct, coupled with low social status, explains why authors such as Gregory hardly ever considered identifying these groups separately. Why should his reading audience be concerned with details of minute differences among the hired help? Instead, when mentioning *matricularii* and lesser clerics guarding churches, the author generally opted for what he must have thought an appropriately ambiguous terminology, words such as *custodes* and *aeditui*. For example, Gregory recorded how church guards once apprehended a thief who had infiltrated the shrine of Saint Julian,

89. Greg. Tur., *Hist.* 6.11.
90. Greg. Tur., *Hist.* 6.11 (*MGH*, SRM 1.1, 281).
91. Greg. Tur., *Hist.* 6.11 (*MGH*, SRM 1.1, 281).

determined to steal a jeweled cross and curtains adorning the holy man's tomb:

> [A thief] put the bundle under his head; then, drowsy and weighed down by his sin, he fell asleep. In the middle of the night the custodians walked through the holy church and saw in a corner one jewel from the cross, shining just like a star in heaven. They were disturbed and fearfully came closer. Once they brought a candle, they found the man lying there with the stolen objects that he could not carry away. During the night the man was kept in custody; then at daybreak he confessed everything that he had done. He claimed that he had become weary and fallen asleep because after walking around the church for a very long time, even with a torch he could not find a door through which he might exit.[92]

This anecdote depicts what would have been a common scene, *custodes* diligently guarding a funerary shrine, defending against the all too common practice of grave robbery.[93] Gregory left too few clues to determine whether the guards were *matricularii*, *ostiarii*, or *fossores*, but why would they not have consisted of some combination of the three?[94] By divorcing this anecdote from its hagiographical trappings, the not uncommon behavior of *custodes* employing violence again becomes plausible. Perhaps when they discovered the culprit, these guards helped him to his premature nap and held him until morning.

Just as the Bishop of Tours commonly offered ambivalent terminology in reference to church custodians, so too did he often ambiguously

---

92. Greg. Tur., *VJ* 20 (*MGH*, SRM 1.2, 123): "… positum capiti sarcinam, peccati sopore conpraessus, obdormivit. Media vero nocte circumeuntes custodes sanctam basilicam, aspiciunt in angulo unam gemmam crucis tamquam iubar caeleste regulgere; obstupefacti accedunt comminus cum timore, admotoque cereo, inveniunt personam cum rebus furatis, quas auferre non potuerat, inibi decubare. Denique, sub custodia eum illa nocte detentum, mane facto cuncta quae fecerat patefecit, adserens se lassum obdormisse, eo quod diutissime circuiens cum fasce basilicam, ostium unde egrederetur repperire non poterat." Trans. by Van Dam, *Saints and their Miracles*, 177.

93. Bonnie Effros, *Caring for Body and Soul*, 54, proposes that the tendency among hagiographers to forego mention of royal intervention in portrayals of grave robbers being captured at churches "likely stemmed from fear that a king might benefit from such a precedent to interfere in bishops' or abbots' households." Alternatively, or complementarily, perhaps these images reflect how ecclesiastics simply found it more effective to turn loose their *aeditui templum* on such pillagers rather than petition for the aid of royal agents.

94. Perhaps the clerics among the guards numbered only *ostiarii*, as Gregory's terminology suggests.

identify the violent men who defended powerful ecclesiastics. Gregory would have assumed that given a proper context, readers would recognize readily those he labeled *pauperes*, *servientes*, or *clerici* for what they were, the bishop's mob. An explicit example of this is to be found back at Marseilles in 581, not long after Theodore recovered his see. Governor Dynamius convinced King Guntram to permit him to seize Theodore a second time.[95] Unable to remove the prelate from the fortified city, Dynamius bided his time until the day arrived when the bishop led a procession to dedicate an oratory outside the walls. A group of armed men (*armati*) ambushed the processors, surrounded Theodore, and knocked him from his steed. The bishop's companions (*comites*) fled, while Dynamius' troops "bound his servants and cut down his clerics."[96] In this instance, the bishop's force proved no match for the governor's soldiers. But given the violent atmosphere permeating Marseilles at the time, and assuming Theodore was not so foolish as not to suspect Dynamius of a subterfuge, one wonders whether this procession included nothing more than docile high clergy. That some of Theodore's clerics were "cut down" suggests they might have put up a fight, and that the bishop's servants were tied up implies there might have been reason to constrain them. A considerable portion of the men Gregory here termed *servientes* and *clerici* likely included the *pauperes* and lesser clerics upon whom Gallic bishops relied for physical protection.

If a bishop's retinue were powerful enough that it might hope to stand toe to toe with a royal agent's armed band, it must have been quite effective when brought to bear against more quotidian opponents such as renegade preachers. Indeed, Gregory recorded that in 590 a person claiming to be Christ stirred up the southern Gallic countryside and amassed a following of more than 3,000 people including peasants and clerics while en route from Arles to Le Puy. Gregory set the scene for the ultimate confrontation between this preacher and a bishop by using military imagery: "[The false-Christ] positioned each army about the surrounding basilicas, marshalling a battle line, as if readying to make

95. Greg. Tur., *Hist.* 6.11.
96. Greg. Tur., *Hist.* 6.11 (*MGH*, SRM 1.1, 282): "…servientes alligant, clericos caedunt."

war against Aurelius who was then the bishop of the place. ..."[97] Could such an upstart, even an unusually influential one, prove a match for a Gallic bishop? Although momentarily taken aback (*stupens*), Bishop Aurelius did not waver: "He sent forth his strong men" (*direxit ... viros strenuos*).[98] The leader among these then approached the false prophet, bent as if to kiss his knees, and pounced. He seized the culprit and ordered his fellows to strip him bare and cut him down with a sword. Gregory smugly remarked: "So fell and died that Christ who better ought to be called Antichrist."[99] It was a beginner's mistake on the part of the preacher to challenge a bishop and allow strangers to approach so near to his person. As for the prelate, he likely was wise in his selection of those who infiltrated the enemy ranks. Who better for a bishop to send to deceptively mingle among a multitude of rustics if not a group of *pauperes* and lower clerics? And who better for a bishop to take out a troublesome pseudo-Christ if not his own *viri strenui*? In Barbarian Gaul, the two were one and the same.

Gallic bishops, Gregory in particular, sometimes have been characterized as pusillanimous hurlers of somewhat empty threats of saintly retribution, unable actually to defend themselves.[100] Likely contributing to this notion of "the usually peaceful bishop" is the counter-example of two famous, and supposedly unusual, notoriously warlike prelates. The brothers Salonius and Sagittarius, Bishops of Embrun and Gap, respectively, first appear in the *Historiae* battling Lombards alongside the Patrician Mummolus. Gregory was critical of their conduct: "Rather than be admonished by the heavenly cross, they were armed

---

97. Greg. Tur., *Hist.* 10.25 (*MGH*, SRM 1.1, 518): "... ad basilicas propinquas cum omni exerictu restitit, instruens aciem, qualiter Aurilio, ibidem tunc consistentem episcopo, bellum inferret ..."

98. Greg. Tur., *Hist.* 10.25 (*MGH*, SRM 1.1, 518–19).

99. Greg. Tur., *Hist.* 10.25 (*MGH*, SRM 1.1, 519): "... ceciditque Christus ille, qui magis Antechristus nominare debet, et mortuus est ..."

100. E.g., Giselle de Nie, "The Spring, the Seed and the Tree: Gregory of Tours on the Wonders of Nature," *Journal of Medieval History* 11 (1985), 110, describes Gregory as "unarmed" and "utterly dependent" upon interpreting natural events as divine aid and threats. In idem, "Caesarius of Arles and Gregory of Tours: Two Sixth-Century Gallic Bishops and 'Christian Magic,'" in *Cultural Identity and Cultural Integration: Ireland and Europe in the Early Middle Ages*, ed. Doris Edel (Portland, OR: Four Courts, 1995), 182, she refers to Gregory as "unarmed in a violent society in which every self-respecting man either carried arms himself or had a body-guard. Gregory had Saint Martin." Yes, he had Martin, but I contend he also had a bodyguard!

with the worldly helmet and breastplate, and what is worse, it was said that they killed many by their own hands."[101] Later the brothers' force (*cohors*) armed with swords and arrows assailed Bishop Victor of Saint-Paul-Trois-Châteaux during his birthday party, beat his servants, and robbed his house.[102] Prelates attending two church councils, Lyons (567/73) and Chalon-sur-Saône (579), condemned their more recent misbehavior. At the latter synod, bishops realized that accusing the two of adultery and murder would not suffice to rid of them, so they added a charge of treason, and thereby managed to depose the pair. Gregory's dislike of Salonius and Sagittarius ran deep. The two had been deacons at Lyons under Bishop Nicetius, perhaps at the same time Gregory had been deacon there. Had they been opponents of their own pontiff? Would they have been supporters of Priscus when the latter "stole" the family see from Gregory's kin? Gregory's ire derived from a heartfelt conviction that the pair neglected their pastoral duties, and from a possibly prejudiced belief that they were gluttonous fornicators. Regarding their pugnacious conduct, Gregory took offense at the brothers' delight at riding into combat and their willingness to assail a fellow bishop. But Gregory would not have criticized them for retaining strong men who might properly defend their churches and the poor. He realized that the violent nature of Barbarian Gaul required prominent figures, including bishops, to surround themselves with bodyguards. Thus, he recorded without complaint how Bishop Magneric of Trier in 590 relied on his henchmen to save him when suddenly it happened that the prelate found himself in his own residence being held at sword-point.[103] A fugitive duke, Guntram Boso, had claimed sanctuary in the city and threatened to slay the bishop if he did not negotiate a pardon with King Guntram's soldiers, who were camped outside the edifice. The ostensibly "bishop-loving" and "church defending" King Guntram apparently became thoroughly exacerbated by this situation, and so he directed his troops to burn down the house, atop both duke and bishop if necessary.

---

101. Greg. Tur., *Hist.* 4.42 (*MGH*, SRM 1.1, 175): "… qui non cruce caelesti moniti, sed galea ac lorica saeculari armati, multos manibus propriis, quod peius est, interfecisset referuntur."
102. Greg. Tur., *Hist.* 5.20.
103. Greg. Tur., *Hist.* 9.10.

Learning of the king's command, Magneric's *clerici* decisively acted; they rushed the church doors, wrested their patron from the grasp of the desperate duke, and dragged him out to safety.[104] These *clerici* must have possessed a special fortitude to be willing to dash into a building and steal their patron from a sword wielding general and his henchmen. That Magneric's clerics were of such a disposition was not simply fortunate; it was typical.

An instance in which Gregory's clerical underlings aided their patron involved goings on at Tours in 580 while the bishop was standing trial at Berny-Rivière in regard to Leudast's claim that he had committed treason.[105] The senior cleric in this conspiracy was the wily pauper turned archdeacon, Riculf. Anticipating that he finally would replace Gregory as bishop, Riculf took an inventory of the church plate and began dealing with the clergy accordingly: "To the higher clergy he presented gifts, including vineyards and fields. But to the lesser clerics he gave many beatings and lashes, striking with his own hand."[106] Apparently the pugnacious Riculf, who himself might once have been a *matricularius* under Bishop Eufronius, figured that bribes could turn the higher clerics to his support, but it would require a heavy hand to beat the loyalty out of the faithful and potentially violent lower clerics.[107] Even after Gregory returned to Tours, exonerated of all charges, Riculf continued to act contemptuously to the point of threatening to kill the bishop. After meeting with his suffragan prelates, Gregory had Riculf confined to a monastery. Here the author offered no details for how he actually managed to subdue and deport the belligerent foe. But one can scarcely doubt that Gregory's lesser *clerici* and *matricularii* were not eager to oblige their patron in ridding him of this troublesome priest. At the end of the sixth century, any properly prepared bishop knew to keep a corps of *viri strenui* at hand. If it happened that some of these strong men

104. Greg. Tur., *Hist.* 9.10 (*MGH*, SRM 1.1, 425).
105. Greg. Tur., *Hist.* 5.49.
106. Greg. Tur., *Hist.* 5.49 (*MGH*, SRM 1.1, 262): "Maiores clericos muneribus ditat, largitur vineas, prata distrubuit; minoribus vero fustibus plagisque multis etiam manu propria adfecit ... ."
107. On the possibility of Riculf's having been a *matricularius*, Gregory wrote that Eufronius had elevated him *de pauperibus*; Greg. Tur., *Hist.* 5.49 (*MGH*, SRM 1.1, 262).

might simultaneously remind others of the metaphorical connection between church and poor, so much the better.

OPPORTUNITIES FOR *MATRICULARII* AND CHURCH *CUSTODES*

Social opportunities for *matricularii* principally lay in the perquisites they received for performing their duties: the assurance of food and drink, the security of lodging, and income. Beyond mundane compensations, however, the registered poor could achieve satisfaction through participation in saints' cults and even social advancement into the clerical ranks. Like common *pauperes*, some *matricularii* obtained the benefits concomitant with being healed by a saint. When a pauper from Angers was struck deaf and dumb, he joined the *matricula* at Candes.[108] After six years passed, Saint Martin appeared in a dream to the *matricularius* and restored his speech: "Immediately, a certain man materialized dressed in a bishop's garb. Upon laying hands and making the sign of the cross of Christ on his brow, [Martin] said: 'The Lord has healed you. Rise and hasten to the basilica and give thanks to God.'"[109] Here the former mute's very gratitude would have conferred upon him a special status by making of his voice a testament to the healing *virtus* of the saint. If the pauper actually described Martin "clothed in a bishop's robe" as Gregory recorded in the text, then the seasoned *matricularius*, like Foedamia of Brioude, would have provided his ecclesiastical patron a service by confirming the very aristocratic image of the saint that Bishop Gregory was trying to impose on the community.

The registered poor would have been as eager to inform bishops of miraculous episodes as other *pauperes* were to apprise hagiographers about healings. Because *matricularii* were a constant fixture at churches, none was in a better position to report miracles than they. In fact, they along with lesser clerics were a principal source for many

---

108. Greg. Tur., *VM* 3.23. Pietri, *La Ville de Tours*, 719, identified this *pauper* as a *matricularius*, as did Van Dam, *Saints and their Miracles*, 269.

109. Greg. Tur., *VM* 3.23 (*MGH*, SRM 1.2, 188): "Et statim visus est ei vir quidam sacerdotali habitu comptus, gangens eum et crucem Christi fronti eius inponens, ait: 'Dominus te sanum fecit. Surge et propera ad ecclesiam et age gratias Deo tuo.'"

of the contemporary miracles recorded in Gregory's hagiography. The bishop admitted: "Whenever a report surfaces that the blessed bishop's power has been present, I send for the shrine's guards to find out what has transpired. ..."[110] Thus the "trustworthy men" (*viri fideles*) whom Gregory confessed brought so many miracles stories to him likely included both *matricularii* and lesser clerics.[111] Because many miracle stories passed through the *custodes* before they made their way to Gregory, it is not unlikely that the content of his *Miracula* was influenced somewhat by the witnesses' desire to have their experiences depicted and preserved in literary form. So long as the stories rang true, contributed to the repute of the saints, and encouraged proper respect for the holy patrons, why would a hagiographer not include them? As was mentioned, the tale of the thief who "fell asleep" after he could not find an exit to the shrine of Saint Julian may preserve in fanciful form several *custodes'* actual capture of such a man. Similarly, one guard received a rare benefit after apprehending a thief inside a church not only by having his story told in a *Vita* but by having his name included in the account. Reportedly Baudegisilus was wakened through a dreamed visitation from Saint Gaugericus of Cambrai (died ca. 623), and thereby he was able to prevent a man from robbing the saint's tomb.[112] This thief managed to escape punishment, however, by obtaining sanctuary at another church. In another miracle tale reeking of custodial involvement, the offending party was not so fortunate. According to Gregory, when King Sigibert's army besieged Paris in 574, a soldier entered the church of Saint Denis and had the

---

110. Greg. Tur., *VM* 3.45 (*MGH*, SRM 1.2, 193): "Cumque rumor surrexerit, beati antestitis apparuisse virtutem, vocatis ad nos custodibus aedis, quae sunt acta cognoscimus ..." Luce Pietri, *La ville de Tours*, 364–66, suspected that these *custodes* were *ostiarii*, but given the similarities of place and function there is no reason to doubt that the guards would not have included *matricularii*.

111. See, e. g., Greg. Tur., *VJ* 34, 35. It was an *aedituus* at the church of the martyr Saint Ferreolus at Vienne who informed Gregory how the head of Saint Julian came to be buried separately from its body at that church; Greg. Tur., *VJ* 2 (*MGH*, SRM, 1.2, 114).

112. *Vita Gaugerici* 15; and see Effros, *Caring for Body and Soul*, 53–54. While the anonymous hagiographer had to admit that the thief escaped immediate punishment, he was able smugly to report that the man died soon after the crime. Furthermore, just as he positively commemorated the church guard for doing his duty, so too did the author permanently malign the memory of the thief, and perhaps his surviving family members also, by publicizing his name, Launericus, in the account.

audacity to climb atop the tomb and attempt to pry loose a golden, ornamental dove, but his plan went awry: "Because there was a tower on top of the tomb, the man's feet slipped on each side. He crushed his testicles, stabbed himself in the side with his spear, and was found dead. Let no one doubt that this happened not by chance, but by the judgment of God."[113] I think Gregory sometimes exhibited a wicked sense of humor! Indeed, assuming Saint Denis' temple guards were of the usual caliber among Gallic *aeditui*, there is little doubt that the mutilation and death of this soldier happened "by chance"![114]

A similar suspicion arises in connection with another episode that attests specifically to the loyalty that made *matricularii* so valuable to their patrons. According to Gregory, the registered poor at Tours once left a custodian to collect alms at the colonnade at Saint Martin's church. When the man received a small gold coin from one of the faithful, he pocketed it. Hearing that someone had left a donation, the other *pauperes* returned and demanded that the suspect declare his innocence before the saint's tomb. No sooner had the custodian begun to speak than he fell to the ground in pain and confessed his misdeed: "'I committed perjury regarding that *trians* that the paupers asked about, and so vengeance is promptly striking me. Still, I request that you give the coin back to the *matricula*.' When the coin was given back, immediately the man lost his spirit."[115] Not only did this poor man attempt to steal from the *matricularii*, but he also presumed he could circumvent the authority of the holy arbiter, Martin. Had the pauper survived, or had he been permitted to survive, perhaps he would have attributed the assault to a demon, as the aforementioned trespasser on property of the *matricula* at Tours had done. For Gregory, stealing from a poor box was

---

113. Greg. Tur., *GM* 71 (*MGH*, SRM 1.2, 86): "... elapsisque pedibus ab utraque parte, quia turritum erat tumulum, conpressis testiculis, lancea in latere defixa, exanimis est inventus. Id non fortuitu contigisse, sed iudicio Dei gestum, nullus ambigat." Trans. by Van Dam, *Gregory of Tours, Glory of the Martyrs*, 95.

114. Gregory revealed his lighter side by telling a miracle story about a ferrier who prayed to Saint Martin, who in turn caused a large fish to leap from a whirlpool into his boat; Greg. Tur., *VM* 2.16.

115. Greg. Tur., *VM* 1.31 (*MGH*, SRM 1.2, 153): "'Triantem illum quem pauperes requirebant periuravi, et ideo me praesens vindicta flagellat; sed rogo, ut eum accipientes reddatis matriciolae.' Quo reddito, statim amisit spiritum."

no laughing matter. The bishop concluded the anecdote by consigning the poor malefactor's soul to hell.[116]

Rather than risking life and limb by taking from a poor box, *matricularii* otherwise could improve their social lot by entering into lesser clerical orders. Becoming a cleric did not guarantee a dramatic change in one's economic situation. For example, there was a lame man from Bourges named Leuboveus, who despite already being a cleric had to drag himself to Tours because his poverty prevented him from renting a porter.[117] But if the transition from *matricularius* to *clericus* did not necessarily entail economic improvement, it could bring about elements of increased prestige. Rising up the pecking order of church guardians involved several factors that could foster a greater sense of worth. First, prospective clerics underwent ceremonies of initiation that marked their transition from the *saeculum* to the clergy. According to the *Statuta ecclesiae antiqua*, entering the *ordo ostiariorum* included a meaningful ordination ritual conducted by the archdeacon in the bishop's presence.[118] Second, clerics of all ranks distinguished themselves from the laity by wearing the tonsure. Lesser clerics who lacked economic clout might regard this mark as a meaningful status symbol as much or more than did their upper-class brethren. Thus, when Gregory described how Saint Martin healed the slave Veranus, he depicted the servile person receiving the following benefits: "[Veranus's] head was tonsured, he received his freedom, and now he serves the needs of the blessed lord [Martin]."[119]

116. Greg. Tur., *VM* 1.31 (*MGH*, SRM 1.2, 153): "Quae invida quondam vidua duobus minutis caeleste regnum mercanti fueras [Mark 12: 42–44; Luke 21: 1–4], hunc per unum triantem *ad ima* praecipitas," with my italics. This perjuring pauper is one of but eight individuals whom Gregory directly consigned to hell using a term for the underworld; Jones, "Death and Afterlife in the Pages of Gregory of Tours" (forthcoming). I am not proposing that every miracle needs to be explained away in the old "positivist" manner. But I do think it is a worthwhile endeavor, one of many credible approaches to hagiographical evidence, to consider how Gallic miracle stories may confirm details from other sources about the behavior of people associated with churches. Because other evidence suggests that church custodians used violence to defend patrons, I think it important to consider whether hagiographical anecdotes can be read to substantiate this behavior.

117. Greg. Tur., *VM* 2.7 (*MGH*, SRM 1.2, 161). A miraculous recovery of this man's feet occurred in 574, on the day that Kings Sigibert, Chilperic, and Guntram made peace with one another. On the political implications of this and two other miracles at the tomb of Saint Martin on that day, see Van Dam, *Saints and their Miracles*, 232, n. 53.

118. *Statuta ecclesiae antiqua*, c. 97.

119. Greg. Tur., *VM* 2.4 (*MGH*, SRM 1.2, 161): "Qui, tonsurato capite, accepta libertate, beati domni usibus nunc deservit."

Here perhaps the bishop expected low-ranking members of his audience to be as impressed by mention of the tonsure as by the fact that Veranus was free. Third, by becoming a lesser cleric, one might achieve greater intimacy with an ecclesiastical patron and a holy patron. Perhaps elevation from *matricularius* to *clericus* included a move from the *domus pauperum* to the *domus ecclesiae*. Clerics and servants who had personal contact with a bishop would be privy to even more opportunities to enjoy a saint's favor. For example, Gregory commonly administered his healing concoction of water and dust from the tombs of his patron saints to his personal servants and attendant clerics, and he included accounts of their recoveries in the *Miracula*.[120] Becoming a cleric also might increase one's opportunity to be buried in the vicinity of a saint, which would be regarded as improving one's likelihood for salvation.[121] At Trier, separate commemorands offered rare mentions of occupation for two *ostiarii* buried at extra-mural cemeteries for devotees to particular cults.[122] Ursatius (sixth or seventh century) was interred in the northern cemetery of Saints Paulinus and Maximinus, while an anonymous doorkeeper (unknown date) was buried at the city's southern cemetery of Saint Eucherius.[123] How many more tombs at extra-mural cemeteries that do not have epitaphs mentioning occupation might have held the remains of lesser clerics? Presumably, these *ostiarii*, and perhaps many other devoted low clergy buried in graveyards of the holy, enjoyed true satisfaction knowing that their proximate patron saint would one day advocate their souls' entry into heaven, as did a confident Gregory of Tours.[124]

120. Servants: Greg. Tur., *VM* 3.12, 59; clerics: Greg. Tur., *VM* 1.33, 3.52.
121. Handley, *Death, Society and Culture*, 155.
122. The epitaphs read *ustiarii* (sc. *ostiarii*); Handley, "Beyond Hagiography: Epigraphic Commemoration," 194.
123. Ibid. About this duo, Handley, ibid., 194–95, writes: "If they were buried in the cemeteries where they held their posts, then an argument could be made that the ecclesiastical organization of Trier included the appointment of officials with responsibility for overseeing burial there. Clerical control over these cemeteries and over burial must be envisaged."
124. For Gregory's certainty that Saint Martin would protect him in the afterlife, see Greg. Tur., *Hist.* 10.31. In the seventh century, confident notions of direct entry to heaven waned as anxious ideas connected to the notion of purgatory increased; Effros, *Caring for Body and Soul*, 162–68.

Conclusion

In the final analysis, an ecclesiastical need to project an image of continued association between church and poor resulted in a relationship of mutual exploitation between clerical patrons and *pauperes*. Undoubtedly some powerful ecclesiastics anxiously labored to maintain the church's traditional charge to tend to the poor at a high standard. Not only did Caesarius of Arles devote entire lessons to almsgiving, but individual mentions of succoring the poor permeated many more of his sermons.[125] Caesarius stressed the redemptive properties of almsgiving, and he emphasized care for the poor along with other acts of compassion such as welcoming strangers and reconciling with enemies.[126] But Caesarius's monastically oriented reform agenda and centralized episcopal management style were atypical and could not compete with other forms of piety in an age of increasingly popular saints' cults.[127] Gregory of Tours' solution to the poor probably was more widely appreciated. Gregory invited *pauperes* to join him in venerating saints at churches, for him the only true source for compassion and salvation.

Indeed, what compassion for the poor was to be had in Barbarian Gaul was found primarily at its churches. This usually came in the form of temporary breaks from a difficult mundane existence, through participating alongside one's neighbors in church services and attending festivals. Compassion for some would be the attention and consideration that clerics and the faithful provided ailing people.[128] Day after day, *pauperes* lay about Gallic churches awaiting miracles that did not happen. Meanwhile, clerics were patient, obliging, and nurturing. Thus visitors to the church of Saint Martin at Tours provided for Palatina three months until her legs were cured.[129] Almsgivers at the shrine of Saint Julian sustained Anagild for an entire year before he was healed,[130]

---

125. Sermons about almsgiving: Caes. Arel. *Serm.* 25–27; Klingshirn, *Caesarius of Arles: The Making of a Christian Community*, 186–89.
126. Klingshirn, *Caesarius of Arles: The Making of a Christian Community*, 187.
127. De Nie, "Gregory of Tours and Caesarius of Arles," 194–96.
128. Van Dam, *Saints and their Miracles*, 115: "[Saints'] healings emphasized caring over curing."
129. Greg. Tur., *VM* 2.4.
130. Greg. Tur., *VJ* 12.

and let us not forget Foedamia, who received succor from that same congregation eighteen years until Julian healed her paralysis. In the meantime, the clergy provided her a couch upon which she lay in the church's colonnade.[131] Although miracles likely were uncommon, they were momentous events. They offered Gallic inhabitants "flickering opportunities for the realization of hopes and dreams in an otherwise bitter life."[132] This was especially so for the poor, who more acutely felt the sting of nature and succumbed to human inhumanity. For poor people, healing by a saint brought both physical and psychological relief, forgiveness of sins, and reintegration into communal activities. For some it resulted in social advancement in the form of entry into the lower clergy, but more often it afforded a kind of prestige by which healed *pauperes* were honored by becoming testaments to the *virtutes* of their communities' holy patrons.

But therein lies the catch; the compassion that ecclesiastics offered the poor was conditional, available only at the cost of conforming to a prelate's will or entering into clientage. After a war in 508 between Goths and Franks, Caesarius pleaded for alms and sold the church plate to feed the impoverished about Arles, and he also redeemed captured soldiers.[133] But Caesarius expected these released captives to return the favor to their new patron by supporting his reform agenda from which they benefited. Paupers long associated with churches knew what wheels to grease. They realized, whether subconsciously or otherwise, that the crowds attending saints' festivals expected miracles, and they knew where and when they needed to happen. They knew that the bishop wanted visitors to think that the saints looked like aristocrats. They realized that by assisting the ecclesiastics, they probably would enjoy at best a marginal degree of social improvement. But their life could improve by becoming closer to the community's powerful patrons. The church became the livelihood of the registered poor, and some among them developed a zeal that equaled in intensity their bishops' desires to defend its treasures and

131. Greg. Tur., *VJ* 9.
132. Van Dam, *Saints and their Miracles*, 115.
133. Cyprian of Toulon et al., *Vita Caesarii* 1.32; Klingshirn, *Caesarius of Arles: The Making of a Christian Community*, 114–15.

promote its saints. Gregory learned that he could rely upon the *custodes ecclesiae* for a nearly endless supply of material to record in his annalistic account of the posthumous deeds of Saint Martin. Not unlike bishops across Gaul, he wisely valued his *viri strenui*. As a writer, he repaid them, in the *Historiae* by depicting their actual heroics and in the *Miracula* by sharing in hagiographical fashion their successful efforts to guard church property. When it came to promoting the *virtutes* of Gregory's sometimes vengeful saints, his proximate *pauperes* shared in the commitment.

HEALING AND AUTHORITY I: PHYSICIANS

CHAPTER SEVEN

In these days Austrechild, King Guntram's wife, was taken by this plague. … As Herod had done before her, she is said to have made this last request to the king: "I should still have some hope of recovery if my death had not been made inevitable by the treatment prescribed for me by these wicked doctors. It is the medicines which they have given me which have robbed me of my life and forced me thus to lose the light of day. I beseech you, do not let me die unavenged. Give me your solemn word, I beg you, that you will cut their throats the moment that my eyes have closed in death. If I have really come to the end of my life, they must not be permitted to glory in my dying. …" As she said this, she died. When the funeral was over, the King was forced by this dying wish of his evil consort to commit the foul deed which she begged of him. At his orders the two doctors who had lavished their skill upon her were put to the sword… .

GREGORY OF TOURS, *Historiae* 5.35[1]

1. Greg. Tur., *Hist.* 5.35 (*MGH*, SRM 1.2, 241–42): "His diebus Austrigildis Guntchramni principis regina ab hoc morbo consumpta est. … Fertur enim Herodiano more regem petisse, dicens: 'Adhuc spes vivendi fuerat, si non inter iniquorum medicorum manus interissem; nam potionis ab illis

An underappreciated feature of the West in Late Antiquity is the continued, even thriving, operation of physicians. Modern scholarship has focused less on physicians *per se* than on medical techniques, and the conclusions of those who have considered doctors, especially those in Gaul, have been fraught with inaccuracies. Some have speculated that the occupation suffered a general decline in prestige immediately following the disappearance of the Western Empire.[2] Perhaps the most pessimistic view was that of O. M. Dalton who regarded Gallic physicians as a particularly maligned group, ever subject to being robbed of patients and fees and otherwise humiliated by deceased saints.[3] Citing an episode from Gregory of Tours' *Historiae*, specifically this chapter's introductory quote in which Queen Austrechild on her deathbed demanded that doctors who could not cure her be executed, Dalton concluded that physicians risked "bodily harm or even death at the hands of the ignorant and violent Franks, or their relations."[4] He further imagined that physicians had to resort to "moral degeneration" to maintain their position, as when Queen Fredegund offered Bishop Praetextatus of Rouen the services of her doctors because she expected them to finish the job that an assassin seemingly had failed.[5] Disparaging passages are not unique to Gregory's works; various hagiographers discredited members of the profession. But authors of saints' lives criticized others such as counts and prison guards, too, without actually intending to challenge their authority in society.[6] So were Gallic physicians as put upon as some have surmised? This chapter will investigate how physicians faired in

acceptae mihi vi abstulerunt vitam et fecerunt me hanc lucem velociter perdere. Et ideo, ne inulta mors mea praetereat, quaeso et cum sacramenti interpositione coniuro, ut, cum ab hac luce discessero, statim ipse gladio trucidentur; ut, sicut ego amplius vivere non queo, ita nec ille post meum obitum glorientur ...' Haec effata, infilicem animam tradidit. Rex vero, peracto ex more iusticio, oppressus iniquae coniugis iuramento, implevit praeceptum iniquitatis. Nam duos medicos, qui ei studium adhibuerant, gladio ferire praecepit ..." Trans. based on Thorpe, *Gregory of Tours, History of the Franks*, 298–99.

2. E. g., Riché, *Education and Culture in the Barbarian West*, 70.

3. O. M. Dalton, *The History of the Franks, by Gregory of Tours*, 2 vols. (Oxford: Clarendon, 1927), 1: 418–21, contrasted evidence from the letters of Gregory the Great and the works of Gregory of Tours, and concluded that physicians were appreciated in Italy but oppressed in Gaul.

4. Ibid., 419–20; Greg. Tur., *Hist.* 5.35.

5. Dalton, *History of the Franks*, 1: 420. Indeed, this is the very idea Gregory of Tours wanted readers to come away with. See Greg. Tur., *Hist.* 8.31.

6. See the discussion in Chapter Five between pp. 208 and 209.

Barbarian Gaul. It will begin by establishing a context through considering the status of physicians across the late ancient Mediterranean. Then it will analyze the general social predicament for Gallic doctors and the extent to which they were threatened by potential competitors for healing authority, folk healers and saints.

PHYSICIANS IN LATE ANTIQUITY

Physicians achieved a level of prestige and status in Late Antiquity that practitioners in the Roman Republican era would have envied. During the late Republic and early Empire, most doctors across the Mediterranean were of Greek background.[7] Cato regarded physicians as foreigners (i.e., Greeks) and medicine as an alien skill.[8] Most early doctors were either slaves or freedmen.[9] Private physicians commonly served in the households of prominent Romans.[10] For example, Cicero's personal physician Alexio probably was a freedman, as was Cato's doctor, Cleanthes.[11] Similarly, public doctors serving in municipalities in the early Empire usually were of slave and freedman status.[12] Regarding the occupation as a whole, Cicero wrote that physician was an honorable occupation for persons of appropriate (i.e., low) station.[13] In Rome, physicians endured the stigma of "other" for being foreigners, dispensers of strange medicines, and bearers of low status. The xenophobic Cato forbade his son to seek out physicians, and Pliny echoed Cato's accusation that doctors were able to get away with murder.[14] Horace and Martial delighted in satirizing doctors. The latter wrote of a certain oculist: "Now you are a gladiator; before you were an oculist. You did as a doctor what you do as a gladiator."[15]

---

7. Ralph Jackson, *Doctors and Diseases in the Roman Empire* (Norman and London: University of Oklahoma Press, 1988), 56.
8. Pliny, *Historia naturalis*, 29.6.
9. Jackson, *Doctors and Diseases*, 56.
10. Susan Treggiari, *Roman Freedmen During the Late Republic* (Oxford: Clarendon Press, 1969), 130.
11. Ibid., 130, 254.
12. Ibid., 130.
13. Ibid., 129, but with my own interpretation of Cicero undermining the compliment.
14. Pliny, *Historia naturalis*, 29.7–8.
15. Martial, *Epigrams* 8.74 (Ker, ed. and trans., 2: 58): "Oplomachus nunc es, fueras opthalmicus ante. Fecisti medicus quod facis oplomachus."

Despite continued negative literary characterizations, the reputation and social status of doctors improved throughout the Imperial age. A higher percentage of physicians included people of free status and considerable wealth. In the West, doctors increasingly were either free *peregrini* from the East or Greeks born into Roman citizenship. Julius Caesar offered Roman citizenship to lure Greek doctors to Rome, and Augustus promised tax exemptions to entice them to the Eternal City.[16] Such policies presumably made the occupation attractive for persons of free rank. Famous physicians who answered the call to relocate westward included Xenophon of Cos, who acquired wealth and influence as a court physician for the emperor Claudius.[17] Galen, who was born to a wealthy family at Pergamum, already was a Roman citizen when he came to the capital city to act as court physician for Marcus Aurelius.[18] Despite such outstanding examples, it appears that in the late second century the majority of doctors remained people of low rank. Galen complained that free doctors trained numerous slaves in their profession and thereby debased the field.[19]

Into the Late Ancient era, physicians continued to improve in status and prestige, so much so that some doctors achieved aristocratic rank. The highest level of social advancement for doctors was that attained by personal physicians of emperors, "Physicians of the Sacred Palace" (*archiatri sacri palatii*). When appointed to that office, doctors received the senatorial rank of "Count of the First Order" (*comes primi ordinis*), and upon retirement they rated as *viri spectabiles*.[20] Later, court physicians received ever-more-lofty titles, as did Theodorus, care giver for the emperor Maurice from 593 to 597, a *vir gloriosissimus*.[21] A larger number of doctors who achieved respectable rank and wealth were municipal physicians, called *archiatri*.[22] Among the most rewarded of these were

---

16. Suetonius, *De vita caesarum, Divus Iulius* 42; *Divus Augustus* 59.
17. Jackson, *Doctors and Diseases*, 56.
18. Ibid., 60–61.
19. Treggiari, *Roman Freedmen during the Late Republic*, 130.
20. *CTh* 6.16.1 (a. 413). See also *CTh* 13.3.16 (a. 414).
21. *PLRE* 3: 1259, s. v., "Theodorus 44."
22. Vivian Nutton, "*Archiatri*, and the Medical Profession in Antiquity," *Papers from the British School at Rome* 45 (1977), 218–26, offers an in-depth chronological and territorial analysis of *archiatri*, including a prosopography of physicians mentioned on inscriptions, papyri, and coins.

physicians appointed to posts throughout the city of Rome. Emperor Valentinian I, who established the capital city's college of *archiatri*, was concerned that these physicians might take advantage of their new-found influence and dote only over wealthy patients. The emperor also worried that politics would dictate access to the influential posts rather than merit.[23] Emperors awarded municipal doctors a rank and status comparable to that of other eminent officials. One constitution of the Theodosian Code classified physicians alongside state-appointed grammarians and professors of literature.[24] Constantine and other emperors felt obligated to exempt physicians from onerous curial duties and military service.[25] Not only do late Roman constitutions attest to the high regard physicians had acquired, but they also may indicate that residents of the late West were beginning to worry about the possibility of a scarcity of the professionals. Perhaps a universally perceived need for doctors' care contributed to the fact that in both East and West, municipal physicians, like those at Rome, could demand high fees from patients in addition to their state salaries.[26]

In addition to amassing considerable wealth, many late ancient doctors participated in activities indicative of people of high status. Some became noted for their education, teaching, and knowledge of philosophy. Agapius, a native of Alexandria who practiced medicine at Constantinople, was admired in both of those cities for his knowledge of grammar and rhetoric.[27] A. Lurius Geminius in Africa studied medicine and rhetoric, while the renowned physician Gessius studied medicine and philosophy.[28] Agapius described an erudite person named Sergius as "philosopher, translator of books, author of numerous works, and also a

23. *CTh* 13.3.8 (a. 368/370).
24. *CTh* 13.3 is entitled "De medicis et professoribus."
25. *CTh* 13.3.3 (a. 333). See also *CTh* 11.16.18 (a. 412); *CTh* 13.3.2 (a. 326); *CTh* 13.3.12 (a. 379); 13.3.15 (a. 393); and *CTh* 13.3.16 (a. 414).
26. Jones, *Later Roman Empire*, 2: 1012, suggested that public doctors' salaries were based on the importance of the cities in which they practiced. He cited the annual salary of Flavius Phoebammon, a municipal doctor at Antinoe in Egypt, to be 60 *solidi*, while Justinian paid five public doctors assigned to Carthage 50 to 99 *solidi* each.
27. *PLRE* 2: 32, s. v., "Agapius 2": active mid to late fifth century.
28. Geminius: *PLRE* 3: 508–9: dates fourth to sixth century; a Christian. Gessius: *PLRE* 2: 510–11, s. v., "Gessius 3": late fifth century.

doctor."[29] Sergius was educated in medicine and theology at Alexandria, read both Greek and Syriac, and became an intimate of Pope Agapetus's. Perhaps even more influential was Justinian's physician, Iron. The emperor selected this doctor's system for dating Easter after he bested several Alexandrian philosophers in a debate on the matter.[30]

One literary pursuit essential for late ancient doctors was to preserve and disseminate the expertise of past medical luminaries. The early seventh-century doctor Stephanus of Athens commented prolifically on medical texts.[31] Physicians in the West needed translations of early Greek medical texts. Thus, Cassius Felix in Africa translated Galen's corpus into Latin in 447, and Mustio did the same for the writings of Soranus.[32] But highly educated physicians did not simply rely upon the medicine of long-deceased renowned authors; rather, they contributed to a continuous output of manuals that contained old, updated, and new medical knowledge. One famous physician and teacher of medicine was Oribasius, a native of Pergamum and friend of the Emperor Julian's, who traveled with the ruler to Gaul, and while there wrote his (still extant) seventy-volume *Collectiones medicae*.[33] Orabasius's Greek text appeared in Latin translation at Ravenna in the sixth and seventh centuries.[34] His work received citation by Aetius of Amida, author of a sixteen-book medical discourse.[35] Aetius, in turn, found mention in the twelve-book *Therapeutica* written by Alexander of Tralles in the late sixth century. Alexander was an Eastern physician who traveled extensively compiling medical knowledge, with visits including Italy, Spain and Gaul. Eventually he settled in Rome, where he practiced medicine and compiled his voluminous medical works.[36] A contemporary who located to Italy was Anthimus, a Greek physician employed at the Ostrogothic court who penned a dietary *regula* that has survived.[37]

29. *PLRE* 3: 1123–24, s. v., "Sergius 1": early to mid-sixth century.
30. *PLRE* 3: 717, s. v., "Iron."
31. *PLRE* 3: 1194–95, s. v., "Stephanus 52."
32. Cassius Felix: *PLRE* 2: 461, s. v., "Cassius Felix 13"; Mustio: *PLRE* 2: 769.
33. *PLRE* 3: 563–4, s. v. "Oribasius."
34. Riché, *Education and Culture in the Barbarian West*, 70.
35. *PLRE* 2: 20, s. v., "Aetius 5 (of Amida)": mid-fifth to mid-sixth century.
36. *PLRE* 3: 44–45, s. v., "Alexander 8 (of Tralles)."
37. *PLRE* 2: 100, s. v., "Anthimus 3."

Given doctors' potentially high status and penchant for literary production, it should not be surprising that some late ancient doctors participated in lofty literary circles. For example, the prolific, blue-blooded
letter writer Symmachus wrote to Dionysius, a physician at Rome, com-
mending students to him.[38] Many extant letters addressed to physicians
came from eminent bishops. For example, a grateful Augustine of Hippo
wrote a letter to Maximus, a North African doctor, and another to an
aged *archiater* named Dioscurus, congratulating both for converting
to Catholicism.[39] Augustine also wrote a flattering epistle to his friend
Gennadius, a doctor at Rome and Carthage whom the bishop admired
for his charitable acts.[40] In Gaul, the physician Helpidius of Bordeaux
was the addressee of letters from Bishops Ennodius of Pavia and Avitus
of Vienne.[41]

Complementing friendship with influential magnates, some doctors
obtained high positions in secular bureaucracies. For example, Caesarius,
the brother of Gregory of Nazianzus, located to Constantinople, where
he achieved renown as a doctor, eventually serving as court physician
for Constantius II and then for Julian. Unlike the physician Oribasius,
Caesarius was a Christian, and so when he refused to apostatize,
Julian expelled him from court. But after 363, he returned to court
under Valens, and in 368 he received the post of *comes thesaurorum* in
Bithynia.[42] Even more successful was Helvius Vindicianus, a famous
physician from Carthage and acquaintance of Augustine. He served
as *proconsul Africae* between 379 and 382 and therefore ranked as *vir
spectabilis*.[43] In Gaul, Iulius Ausonius, father of the poet Ausonius, was
a doctor at Bazas and Bordeaux and was a *curialis* for both cities. In 377,
he acted as *praefectus praetorio Illyrici*, and thus he became a *vir inlustris* a
full year before his famous son obtained the office of *praefectus praetorio*

---

38. *PLRE* 2: 363, s. v., "Dionysius 1."
39. Maximus: *PLRE* 2: 745, s. v., "Maximus 5"; Dioscurus: *PLRE* 2: 367, s. v., "Dioscurus 3."
40. *PLRE* 2: 502, s. v., "Gennadius 2."
41. *PLRE* 2: 537, s. v., "Helpidius 6." For more on Helpidius, see the discussion in this chapter between
    pp. 280 and 281. For eastern correspondence between physicians and bishops, see, e. g., *PLRE* 2: 575,
    s. v., "Hymnetius"; *PLRE* 2: 995, s. v., "Sergius 8."
42. *PLRE* 1: 169–70, s. v., "Caesarius 2."
43. *PLRE* 1: 967, s. v., "(Helvius) Vindicianus 2."

Galliarum, Italiae et Africae.[44] In their capacity as agents of state, doctors proved particularly worthwhile as ambassadors. Evidence is especially prevalent for sixth-century physicians serving as envoys to Persia.[45] The consummate doctor-envoy was a court physician named Zacharias of Sura. Between 574 and 579 he served on four important embassies; the first two ventures secured four years of peace between Byzantium and Persia, but the latter two failed. In 580, just before Zacharias disappears from history, he was again on embassy looking to arrange a peace between the empires.[46] Physicians in the West apparently were thought no less suitable as envoys. Thus the *archiater* Anthimus represented the Ostrogothic ruler Theodoric the Great on embassy to the Merovingian court of King Theuderic.[47]

As Anthimus's example attests, the disappearance of Western imperial rule did not mark an end for physicians acquiring distinction; they continued to discover promising opportunities at royal courts and through the church. Royal emulation of imperial court composition included kings maintaining personal physicians. For example, Theodoric the Great established the post of chief court physician with the title "count of physicians," *comes archiatrorum.*[48] The formula for creation of this office

44. *PLRE* 1: 139, s. v., "Iulius Ausonius 5." The son Ausonius served as consul in 379; *PLRE* 1: 140–41, s. v., "Decimius Magnus Ausonius 7." Iulius Ausonius's father-in-law was a noble Aeduan astrologer. Ausonius's sister-in-law also practiced medicine. For an excellent look into the kind of medicine practiced by Ausonius and an examination of his druidic relations, see Aline Rouselle, "From Sanctuary to Miracle-Worker: Healing in Fourth-Century Gaul," in *Ritual, Religion, and the Sacred,* ed. Robert Forster and Orest Ranum, trans. by Elborg Forster (Baltimore and London: Johns Hopkins University Press, 1982), 103–05. M. K. Hopkins, "Social Mobility in the Later Roman Empire: The Evidence of Ausonius," *Classical Quarterly* 11 (1961), 241, supposed Ausonius "may have been the son of an eastern Greek-speaking doctor, originally a slave but freed." Given the improvements to doctors' reputations and status by the fourth century, I see little reason to suspect his origins would have been so low.

45. R. C. Blockley, "Doctors as Diplomats in the Sixth Century," *Florilegium* 2 (1980), 93–95, suggested that physicians were utilized as envoys to Persia because of their training in literature, philosophy and oratory, high rank, and medical skills, which the Persians greatly admired.

46. Ibid., 91–93; *PLRE* 3: 1411–12, s. v. "Zacharias 2." Other physician-envoys to Persia include Uranius: Blockley, "Doctors as Diplomats," 91; *PLRE* 3: 1393, s. v., "Uranius," where Martindale is wrong to deny Uranius was a doctor. Stephanus of Edessa: Blockley, "Doctors as Diplomats," 90–91; *PLRE* 3, 1185, s. v., "Stephanus 9." An eastern physician-envoy who ventured north of the Danube was Theodorus: *PLRE* 3: 1258–59, s. v., "Theodorus 43."

47. The title of Anthimus's dietary tract, which appears in letter form, mentions his role as legate: *Epistula Anthimi viri inl(ustris) comitis et legatarii ad gloriosissimum Theodericum regem Francorum de observatione ciborum.*

48. Cassiodorus, *Variae* 6.19. Compare with the imperial *archiatri sacri palatii,* who are called in one constitution *comites archiatrorum*; *CTh* 11.18.1 (a. 409).

offers high praise for the profession of physician in general: "Among the most useful skills that the divine has offered for sustaining the indignity of human frailty, it seems that none offer anything comparable to what the doctor is able to confer."[49] In Gaul, Clovis maintained a personal doctor named Tranquilinus who was well educated and noted for his skill at medicine.[50] King Chilperic's chief physician (*primus medicorum in domo*) Marileifus possessed property and much wealth, and Peter, physician for the Merovingian Theuderic II, hobnobbed with the likes of Protadius, the king's *maior domus*.[51] Other doctors acquired high ecclesiastical office. While many physicians are known to have become deacons and priests, some could aspire to the position of bishop.[52] For example, an Eastern physician named Paulus relocated to Visigothic Spain, where he became Bishop of Mérida.[53] There a desperate *vir inlustris* convinced Paulus to perform upon his wife an operation whereby the physician sliced open the woman to remove a fetus. Because the patient survived, the grateful senatorial couple bequeathed to the prelate all their possessions, and according to the hagiographer, by virtue of this gift Paulus became the most powerful person in Mérida.[54]

Not only did individual late ancient physicians attain prestige and high office at a level not available to past doctors, but the overall socioeconomic lot for physicians also appears to have improved. Epigraphic evidence suggests that late ancient doctors typically were of free status. For example, Pastor, a fifth- or sixth-century doctor at Rome simply

---

49. Cassiodorus, *Variae* 6.19 (*CCL* 96, 247–48): "Inter utillimas artes, quas ad sustentandam hunmanae fragilitatis indigentiam divina tribuerunt, nulla praestare videtur aliquid simile quam potest auxiliatrix medicina conferre."

50. *Vita Severini* 1 (*MGH*, SRM 3, 168–69): "Erat autem ibidem homo in domo regis nomine Tranquilinus doctor et omni sapientia plenus honores arte medicinae gerebat."

51. Marileifus: *PLRE* 3: 830, s. v., "Marileifus." Peter: *PLRE* 3: 1011, s. v. "Petrus 57." Fredegar styled Peter *archiatrus* and depicted the doctor playing dice with Protadius in the king's tent when Theuderic's soldiers stormed it and killed the mayor of the palace; Fredegar, *Chron.* 4.27.

52. Doctor and deacon: Iulianus: *PLRE* 2: 638, s. v., "Iulianus 10"; Dionysius: *PLRE* 2: 363, s. v., "Dionysius 3"; Andronicus: *PLRE* 3: 81, s. v., "Andronicus 6; Anouthis: *PLRE* 3: 84. Doctor and priest: Petrus: *PLRE* 2: 866, s. v., "Petrus 9"; Theotecnus: *PLRE* 2: 1111, s. v., "Theotecnus 1." On the attractions for converting medical practitioners into church personnel, see Rapp, *Holy Bishops in Late Antiquity*, 177–78.

53. *PLRE* 3: 980, s. v., "Paulus 22." For an eastern doctor turned Nestorian patriarch in Persia, see *PLRE* 3: 714, s. v., "Ioseph 2." The son of an Italian doctor in the mid-sixth century became Pope Boniface IV; *PLRE* 3: 663, s. v., "Ioannis 51."

54. *Vitae patrum Emeretensium* 4.2.

styled *medicus* on his epitaph must have possessed some wealth and clout to have a tomb placed in the cemetery of Saint Valentinus.[55] Likewise, the three children of Sarmana, a fourth- or fifth-century *medica* from the Rhineland, had the financial wherewithal to erect an epitaph for their aged mother.[56] A late sixth- or early seventh-century doctor named Gregorius found mention on a papyrus listing minor Roman officials.[57] Flavius Ioseph, who was both a doctor and soldier, perhaps was identical with a man named on a list of centurians and soldiers.[58] Furthermore, it has been suggested that the *ingenuus* thaumaturge Martin of Tours, who began his career as a soldier, was a military *medicus*.[59] Late ancient physicians, then, were not unlike grammarians and clergymen; while a few standouts achieved social eminence, the average doctor was "very much a 'middling' person."[60]

While evidence for free physicians prevails, examples of slave and freedmen doctors, so prominent in the late Republic and early Empire, lessen in late ancient sources. Training people of servile status in the art of medicine seemingly did continue, however, as a seventh-century Visigothic law attests.[61] But apparently this practice no longer occurred to the extent it had in the past when Galen bemoaned it, for more recent writers no longer depicted the occupation as a profession fit for slaves. Even authors who were doubtful of physicians' remedies did not use social status as a foil. Indeed, becoming a doctor in Late Antiquity likely propelled persons of low status into higher socio-economic ranks. For example, one of only a few individual doctors in the West whose family is known to have been servile was Chilperic's physician, Marileifus, about whom Gregory of Tours commented that his father had been a

55. *PLRE* 2: 836, s. v., "Pastor."
56. Handley, *Death, Society and Culture*, 41, 191, proposes that Sarmana was probably a female physician, or perhaps a wet nurse. She died at around seventy years of age and was interred at Gondorf. See also Handley, ibid., 194, for the epitaph of [Reccar]edus, a physician of sixth-century Mérida who died at age twenty. Raising epitaphs was not an inexpensive enterprise. See ibid., 39.
57. *PLRE* 3: 552, s. v., "Gregorius 11."
58. *PLRE* 3: 715, s. v., "Fl. Ioseph 5."
59. Rouselle, "From Sanctuary to Miracle-Worker," 110–11.
60. Brown, *Poverty and Leadership*, 49, uses these words to characterize the status of churchmen. For the social status of grammarians, see Kaster, *Guardians of Language*, 99–134.
61. *Lex Visigothorum* 11.1.7 (*MGH*, LL 1.1, 402): "Si quis medicus famulum in doctrinam susceperit, pro beneficio suo duodecim solidos consequatur."

slave attached to a church.[62] Marileifus advanced high above servile rank, for by the 580s he was known for having enormous wealth in the form of horses, gold, and silver. This royal physician's example would suggest that in Barbarian Gaul, as across the Mediterranean, becoming a physician could confer riches and distinction upon a person. Indeed, one Gallic preacher thought to stress divine magnanimity to his congregation by referring to God in a simile as being "like a good doctor" (*quomodo bonus medicus*).[63] If God's being a physician was good, then being a physician could not be bad.

GALLIC PHYSICIANS AND POTENTIAL PROBLEMS

For all of their potential prestige, physicians in Gaul still faced dilemmas that were part and parcel of the healing profession. Even doctors in the loftiest positions might be regarded only as worthy as their last success or failure, as the sorry tale of Austrechild's caregivers to attests.[64] Furthermore, when separated from his powerful patron, a physician might not be able to demand the kind of respect that a more militant person could. Chilperic's chief physician Marileifus possessed two qualities that, when combined, could invite trouble in Gaul – much movable wealth and little to no military prowess. The doctor proved such easy prey that he was robbed on at least three occasions.[65] In the first instance, in 577, Chilperic's rebellious son Merovech attacked the doctor reportedly on the advice of King Guntram in retaliation for Leudast's having waylaid and slain several of Merovech's retainers.[66] The second and third thefts happened after Chilperic's demise when Childebert II's

---

62. Greg. Tur., *Hist.* 7.25. Augustine mentioned a socially low doctor in the service of Innocentius of Carthage who differed with the opinion of more established physicians that the noble patient would need a second operation to remove a rectal fistula. The master and others belittled the household doctor's prognosis, but later a visiting Alexandrian specialist confirmed it; Aug., *De civitate Dei* 22.8. For an Egyptian doctor who possibly was a slave, see *PLRE* 2: 721, s. v., "(I)saeus."

63. Caes. Arel., *Serm.* 17.4 (*CCL* 103, 81).

64. According to Visigothic law, physicians who failed to obtain a cure or who harmed their patient had to forfeit payment or pay a fine; *Lex Visigothorum*, 11.1.4, 6.

65. Compare Marileifus's woes with those of a Sicilian doctor belabored by continual lawsuits who appealed to Pope Gregory I to help him keep his possessions; *PLRE* 3: 105, s. v., "Archelaus 3."

66. Greg. Tur., *Hist.* 5.14. Marileifus was traveling en route from Chilperic's court to Poitiers, and although he lost his movables, he was able to save his life by taking sanctuary at Saint Martin's basilica. Gregory negotiated the doctor's safe passage to Poitiers.

duke Gararicus stole the doctor's wealth. The last assault left Marileifus completely destitute, so that he again had to rely on the church for employ along with his servile relatives.[67] Because Marileifus's assailers were enemies of Chilperic's, these misfortunes should be interpreted to indicate the dangers a Gallic courtier might incur, not as evidence for a widespread lack of respect for physicians.[68] A more realistic difficulty for physicians was that they did not monopolize the art of healing. Three potential challenges to their healing authority were do-it-yourself medicine, folk healers, and saints.

As had happened regularly throughout the Roman past, some late ancient people opted for home remedies over physicians' care. Indeed, one Gallic aristocrat of the late fourth and early fifth century who gathered medical knowledge was Marcellus of Bordeaux. In 394/95, he served as *magister officiorum* under Theodosius I. Shortly after 401, he wrote *De medicamentis*, a compendium of prescriptions, although he was not a doctor.[69] Not only did Marcellus copy prescriptions from earlier texts, but also he added what he thought were effective contemporary Gallic remedies gathered *ab agrestibus et plebeis.*[70] He claimed to have written the text so that his sons would not have to rely on medical charlatans.[71] Marcellus's intentions recall Cato's distrust of physicians, and while his words may indicate a lingering suspicion toward the craft among aristocrats, perhaps they merely echo a literary *topos*. For Marcellus

---

67. Greg. Tur., *Hist.* 7.25. Gregory's portrayal of Marileifus compares with other testimonies of dilemmas incurred by King Chilperic's retainers, especially Count Leudast. I strongly suspect that Gregory had a strong personal animus for this particular physician. Not only did the author devote two anecdotes to his being assaulted, but also he emphasized Marileifus's servile origin as he did with Leudast. It suited Gregory's literary agenda to portray people whom he thought were bent on greedily amassing properties as succumbing to some mishap. One may wonder, however, whether after 585, the destitute Marileifus would not have begun to use his valuable medical expertise to begin building up his wealth again.

68. I echo the estimation of Valerie J. Flint, "The Early Medieval 'Medicus', the Saint – and the Enchanter," *Journal of the Society for the Social History of Medicine* 2 (1989), 132–33: "the early Merovingian '*medicus*' seems likely to have been a familiar and distinguished, skilled, and sometimes learned figure, much sought after."

69. Marcellus of Bordeaux, *De medicamentis*, ed. Maximilian Niedermann, Corpus Medicorum Latinorum 5 (Leipzig and Berlin: B. G. Teubner, 1916). See *PLRE* I: 551–52, s. v., "Marcellus 7"; Rouselle, "From Sanctuary to Miracle-Worker," 101–02.

70. Marcellus of Bordeaux, *De Medicamentis* (Niedermann, p. 3); cited by Rouselle, "From Sanctuary to Miracle-Worker," 125.

71. Rouselle, "From Sanctuary to Miracle-Worker," 102.

otherwise warned readers that they should not attempt the cures in his book without the supervision of physicians![72] Another Gallic aristocrat who displayed some knowledge of medicine was Gregory of Tours. He afforded minute physiological details, for instance, when he described the effects of plague on bodies, and when he recounted healings of common ailments such as gout, cataracts, and fevers.[73] For example, regarding an onslaught of plague that overran Gaul in 580, he offered the following observation:

> Those who caught it had a high temperature, with vomiting and severe pains in the small of their back: their heads ached and so did their necks. The matter they vomited up was yellow or even green. … as soon as cupping glasses were applied to their shoulders or legs, great tumours formed, and when these burst and discharged their pus they were cured. …The epidemic began in the month of August. It attacked young children first of all and to them it was fatal.[74]

Venantius Fortunatus likened his medically adept friend Gregory to a *medicus*,[75] and Bede was so impressed with his medical erudition that when he defined dysentery he cited Hippocrates and Gregory of Tours![76] Perhaps Gregory honed his knowledge by consulting texts such as Marcellus's book, or perhaps he learned about medicine through discussions with an *archiater* at Tours named Armentarius. In either case,

---

72. Marcellus of Bordeaux, *De medicamentis*, 12–15; with Raymond Van Dam, *Leadership and Community in Late Antique Gaul*, 129–30.

73. Plague: Greg. Tur., *Hist*. 4.5, 4.31, 5.34, 35, 6.14, 9.22, 10.23, *GM* 50, *VM* 2.52. Gout: Greg. Tur., *Hist*. 5.42. Cataracts: Greg. Tur., *Hist*. 5.6. Fevers: Greg. Tur., *VJ* 3, *VM* 2.22, 2.32, 3.50, 3.60, 4.37, *VP* 6.6, 7.2, 14.2.

74. Greg. Tur., *Hist*. 5.34 (*MGH*, SRM 1.1, 238–39): "Erat enim his qui patiebantur valida cum vomitu febris renumque nimius dolor; caput grave vel cervix. Ea vero quae ex ore proiciebantur colore cricei aut certe viridia erant. …missae in scapulis sive cruribus ventosae, procedentibus erumpentibusque visicis, decursa saniae, multi liberabantur. …Et quidem primum haec infirmitas a mense Augusto initiata, parvulus adulescentes arripuit lectoque subegit." Trans. by Thorpe, *Gregory of Tours, History of the Franks*, 296.

75. Ven. Fort., *Carm*. 8.11.1 (*MGH*, AA 4.1, 196).

76. Bede, *Retractio in actus apostolorum* 28.8 (Laistner, ed., *Bedae venerabilis Expositio Actuum apostolorum et Retractatio*, 145–46). A perusal of Gregory's text suggests a theological perspective strongly affected his analysis of the ill and dying. In particular, Gregory was fond of indicating a recurrence of the number three in the days it took for people, especially wicked ones, to succumb to illness. See e. g., *Hist*. 5.5 (twice), 6.6, 8.40, 9.30, *GC* 6, 13, 66, *VP* 4.3. No doubt Venantius and Bede would not have found this discrepancy problematic.

he was informed enough to know that scammony purged the stomach, hyssop the lungs, and pyrethrum the head.[77] Likewise, he was familiar with medical terminology such as physicians' use of the word "epilepsy" for what the *rustici* called "falling sickness."[78] Such possession of limited medical knowledge by non-professionals, however, likely did not pose a threat to physicians' care. Even Gregory's works, which contain some of the most inflammatory remarks about doctors in all Late Antiquity, do not hint that the bishop ever treated an illness with a home remedy unless a physician or a saint sanctioned it. Thus the existence of medical manuals did not necessarily translate into use of them to a point where they could threaten the livelihood of Gallic doctors.

But if physicians faced no threat from do-it-yourself medicine, they must have regarded rival healers with some suspicion. One kind of healer who likely infringed somewhat upon their occupation was the disestablished medical practitioner, "root doctors" and the like. Certainly doctors lost some patients to them, if only those who turned to alternative medicine to avoid what might be perceived as terrifying procedures, as when physicians drew blood from patients or inserted pointy instruments into their eyes.[79] But all in all, folk healers could not seriously challenge physicians, for the two kinds of healer maintained separate identities, and they operated using different medical techniques upon rather different patient pools.[80] Gallic authors employed a vocabulary that readily distinguished between established and disestablished medical practitioners. While elite writers uniformly referred to physicians as *medici* and *archiatri*, they consistently labeled or denigrated folk healers with terms that associated their ministrations with magic such as *incantatores* and *malefici*.[81] Maintaining separate identities between

---

77. Greg. Tur., *VM* 3.60 (*MGH*, SRM 1.2, 197): "…quod mundat ventrem ut agridium, pulmonem ut hisopum, ipsumque caput purgat ut pyretrum."
78. Greg. Tur., *VM* 2.18 (*MGH*, SRM 1.2, 165): "Quod genus morbi ephilenticum peritorum medicorum vocitavit auctoritas; rustici vero cavidum dixere, pro eo quod caderet." For Gregory's knowledge of medical terminology, see Max Bonnet, *Le Latin de Grégoire de Tours* (Paris: Hachette, 1890), 218–20.
79. For the horrific treatments of oculists, see Greg. Tur., *VM* 2.19.
80. Flint, "The Early Medieval 'Medicus', the Saint – and the Enchanter," 139, perceived folk healers to be a greater intrusion upon physicians than do I.
81. By the sixth century, favoring Greek-influenced physicians over traditional healers, and linking the latter with magic, had a long past. The third-century jurist Ulpian offered strong words to separate

proper physicians and folk healers was a longstanding practice that resulted in part from differences in training and techniques.[82] While folk healers applied poultices and dispensed potions and salves, which doctors sometimes prescribed, too, only physicians performed surgeries and bloodlettings. Indeed, phlebotomy was the cornerstone of Greek medicine, a practice that remained solely within the domain of the *medicus*.[83] Just as the gourd-like shape and (typically) bronze composition of the cupping vessel would have stood out among any other sort of chalice, so too would its image on a storefront sign or its actual presence in an office interior inform a patient that the healer was a practitioner of traditional Greek procedures.[84] Otherwise, while a few hagiographical vignettes depict physicians and folk healers attending the same patients, other evidence indicates that the two had a largely separate clientele. Sources consistently characterize doctors as being located in cities and desiring to attend wealthy and influential patients. Gallic writers commonly depicted individual doctors caring for powerful persons including kings, courtiers, and high ecclesiastics.[85] Whenever people of low status managed to obtain a physician's care, they usually did so only by virtue of a patron's aid. For example, when a servant at Radegund's nunnery at Poitiers suffered groin pains, his mother appealed to the queen, who

the two: "Some will perhaps regard as doctors those who offer a cure for a particular part of the body or a particular ill, as, for instance, an ear doctor, a throat doctor, or a dentist. But one must not include people who make incantations or imprecations or, to use the common expression of imposters, exorcisms. For these are not branches of medicine, even though people exist who strongly assert that such people have helped them." *Digesta* 50.13.1 (Mommsen et al., 4: 929).

82. I am familiar with only one instance in which a late ancient physician is implicated as a sorcerer. When the aged Emperor Justin II fell ill, courtiers called upon an apparently prominent healer named Timotheus, a Jewish healer who presented himself as a doctor but whom the hagiographer for Symeon Stylites the Younger perceived to be a demon worshipping practitioner of sorcery; *PLRE* 3: 1327, s. v., "Timotheus 3"; Matthew W. Dickie, *Magic and Magicians in the Greco-Roman World* (London and New York: Routledge, 2001), 292.

83. For bloodletting, see, e.g., Greg. Tur., *Hist.* 5.6, 5.34, 6.15, 7.22; *VM* 2.60, 4.2; Ven. Fort., *Carm.* 6.10; *Vita Germani* 60. On bloodletting as an essential part of Greco-Roman medical practice, see Jackson, *Doctors and Diseases*, 70.

84. Jackson, *Doctors and Diseases*, 72. Ibid., 56–85, is an exceptional examination of physicians' tools in the Roman era. For doctors' equipment in the Merovingian age, see Fay Ross Dwelle, "Medicine in Merovingian and Carolingian Gaul," unpublished Ph.D. diss. (Chapel Hill, NC: University of North Carolina, 1934), 89.

85. Bishops: Greg. Tur., *Hist.* 5.5; *VM* 2.1; Ven. Fort., *Carm.* 10.6; priests: Greg. Tur., *Hist.* 7.22; royalty: Greg. Tur., *Hist.* 5.35, 7.25, 8.31; count: Greg. Tur., *GM* 84.

in turn summoned the *archiater* Reovalis.[86] If Gallic physicians tended to neglect poorer patients, they fell over themselves to attend wealthy ones. Thus, when Sidonius Apollinaris's noble relation Severiana contracted a cough and a fever, the bishop wrote: "Therefore (under Christ's guidance) we are taking ourselves and our whole household away from the heat and the oppressiveness of the city, and at the same time escaping from the counsels of the physicians, who attend and contend at the bedside."[87] Of course, physicians preferred important patients because they could extract large payments from them.[88] Gregory called doctors' care "expensive relief" (*confortatio sumptuosa*), and Caesarius of Arles wrote that people could gain their attention only *cum ... granda expensa*.[89] Meanwhile, the same sources portray folk healers usually tending slaves and peasants in a rural venue. Gregory characterized the habit of resorting to *incantatores* as a "peasant custom" (*mos rusticorum*).[90] This is not to say that an unusually successful enchanter could build a reputation and thereby attract a wealthier clientele.[91] But by and large, physicians and folk healers tended to patients of different locales and status. Judging by the sources, a potentially greater rival for Gallic physicians was another unconventional healer, the saint.

PHYSICIANS, BISHOPS, AND SAINTS

According to our undoubtedly biased ecclesiastical sources, the most socially prominent potential rivals for doctors were saints. By the late sixth century, bishops usually were the most distinguished individuals of a Gallic community. They and hagiographers augmented ecclesiastics' authority by encouraging recognition of saints as healers. In addition to metaphorically touting saints as doctors, some clerics calumniated

---

86. Greg. Tur., *Hist.* 10.15.
87. Sid. Ap., *Ep.* 2.12.3 (Anderson, ed. and trans., 1: 472–73): "Igitur ardori vicitatis atque torpori tam nos quam domum totam praevio Christo pariter eximimus simulque medicorum consilia vitamus assidentum dissidentumque ..."
88. E. g., *CTh* 13.3.8.
89. Greg. Tur., *VM* 2.1 (*MGH*, SRM 1.2, 159); Caes. Arel., *Serm.* 5.5 (*CCL* 103, 29). A count from Brittany reportedly squandered his fortune on doctors; Greg. Tur., *GM* 84.
90. Greg. Tur., *VM* 1.26 (*MGH*, SRM 1.2, 151). Van Dam, *Saints and their Miracles*, 220, interprets *rustici* in this instance as "nonbelievers" instead of "commoners" or "country folk."
91. E. g., Greg. Tur., *Hist.* 5.14, 7.44.

physicians, whom they perceived as rivals of the holy healers. But just how far were powerful ecclesiastics willing to go to champion saints as the most effective healers of their communities?

The Gallic bishop who most vociferously criticized physicians was Gregory of Tours. One such as he with a mind to make his patron saint the principal healer of the community could do much toward this end. First, Gregory himself served as a witness to the healing power of his holy patron Martin by recording how the saint repeatedly cured him of afflictions such as headaches, stomach aches, and a swollen tongue and lips.[92] On an occasion graver than most, Martin delivered the bishop from a deadly bout of dysentery, while on the lighter side, Martin once dislodged a fish bone that had been stuck in his throat for three days![93] Gregory also touted Martin's healing *virtus* by speaking publicly about it. Whether at home or traveling abroad, he communicated to distinguished dining companions stories of the saint's curative abilities.[94] To confirm Martin's powers, Gregory brought along relics on his travels. He carried, perhaps in a locket around his neck, Martin's *post mortem* panacea, dust from the holy man's tomb. Gregory purported that this dust mixed with water or wine made for a powerful unguent. He dispensed the dust to persons of every social level – fellow bishops, Austrasian courtiers, and even slaves – in hopes of convincing all that the saint was a healer the people of Gaul should trust.[95] Of course, Gregory also advertised Saint Martin's reputation as a healer by commemorating his miracles in writing. Most of the miracles he recorded in the *Four Books on the Miracles of the Blessed Bishop Martin* were healings.[96] Gregory sometimes touted the saint as a *medicus*, and once in a particularly authoritative vein he deemed Martin "the true doctor," as if there could be no other.[97] People who lived about Tours responded

---

92. Stomach aches: Greg. Tur., *VM* 2.1, 4.1; swollen tongue and lips: *VM* 4.2; eye and headache: *VM* 2.60; toothache and headache: *VM* 3.60.
93. Fever and dysentery: Greg. Tur., *VM* 2.1; fishbone: *VM* 3.1.
94. Gregory visiting Saintes: Greg. Tur., *VM* 4.31; Spanish envoys visiting Tours: *VM* 3.8.
95. Bishop: Greg. Tur., *VM* 3.60; courtier: *VM* 4.28; slave: *VM* 3.60.
96. See Corbett, "*Praesentium signorum munera*," 54–61.
97. Martin as *medicus*: Greg. Tur., *VM* 2.13, 3, *praef.*, 3.21; Martin as "true doctor": Greg. Tur., *VM* 2.52 (*MGH*, SRM 1.2, 177): "verum … medicum." Venantius Fortunatus also used the metaphor of saint

to Gregory's appeals that they seek Martin's curative powers. The bishop gathered evidence from the shrine's miracle register to show that hardly a year passed without Martin's extending his healing touch upon some fortunate few.[98] Visitors received miracles at Martin's tomb especially during festival days in the saint's honor.[99]

In addition to extolling the healing powers of Martin and many other saints, Gregory sometimes railed against rivals of the holy healers, including physicians. For example, after he described how Martin healed the cataracts of a man whom a doctor could not cure, Gregory inveighed against the profession at large:

> When have physicians with their instruments ever performed something like this, since they put forth more pain of affliction than comforts; for the eye is stretched and prodded with darts, and first they must fashion engines of death in order to bring the light to it? And if caution is bypassed during this effort, a wretch is saddled with eternal blindness. In contrast, the instrument of the blessed confessor is goodwill, and the only unguent is his power.[100]

According to Gregory, not only might Martin's remedies prove more effective and less painful than doctors' treatments; they also constituted a kind of medicine superior to what physicians could offer. This argument depended upon beliefs common among members of Gallic society that illnesses were manifestations of sin, and that guilt must necessarily accompany illness.[101] Therefore, a doctor who tended to bodily wounds could only address symptoms, whereas a holy healer mended symptom and cause, illness and sin: "This [dust from Martin's tomb] bests the cleverness of physicians, is superior to the sweetness of aromatics, and is

as doctor: e.g., Germanus of Paris: Ven. Fort., *Vita Germanii* 49, 51, 55; Saturninus of Toulouse: Ven. Fort., *Carm.* 2.7.20.

98. For Gregory's reliance on a miracle register, see Shanzer, "So Many Saints – So Little Time," 25–27.

99. For the extent of dissemination of Martin's cult and its appeal to pilgrims, see Van Dam, *Saints and their Miracles*, 117-28; Handley, *Death, Society and Culture*, 139-42.

100. Greg. Tur., *VM* 2.19 (*MGH*, SRM 1.2, 166): "Quid umquam tale fecere cum ferramentis medici, cum plus negotium doloris exserant, quam medellae, cum, distentum transfixumque spiculis oculum, prius mortis tormenta figurant, quam lumen aperiant? In quo cautela fefellerit, aeternam misero praeparat caecitatem. Huic autem beato confessori voluntas ferramentum est, et sola virtus unguentum." See also Greg. Tur., *GM* 30.

101. Van Dam, *Saints and their Miracles*, 86–89.

more potent than the strength of all unguents.... . For it not only makes weak limbs strong, but, even better than this, it wipes away and lifts off those stains of [sinners'] consciences."[102] When Gregory described the *virtutes* of two physicians turned saints, Cosmas and Damian, he forewent the usual tale of how the holy doctors while living attended people without pay; instead, he commented that the pair as deceased saints healed the sick "only by the merit of their powers and by the inter-vention of their prayers."[103] Gregory's emphasis on the physician-saints' performing miracles after their death resulted from his program of convincing people to revere relics, many of which the bishop and his clergy housed in churches throughout the Touraine.[104]

Beyond calumniating the medical profession in general, Gregory recorded specific instances in which saints prevailed after physicians faltered. For example, he preserved an account of how Saint Martin accomplished what the *archiater* Armentarius could not. After Gregory contracted dysentery, the doctor's antidotes failed and the bishop despaired: "I summoned the *archiater* Armentarius and told him: 'You have put forth every skill of your craft, and now you have shown the potency of all of your unguents, but these worldly stratagems have profited me nothing as I am perishing.'"[105] As a last resort, Gregory sent a deacon to take dust from Martin's tomb and mix it with water, and within hours of drinking the potion he recovered his health. Similarly, Gregory described another incident in which a saint's ministrations healed a patient whose condition had worsened after a visit to physicians. A slave of Bishop Phronimius of Agde's who suffered severe epileptic

---

102. Greg. Tur., *VM* 3.60 (*MGH*, SRM 1.2, 197): "Quod medicorum vincit argutias, aromatum suavitates superat ungentorumque omnium robur supercrescit... Etiam non solum membra debilia solidat, sed, quod his omnibus magis est, ipsas illas conscientiarum maculas abstergit ac levigat."

103. Greg. Tur., *GM* 97 (*MGH*, SRM, 1.2, 103–4): "... solo virtutum merito et orationum interventu ..." Cosmas and Damian were martyred at Cyrrhus in Cilicia, traditionally during Diocletian's persecution. With the exception of Gregory, hagiographers noted how they refused payment from patients. Their cult spread into the West via Rome and thrived in the Middle Ages. See *The Book of Saints*, compiled by the Benedictine monks of St. Augustine's Abbey, Ramsgate (Wilton, CN: Morehouse, 1989), 139.

104. Greg. Tur., *Hist.* 10.31.

105. Greg. Tur., *VM* 2.1 (*MGH*, SRM 1.2, 159): "...vocavi Armentarium archiatrum et dico ei: 'Omnem ingenium artificii tui inpendisti, pigmentorum omnium vim iam probasti, sed nihil proficit perituro res saeculi.'"

attacks was taken to doctors, who prescribed a variety of remedies. The attacks subsided for a few months, but then returned worse than before. Finally the bishop sent the man to Lyons, and there, after lying before the tomb of Saint Nicetius, he received a permanent cure.[106] Another story in which it seems a physician really botched the treatment of an influential courtier comes from Venantius Fortunatus:

> When Attila, *vir inlustris* and *domesticus* of the royal palace, fell in a bath, he severely broke his arm and bent his entire hand from the humerus. The doctor who was summoned desired to give him care, but when a vein on his chest was opened, nearly all the blood of life poured out in an instant. It was announced to Bishop [Germanus of Paris] that the man was near death. The old man hurried by the impulse of piety, and found Attila laid out, crying tears without hope, overwhelmed and with his eyes closed. Germanus was scarcely able to pry open the throat with the handle of a little knife. First he gave a prayer, and then he placed into his mouth small amounts of cold water, once, twice, and thrice. While awaiting what would be the outcome of the matter, he sat by the bed. Hardly an hour passed when the gasps renewed, and the out of breath man roused. When the breaths assumed a smooth motion, Germanus drew back. The [patient's] chest relaxed and the movement of the throat returned [to normal] with breath rushing in and gradually increasing, so life was restored from death.[107]

In this instance, the saint in question, Bishop Germanus, was still alive when he exhibited his healing authority. Furthermore, the cure seems to have been less miraculous than medical. Thus, here a hagiographer depicted a saintly bishop's besting a doctor at his own game. Not to be

---

106. Greg. Tur., *VP* 8.8.
107. Ven. Fort., *Vita Germani* 60 (*MGH*, AA 4.2, 23–24): "Attila vir inluster ac regalis aulae domesticus conruens in balneo laeso graviter brachio conputruerat ipsa tota manus ab humero. Qui medico adhibito, dum curam velit inpendere, rupta vena viscerum paene omnis in momento vitae sanguis effusus est. Nuntiatur pontifici hominem esse in funere, pietatis inpulsu occurrit senior, quem lacrimis conclamantum sine ulla spe oculis clausis onbpressum invenit expositum. Cuius vix adaperit faucews cum cultelli manubrio, oratione prius data intulit ei in ore paulolum aquae frigidae semel, secundo vel tertio. Transacta fere hora redivivo singultu exanimatus concutitur, molli motu anhelitus evocatus reducitur. Faucium meatus relaxatis visceribus, spiritu intercurrente reduciter, paulatim convaliscens vita de morte revertitur …"

outdone when it came to showing up physicians in writing, Gregory offered a tale in which a doctor undid a miracle performed by Saint Martin. Leunastes, an archdeacon from Bourges, became blind in both eyes from cataracts. When physicians failed to heal him, the cleric traveled to Saint Martin's basilica, and after remaining there several months he recovered some of his sight. But back at home, Leunastes let a Jewish doctor bleed his shoulders, expecting that this would improve his vision. Instead, the archdeacon became blind again. He returned to Martin's basilica and lay there a long time, but never regained his sight. Gregory concluded the tale with a rebuke for the insufficiently reverent archdeacon and an admonition for his readers: "This man would have persisted in health, had he not preferred [the cure of] a Jew over divine power. ... Therefore, let this incident teach every Christian, so that whenever one will have deserved to receive heavenly medicine, he will not then look to earthly solutions."[108] This anecdote provides a context for Gregory's animosity toward physicians. First, the fact that Gregory blamed the loss of sight on Leunastes' own faithlessness and not on the physician's care reveals how the author was more concerned to prove that people must respect the saints than he was to argue that doctors' treatments regularly failed. Second, in this passage Gregory trumped any disparagement for physicians by referring to the doctor as a *Iudaeus*. Jews apparently were a group for whom the bishop harbored considerable animus, but the same cannot be said about his actual feeling for doctors.[109]

---

108. Greg. Tur., *Hist.*, 5.6 (*MGH*, SRM 1.1, 203): "Nam perstiterat hic in sanitate, si Iudaeum non induxisset super divinam virtutem. ... Ideo doceat unumquemque christianum haec causa, ut, quando caelestem accipere meruerit medicinam, terrena non requirat studia."

109. Elsewhere Gregory referred to a Jew (perhaps another doctor) who belittled the healing powers of Martin as a *serpens antiquus*; Greg. Tur., *VM* 3.50 (*MGH*, SRM 1.2, 194). Gregory's criticisms of Bishop Cautinus of Clermont included an accusation of the latter's overt familiarity with that community's Jews; Greg. Tur., *Hist.* 4.12. In 576 Gregory's friend Bishop Avitus forcibly converted members of that same Jewish community at Clermont, which action Gregory supported; Greg. Tur., *Hist.* 5.11. On Gregory's representations of Jews, see Avril Keely, "Arians and Jews in the *Histories* of Gregory of Tours," *Early Medieval Europe* 2 (1997), 103–15. Michael Toch, "The Jews in Europe, 500–1050," in *The New Cambridge Medieval History*, v. 1, c. 500–c. 700, ed. Paul Fouracre (Cambridge: Cambridge University Press, 2005), 550–53, proposes a minimal presence of Jews in late ancient Gaul and Spain. While accepting that there were Jewish settlements at Narbonne, Arles, and Marseilles, he denies such for central, western, and northern Gallic towns, except possibly Clermont; ibid., 553. While Toch's central thesis for Gaul and Spain appears sound, his reticence to accept literary evidence seems a little extreme, particularly as it includes evidence from multiple sources – namely, Gregory and Venantius – for Jews at Clermont. Gregory estimated that Avitus baptized

The disdain Gregory heaped upon physicians in his hagiography was in fact merely a posture intended to convince readers of the claim that saints were effectual healers in their communities.[110] For passages in which he was not promoting a saint's healing *virtus*, Gregory readily dispensed with criticisms. Thus, when he related in the *Historiae* how physicians failed to cure King Theudebert, rather than lashing out against them he instead commented that they did their best. Indeed, Theudebert's doctors in this instance could not possibly have saved the ruler's life, thought Gregory, because God was summoning the goodly king to heaven.[111] Indeed, looking beyond Gregory's occasional obligatory hagiographic harangue, one finds that the bishop actually had high regard for the profession. First, Gregory repeatedly turned to doctors for medical treatment. The anecdote has already been cited in which he sought Armentarius's aid when he feared for his life because of a severe fever and dysentery in 573. Seven years later in 580, Gregory suffered a recurring pain in his eyes and temples, and so he twice touched his head to the curtains in Martin's church. After these efforts failed, he next resorted to bloodlettings, two in three days.[112] Only after the second treatment failed did he realize he ought not to have considered letting a physician tend him. Attributing the idea of seeking out a doctor to demonic deception, he finally rushed to Martin's tomb, where he soon recovered his health.[113] It is significant to note that several years after this lapse in judgment, Gregory again considered phlebotomy to treat

more than 500 Jews in 576; Greg. Tur., *Hist.* 5.11. A poem that he had Venantius compose for Avitus was intended to exonerate the friend from this ugly and actual incident; see Brian Brennan, "The Conversion of the Jews of Clermont in AD 576," *Journal of Theological Studies* 36 (1985), 321–37. In contrast to the hostile mention of Cautinus cavorting with Clermont's Jews, Gregory when describing the funeral of his uncle Gallus disclosed in a rare moment of generosity that the city's Jews joined the procession and mourned the bishop's passing; Greg. Tur., *VP* 6.7. That a substantial number of Jews was resident at Clermont is not merely a possibility; it is a certainty.

110. Flint, "The Early Medieval 'Medicus', the Saint – and the Enchanter," 135–36. Flint, ibid., 136, commented: "[T]he fact that the 'medicus' *is* so important as a foil to the saint is very strong testimony indeed to the importance of [the doctor's] social status in reality."

111. Greg. Tur., *Hist.*, 3.36; Jones, "Death and Afterlife in the Pages of Gregory of Tours," (forthcoming).

112. Greg. Tur., *VM*, 2.60.

113. Since Gregory's pain did not increase after he sought a physician for a problem that Saint Martin had not permanently fixed, it would seem that Martin was more forgiving toward the bishop than he had been toward the aforementioned Archdeacon Leunastes, who was left blind after consulting a Jewish doctor. But as Gregory rationalized, his own case resulted not from faithlessness but from a demon!

a swollen tongue and lip; however, this time he overcame the tempta-
tion.[114] If reservations about consulting physicians increased for Gregory
late in life, there is no reason to think they would have for his friend
Venantius. The latter composed an ode to phlebotomy in which the
poet's only concern was that after letting blood from his arm, he would
be unable to hold a quill.[115]

In addition to frequenting doctors, Gregory and company sometimes
cast physicians in a positive light. For example, the bishop mentioned
"the many skills of doctors" (*medici multa studia*) and "the authority of
skilled doctors" (*auctoritas peritorum medicorum*).[116] He even preserved
in writing several highlights of Gallic physicians in action. For example,
in 584, Chilperic's treasurer Eberulf beat one of Gregory's priests to the
point of death, but fortunately physicians were nearby: "... it seemed the
[priest's] soul was about to depart, and perhaps it would have, if the cupping glasses of the doctors had not revived him."[117] Likewise, Gregory
admitted that doctors comforted people during the plague in 580 and by
virtue of their bloodlettings "many were cured" (*multi liberabantur*).[118]
Gregory recorded these episodes not in the *Miracula* but in the *Historiae*.
Because in these particular instances he was narrating and not pointedly
arguing for the reality of saintly *virtutes*, here he allowed glimpses of
his actual appreciation for physicians' skills. Even if Gregory personally
favored Martin's healing over doctors' remedies, he did not deny the
positive role the latter often played in society.

The relatively innocuous rhetoric afforded physicians by hagiographers such as Gregory and Venantius was more than offset by the
attitudes of other Gallic bishops who outwardly embraced the occupation, such as Caesarius of Arles. Because Caesarius was little inclined
to promote the *virtutes* of deceased saints, his writings lack the invectives against doctors designed to promote the healing authority of holy
persons. His sermons contain generally favorable characterizations of

114. Greg. Tur., *VM* 4.2.
115. Ven. Fort., *Carm.* 6.10.
116. Greg. Tur., *Hist.* 3.36 (*MGH*, SRM 1.1, 131); *VM* 2.18 (*MGH*, SRM 1.2, 165).
117. Greg. Tur., *Hist.*, 7.22 (*MGH*, SRM 1.1, 341): "...paene animam reddere videretur; et fecissit forsitan, si ei medicorum ventusae non subvenissent."
118. Greg. Tur., *Hist.* 5.34 (*MGH*, SRM 1.1, 239).

physicians and their craft.[119] This is not to say that Caesarius was averse to pointing out doctors' shortcomings, including an imperfect success rate and a notorious habit of holding out for cash: "When bodily doctors refuse to come to the sick, dearly beloved, they are begged with great humility, and rewards and gifts are promised, even though it is doubtful whether their remedies will be beneficial."[120] This statement does not express a distrust of physicians so much as it realistically indicates the hit-or-miss nature of medicine in the age. Elsewhere, Caesarius offered positive words on doctors: "The iron implements of the physician are harsh, but they make men well."[121] The bishop even likened God to a well-intentioned doctor: "Truly, dearly beloved, God does not want to kill the sinner, but his sin. Like a good doctor He wants to strike the disease, not the person who is ill."[122]

Like Gregory, the Bishop of Arles often used metaphors of healing, but Caesarius's metaphorical language did not make saints into physicians. Rather, Caesarius proposed that there were two kinds of healer, those of the body and those of the spirit – that is, actual physicians and clerics. Caesarius's sermons usually presented each kind of healer as having his own sphere of influence. Bodily physicians rightly tended to bodily maladies, while spiritual doctors mended souls: "Like sick people who seek bodily health from physical doctors, [sinners] may desire remedies for their souls from spiritual ones."[123] Unlike the verbal imagery advanced by hagiographers, Caesarius's metaphor with its separate spheres of influence tended to negate the potential for rivalry over

---

119. Flint, "The Early Medieval 'Medicus', the Saint – and the Enchanter," 131–32.
120. Caes. Arel., *Serm.* 5.5 (*CCL* 103, 29): "Nam illud quale est, fratres carissimi, quod medici corporum, quando ad aegrotos venire dissimulant, cum grandi humilitate rogantur, praemia et munera promittuntur; et tamen dubium est utrum aliquid illorum medicamenta prificant ..." Trans. by Mary Magdeline Mueller, *Saint Caesarius of Arles: Sermons*, 3 vols. (New York: Fathers of the Church, 1956; Washington: Catholic University of America Press, 1964–1973), 1: 37.
121. Caes. Arel., *Serm.* 207.4 (*CCL* 104, 831): "Dura quidem sunt medici ferramenta, sed sanos faciunt ..."
122. Caes. Arel., *Serm.* 17.4 (*CCL* 103, 81): "Deus enim, fratres carissimi, non peccatorem vult occidere, sed peccatum; et, quomodo bonus medicus, morbum vult percutere, non aegrotum ..." Trans. by Mueller, *Saint Caesarius of Arles: Sermons*, 1: 92.
123. Caes. Arel., *Serm.* 43.9 (*CCL* 103, 194): "...et quomodo aegrotantes a carnalibus medicis requirunt sanitatem corporum, sic ab spiritalibus medicamenta desiderent animarum." Trans. by Mueller, *Saint Caesarius of Arles: Sermons*, 1: 220.

healing authority. But this did not mean the skills of the two kinds of healer were equally effective, for whereas medicine prescribed for the body could fail, spiritual medicine could not prove powerless. Caesarius wrote: "It is uncertain whether a physical doctor can relieve a sick man; however, if spiritual medicine is willingly received, without any doubt the soul is revived even if it was wounded by many sins or was dead."[124] Caesarius relied on both his community's understanding of medical practices and his healing metaphor to advance difficult subjects before his congregation.[125] For example, he used his urban audience's familiarity with physicians' care to explain why they had to endure harsh sermons. He commented how listeners were well aware that the ill willingly endured brief discomfiture such as bitter potions and burning cauterizing to recover physical health, and so they should realize that spiritual doctors would have to excise sin by prescribing harsh medicine in the form of "acerb reproof" (*asperam castigationem*)."[126] One "bitter pill" Caesarius frequently administered was a reminder of impending Judgment Day. Knowing there were those who would question why he had to raise the unsavory topic repeatedly, the preacher was ready with a comparison to the doctor's craft:

> Moreover, notice that physicians of the body, whenever patients who are physically ill come to them, take away everything that seemed agreeable. What is pleasant for a well man is forbidden. For example, they do not allow the person to take anything cold, or sometimes they are compelled to drink very bitter medicines, and wounds frequently are cut with exceedingly rough or sharp

---

124. Caes. Arel., *Serm.* 5.5 (*CCL* 103, 29): "Carnalis enim medicus utrum relevare possit aegrotum, incertum est: spiritalis vero medicina si libenter accipiatur, absque ulla dubitatione, etiamsi multis peccatis vulnerata sit, etiamsi mortua sit, anima suscitatur." Trans. by Mueller, *Saint Caesarius of Arles: Sermons*, 1: 37.

125. Perhaps residents of cosmopolitan Arles and its environs had greater familiarity with physicians' care and better access to doctors than did people living elsewhere in Gaul. Bishop Maximianus of Trier requested that Avitus of Vienne ask Caesarius to recommend a doctor to him; Avitus of Vienne, *Ep.* 11. While he was still a monk at Lérins, Caesarius traveled to Arles in search of a remedy for a fever; Cyprian of Toulon et al., *Vita Caesarii* 1.7. John Riddle, "Theory and Practice in Medieval Medicine," *Viator* 5 (1974), 159, challenges historians to abandon speculating on the location of formal medical schools and their "decline" in Late Antiquity, since such institutions likely never existed in the Roman world.

126. Caes. Arel., *Serm.* 5.5 (*CCL* 103, 29).

instruments. What earthly doctors do for the sake of bodily health, spiritual physicians try to practice for the salvation of souls.[127]

For all the differences between Caesarius's two kinds of healer, their spheres of influence were not completely distinct. Caesarius thought it necessary for the inferior, bodily sphere to yield to the superior, spiritual one on holy occasions, especially on Rogation Days, during which clerical rituals would be healing souls.[128] Proper observance of this sacred time could result in, among other things, bodily healing: "If we are entirely devoted to God and humbly implore His mercy, through the mercy of God we may deserve to be *healed of all our infirmities*, rescued from all of our sins, set free from the very frequent flooding of waters."[129] Because of the special opportunities afforded by the Rogations, Caesarius was adamant about church attendance on these days: "No one should leave the Church, which is the school of the heavenly physician, or desert the spiritual camp because he is involved in earthly activities."[130] Specifically, Caesarius warned that people were not to work, gamble or gossip during Rogation days, nor were they to seek out physicians. The bishop admonished: "On these three days, no one should let himself be bled or accept a potion, unless perchance a very critical illness makes this necessary."[131] Caesarius enacted this prohibition because frequenting a doctor implied

---

127. Caes. Arel., *Serm.* 57.1 (*CCL* 103, 251): "Et hoc adtendite, fratres, quia cmnes carnales medici, quotiens ad eos qui in corpore aegrotare videntur veniunt, omnia quae eis delectabilia esse videbantur abscidunt, et quod dulce est ad integrum interdicunt; aliquotiens etiam frigidum accipere non permittunt, interdum et amarissimas potiones bibere cogunt, et asperrimis vel acutissimis ferramentis eorum vulnera frequenter incidunt. Hoc ergo, quod pro sanitate corporum carnales medici faciunt, pro animarum salute spiritales medici exercere contendunt." Trans. by Mueller, *Saint Caesarius of Arles: Sermons*, 1: 282.
128. Caes. Arel., *Serm.* 207.1, 209.4; Klingshirn, *Caesarius of Arles: The Making of a Christian Community*, 177.
129. Caes. Arel., *Serm.* 207.3 (*CCL* 104, 830): "... ut ad integrum deo vacantes, et misericordiam illius suppliciter exorantes, et a cunctis infirmtatibus sanari, et a peccatis omnibus erui, et de tam frequenti inundatione aquarum mereamur per dei misericordiam liberari." Trans. by Mueller, *Saint Caesarius of Arles: Sermons*, 3: 85, with my italics.
130. Caes. Arel., *Serm.* 207.2 (*CCL* 104, 829): "... nullus ecclesiam, quae est caelestis medici scola, occupatus terrenis actibus derelinquat, nullus castra spiritalia deserat." Trans. by Mueller, *Saint Caesarius of Arles: Sermons*, 3: 84.
131. Caes. Arel., *Serm.* 207.3 (*CCL* 104, 830): "Nemo in istis tribus diebus aut sanguinem tollat aut potionem accipiat, nisi forte hoc infirmtas nimium periculosa conpellat." Trans. by Mueller, *Saint Caesarius of Arles: Sermons*, 3: 85.

placing emphasis on the physical, the very matter one was not supposed to stress during Rogation Days. But note the exemption clause in the previous passage. The zealous Bishop of Arles was reasonable enough to allow people even during the Rogations to seek a doctor if faced with a life or death scenario. Thus, while Caesarius believed the business of spiritual physicians undoubtedly was more important than that of bodily ones, he expected of the latter only that they acquiesce to the spiritual doctors a mere three days per annum: "It ought to be enough for us, brethren, that throughout the space of the entire year we are busy with some bodily advantage or need; at least on these three days, let us reflect more carefully on the salvation of our soul."[132] Otherwise, Caesarius acknowledged physicians as the principal bodily healers of his community.[133]

However, physicians at Arles did have to share the limelight with one particularly prominent ecclesiastical healer. While Caesarius apparently was not a passionate promoter of saints' cults, he regarded his own body as a channel for God's medicinal powers.[134] There is no evidence that Gregory of Tours ever claimed this honor for himself. Caesarius thus responded to requests that he try to heal sick persons, and he diagnosed patients "like a good physician" (sicut bonus medicus).[135] He healed the infirm by using "ecclesiastically approved techniques: praying, anointing with consecrated oil, blessing with holy water, laying on hands, or making the sign of the cross."[136] But Caesarius's personal wonder-working would have posed no threat to physicians. First, the bishop shied away from taking credit for any cures, attributing any successful outcomes to

---

132. Caes. Arel., *Serm.* 209.4 (*CCL* 104, 837): "Debet nobis sufficere, fratres, quod per totum spatium anni pro utilitate vel necessitate corporis occupamur: vel in his tribus diebus de salute animae nostrae adtentius cogitemus." Trans. by Mueller, *Saint Caesarius of Arles: Sermons*, 3: 92–93.

133. Caesarius did advise ill people to seek remedies for their afflictions at churches where priests could administer holy oil and pray for them. See, e.g., Caes. Arel., *Serm.* 19.5. But whenever he preached in this vein, the bishop had in mind opposition to folk healers.

134. For Caesarius's "lukewarm" attitude toward use of relics, see Klingshirn, *Caesarius of Arles: The Making of a Christian Community*, 166–67. For Caesarius's attributing successful cures he performed to God rather than himself, see, e.g., Cyprian of Toulon et al., *Vita Caesarii* 1.40, 2.3, 2.20.

135. Cyprian of Toulon et al., *Vita Caesarii* 1.17 (Morin, ed., 2: 302).

136. Klingshirn, *Caesarius of Arles: The Making of a Christian Community*, 164. For Caesarius as miracle worker, see idem, 161–70.

God.[137] Second, despite any successes he was but one person, the very person, no less, who from his pulpit encouraged members of his congregation to take ill family members to physicians.[138]

Another matter for Arles' doctors was the inevitable insistence that the relics of Caesarius could heal patients. Even before the bishop's death, some of Caesarius's more zealous disciples – namely, his eventual hagiographers Messianus and Stephanus – were intimating that pieces of the bishop's clothes could be used as medicinal curatives.[139] Upon the prelate's death, these two authored the second of two books of the saint's *Vita*. Just as Gregory would later do for Saint Martin, the pair offered a healing metaphor to promote Saint Caesarius as the "skilled physician" of the community.[140] Also like Gregory, Caesarius's hagiographers preserved in writing how their holy healer sometimes prevailed when physicians faltered. For example, they related that Bishop Caesarius while alive once anointed with holy oil a slave of the patrician Parthenius and thereby cured him of epilepsy. The authors concluded the tale with the obligatory hagiographical poke at the medical profession: "Through his servant [Caesarius], Christ had restored him to good health after the treatment of a physician of this world had failed."[141] Depictions of Caesarius healing patients with prayer and holy oil are among a scant number of miracles that can be corroborated to show that not all accounts of healings were literary fictions, for the images conform to the techniques Caesarius espoused in his sermons.[142] Interestingly, Gregory of Tours, who began writing his *Miracula* almost thirty years after publication of the *Vita Caesarii*, did not include Caesarius in his book of Gallic confessors. Caesarius did not maintain a lasting reputation as a holy healer as did Saint Martin. This likely resulted in part because Martin's cult enjoyed an unprecedented string of capable promoters,

---

137. Klingshirn, ibid., 165, notes that attributing miracles to God would have provided Caesarius a way out whenever his efforts failed.
138. E.g., Caes. Arel., *Serm.* 52.5.
139. E.g., Cyprian of Toulon et al., *Vita Caesarii* 2.13–15.
140. Cyprian of Toulon et al., *Vita Caesarii* 2.34.
141. Cyprian of Toulon et al., *Vita Caesarii* 1.49 (Morin, ed., 2: 316–17): "ut quem cessante cura terreni medici per servum suum Christus reddiderat sanitati ..." Trans. by Klingshirn, *The Caesarius of Arles: Life, Testament, Letters*, 34. See also *Vita Caesarii* 2.40, 41.
142. Klingshirn, *Caesarius of Arles: The Making of a Christian Community*, 162.

while Caesarius's perhaps did not. But if the residents of Arles never developed a lasting need to imagine their former bishop as a formidable holy healer, they did not abandon their appreciation for bodily physicians.

PHYSICIANS SUCCEEDING

Most physicians in Gaul probably enjoyed a modest to wealthy socio-economic position, numbering among the well-to-do *ingenui*. As elsewhere in the Late Ancient Mediterranean, Gallic doctors achieved a level of wealth and status few physicians could have aspired to in the Classical era. While some displayed a noble air by joining in aristocratic pursuits such as participation in literary circles, most physicians worked toward moderate respectability through accumulating riches. The prestige and popularity of physicians continued unabated into the early Medieval period.[143] For example, the biographer of Saint Bonitus of Clermont (d. 706) tellingly remarked, "...as great a multitude of sick people flocked together with the faithful congregation at the body of the holy bishop [i. e., at his tomb] as [would attend] the lecture of a very eminent physician."[144] Thus even Gallic hagiographers eventually admitted plainly to the profession's prestige. While their pursuit of influence and wealth through attendance upon affluent patients caused continuous complaints that doctors disregarded the poor, there was no general antipathy toward the profession. Indeed, writers such as Gregory included anecdotes about physicians being mistreated precisely because doctors were thought to be significant members of society, and tales of physical assaults upon them were scandalous. For example, in one of only two entries for the year 581, a contemporary of Gregory's, the chronicler Marius of Avenches, offered readers the notorious tale of Austrechild demanding the execution of her doctors, and in the seventh century, the chronicler Fredegar still found the incident worthy of remembrance.[145]

---

143. For the continued importance of physicians into the Carolingian period, see Flint, "The Early Medieval 'Medicus,' the Saint – and the Enchanter," 133.

144. *Vita Boniti* 38 (*MGH*, SRM 6, 137): "... quanta infirmantium multitudo fideli concursu ad corpus sancti sacerdotis velud ad scolam medici probatissimi confluebant ..."

145. Mar. Avent., *Chron.*, s. a. 581, c. 1 (*MGH*, AA 11, 239). Marius provided the names of Austrechild's physicians, Nicholas and Donatus. In the second anecdote for this year Marius mentioned the

Gallic physicians survived all challenges to their healing authority. Neither the availability of medical manuals nor rustic people's reliance on folk healers could translate into widespread abandonment of physicians' care. The techniques that doctors mastered in surgery and bloodletting were skills that unqualified medical practitioners could not duplicate. Even the culturally dominant ecclesiastics who championed the healing *virtutes* of invisible holy patrons did not press an actual rivalry with physicians.[146] Gregory of Tours, Venantius Fortunatus, and Caesarius of Arles all appreciated the physician's art. For their part, doctors did not necessarily discount the possibility that saints could heal.[147] For example, according to the *Life of Saint Severinus of Agaune*, when King Clovis's skilled *medicus* Tranquilinus realized that he and other doctors could not cure the king of a lingering (two-year) fever, the physician himself advised the ruler to seek a cure from the holy abbot.[148] Another doctor and proponent of saints was the *archiater* of Poitiers Reovalis, upon whom Queen Radegund relied for care of residents at her nunnery. According to the nun Baudonivia, the queen authorized the doctor to travel to Jerusalem to obtain a relic of the martyr Mammas.[149] Reovalis obligingly ventured east and met the patriarch. During a special ceremony, the physician was permitted to run his hands over the limbs of the martyr's corpse until the saint let him know what relic he might take – the little finger of the right hand, as it turned out. When Reovalis presented Radegund with the "heavenly gift," she behaved ecstatically and ordered her community to join in a week of devotional exercises. The queen owed her joy to the helpful and honorable *medicus*. After

execution of the patrician Mummolus and his family; *Chron.*, s. a. 581, c. 2. Fredegar, *Chron.* 3.82, relied on Gregory's text for his version of the episode.

146. For continued criticism of physicians as a hagiographical theme into the High Middle Ages, see Klaus Bergdolt, "Die Kritik am Arzt im Mittelalter – Beispiel und Tendenzen vom 6. bis zum 12. Jahrhundert," *Gesnerus* 48 (1991), 43–63. Bergdolt's assertion that early medieval Christians were suspicious of medicine because they associated it with paganism is unconvincing, certainly so for Merovingian Gaul.

147. The assertion by Flint, "The Early Medieval 'Medicus,' the Saint – and the Enchanter," 142–43, that physicians felt intimidated by enchanters and needed to "join" with saints versus them is, I think, invalid, arising as it does from Flint's assumption that many folk healers were socially prominent pagans; e.g., ibid., 130. For my contrary assessment, see the discussion in Chapter Eight.

148. *Vita Severini* I (*MGH*, SRM 3, 169).

149. Baudonivia, *Vita Radegundis* 14 (*MGH*, SRM 2, 387).

Radegund's death in 587, Reovalis remained an influential figure about the convent. In 590, he testified in support of the Abbess Leubovera, thereby frustrating the ridiculous accusation of a rebellious nun that she maintained eunuchs in the nunnery.[150] Finally, Reovalis capped off his reputation within the religious circle at Poitiers by becoming a priest. Writing in the early seventh century, Baudonivia not only attested that the aged *archiater* was still living, but respectfully identified him as a *vir venerabilis*.[151]

Another Gallic physician intimately involved with ecclesiastics was Helpidius of Bordeaux, who was both an *archiater* and *diaconus*.[152] In the early sixth century, Helpidius served at the court of Theodoric the Ostrogoth, where he held the rank of *vir inlustris*. He was addressee of several letters from episcopal friends Ennodius of Pavia and Avitus of Vienne, and he was a compatriot of Caesarius of Arles'. The relationship between these bishops and the influential physician was reciprocal. For example, when the son of a friend of Avitus fell ill, the bishop appealed to Helpidius to cure the boy: "May Christ grant that by exalting and praising your supreme command of this art (i.e., medicine), Italy may owe its fame for medicine and Gaul the health of this child to you."[153] Likewise, when Helpidius's house at Ravenna became infested by demons, the *archiater* turned to the friend who could best attend to that kind of dilemma, a wonderworking bishop. Caesarius' hagiographers wrote:

> The deacon Helpidius, who was a physician and was very close to the king and zealously served him, suffered from a demonic infestation. He was not only worn out by various other afflictions, but he was also frequently assaulted by showers of stones in his own house. He convinced the holy man of God that he deserved to be freed from this distress by his prayers. Upon entering his house to purify it, Caesarius sprinkled it with holy water and so thoroughly delivered it

---

150. Greg. Tur., *Hist.* 10.15.
151. Baudonivia, *Vita Radegundis* 14 (*MGH*, SRM 2, 386).
152. *PLRE* 2: 537, s. v., "Helpidius 6."
153. Avitus of Vienne, *Ep.* 38 (*MGH*, AA 6, 67): "Tribuat Christus, ut exultando atque impensius laudando in hac cura magisterio tuo simul tibi et Italia medicinae opinionem et Gallia pueri debeat sanitatem." Trans. by Shanzer and Wood, *Avitus of Vienne: Letters*, 361.

from the perils of its previous distress that nothing similar has ever happened there since.[154]

It has been proposed that this anecdote offers evidence of its hagiographers' desire to diminish the vocation of physician, but this can hardly be the case.[155] First, the writers' mention of Helpidius's being a doctor, like their indication of his familiarity with the king, was part and parcel of the authors' providing social credentials for the subject in order to impress readers with the quality of the saint's friends. Second, in no way can Caesarius' performance of an exorcism on Helpidius's house reflect negatively upon the physician's medical competence, nor upon the medical profession in general. Otherwise, referring back to Avitus's letter, the fact that the bishop had to seek medical aid from a physician living in Italy seems to indicate a lack of doctors, or perhaps specialists, in southern Gaul.[156] Alternatively, perhaps the letter, like the exorcism story, reflects more the mindfulness of aristocratic friends to rely exclusively upon one another's support and the lengths to which they would go to maintain contact, even if more expedient remedies, i. e., Gallic doctors or Italian exorcists, were at hand. Helpidius, Avitus, and Caesarius – and perhaps even the episcopal hagiographers who preserved the exorcism episode – regarded one another as friends, and each bore a profound respect for the others' special talents.

Finally, even the doctor Armentarius at Tours likely was an esteemed figure in Gregory's circle. Although Gregory depicted this physician as failing to cure him of an illness that Saint Martin subsequently healed, even in this negative presentation, the author positively noted Armentarius's capabilities, *omnem ingenium artificii tui.*[157] Gregory's doctor was no household servant in the mode of the freed physicians of

---

154. Cyprian of Toulon et al., *Vita Caesarii* 1.41 (Morin, ed., 2: 313): "Medicus etiam diaconus Helpidius, regiae potestati ac sedulo famulatu intimus, diabolica infestatione non solum reliquis diversis invidiis fatigatus, sed et saxorum quoque imbre in domo sua crebrius adpetitus, sanctum dei exorat, ut a vexatione ipsa eius merertur orationibus liberari. Cuius domum sanctificaturus ingrediens, benedictae aquae infusione respersit, atque ita consuetae vexationis discriminibus liberavit, ut ultra ibi nihil tale contingerit." Trans. by Klingshirn, *Caesarius of Arles: Life, Testament, Letters,* 30.
155. *Contra* Flint, "The Early Medieval 'Medicus', the Saint – and the Enchanter," 136, n. 29.
156. Shanzer and Wood, *Avitus of Vienne: Letters,* 359.
157. Greg. Tur., *VM* 2.1 (*MGH,* SRM 1.2, 159).

Cicero and Cato's era; rather, he was an *archiater*, a municipal physician, one of the most prominent members of his profession. Like other prestigious doctors, Armentarius may have been of noble stock, like Helpidius. Were he an aristocrat, given that his name is similar to that of Gregory's mother Armentaria, he may well have been a relation of Gregory's.[158] Perhaps Armentarius was among the *medici* whom Gregory positively depicted using cupping glasses to save the life of his own priest, who had been beaten to the point of death by Eberulf.[159] Regardless of whether he was a relative or not, his presence reveals that even in the company of the Gaul most notorious for vilifying doctors, one might witness a competent physician enjoying success, wealth, status and influence.

158. Van Dam, *Saints and their Miracles*, 92, n. 46, proposed this possibility. Heinzelmann, *Bischofs-herrschaft in Gallien*, 213–14, and Mathisen, "The Family of Georgius Florentius Gregorius," 92–93, n. 10, did not include the *archiater* in their lists of "noteworthy Armentarii" possibly related to Gregory. Riché, *Education and Culture in the Barbarian West*, 520, identified the *archiater* Armentarius with "unus ex clericis meis, Artmentarius ... eruditus in spiritualibus scripturis;" Greg. Tur., *VM* 1.33 (*MGH*, SRM 1.2, 154). This identification is unlikely, as the latter passage seems to depict a servile cleric, although one cannot be positive that this cleric was of low status. Of course, if he were, the passage would then serve to remind us that having the name Armentarius and living at Tours need not mean that one was related to Gregory!

159. Greg. Tur., *Hist.* 7.22.

HEALING AND AUTHORITY II: ENCHANTERS

CHAPTER EIGHT

There was in this time a woman possessing the spirit of the python, who generated much [wealth] for her masters by divining [answers] to questions. On account of her service she advanced in their gratitude; she was freed and permitted to act as she pleased. If anyone suffered from theft or some other evil, immediately she would declare where the thief was hiding, to whom he had delivered the goods, or whatever else had transpired. Daily she accumulated gold and silver. She went about bedecked with jewels so that the people thought her something of a goddess.

GREGORY OF TOURS, *Historiae* 7.44[1]

Late Antiquity had no lack of people who claimed an ability to supernaturally secure health, wealth, love, revenge, and hidden knowledge.[2]

---

1. Greg. Tur., *Hist.* 7.44 (*MGH*, SRM 1.1, 364–65): "Fuit tunc temporis mulier, quae spiritum pithonis habens multum praestabat dominis divinando questum eoque in gratia proficit, ut, ab his libera facta, suis voluntatibus laxaretur. Si quis enim aut furtum aut aliquid mali perferret, statim haec, quo fur abiit, cui tradedit vel quid ex hoc fecerit, edicebat. Congregabat cotidie aurum argentumque, procedens in ornamentis ita ut putaretur esse aliquid divinum in populis."
2. Much literature on late ancient magic subsequent to 1991 is to some extent a commentary on the insights of Valerie Flint, *The Rise of Magic in Early Medieval Europe* (op. cit.). For Greek and Roman

Such persons predicted future events, elucidated on the past, interpreted dreams, affected weather conditions, healed physical afflictions, caused afflictions, identified this-worldly evildoers, and got rid of other-worldly evildoers. Late ancient magicians were a varied lot: Christian and pagan, clergy and laity, male and female, bishop and slave, philosopher and athlete. While acquisition of wealth and local repute motivated some to contact the supernatural, as apparently was the case for the diviner of this chapter's introductory quote, others claimed such abilities in order to augment their control over society. Practitioners of esoteric arts chanced having to reckon with powerful secular officials and ecclesiastics, but if they fared as successfully as the prognosticator described here, then presumably their efforts will have been worth the risk.

This chapter explores the behaviors and opportunities of a sub-set of persons who appealed for, or demanded, supernatural aid, people whom Gallic litterateurs labeled neutrally "enchanters" (*incantatores*) or sinisterly "sorcerers" (e.g., *malefici*). As with the previous chapter (Seven) on physicians, this one will begin by establishing a context though briefly considering the "magic-using" professions in Late Antiquity. It then will focus on the social conditions of *incantatores* in Barbarian Gaul, including potential problems they might encounter.[3] Because healing was an important practice among many enchanters, they, like physicians, would potentially have had to contend with ecclesiastics, especially promoters of saints' cults desirous of monopolizing healing authority in their communities.

magic up to Late Antiquity, see Fritz Graf, *Magic in the Ancient World*, trans. by Franklin Philip (Cambridge, MA, and London: Harvard University Press, 1999).

3. Henceforth I shall privilege use of the term with the most neutral ring to it, "enchanter" (*incantator*), following Flint, "The Early Medieval 'Medicus', the Saint – and the Enchanter," 140, n. 43. Furthermore, I shall use the words "magic" and "magical" in a neutral sense, akin to "wonder" and "wondrous" but implying human involvement. I will not offer the word "magic" in the sense of a strict magic/religion dichotomy, where the former involves manipulation of supernatural forces and the latter supplication, except to imply an author's use of the term in that sense. On definitions for "magic," see Richard Kieckhefer, *Magic in the Middle Ages* (Cambridge: Cambridge University Press, 1989), 8–17, especially at 14–15; and see the discussion in this chapter between pp. 287 and 292.

ENCHANTERS IN LATE ANTIQUITY

In the late Roman world, people from all levels of society, famous and obscure, tested an ability to invoke or manipulate invisible powers for all manner of reasons. According to Porphyry, the renowned philosopher Plotinus accepted the invitation of an Egyptian priest to enter the temple of Isis at Rome and come face to face with his own familiar spirit. The rite involved an apprentice's keeping hold of two chickens, which apparently were to be sacrificed to appease the entity. The summoned familiar did manifest, and much to the amazement of the conjuror, Plotinus's genius turned out to be not a mere lesser spirit but a god.[4] On a more mundane level, according to Ammianus Marcellinus, an imperial secretary admitted to killing an ass as part of a remedy to overcome baldness.[5] The famous eastern orator Libanius professed to using magic, and although he insisted that his craft was of a beneficial variety, nevertheless he more than once had to stave off a charge of necromancy.[6] Because certain magical practices were suspect and could bring unwanted attention from law enforcement, powerful Romans likely tended to avoid personal participation in many such activities. A senator might circumvent the taint of magic and yet enjoy its fruits by apprenticing slaves to a master magician.[7] Most ancient enchanters were of middling to low social rank. Old women of generally low and servile status were regarded as the Ancient Mediterranean's appropriate type of person to consult for tending the ill with poultices and incantations, for remedying distress caused by nightmares, and for identifying and curing bewitchment by the Evil Eye.[8] From the second century CE urban-dwelling stage performers,

---

4. Georg Luck, "Witches and Sorcerers in Classical Literature," in *Witchcraft and Magic in Europe: Ancient Greece and Rome*, ed., Bengt Ankarloo and Stuart Clark (Philadelphia: University of Pennsylvania Press, 1999), 148–49.

5. Amm. Marc., *Res gestae* 30.5.11.

6. A. A. Barb, "The Survival of Magic Arts," in *The Conflict between Paganism and Christianity in the Fourth Century*, ed. Arnaldo Momigliano (Oxford: Clarendon, 1963), 115–16.

7. Amm. Marc., *Res gestae* 26.3.4.

8. Dickie, *Magic and Magicians*, 108–09, 190–91, 245–47, 281–84, 309–11. On late ancient healers and amulet makers, Dickie, ibid., 281–84, 304–11, notably makes good use of the sermons of John Chrysostom, Augustine, and Caesarius of Arles among other sources.

wrestlers, and charioteers were living in an endemically magic-using *demi-monde.*[9] Charioteers in particular might have scoffed at the risk that magic could attract threatening legal attention; despite the danger, they embraced rumors of sorcery, which added to their attention-getting mystique.[10] Among several chariot riders from the pages of Ammianus was Auchenius, an alleged maker of poisons who sold his draughts to customers of senatorial rank.[11] Athanasius was a charioteer whose magical craft came to the attention of Emperor Valentinian, and so he paid a fatal price.[12] Another sub-set of urban magician whom sports fans turned to, perhaps more numerous than athletes, was curse manufacturers. Enthusiastic boosters commonly resorted to these magicians in hopes that their spells would thwart the horses and jockeys of rival chariot factions. The usual means to accomplish this famously involved interring lead tablets cursing opposing riders and horses by name (*defixiones*), but a fan might expect a higher chance for success if the magician performed a more dramatic procedure such as placing a curse inside the body of a ritually sacrificed cat.[13] An even larger body of enchanters would have been those persons who secured supernatural aid to assess the future and heal the sick. Healers commonly inscribed short formulae on amulets made from herbs and magical gems, and they filled papyrus pages with lengthy spells that conferred protection when recited.[14] While there

---

9. Ibid., 293–301.
10. *CTh* 9.16.11 (a. 389) mandates the arrest of magicians and refers specifically to charioteers. According to Cassiodorus, *Variae* 3.51.2, charioteers took sorcery accusations as a high honor.
11. Amm. Marc., *Res gestae* 28.1.27.
12. Amm. Marc., *Res gestae* 29.3.5. Peter Brown, "Sorcery, Demons, and the Rise of Christianity from Late Antiquity into the Middle Ages," in *Witchcraft Confessions and Accusations*, ed. Mary Douglas (London and New York: Tavistock, 1970)," 24–26, suggested that indeterminate status accompanying occupations such as professor and charioteer – e. g., the latter being both client of aristocrats and potential mob leader – contributed to their identification as sorcerers. Alternatively, the charioteer's world simply was one in which many ferociously competitive people practiced a lot of magic. See Amm. Marc., *Res gestae* 26.3.3, for a charioteer executed after it was discovered that he had apprenticed his son to a master poison manufacturer (*veneficus*). The ancient prostitute's *demi-monde*, like that of athletes and entertainers, was similarly competitive and likewise very magically prolific; Dickie, *Magic and Magicians*, 300–03.
13. For a mundane curse of charioteers and the cat ritual, see Georg Luck, *Arcana Mundi: Magic and the Occult in the Greek and Roman Worlds, A Collection of Ancient Texts*, 2nd ed. (Baltimore and London: Johns Hopkins University Press, 2006), 128–29, 135–36.
14. Isidore of Seville imagined that all magicians practiced healing and most studied divination; Flint, *Rise of Magic in Early Medieval Europe*, 53.

certainly were enchanters who specialized either in divination or curing, late ancient wonderworkers frequently combined these two practices. For example, the usual ministrations of one institutionalized band of healers, the priests of Asclepius, involved "incubation," a composite practice of dream interpretation and cure; but priests of the popular healing god also pronounced oracles, too.[15]

As inhabitants across the Mediterranean heartily performed a variety of wonders, all the while some debated what practices constituted "magic" and what "religion." Through the early centuries of the Common Era, pagans and Christians adapted terminology for the classical Greek concept of "daimones" to define both. "Religion," by which term one usually identified one's own belief system, relied on the aid of good "daimones" or angels, while "sorcery," a label one attached to objectionable practices, implicated competitors with dependence upon evil "daimones," or demons.[16] A further distinction could be drawn by arguing that a "religious" person submitted to the divine will, whereas a "sorcerer" compelled the divine to satisfy the individual's will.[17] Such a debate ensued between two distinguished Neo-Platonists, Porphyry and Iamblichus, over theurgy. Iamblichus supported the theurgists, a group who appealed to supernatural entities to help them achieve the ultimate goal of purifying the human soul, thereby enabling its subordinate union with the divine.[18] Iamblichus listed theurgist rituals to include

> incantations, ecstatic trances and dreams, frenzies and dances (accompanied by flutes, cymbals and tambourines), the consulting of oracles, the interpretation of entrails of sacrificed animals and of the calls and flights of birds, the calling up of visions on reflecting surfaces such as mirrors or pools of water, conjuring with 'signatures'

15. Robin Lane Fox, *Pagans and Christians in the Mediterranean World from the Second Century AD to the Conversion of Constantine* (New York: Alfred A. Knopf, 1986), 206. For continued combination of healing and divining through the Middle Ages, see Kieckhefer, *Magic in the Middle Ages*, 57–64.
16. Valerie Flint, "The Demonisation of Magic and Sorcery in Late Antiquity," in *Witchcraft and Magic in Europe: Ancient Greece and Rome*, ed. Bengt Ankarloo and Stuart Clark (Philadelphia: University of Pennsylvania Press, 1999), 179.
17. Barb, "Survival of Magic Arts," 101; Kieckhefer, *Magic in the Middle Ages*, 15.
18. Flint, "Demonisation of Magic and Sorcery," 285.

or mantic signs, or wands, enquiring into the future by means of scattered pebbles or grain, or the movements and dispositions of the stars.[19]

While Iamblichus claimed that the entities to which theurgists appealed were good, as evidenced by the practitioners' kindly activities, his younger contemporary Porphyry suspected the powers in question to be deceitful "daimones."[20]

Similarly, some pagans accused members of the Christian sects of sorcery. One such charge stirred the third-century apologist Origen to pen *Against Celsus* in which he fended off the philosopher's estimation that Christians relied on demonic magic, while Eusebius of Caesarea in his *Proof of the Gospel* countered accusations that Christ had been a mage.[21] More than half a century later, Augustine of Hippo composed *Against Faustus* to refute the Manichean's charge that Christ had been a sorcerer, and in *City of God* the bishop objected to contemporary pagan accusations that Saint Peter had been a magician.[22] In like manner, late ancient Christians associated pagan rituals with demon worship, as some had done from that faith's inception, but the Church Fathers went farther than their earliest brethren by making the connection among paganism, demons, and magic inseparable in the Christian mind. Thus, a pagan soothsayer's accurate prediction of the destruction of the temple of Serapis in 391 occasioned Augustine to compose *On the Divination of Demons*, in which he explained that pagan prognostications were able to succeed because airy demons speedily carried information and possessed the body of a diviner, who in turn could pronounce the

---

19. Ibid., 286.
20. Ibid., 287. Luck, "Witches and Sorcerers," 149–52, offers highlights of several magic-using theurgists as described by the biographer Eunapius. Iamblichus reportedly impressed students when two divine entities manifested, and embraced him. The Emperor Julian selected Maximus of Ephesus to be his tutor after hearing how the mage had animated a statue of the goddess Hecate. Maximus was executed in the reign of the Christian ruler Valens. The philosopher Sosipatra was tutored by two otherworldly spirits, and while lecturing she telepathically witnessed a lover survive a carriage crash. Sosipatra's son Antoninus was also clairvoyant, and among other noteworthy deeds he predicted the destruction of the Serapeum in 391. For more on theurgy, see Luck, *Arcana Mundi*, 51–54, 164–73.
21. Flint, "Demonisation of Magic and Sorcery," 307, 315.
22. Ibid., 317; Augustine, *De civitate dei* 18.53.

heretofore unknown knowledge.[23] Likewise, the bishop of Hippo's *City of God* was a tour de force containing passages that regularly stressed how Christians practiced "right religion" by worshipping God, while pagans revered demons whether they realized it or not. Augustine linked magicians and demons by writing that the latter "cherish 'the thousand arts of injuring' [Aeneid 7.338] that the magicians practice in their sorceries and that innocence detests. ...."[24]

Late ancient Christians also leveled charges of witchcraft against their own. While accusations of sorcery likely played a minimal role in contributing to the decline of institutionalized paganism, they apparently were effective in the victory of orthodoxy (i. e., a hierarchical and bishop-led church) over heterodoxy. For example, the (second to fourth) centuries-long contest between bishops and Gnostic Christians involved production of pamphlets that highlighted a magical contest between the Apostle Peter, orthodox champion, and Simon Magus, represented as a Gnostic and demonically empowered sorcerer.[25] In late fourth-century Spain, another heresy that deemphasized episcopal leadership (although it did not deny it) was Priscillianism. Opponents justified execution of the heresiarch Priscillian of Avila and then squelched the movement in Spain and Southern Gaul by casting leader and followers as practitioners of sorcery, hence "demonizing" their behavior.[26] An eager advocate of Priscillian's condemnation was Magnus Maximus, imperial usurper at Trier who hoped to shore up political support among Spanish and Gallic bishops by championing orthodoxy. Priscillian's death came at the end of a fourth-century "flash-point" in which emperors were allowing secular officials to level rampant accusations of witchcraft as part of a ploy to augment imperial power.[27] Perhaps the most volatile late Roman purges of enchanters happened under Constantius II (337–361) and the

23. Flint, "Demonisation of Magic and Sorcery," 318.
24. Ibid., 319.
25. Ibid., 300–02.
26. E. g., Sulp. Sev., *Chron.* 2.46–48 (*CSEL* 1, 99–101).
27. Brown, "Sorcery, Demons, and the Rise of Christianity," 20; and see Dickie, *Magic and Magicians*, 270–71, who writes: "The circumstances of Priscillian's trial are so extraordinary that it would be unwise to draw any general conclusions from it." Another cleric tried for sorcery by a civil court and burned at the stake was an early seventh-century priest from Constantia, Cyprus; ibid., 271–72.

siblings Valentinian I (364–375) and Valens (364–378).[28] According to Ammianus Marcellinus, a notorious series of trials in 371 originated with charges against two diviners, Hilarius and Patricius, who appear to have been hired to divine the name of Valens' successor. As the story goes, a disturbance foiled the conjuration, and subsequently the pair was convicted, tortured, and executed. But instead of ending imperial suspicions, their deaths precipitated a witch-hunt that resulted in the arrest, torture, and execution of hundreds.[29]

Unlike politically motivated emperors, many other prominent Christians did not approve of harsh, especially fatal, measures against suspected magicians.[30] Bishop Martin of Tours, for example, famously condemned those who condoned Priscillian's execution, and Sulpicius Severus echoed his sentiments.[31] Martin and Sulpicius's criticism of capital punishment in this politically charged case arose in part from their general opposition to any secular tribunal handling ecclesiastical affairs. Another reason Christians advocated extending a general leniency toward suspected enchanters would have been a pious desire to afford suspects the opportunity to receive exorcisms and repent, or convert. A more self-interested reason to oppose harsh measures was because Christians could not escape their own obvious associations with *magia*. After all, when Martin of Tours attempted to protect crops from hailstorms, as

---

28. Constantius II: *CTh* 9.16.4 (357), metes out capital punishment for consulting a soothsayer, astrologer or diviner; *CTh* 9.16.5 (357), fatal curse upon conjurers of spirits; *CTh* 9.16.6 (357/58), denies exemption from torture and punishment for any member of the imperial retinue caught acting as a mage, sorcerer, soothsayer, diviner, augur, astrologer, or dream interpreter. Valentinian I and Valens: *CTh* 9.16.7 (364), forbids suspect prayers, rituals, and sacrifices at night; *CTh* 9.16.8 (370 or 373), forbids astrology; *CTh* 9.16.9 (371), only form of divination that is of a harmful intent; *CTh* 9.16.10 (371), concerning jurisdictions of sorcery trials for persons of senatorial status.

29. Amm. Marc., *Res gestae*, 29.1.1–44; and see Barb, "Survival of Magic Arts," 111–14. Ammianus complained that under Constantius, people might be put to death for the most benign of reasons, including consulting a soothsayer to interpret a mouse squeaking or a weasel passing by or wearing innocuous amulets, and one could be accused of necromancy simply for walking past a graveyard; Amm. Marc., *Res gestae*, 16.8.2, 19.12.14. Matthew Dickie, *Magic and Magicians*, 253–55, explains that Ammianus likely was attempting to characterize Constantius and Valens' reigns as imbued with an atmosphere of terror, and so it is unclear whether people actually were being killed for trivial magical behavior. Dickie, ibid., 355–57, interprets the legal evidence to show that in contrast to Ammianus's assertions, the Constantinian and Valentinian rulers in fact were concerned only to repress those kinds of magic that potentially could threaten social stability and the regime.

30. Ammianus and Libanius were struck by Christians' leniency toward suspected sorcerers; Flint, "Demonisation of Magic and Sorcery," 322–23.

31. Sulp. Sev., *Chron.* 2.50–51.

Sulpicius Severus claimed he did, he cannot have been acting much differently than a traditional weather changer (*tempestarius*).[32] One prominent fifth-century Christian with a learned interest in the occult not unlike the theurgists who consulted the *Chaldaean Oracles* was Bishop Sophronius of Constantia, who put a sub-deacon and two deaconesses to work making copies of astrological tomes.[33] Sophronius otherwise presided over several rituals to inquire of conjured spirits about his son's whereabouts. To that end, the bishop assisted by a deacon conducted a ceremony in which the prelate incanted magic words into the ear of a naked boy, a servant's son, who in turn was to act as a medium and read the contents of a bowl containing water and oil placed on a specially prepared table. After this, the boy was called upon to peer into a hole filled with water and oil behind a door, in which he witnessed the bishop's son riding a mule on a return journey from Constantinople. This viewing was confirmed in yet another ritual by which the boy gazed into a properly arranged egg yoke. For his troubles, the boy medium suffered hallucinatory trauma, which ended only after undergoing purificatory rituals at churches for eight months.[34]

Some ecclesiastics tried to rid their ranks of what many would have acknowledged as inappropriate magic through depositions at councils and canon legislation.[35] For example, Sophronius's behavior came to light through the proceedings of the Council of Ephesus (449), where the bishop was accused of heresy, sorcery, and astrology.[36] Bishops attending the Council of Laodicea (375) forbade clerics of all orders

---

32. Sulp. Sev., *Dialogi* 3.7.
33. Dickie, *Magic and Magicians*, 278.
34. Luck, "Witches and Sorcerers," 155–56; Dickie, *Magic and Magicians*, 277–79.
35. Dickie, *Magic and Magicians*, 257–72.
36. Luck, "Witches and Sorcerers," 155; Dickie, *Magic and Magicians*, 267, 269–70. The evidence mounted against Sophronius also details how he tried to identify a thief at first by conducting a traditional exercise by which suspects had to choke down cheese and bread. After this ordeal failed to provide an answer, the bishop finally identified the thief through the ritual of peering into a magically prepared bowl of water and oil; Luck, "Witches and Sorcerers," 155. Another Christian prelate accused of sorcery was a Bishop Paulinus, whom bishops attending the Council of Serdica (343) deposed. Paulinus had a cache of magical books, which were burned; Dickie, *Magic and Magicians*, 276–77. Two bishops whose sorcery charges at church councils were products of acute theological conflict, not because they studied the occult, were Athanasius of Alexandria, deposed at two Arian controlled synods, and the Nestorian Ibas of Edessa; ibid., 267–69, 275–76.

from being magicians, charmers, soothsayers, and astrologers, and they also condemned fabrication of amulets.[37] But in East and West, clerically manufactured amulets with accompanying invocations for Christ to deliver health and prosperity simply kept coming.[38] Indeed, some Christians, convinced that their religion already had triumphed over paganism, saw no harm in admitting to a likeness between holy wonderworkers and magicians. Thus Jerome did not hesitate to depict Saint Hilarion engaged in the quintessential magical deed, contributing to a chariot team's victory at a hippodrome![39] Because it would be impossible to fully disassociate Christianity from magical practices, Augustine proposed a subtle, tripartite characterization for wonder-workers: "… magicians perform wonders (*miracula*) one way, good Christians another, and evil Christians another. Magicians do this through private contracts, good Christians through public righteousness, and evil Christians through the symbols of public righteousness."[40] Here Augustine denied the three kinds of wonder-worker neither efficacy of their practices nor similarity among their procedures (e.g., making the sign of the cross, which both orthodox and heretical Christians would have done). It would take an acute mind such as his to be able to know the difference between angelically inspired *miracula* and demonic *magia*. Hence, for Augustine, the solution to distinguishing "religion" from "magic" was to be had less by relying on human sensibilities than through convincing ordinary people to accept the judgment of wise Christian betters such as himself.

37. Barb, "Survival of Magic Arts," 107; Dickie, *Magic and Magicians*, 280.
38. For several examples of Christian amulets, see David Frankfurter, "Amuletic Invocations of Christ for Health and Fortune," in *Religions of Late Antiquity in Practice*, ed. Richard Valantasis (Princeton, NJ, and Oxford: Princeton University Press, 2000), 340–43.
39. Jerome, *Vita Hilarionis* 20; with Flint, "Demonisation of Magic and Sorcery," 341. Whereas a pagan leader of a chariot faction at Gaza relied on a magician who used incantations to curse opponents' horses and make them fail, Saint Hilarion, responding to the petition of a Christian horse owner, Italicus, provided a humble drinking cup, the contents of which when sprinkled upon the horses empowered them for the victory. After the race, some disgruntled losers demanded that Hilarion be tried as a sorcerer, apparently to no avail, but others joined the winners by converting to Christianity.
40. Augustine, *De diversis quaestionibus octoginta tribus* 79 (*CCL* 44A, 229): "Quapropter aliter magi faciunt miracula, aliter boni christiani, aliter mali christiani: magi per privatos contractus, boni christiani per publicam iustitam, mali christiani per signa publicae iustitiae."

Magic in Barbarian Gaul

As Western imperial rule waned, magical practices persisted unabated.[41] Gallic authors inherited from classical and patristic writers a wide array of terms to describe wonder-workers, and their words hint to a continued diversity of magical practice. Included in their vocabulary were magicians (*magi*), enchanters (*incantatores, praecantatores*), sorcerers and witches (*malefici, striae, strigae*), lot casters (*sortilegi*), weather changers (*tempestarii*), astrologers (*astrologi, genethliaci, horoscopi, mathematici*), and soothsayers and diviners (*(h)arioli, (h)aruspices, divini, auspices, augures, caragii, pithonissae, salisitores*). Like their terminology for identifying enchanters, our Gallic authors' manner of, and justification for, condoning *miracula* and condemning *magia* arose in part out of emulation of earlier writers. First, they espoused an emerging pseudo-history linking magic, paganism, and demons. Latin historians and chronographers, for example, relied on Jerome's translation of Eusebius's chronicle to understand that past. For example, it was through Jerome that Gregory of Tours realized that the Devil had inspired Noah's grandson Chus, equated with Zoroaster, to invent both pagan idolatry and "every magic art" (*totius artis magicae*).[42] These accounts would have helped

---

41. John O. Ward, "Witchcraft and Sorcery in the Later Roman Empire and the Early Middle Ages: An Anthropological Comment," in *Witchcraft, Women and Society*, ed. Brian P. Levack (New York and London: Garland, 1992), 12–14, indicates that similarities in late Roman and post-Roman societies, both "fraught with social change and tension," contributed to continued magic in the latter period. Ward opposes the apparent contention of Peter Brown, "Sorcery, Demons and the Rise of Christianity," 27, that sorcery waned from the fourth to sixth centuries as late Roman society in the West "grew more stable and defined." I say apparent because Brown seems to have been suggesting a correlation between sorcery accusations and people engaging in magical practices. While politics certainly might have caused the number of witchcraft accusations to rise, I see no necessary correlation between political atmosphere and the practice of magic. Then, as now, so long as people become ill, the weather sours, and information needs to be known, there will be wonder-workers convincing themselves and others that they can overcome natural limitations and/or access divine aid to resolve these problems.

42. Greg. Tur., *Hist.* 1.5 (*MGH*, SRM 1.1, 7). A more detailed analysis of the origin of magic with which Gregory presumably was familiar was John Cassian, *Conferences* 8.21. Gregory's near contemporary, Isidore of Seville, attributed the invention of magic to Zoroaster and the spread of sorcery to the Assyrian monarch Ninus; Isidore of Seville, *Etymologiae* 8.9, 18.1, with Flint, "The Demonisation of Magic and Sorcery in Late Antiquity," 312. Peter Brown, "Sorcery, Demons, and the Rise of Christianity," 35, attributed the origins of a lasting association of witchcraft and diabolism to the sixth century, but that century's writers' indebtedness to earlier patristic authors necessitates this being dated to an earlier era.

ecclesiastics explain the widespread nature of what they perceived as wrongful magical phenomena happening in their own age. Second, Gallic ecclesiastics estimated their own magical behaviors and those of favored wonder workers to be heavenly inspired, while they deemed those of opponents to be demonic, just as Augustine had done. Thus Gregory recalled how as a child he had burned the heart and liver of a fish and applied the compound to his father Florentius's body to relieve him of gout.[43] Although this activity seems a patent incident of *magia*, Gregory thought the remedy to be "religious," for he learned of it in a legitimate text, the Book of Tobit. Furthermore, Gregory will have reasoned that his was an appropriate action because he was following the advice of a saint who had appeared in a dream and told him to consult the holy tome. A year earlier, that same saint had helped Gregory tend to his father's gout by telling him to write a (magical?) name on a wooden block and place it under the sufferer's pillow.[44] Conversely, Caesarius of Arles admonished ill people not to seek out those who would adorn them with phylacteries and letters (*caracteres*), because he considered all such remedies to be "diabolic" (*diabilica*) in nature.[45] What would Caesarius have thought about Gregory's remedies for his father's ailments?

While Gallic authors followed classical and patristic models to condemn "magic," neither their reliance on earlier texts nor subsequent early medieval reuses of our writers' compositions (e.g., Saint Ouen's copying sections of Caesarius's sermons to condemn "superstition") need cause one to conclude that depictions of magic use in Gallic sources constitute nothing more than literary convention.[46] Rather, Caesarius, Gregory,

---

43. Greg. Tur., *GC* 39.
44. Greg. Tur., *GC* 39.
45. Caes. Arel., *Serm.* 50.1 (*CCL* 103, 225).
46. On Caesarius borrowing patristic literature to condemn magic, and for early Medieval writers borrowing Caesarius, see Hen, *Culture and Religion in Merovingian Gaul*, 162–72. The strongest claim that repeated early Medieval prohibitions of magic merely constitute a continuance of literary themes and so offer no evidence for actual behavior is that of Dieter Harmening, *Superstitio. Überlieferungs- und theoriegeschichtliche Untersuchungen zur kirchlich-theologischen Aberglaubensliteratur des Mittelalters* (Berlin: Erich Schmidt, 1979), 49–73. Yitzhak Hen, *Culture and Religion in Merovingian Gaul*, 171–72, takes a novel approach in arguing that the condemnations represent a "mental reality," meaning that the proscribed "superstitious" practices were no longer being conducted by Gauls, but because the authors' territories were newly converted and adjacent to still pagan lands such as "Frisia, Thuringia, Bavaria and Alemania," worried clerics had reason to continue condemning the behaviors. I am hard

and other authors who condemned particular magical practices were commenting in a prejudiced manner on actual behaviors that the Gauls inherited from the late Roman period. Our literary sources, and even material evidence, indicate the kind of activities wonder-workers maintained, and those that were abandoned. One victim of the times was magic associated with games and races, which would have disappeared with patronage of these popular productions. Archaeology indicates that all Gallic arenas and most hippodromes were defunct well before the establishment of the Barbarian kingdoms. The last operable horse track in Gaul was at Arles, and it ceased functioning in the mid-sixth century.[47] Presumably the once common burial of tablets designed to curse charioteers and other athletes vanished with these sports venues. A magical practice that did persist was averting inclement weather, an activity condemned in Gallic preaching. Attesting to this activity in the early medieval West is a talisman composed of two slate tablets buried in a field of late eighth- or early ninth-century Spain by a *servus Dei* named Auriolus. This *tempestarius* intended to prevent an onslaught of hail by appealing to archangels to hold back the clouds and adjuring Satan not to damage the region's crops.[48] Two magical practices that likely met with less clerical disdain were incubation and exorcism. In the Barbarian era, both of these practices typically happened at churches, where

pressed to imagine Caesarius preaching against practices that he was not convinced certain members of his own congregation were not engaged in. Caesarius was responding to people in his community who were acting like Gregory! A sound interpretation of the reoccurrence of prohibitions of magic is that of Rob Meens, "Magic and the Early Medieval World View," in *The Community, the Family and the Saint*, ed. J. Hilland and M. Swan (Turnhout: Brepols, 1998), 286, who concludes that repeated descriptions of so-called "superstitious" practices "sometimes reveals interesting aspects of actual behaviour."

47. On the demise of chariot racing in Gaul, see Hen, *Religion and Culture in Merovingian Gaul*, 219–26. This decline typified a wider late antique trend of disappearance of arena spectacles and horse racing throughout the Roman provinces; ibid., 217. An exception was Ostrogothic Italy, where chariot racing remained popular and hippodromes operative; Cassiodorus, *Variae* 1.20, 3.51; Hen, *Religion and Culture in Merovingian Gaul*, 220. Gregory of Tours disapprovingly related that King Chilperic was intent upon building arenas to hold spectacles at Soissons and Paris, but these measures likely failed; Greg. Tur., *Hist.*, 5.17; Hen, *Religion and Culture in Merovingian Gaul*, 225–26. One group from the ancient magic-using entertainment *demi-monde* that survived through the Barbarian era and perhaps kept practicing magic was actors. Although theaters disappeared from Gaul in the fifth century, traveling mimes and pantomimes continued to attract crowds and disconcert ecclesiastics through the Merovingian age; ibid., 226–31.

48. Smith, *Europe after Rome*, 77.

clerics so monopolized them that Gallic litterateurs scarcely would have thought to question whether the activating power was holy or demonic.[49] Three common magical practices that frequently occurred away from churches, and therefore fostered suspicion from ecclesiastical litterateurs, were potion manufacture, divination, and healing. About the latter two exercises, performers of one kind of magic frequently engaged in the other, as earlier had been the case. For example, Gregory related that one soothsayer's remedy for a fever involved not only applying ligatures but also casting lots.[50] I contend that there is no more reason to doubt that actual behaviors lie behind Gregory's portrayals of contemporary enchanters such as this than there is to deny that he actually administered draughts of dust from Saint Martin's tomb mixed with water to sufferers of various ailments. About wonder-workers, while the composers of *Vitae* would have imagined that they could readily discern saints from sorcerers, in actuality it would not have been a simple matter or even a concern for most inhabitants of Gaul to make such a drastic distinction. Nevertheless, many undoubtedly conducted magical arts, and so it remains to consider what difficulties such persons faced.

As happened throughout Late Antiquity, so in Barbarian Gaul, wonder-workers of high social rank, even when associated with the culturally dominant religion, sometimes were accused of witchcraft. Hagiography readily attests that healing was an important component of the repertoire of Gauls who came to be regarded as saints, even socially prominent ones. As has been considered, Caesarius of Arles was a politically astute and busy bishop, and yet evidence from his sermons corroborates depictions from his *Vita* to show how the bishop found time to try to cure ill people.[51] Caesarius argued that he and his clerics alone among the members of his diocese possessed the authority to appeal to Christ for the power to heal. Thus, while literary convention undoubtedly obligated his hagiographers to include episodes of the bishop healing in order to "prove" Caesarius's sainthood, nevertheless,

49. Incubation: Hen, *Religion and Culture in Merovingian Gaul*, 112–13; exorcism: e. g., Greg. Tur., *VJ* 30; *VM* 2.18, 28, 37, 4.24.
50. Greg. Tur., *VJ* 46a.
51. See the discussion between pp. 276 and 278.

the portrayals confirm how the aristocratic wonder-worker did attempt this magical behavior, which at least loosely resembled the ministrations of those sometimes deemed *malefici*. Indeed, one Gallic aristocrat who proved incapable of eluding the label of "witch" was Geneviève of Paris.[52] In childhood, Geneviève had been consecrated as a virgin by none other than Bishop Germanus of Auxerre.[53] Early on, she took to wonder-working, but from the start her magical efforts bore a sinister quality. The first miracle recorded in Geneviève's *Life* explains how her mother refused to allow the pious child to attend a saint's festival, and when she went so far as to strike the daughter, the woman became blind.[54] Geneviève was cognizant that her own power had harmed her mother, but it would be nearly two years before she realized a solution; in the end, the youth blessed a cup of water and gave it to the mother, who recovered her sight. As she aged, Geneviève mastered her *virtus* while she expanded her magical repertoire. Her craft included cursing people, healing (sometimes those whom she had cursed), changing the weather, reading people's thoughts and divining secrets, opening doors and gates, lighting candles, and prognosticating.[55] In 451, Geneviève famously prophesied that Paris would survive Attila's invasion of Gaul.[56] Because of her high social stature, Geneviève was able to back her prediction by preventing the frightened Parisians from relocating their movables and their persons to other towns. Amid the anxiety of the approaching horde, some citizens accused Geneviève of being a false prophet, and they even prepared to execute her by stoning or drowning. Geneviève was rescued, however, when a clerical ally from Auxerre arrived to defend her reputation and actions.[57] The Huns did not attack Paris. Writing seventy years after the Hunnic onslaught and eighteen years after Geneviève's death in 502, an anonymous hagiographer

---

52. Cf. Mathisen, *People, Personal Expressions, and Social Relations*, 1: 211–12, 228–31, 2: 169, 184.
53. *Vita Genovefae* 2–6.
54. *Vita Genovefae* 7.
55. More possible curses followed by healings: *Vita Genovefae* 24, 34, 43–44; averting storms: 50–51; reading minds and divining secrets: 8, 17–19, 31, 48; opening gates and doors: 26, 28; lighting candles: 22, 23; prognostication: 12–14.
56. *Vita Genovefae* 12.
57. *Vita Genovefae* 12–13. See also *Vita Genovefae* 11 for earlier criticisms of the Parisian wonder-worker.

interpreted Geneviève's prognostication as a miracle.[58] But even in 520, the biographer had to admit to lingering suspicions about Geneviève's behaviors: "And to many in this world she clearly revealed their secret thoughts, which, on account of disdainful people, it is better to pass by in silence rather than to point out to the envious, who have a penchant for slander. For when they resent good people, they reveal their own superstitious mentality."[59] Judging by this admission that the influential woman had her detractors, Geneviève's wondrous activity must have been thought to be magic by some and miracle by others. In the realm of opinion she was both a saint and a witch, but a reputation for holiness eventually won out. A positive image was facilitated by her being an aristocrat and by the fact that she enjoyed a string of socially influential friends and supporters. These included not only the ecclesiastics of Auxerre, who provided aid during her early and middling years, but also Clovis and Clotild, who likely were acquainted with the aged matron, and who certainly contributed to Geneviève's sanctification by burying her in their funerary basilica dedicated to the Holy Apostles, where they themselves would be interred *ad sanctae*.[60]

Geneviève's brush with a charge of witchcraft is unique among stories about Gallic aristocratic saints.[61] Her problematic activity may be compared with another dedicated thaumaturge whom we have encountered, Monegund of Chartres. Recalling that Monegund abandoned her husband and established a women's ascetic community at Tours, the woman impressed the ecclesiastical establishment with an enthusiasm to promote the supernatural beneficence of Saint Martin. For example, when clerics brought forth a blind woman, Monegund questioned: "What is it between you and me, men of God? Does not Saint Martin live here, who each day shines with the work of his miracles? Go

---

58. *Vita Genovefae* 14.
59. *Vita Genovefae* 10 (Mathisen, ed. and trans., *People, Personal Expressions, and Social Relations*, 1: 229, 2: 184): "Pluribus namque in hoc saeculo viventibus secreta conscientia manifestissime declarabat, quod propter adrogantes silere satius quam emulantibus innotescere, qui ingentem devotionem habent conscientiam …"
60. Effros, *Merovingian Mortuary Archaeology*, 214.
61. Two eastern saints of the late sixth/early seventh centuries whose miracles some interpreted as sorcery are Symeon Stylites the Younger and his mother, Martha; Dickie, *Magic and Magicians*, 274–85.

to him and pray that he may deign to visit you. For I am only a sinner; what can I do?"[62] Martin had been given his due, but the blind woman persisted, and so finally Monegund acquiesced; laying hands on eyes, she caused the woman's cataracts to disappear. The blind woman felt assured that the source of Monegund's "grace of healing" (*gratia curationum*) was God given.[63] Unlike the outrageous Geneviève, Monegund humbly limited her ministrations to healings, and she attested that the source of all *virtutes* displayed at Tours was the invisible patron, Martin. The Tourangeaux clergy undoubtedly appreciated how the living healer proved an attraction for pilgrims to Saint Martin's church. Because Monegund's wonders were fully assimilated into the agenda of the clerical establishment, they might even be used to discredit or counter the abilities of local enchanters not affiliated with the cult. For example, Gregory explained that a boy once consumed "poison in a potion" (*maleficium in potione*), presumably a concoction of a local folk healer, and afterward developed snakes in his belly. The youth then came to Tours, where the "blessed woman" (*beatam feminam*) plied her craft: "She touched the boy's stomach, rubbed it softly with her palm and sensed where the malice of the poisonous serpents concealed itself. Then she smeared saliva on a leaf picked from a green vine and after making the sign of the blessed cross over it, placed [the leaf] on his belly."[64] Next the youth took a nap, vomited out the poison, and received a cure. Monegund's magical behavior in this instance was somewhat scripturally based (e.g., John 9, 6). Her success would have supported local clerics' arguments that the *virtus* available at Saint Martin's basilica was far superior to the imperfect and even deadly dealings of non-church-affiliated enchanters.

---

62. Greg. Tur., *VP* 19.3 (*MGH*, SRM 1.2, 289): "Quid vobis et mihi, homines Dei? Nonne sanctus Martinus hic habitat, qui cotidie inlustrium virtutum opere refulget? Illuc accedite, ibi obsecramini, ut ipse vos visitare dignetur. Nam ego peccatrix quid faciam?' Trans. by James, *Gregory of Tours, Life of the Fathers*, 123.

63. Greg. Tur., *VP* 19.3 (*MGH*, SRM 1.2, 289).

64. Greg. Tur., *VP* 19.3 (*MGH*, SRM 1.2, 289): "... ventrem pueri palpat et palma demulcet; sensitque, ibi anguium venenatorum nequitiam latitare. Tunc accepto pampini viridis folio, saliva linivit, fixitque super eum crucis beatae signaculum. Quod ponens super alvum iuvenuli ..." Flint, *Rise of Magic in Early Medieval Europe*, 302, n. 132, interprets this boy to have been a victim of sorcery, which the saint overcame. The drink probably was poison, but perhaps it was a curative potion that went wrong, and so the boy sought Monegund to remedy the enchanter's error.

After Monegund's death, the clergy at Tours were not about to allow the healer's reputation to diminish. To that end, Gregory proclaimed the continued availability of the deceased saint's *virtus* in *Life of the Fathers* and in his book exalting Gaul's many confessors.[65]

Church affiliation did not automatically exempt Gallic clerics from implications of witchcraft by other ecclesiastics. For example, Caesarius of Arles discouraged people from consulting clerical enchanters in his sermons:

> What is deplorable is that there are some who seek soothsayers in every kind of infirmity. …Often enough they receive charms even from priests and religious… See, brethren, how I plead with you not to consent to accept these wicked objects, even if they are offered by clerics. …Even if you are told that the phylacteries contain holy facts and divine lessons, let no one believe it or expect health to come to him from them.[66]

Here Caesarius's plea attests that clerics engaged in magical curative practices using procedures not unlike those of non-clerical folk healers. Churchmen also were implicated in performing harmful *magia*. Thus, when Bishop Droctigisel of Soissons went insane, "many citizens" (*multi civium*) suspected that an archdeacon whom the prelate had dismissed earlier had performed *maleficium* on the prelate.[67] Likewise, when the bishop-elect Silvester died at Lyons, his son accused the deacon Peter, Gregory's brother, of killing the man through *maleficia*.[68] One reason Gallic clerics could not shake an association with *magia* was that church leaders could not arrive at a consensus regarding what magical practices were offensive and what were not. For example, while churchmen almost unanimously acknowledged the legitimacy of exorcisms

---

65. Greg. Tur., *GC* 24.
66. Caes. Arel., *Serm.* 50 (*CCL* 103, 225): "… sed, quod dolendum est, sunt aliqui, qui in qualibet infirmitate sortilegos quaerunt… Et aliquotiens ligaturas ipsas a clericis ac religiosis accipiunt… Videte, fratres, quia contestor vos, ut ista mala, etiam si a clericis offerantur, non adquiescatis accipere… Etiam si vobis dicatur, quod res sanctas et lectiones divinas filacteria ipsa contineant, nemo credat, nemo de illis sanitatem sibi venturam esse confidat …" Trans. by Mueller, *Saint Caesarius of Arles: Sermons*, 1: 254.
67. Greg. Tur., *Hist.* 9.37 (*MGH*, SRM 1.1, 457).
68. Greg. Tur., *Hist.* 5.5 (*MGH*, SRM 1.1, 201).

and incubation, they strongly disagreed about the acceptability of Christianized divinatory practices. Prelates at the Council of Agde (506), over which Caesarius presided, deemed the "numerous clerics and laymen" (*aliquanti clerici sive laici*) who were making ready use of a divinatory tome (apparently of Gallic provenance) called the *Sortes Sanctorum* to be acting "under the name of false religion" (*sub nomine fictae religionis*).[69] The council prescribed excommunication for offenders, and it also meted out the same penalty for any cleric or layperson who opened pages of scripture to assess the future.[70] Despite such objections, other clerics and even bishops simply would have refused to desist in divinatory efforts, for the practices could be quite useful in settling difficult dilemmas, both personal and otherwise. For example, Gregory recorded that around 558, priests at Langres performed the *sortes biblicae* to decide whether or not to permit King Chlothar's rebellious son Chramn to enter Dijon.[71] On a more personal level, when the hermit Patroclus was at a loss about whether to remain in his village or relocate to a remoter place, he turned to lot divination. After placing small notes on an altar, he prayed for three nights and then consulted the cards. The *sortes* dictated that Patroclus abandon his oratory in the overly congested hamlet of Néris and enter the "high solitudes of the forests" (*altas silvarum solitudines*).[72]

If ecclesiastics were unlikely to accuse socially prominent persons of witchcraft, and were ambivalent about fellow clerics immersed in magical behaviors, there was one category of wonder-workers that many could agree to associate with *maleficium*, *incantatores* of low social rank. For example, one impertinent enchanter who passed through Tours and into Gregory's *Historiae* was a fugitive slave.[73] Likewise, a folk healer "who was calling himself a great man" (*qui se magnum quendam esse*

---

69. Council of Agde (506), c. 42 (*CCL* 148, 210–11); and see William E. Klingshirn, "Defining the *Sortes Sanctorum*: Gibbon, Du Cange, and Early Christian Lot Divination," *Journal of Early Christian Studies* 10 (2002), 77–130, especially at 86–87.

70. Council of Agde (506), c. 42. See also Council of Orléans (511), c. 30.

71. Greg. Tur., *Hist.* 4.16. In a much later public episode, clerical representatives from three towns in 678 relied on the *sortes* to peacefully determine which city should receive the remains of Saint Leodegar of Autun; *Passio Leudegarii* 2.24 (*MGH*, SRM 5, 346–48).

72. Greg. Tur., *VP* 9.2 (*MGH*, SRM 1.2, 253–54).

73. Greg. Tur., *Hist.* 9.6.

dicebat) turned out to be a lowborn fraud.[74] Similarly, a canon of the
Council of Narbonne (589) prohibiting *maleficium* tellingly insisted
that penalties should apply whether the offenders were "freed or slaves
or maidservants" (*liberi seu servi vel ancillae sint*).[75] The word *ancilla*
recalls the successful diviner of this chapter's introductory anecdote,
who began her career while still a slave. Gallic sources frequently singled
out women of low status as potential *maleficae*. For example, Gregory
related that Queen Fredegund in 580 responded to a charge that a maidservant had magically murdered her sons Chlodobert and Dagobert by
torturing the slave until she confessed.[76] Likewise, a rumor circulated
in 584 that Chilperic and Fredegund's infant son Theuderic had been
killed in Paris through witchcraft, and so the queen rounded up and
tortured Parisian women with a predictable result: "They confessed that
they were witches and testified that they had caused many to succumb
to death."[77] Similarly, in a rather late example, a hagiographer for Saint
Eligius of Noyon (d. 660) suggested that female textile workers commonly practiced magic.[78] Another group of servile females associated
with witchcraft were women of the Merovingian courts. First and foremost was the slave turned queen, Fredegund herself, whom Gregory
alleged used magical potions to murder her enemies. For example, when
in 586 a nobleman from Rouen threatened the queen with a full inquiry
into the death of Bishop Praetextatus, she in turn invited the accuser for
a drink, a favorite Frankish potable of absinthe mixed with wine and
honey, which was poisoned. The Frank realized the queen's deceit too

---

74. Greg. Tur., *Hist.* 9.6 (*MGH*, SRM 1.1, 417). In Spain, Maximus of Turin (d. ca. 470) in a sermon identified a local sorcerer as "a drunken peasant" (*saucium vino rusticum*); Maximus of Turin, *Serm.* 107.2
(*CCL* 23, 420).

75. Council of Narbonne (589), c. 14 (*CCL* 148A, 257).

76. Greg. Tur., *Hist.* 5.39. This maidservant's daughter was in love with Fredegund's stepson Clovis, so
Fredegund would have perceived the pair as potential rivals for controlling Neustria. The prince had
discredited the queen, so she had him assassinated. Fredegund then humiliated the girl by having her
hair removed and tying her to a stake posted outside Clovis's residence. Finally the queen had the
informant bound to a stake and burned alive.

77. Greg. Tur., *Hist.*, 6.35 (*MGH*, SRM 1.1, 305): "At illae confitentur se maleficas esse, et multos occum-
bere leto se fecisse testatae sunt ..."

78. *Vita Eligii* 2.16a (*MGH*, SRM 4, 706–07). On the convention to associate weavers and binders with
witchcraft, see Flint, *Rise of Magic in Early Medieval Europe*, 226–31.

late, and while fleeing on horseback he died.[79] Gregory did not indicate
here whether Fredegund concocted the poison herself or called upon
a professional *incantator*, but he certainly thought the queen a regular
user of magic to rid herself of opponents. Elsewhere in the *Historiae*,
Gregory depicted an envoy of King Childebert II's calling the queen
Fredegundem maleficam, per quam multi reges interfecti sunt.[80] Another
alleged witch of servile status at court was Septimima, the nurse for King
Childebert II and Queen Faileuba's children. In 589, she joined a band
of conspirators who threatened that Childebert must banish his wife
and mother or else he would die by *maleficiis*.[81] When the coup failed
and the conspirators were captured, Septimima confessed under torture that she earlier had used witchcraft to murder her own husband.[82]
Finally, the chronicler Fredegar characterized Queen Marcatrude, second wife of King Guntram, as a "whore" (*meretrix*) and a "herbalist"
(*herbaria*).[83] In fact, Marcatrude, unlike Guntram's first and third wives,
does not appear to have been of servile origin. Her father was known
to have possessed slaves, the future queen Austrechild among them,
and her brothers held considerable possessions.[84] Nevertheless, Gregory
similarly wrote that Marcatrude murdered her stepson, Gundobad, by
slipping him a poisonous drink.[85]

Episodes of high-profile poisonings at court likely fueled misogynist
clerics' imaginations about *iniquae mulieres* persisting in *maleficia*. These
and other anecdotes linking women and witchcraft, however, should not
be taken to suggest that Gallic women practiced magic more than did
men. But one may conclude tentatively according to the evidence, especially Gregory's corpus, that by the sixth century it was not uncommon
for women to be made scapegoats for witchcraft scares, although such

79. Greg. Tur., *Hist.* 8.31.
80. Greg. Tur., *Hist.* 7.14 (*MGH*, SRM 1.1, 335).
81. Greg. Tur., *Hist.* 9.38 (*MGH*, SRM 1.1, 458).
82. Greg. Tur., *Hist.* 9.38.
83. Fredegar, *Chron.* 3.56 (*MGH*, SRM 2, 108). On the long-lasting involvement of ancient prostitutes
    in magic, from Classical Athens through Late Antiquity, see Dickie, *Magic and Magicians*, 81–87,
    99–106, 178–91, 247–49, 302–03.
84. Father: Greg. Tur., *Hist.* 5.20; brothers: Greg. Tur., *Hist.* 5.17.
85. Greg. Tur., *Hist.* 4.25.

episodes were far more local and less lasting than what would arise in the late Medieval period.[86] Furthermore, it needs be acknowledged that some individuals actually did willingly practice what they well knew was harmful magic. For secular and ecclesiastical magnates who wanted to establish or preserve a law-and-order Christian society atop which they stood, *maleficium* was taken to be a real and proximate threat. This does not mean that most Gallic *incantatores* were socially powerful, much less that they were stalwart pagan holdouts. But because some enchanters claimed the ability to heal, other medical practitioners rivaled them. And because some professed an ability to harm, secular authorities regarded them warily.

ENCHANTERS AND SECULAR AUTHORITIES

Some *incantatores* devoted a degree of their energies to causing damage; some offered curses, while others concocted harmful potions. Gauls were on their guard against persons who magically afflicted bodily harm. For example, Gregory wrote that when a peasant boy approached a passing retinue of monks and suddenly fell to the ground as if dead, the parents, having witnessed what transpired, immediately assumed that their son had been killed by "the exercise of the men's craft [in sorcery]" (*artem suam exercere*).[87] Fear such as this was justifiable in that people did in fact concoct potions to take and prevent life. Not only did some brew poisons for use in assassination efforts; on a more mundane level, enchanters manufactured philters whereby customers might dispose of newborns and induce abortions. Caesarius of Arles condemned as diabolical what likely was common recourse to draughts intended for these purposes.[88] Gallic inhabitants also believed that enchanters,

86. John O. Ward, "Women, Witchcraft and Social Patterning in the Later Roman Lawcodes," *Prudentia* 13 (1981): 99–118, dates the origin of Europeans' making stereotypical correlations between women and magic to the late Roman era. Matthew Dickie, *Magic and Magicians*, 79, interpreting Athenian theater, claims the assumption was already a commonplace in the Classical age. Dickie, ibid., 175, further contends that women likely actually practiced magic more than men.

87. Greg. Tur., *VJ* 45 (*MGH*, SRM 1.2, 132). Gregory explained that in fact the boy had been possessed by a demon, and so it was the presence of Saint Julian through relics carried by a monk that caused the collapse. When the monk placed the reliquary on the youth's head, he expelled the demon in a gush of bloody vomit.

88. Caes. Arel., *Serm.* 52.4.

besides administering potions, caused injury through harmful chants. As was mentioned, Fredegund in 584 became convinced that her infant son had been slain by *maleficia et incantationes*.[89] These fears, too, are understandable, since even prominent wonder-workers unabashedly revealed an ability to harm others with words. For example, when a slave-master refused to take the advice of the "witch-like" Geneviève of Paris and forgive his servant, she threatened that Christ would not aid one who ignored her supplications. Whatever Geneviève prayed for to convince the avenging Angel of the Lord to visit this impertinent person, the hagiographer does not reveal, but after the slave-owner left her presence, he reportedly became feverish, restless, and worse: "With his mouth open like some beast of burden ... spewing saliva, he fell before Geneviève's feet and pleaded that she give him the forgiveness which the day previous he would not extend to the servant."[90] Given, then, that some in Gallic society had no qualms about cursing others and producing fatal ointments, it is no wonder that secular authorities directed their attention to enchanters.

Unlike much of the legislation produced by late Roman emperors, who heaped sweeping condemnations upon all manner of magic user, prohibitions of sorcery contained in Barbarian constitutions are meager in number and directed only against magic that caused bodily harm. For example, Salic law specifically addressed the very kinds of magic employed with harmful intent, cursing, and poison: "He who casts a magic spell over another man or gives him an herbal potion to drink so that he dies, and it is proved against him, shall be liable to pay eight thousand *denarii* (i.e., two hundred *solidi*)."[91] One Salic constitution pertains to sorcery in relation to women and childbirth: "If any woman casts a spell over another woman so that she cannot have children, she shall be liable to pay twenty-five hundred *denarii* (i.e., sixty-two and

---

89. Greg. Tur., *Hist.* 6.35 (*MGH*, SRM 1.1, 205).
90. *Vita Genovefae* 43 (*MGH*, SRM 3, 233): "... aperto ore secut urus ... salivam distillans, ad pedes Genovefae provolutus, veniam quam pridie famulo non dederat, sibi dare precabatur."
91. *PLS* 19.1 (*MGH*, LL sectio 1, 4.1, 81): "Si quis alteri <maleficiis fecerit aut> herbas dederit bibere, ut moriatur, <et ei fuerit adprobatum>, mallobergo touuer(f)o sunt, denarios VIIIM qui facuint solidos CC culpabilis iudicatur <aut certe ignem tradatur>." Trans. by Drew, *Laws of the Salian Franks*, 83. For cases when the victim survived the spell or potion: *PLS* 19.2.

one-half *solidi*)."⁹² It is interesting here that the lawmakers imagined women would be the likely manufacturers of these brews. Likewise, another constitution that singles out female enchanters reads: "If a witch eats a man and it is proved against her, she shall be liable to pay eight thousand *denarii* (i.e., two hundred *solidi*)."⁹³ As odd as these laws on sorcery may seem at face value, their intention and worth arose not so much from an attempt to eradicate unseemly activities as to prevent escalations of social strife. For example, preserving the peace explains at least in part the following law: "He who calls a free woman a witch and is not able to prove it shall be liable to pay three times twenty-five hundred *denarii* (i.e., one-hundred eighty-seven and one-half *solidi*)."⁹⁴ A version of this constitution from one manuscript of Salic law affords the same composition for a free woman slandered as being a whore (*meretrix*).⁹⁵ This suggests that lawmakers were more concerned to discourage violent retribution than to prevent magic or prostitution.

Gregory of Tours described an incident that illustrates the very possibility of violence's expanding because of suspicions of witchcraft. After the death of Fredegund's son in 584, a woman appeared before the queen, charging the patrician Mummolus with *maleficium*.⁹⁶ Gregory explained that Mummolus's difficulties began innocently enough; when a fellow courtier was lamenting that a child had died of dysentery, the patrician commented that he kept a certain herb that if added to a potion would cure such a sufferer. Upon learning this tidbit about Mummolus, the queen rounded up the Parisian women and tortured them until they confessed to murdering the young prince. But their confession also implicated the patrician. Gregory wrote, "They added

---

92. *PLS* 19.4 (*MGH*, LL sectio 1, 4.1, 82): "Si quis mulier altera mulieri maleficium fecerit, unde infantes non potuerit habere, <MMX denarios qui facuint> solidos LXII semis culpabilis iudicetur." The same composition is due from anyone convicted of cursing another; *PLS* 19.3.

93. *PLS* 64.3 (*MGH*, LL sectio 1, 4.1, 231): "Si stria hominem commederit et ei fuerit adprobatum, mallobergo granderba, sunt denarii VIIIM qui faciunt solidos CC culpabilis iudicetur." Trans. based on Drew, *Laws of the Salian Franks*, 125.

94. *PLS* 64.2 (*MGH*, LL sectio 1, 4.1, 231): "Si quis <vero> mulierem <ingenuam> stri(g)am clamaverit et non potuerit adprobare, <MMD> denarios qui faciunt <in triplum> solidos (C)LXXXVII et semis culpabilis iudicetur." Trans. by Drew, *Laws of the Salian Franks*, 125. A man wrongly called a sorcerer was due a payment of only a third that price; *PLS* 64.1 (*MGH*, LL sectio 1, 4.1, 230).

95. See *MGH*, LL sectio 1, 4.1, 231. A free woman slandered as a *meretrix* was due 1,800 *denarii*; *PLS* 30.3.

96. Greg. Tur., *Hist.* 6.35 (*MGH*, SRM 1.1, 305).

what must be believed is without reason: 'Your son, oh queen, we have sacrificed, for the life of the prefect Mummolus.'[97] King Chilperic next ordered Mummolus to be arrested and tortured, but the latter succeeded in exonerating himself in the youth's demise. Mummolus did admit, however, that he employed enchanters to provide him with unguents and potions (*unctionis et potionis*), which enabled him to appear well disposed before the eyes of the royal couple.[98] Although the patrician survived the torture, he died on the return journey to his native Bordeaux. This anecdote reveals how a simple mention of magic carried the potential to mushroom into wholesale slaughter, especially if it happened at a time of duress, as during the plague of 584.[99]

But were the Parisian *incantatores* making helpful or harmful magic? It seems Fredegund assumed that one who could make a cure for dysentery should be suspected of making poisons, too. And what of the unguent that made Mummolus charming? Because this bewitching kind of magic, akin to a love potion, would have caused another to act regardless of or contrary to his own will, it could be perceived as sinister. In a Christian context, another reason Gauls should have been suspicious of charming magic and love potions was that they might prove inimical to a person trying to preserve his chastity.[100] At any rate, it was a desire to prevent volatility of the sort that happened at Paris that caused makers of Salic law to legislate against witchcraft. In a similar vein, other mentions of sorcery in Barbarian law were designed to afford protection for women. Two Burgundian constitutions dictated that a man could divorce his wife only if he could prove that she had committed adultery or murder, performed witchcraft, or violated a gravesite.[101] These

---

97. Greg. Tur., *Hist.* 6.35 (*MGH*, SRM 1.1, 306): "... addentes, illud, quod nulla ratione credi patior: 'Filium,' aiunt, 'tuum, o regina, pro Mummoli praefecti vita donavimus.'

98. Greg. Tur., *Hist.* 6.35 (*MGH*, SRM 1.1, 306).

99. During an earlier epidemic in 580, Chilperic and Fredegund lost two infant sons, Chlodobert and Dagobert. On that occasion, the royal couple blamed their loss on their own misdeeds, and so they gave alms to cathedrals, churches, and the poor; Greg. Tur., *Hist.* 5.34. Making an accusation of sorcery four years later would have enabled Fredegund to disassociate herself, consciously or otherwise, from any guilt for the death of the third child.

100. E.g., Caes. Arel., *Serm.* 1.12. For early Medieval condemnations of love magic, see Flint, *Rise of Magic in Early Medieval Europe*, 231–39.

101. *Liber constitutionum* 34.3 (*MGH*, LL sectio 1, 2.1, 68): "adulterium, maleficium vel sepulchrorum violatricem;" *Lex Romana Burgundionum* 21.3 (*MGH*, LL sectio 1, 2.1, 144): "homicidam ... aut sepulchrum violatorem, aut veneficium."

laws were not intended to punish witches *per se*; rather, they provided defenses for wives whose spouses might try to abandon them without proper cause.[102] In the final analysis, then, Gallic *incantatores* could become embroiled in criminal procedures, and if convicted they faced brutal penalties in the form of corporal and capital punishment. But fortunately for them, kings and counts were not stridently "out to get" enchanters. A greater problem for such wonder-workers would have been institutionally established healers opposed to random people dispensing magical medicines.

Folk Healers and Physicians

Judging by the available sources, healing was the principal skill included in most wonder-workers' repertoire. Isidore of Seville conjectured that all enchanters dabbled in magical medicine.[103] The numerous hagiographical anecdotes that portray *incantatores* tending to the sick must offer at least some semblance of their actual ministrations. They also attest to Gallic society's considerable recourse to remedies beyond those available at churches and physicians' offices. The medical procedures of enchanters involved traditional techniques, including application of salves and plasters, hanging protective amulets and ligaments about a patient's neck, and dispensing potions. Magical incantations were either spoken or inscribed on curative implements. For example, one *hariolus* summoned to cure a boy's fever "murmured [a chant], cast a fortune, [and] hung ligatures around [the patient's] neck. ..."[104] Likewise, when a youth suffered a spasm and lost his senses, his parents sought ligaments and potions "from lot-casters and magicians" (*a sortilegis et hariolis*).[105] Similarly, a *hariolus* tending an ill woman from the Touraine applied "ligaments of herbs" (*ligamina herbarum*) to her body and offered

---

102. A man who left a spouse who proved to be innocent of these crimes had to leave all possessions to her and their children; *Liber constitutionum* 34.4. According to Wemple, *Women in Frankish Society*, 42, men under Frankish law could more easily divorce their wives, and so no conditions were added for accusing sorcery in Salic law. The substantial composition for wrongly accusing a woman of being a witch might have posed a strong deterrent for husbands contemplating leveling this charge in efforts to abandon wives.

103. Flint, *Rise of Magic in Early Medieval Europe*, 53.

104. Greg. Tur., *VJ* 46a (*MGH*, SRM 1.2, 132): "Inmurmurat, sortes iactat, ligaturas collo suspendit ..."

105. Greg. Tur., VM 1.26 (*MGH*, SRM 1.2, 151).

"chanted words" (*incantationum verba*).[106] These scenes need not be dismissed as mere literary inventions, for they reflect behaviors deeply ingrained among ancient Mediterranean peoples. Despite the Barbarian era's lack of material evidence for curative formulae, which is prolific for the adjacent Late Roman and High Medieval periods, evidence from the principal narrative sources ought to be interpreted as indicating this continuity. Given that Gregory was a widely traveled person and dedicated to understanding and improving in his own way the lot of *humiliores*, and because his own servile associates frequented soothsayers, it is most probable that he was as familiar with the healing techniques of *incantatores* as he was with the operations of physicians. The promises of enchanters to dispense health likely were as prevalent in Gaul as were the hagiographers' repetitious criticisms of them.

However, before we focus on sorcerers and saints, let us briefly revisit the rivalry between folk healers and doctors, or more properly the lack thereof. First, these two kinds of healer likely attended the same patients, if rarely. For example, when a certain Ursio broke his arm, he reportedly resorted to *medici* and *incantatores*.[107] Likewise, when the *vir nobilis* Ruricius became ill, his men carried him to see doctors (*medici*) and then "sorcerers and enchanters" (*maleficos et praecantatores*).[108] For the most part, however, physicians and enchanters participated on separate medical planes. On the one hand, Gallic doctors generally were city dwellers, socially middling to prominent and occasionally wealthy, usually ranking as *ingenui* and sometimes moving in aristocratic circles. They were accustomed to treating rich and influential patients including kings and high ecclesiastics. On the other hand, most enchanters were of low status and typically cared for the social leftovers—servants and peasants.[109] Gregory characterized resorting to *incantatores* as a "peasant

106. Greg. Tur., *VM* 4.36 (*MGH*, SRM 4.36, 208).
107. *Passio Praeiecti* 38 (*MGH*, SRM 5, 247).
108. *Vita Iuniani* 6 (*MGH*, SRM 3, 378).
109. For enchanters' patients: slaves: Greg. Tur., *VJ* 46a; servants: Greg. Tur., *VM* 1.26; peasants: Greg. Tur., *VM* 4.36, *Hist.* 9.6. Valerie Flint, *Rise of Magic in Early Medieval Europe*, 61, characterizes folk healers as "strong and numerous." I agree that they were numerous and even popular, but few among them would have been socially prominent.

custom" (*mos rusticorum*).[110] Similarly, a Spanish contemporary, Martin of Braga, who devoted a tome to criticizing "superstitious" rural behaviors including seeking diviners and folk healers, tellingly entitled his work *De corrrectione rusticorum*.[111]

If ever the realms of doctors and enchanters did meet, it was easier for physicians to encroach upon the territory of the latter, rather than the opposite. Gallic physicians were recognized by their education, especially in Greek medicine, and by an ability to perform technical procedures such as bloodletting and surgery. While few enchanters if any could hope to match the erudition and expertise of established medical practitioners, physicians could and did incorporate "traditional" elements into their repertoire, apparently with some regularity. For example, incantation and the use of amulets were not uncommon elements of Mediterranean physician's care, and physicians in Gaul apparently prescribed traditional water remedies.[112] While Marcellus of Bordeaux advised wearing amulets for nearly every disease in his home medicine book, he tellingly remarked that only physicians should fashion them.[113] Therefore, in the rivalry between physicians and enchanters, however small that competition likely was, the *incantatores* were by far the more disadvantaged of the two. Fortunately for them, their patient pool of underprivileged folk was massive. Unfortunately, another kind of healer with even greater organizational backing had designs for that same socially downtrodden clientele.

ENCHANTERS, ECCLESIASTICS, AND SAINTS

The group that most opposed indiscriminate access to the supernatural was ecclesiastics, but by no means were clerical leaders of the same mind about how to determine whose wonder-working was legitimate. Gregory of Tours, for example, advocated and practiced a piety that admitted to a wide array of wonder-working saints, while Caesarius

110. Greg. Tur., VM 1.26 (*MGH*, SRM 1.2, 151).
111. Martin of Braga, *De correctione rusticorum*12, 16.
112. Dickie, *Magic and Magicians*, 25; Rouselle, "From Sanctuary to Miracle-Worker," 104–06.
113. Rouselle, "From Sanctuary to Miracle-Worker," 106.

of Arles' monastically oriented and text-based piety only allowed for a modest number of clerics to attempt healing.[114] Nor did clerics agree on what constituted miracle and what magic. Caesarius would have scowled at Gregory's seeming support for use of the *sortes biblicae*, but even in the realm of healing, the pair's ideals were worlds apart. Whereas Gregory readily advocated the efficacy of relics to heal and protect in all manner of instances, Caesarius's ideal of a presbyter-centered "spiritual healing" had no place for them.[115] Judging by the ever-increasing popularity of saints' cults, however, Gregory's piety likely was more in keeping with what inhabitants across Gaul expected of their religion.[116] Even in Caesarius's Arles, people of all social levels, including the bishop's own disciples, circumvented the prelate's limitation for availing spiritual authority and incorporated relics into their pious behavior. For example, according to Caesarius's underlings turned hagiographers (the priest Messianus and the deacon Stephanus), an aristocratic woman named Agretia, who suffered from excessive menstrual bleeding, realized her dilemma was identical to that of the woman from Matthew 9:20 who touched the fringes of Christ's clothes, and so "possessing a not dissimilar faith and devotion" (*non dissimilis fide et devotione*), she sought a cure through a like remedy.[117] She "demanded" (*exposcere*) that Messianus procure for her an article of Bishop Caesarius's clothing. Despite being filled with trepidation, Messianus obtained an old garment from the servant in charge of the bishop's wardrobe, Stephanus no less. Caesarius became aware of the subterfuge and confronted the duo. The clerics had been found complicit in a curative exercise that neither involved the presence of God's "appointed ministers" nor corresponded

114. For superb analysis of Caesarius and Gregory's contrasting pieties, see de Nie, "Caesarius of Arles and Gregory of Tours" 183–89.

115. In developing his concept of the priest as "spiritual physician," Caesarius neither emphasized nor alluded to relics. If personally attempting healings confirmed Caesarius's scheme, use of relics would only obfuscate it. William Klingshirn, *Caesarius of Arles: The Making of a Christian Community*, 166, writes, '[I]t is difficult to see how [Caesarius] could have considered the use of ... relics fully legitimate, since they appeared to provide unregulated access to divine power, an objection that informed his opposition to many ostensibly 'pagan' practices as well."

116. De Nie, "Caesarius of Arles and Gregory of Tours,"194–96. For widespread adoption of saints' cults penetrating deep into the Gallic social fabric, see Hen, *Religion and Society in Merovingian Gaul*, 82–120.

117. Cyprian of Toulon et al., *Vita Caesarii*, 2.13 (Morin, ed., 2: 329).

to the bishop's "approved techniques."[118] Potentially the bishop could have accused the pair of acting like sorcerers or of being in league with the Devil. Instead, Caesarius contradicted his own ideals by proposing a compromise by which Messianus, Stephanus, and Agretia might have their relic, and whereby a successful outcome would be attributed to an appropriate holy figure, a dead saint. Stephanus wrote:

> Reverently taking hold of yet another piece of clothing he gave it to me and said, "Go and take both of them to the basilica of lord Stephen, and put them under the altar; leave them there, and in the morning take whichever one you wish to the woman who asked you for it, and bring the other one back to me." I did just as he ordered his unworthy servant to do. ...[119]

Agretia persisted in her demand that Stephanus hand over the cloth. When she finally received it and held it to her bosom, immediately her malady ceased.[120] Although the hagiographers depicted Caesarius's hesitance to allow use of this relic as stemming from the bishop's humble concern that he not be credited with a miracle, in fact the behavior went well beyond the preferred healing techniques that Caesarius had advocated in his sermons, which were limited to prayer, anointing with holy oil, and making the sign of the cross.[121] But if Caesarius thought a biblical basis legitimized his curative techniques, so also was Agretia's solution biblically modeled. Furthermore, although one reads that the "demanding" aristocratic woman pressured Caesarius's clerics to provide the relic, Messianus and Stephanus must have shared Agretia's interpretation of what constituted appropriate Christian wonder-works over Caesarius's, as evidenced by their inclusion of the detailed account in the *Vita*. Caesarius's subordinates continued to disseminate magical aid to the people of Arles in a manner contrary to their bishop's ideals. Eleven

118. Klingshirn, *Caesarius of Arles: The Making of a Christian Community*, 166.
119. Cyprian of Toulon et al., *Vita Caesarii* 2.14 (Morin, ed., 2: 330): "... et cum gradi pietate apprehendens adhuc etiam alium tessellum dedit mihi et dixit; 'Vade, inquit, porta, ambos ad basilicam domni Stephani, et mitte illos sub altare, et ibi maneant, et unum quem volueris porta mane ad eam quae te gogavit, et alium mihi revoca.' Sicut iussit indigno servo duo feci ..." Trans. by Klingshirn, *Caesarius of Arles: Life, Testament, Letters*, 50.
120. Cyprian of Toulon et al., *Vita Caesarii* 2.15.
121. Klingshirn, *Caesarius of Arles: The Making of a Christian Community*, 162.

of the sixteen relic miracles preserved in Caesarius's *Vita* occurred while the bishop was alive. In none but the aforementioned one did Caesarius grant permission or have knowledge of his relics' use.[122] As one might suspect, Messianus and Stephanus usually were intimately involved.

Like Caesarius's disciples and the illustrious urban matron Agretia, humble peasants might also welcome the use of relics to overcome desperate circumstances. For example, Messianus wrote that in the parish of Succentriones, there was a great, ruined bath house that nearby inhabitants believed to be haunted. Passersby would hear their names called, and some even had to dodge falling stones. Caesarius once visited the site, but was called to another church. Then, confessed Messianus:

> ...the cleric whose responsibility it was to carry his staff forgot it. This was the duty of his notaries, in which capacity my useless self was serving. When the inhabitants of the place found it, they joyfully proclaimed that it had been furnished to them by their lord so that they could find something belonging to him. They were amazed, and thanked God, and hung the staff from the wall. And immediately the devil's snare was put to flight, and until the present the adversary has not dared to inflict any wicked evil on anyone in that place.[123]

Here Messianus passed off a supernaturally charged relic to assuage a band of rustics, the very kind of person whom Caesarius was most anxious to discourage from persisting in what he perceived to be superstitious behaviors. The peasants "joyfully" received the relic, and through its prominent display they were able to dispel the maleficent aura associated with the ruin. But what of Caesarius's reservations about using relics? Despite repeated sermonizing, Caesarius could not muster

---

122. ibid., 167.
123. Cyprian of Toulon et al., *Vita Caesarii* 2.22 (Morin, ed., 2: 334): "... clericus cui cura erat baculum illius portare – quod notariorum officium erat – oblitus est, in quo ministerio inutilis ego serviebam. Tunc incolae loci illius, cum eum invenissent, gaudentes dicebant sibi a domino praestitum, ut aliquid illius reperissent. Mirantur, et agunt deo gratias, virgamque ipsam de pariete illo suspendunt; statimque effugatae sunt insidiae diaboli, et ultra nulli in loco illo nequissimum malum facere usque hodie adversarius ipse praesumit." Trans. by Klingshirn, *Caesarius of Arles: Life, Testament, Letters*, 54. Similarly, see *Vita Caesarii* 2.27.

a consensus regarding Christian magic even among clerics who resided in his very bedchamber.

Although ecclesiastics held a variety of opinions about how clerics should distribute supernatural largesse, they were in agreement about one general goal–all churchmen wanted to bolster their local churches' healing authority. To this end they fostered an actual rivalry with healers who were not affiliated with churches. Clerics had a range of options by which they opposed the garden variety of *incantator*, including verbal disparagement and "demonization" in sermons and hagiography, actual promotion of saintly curative powers "in the field," so to speak, and also coercion. First, ecclesiastics used writings and community gatherings at churches to verbally disparage *incantatores*. In his book on Saint Martin's *virtutes*, Gregory belittled folk healers as "fools" (*stulti*), and he sometimes coupled such slurs with assurances that enchanters were incapable of performing wonders.[124] Gregory wrote, "I warn that no one be taken in by *harioli*, because they are never of any use to the infirm. For a dash of dust from [Martin's tomb in] the basilica is more effective than those people and their crazy medicine."[125] Hagiographers especially derided enchanters by preserving and publicizing incidents in which the saints prevailed after their opponents failed. For example, Gregory recalled that when a certain Aquilinus lost his senses, his kin sought ligaments and potions from *sortilegi* and *harioli*, but to no avail: "After there was *no improvement as usual*, [the parents] with grief mounting sought out Saint Martin's prompt beneficence."[126] At the saint's church, Aquilinus prayed, fasted, and begged Martin's assistance, and eventually he regained his sanity. Lectors at Tours will have read accounts of miracles such as this during heavily attended festivals in the saint's honor, and thereby the bishop could hope that some would be convinced of the folk healers' ineffectiveness. If, however, some suspicious listener wished to inquire about the veracity of the miracle, as Gregory

124. Greg. Tur., *VM* 4.36 (*MGH*, SRM 1.2, 209).

125. Greg. Tur., *VM* 1.27 (*MGH*, SRM 1.2, 151): "… monemus, ut nullus sollicitetur ab hariolis, quia nil proderunt umquam infirmis. Plus enim valet parumper de pulvere basilicae, quam illi cum medicamentis insaniae."

126. Greg. Tur., *VM* 1.26 (*MGH*, SRM 1.2, 151): "Sed cum *nihil valeret ex more*, sancti Martini auxilia prompti, dolore cogente, requirunt …" with my italics.

sometimes challenged them to do, then on this instance he would have been able to receive confirmation of the wonder, for upon being cured, Aquilinus remained at Martin's basilica, where "he has served ... up to this day."[127]

Presumably an important part of a client's repayment of debt to an invisible patron involved attesting before pilgrims and attendees at church as to how one had benefited from a saint's medicinal *virtus* after *incantatores* had fallen short. Not only did hagiographers record enchanters' failures, but they also preserved instances when their magic proved injurious to patients. For example, in his book on Saint Julian's *virtutes*, Gregory wrote that during a bout of plague in the Auvergne in 571, one of his own slaves succumbed to disease, and so others of Gregory's servants summoned a *hariolus*, who immediately plied his craft: "He murmured incantations, *cast lots*, hung amulets about [the patient's] neck, and *promised* he would live who in fact was being handed over to death."[128] Gregory had been unaware of these goings on, but when he learned of the servants' wrong-headed recourse to a folk healer he denounced them and then offered his own counter-prediction: "I sighed deeply as I recalled what the Lord said through the prophet Elijah to King Ahaziah; he said: 'Because you have forsaken the Lord God of Israel and you have consulted the god of Ekron, therefore you will not rise from the bed into which you have ascended, but you will die the death.'"[129] Indeed, after the *hariolus* administered his traditional techniques, the young servant's fever intensified, and the lad died. Not only had the soothsayer killed the patient, in Gregory's estimation, but he also had erred in his prognostication, while Gregory, thanks to his biblical knowledge, showed up the enchanter by correctly predicting that the boy would expire. Next, Gregory further discredited this same

127. Greg. Tur., *VM* 1.26 (*MGH*, SRM 1.2, 151): "usque hodie ... deservit." On Gregory's challenging his audience to investigate healing miracles, see *VJ* 46a.
128. Greg. Tur., *VJ* 46a (*MGH*, SRM 1.2, 132): "Incantationes inmurmurat, *sortes iacat*, ligaturas collo suspendit, *promittit* vivere quem ipse mancipaverat morti," with my italics.
129. Greg. Tur., *VJ* 46a (*MGH*, SRM 1.2, 132): "... et cum gravi suspirio illud conmemoro, quod Dominus per Heliam prophetam Oziae regi pronuntiat, dicens: *Quia dereliquisti dominum Deum Israel et consoluisti deum Acharon, ideo de lectulo, in quo ascendisti, non consurges, sed morte moreiris* [2 Kings 1:16]." Trans. based on Van Dam, *Saints and their Miracles*, 191–92.

incantator by appending a related tale of wonder. A few days after the first boy's death, another contracted the plague, but this time Gregory learned of the danger and sent servants to collect dust from Saint Julian's tomb. After mixing this with water and administering the potion, the youth immediately recovered.[130] Obviously Gregory intended these stories to discourage members of his congregation from relying on folk healers; however, these and similar hagiographical episodes attest that consulting enchanters must have been a common phenomenon, for even the servants of an ecclesiastical aristocrat might readily consult them.[131] The passages also indicate how enchanters and clerics were competing for the same patients. Gregory's approach to this contest was to convince readers and listeners of saints' lives that "sorcery" always failed, while the saints always prevailed: "Therefore, all you fools [standing] amongst the people ... understand that whatever the Devil tries to seduce the human race amounts to nothing. ...However, let one seek out patronage from the martyrs whose miracles are declared through health [being distributed] ... and then he will get what he has wanted."[132]

Ecclesiastics need not be passionate promoters of saints' cults to oppose the common practice of seeking out *incantatores*. Dissuasion of people relying on divination and magical healing is a motif found in Caesarius of Arles' sermons, too. Like hagiographers, Caesarius primarily combated enchanters through discouragement on the demand end, from the pulpit haranguing members of his congregation to forego recourse to them. He equated such behavior with sinfulness: "... everyone

---

130. Greg. Tur., *VJ* 46b.

131. Yitzhak Hen, "Paganism and Superstitions in the Time of Gregory of Tours: *Une question mal posée!*," in *The World of Gregory of Tours*, ed. Kathleen Mitchell and Ian Wood (Leiden, Boston, and Cologne: Brill, 2002), 229–40, rightly interprets Gregory's *Historiae*, Caesarius's sermons, and Merovingian hagiography to conclude that there was no active paganism in that world. I do not share Hen's estimation, however, that Gregory's references to behaviors such as consulting the *sortes biblicae* and relying on healers and soothsayers "create the impression that those phenomena were rare and not representative of Merovingian culture" (p. 232). Neither do I subscribe to a notion that such activities may be characterized as "superstitions" or "pagan vestiges." For criticism of interpreting "magic" as a "pagan survival," see Alexander Murray, "Missionaries and Magic in Dark-Age Europe," in *Debating the Middle Ages: Issues and Readings*, ed. Barbara Rosenwein (Malden, MA, and Oxford: Blackwell, 1998), 101–02.

132. Greg. Tur., *VJ* 46a (*MGH*, SRM 1.2, 132): "Intellegite ergo nunc o omnes qui insipientes estis in populo ... quia nihil sunt quae ad seducendum humanum genus diabolus operatur. ...quaerat autem patrocinia martyrum, per quos sanitatem miracula celebrantur ... et quae voluerit obtenebit."

who consults magicians and soothsayers or sorcerers on their own account or for the sake of their household – all who are men of this kind eject Christ from their hearts and bring in the Devil."[133] He admonished people who relied on professional diviners by declaring that "observing omens through soothsayers and prophets and magicians" was a "serious offense" (*crimen aliquod capitale*) akin to murder, which would require "harsh and public cures" (*acriores et publicas curas*), specifically heavy penance and abundant almsgiving.[134] Caesarius further intimidated his flock by declaring that "consulting sorcerers, seers, or charmers, hanging devilish phylacteries, magic signs, herbs, or charms on themselves or their family" would nullify the benefits that the sacraments conferred upon their souls.[135] He even demanded of prominent persons attending church that they whip their servants should they persist in consulting enchanters.[136] This last appeal again attests that most people who relied on *incantatores* were of low social rank. Unlike Gregory, Caesarius did not deny the efficacy of enchanters' abilities; instead, he ratcheted up his rhetoric by likening their practices to other diabolically motivated mortal sins. Thus Caesarius, in one sermon decried: "What need is there to say concerning adultery, murder, robbery, and false testimony that they are part of the Devil's pomp and works...? There is no doubt that to observe omens and to summon charmers, sorcerers, soothsayers, or seers belongs entirely to the pomp and works of the Devil."[137] Caesarius admitted that the *incantatores'* healing techniques sometimes resulted in physical recoveries. But the difference between their "cures" and the

---

133. Caes. Arel., *Serm.* 229.4 (*CCL* 104, 909): "... omnes qui caragios et divinos vel praecantatores aut propter se aut propter suos inquirunt: omnes qui tales sunt, Christum de corde suo proiciunt, et diabolum introducunt." Trans. by Mueller, *Saint Caesarius of Arles: Sermons*, 3: 176–77.

134. Caes. Arel., *Serm.* 197.2 (*CCL* 104, 796): "... si auguria observando per aruspices et divinos atque incantatores." Trans. by Mueller, *Saint Caesarius of Arles: Sermons*, 3: 46. Specific penalties: *Serm.* 197.3.

135. Caes. Arel., *Serm.* 13.5 (*CCL* 103, 68): "... caragios etiam et divinos vel praecantatores inquirere, fylacteria etiam diabolica, characteres aut herbas vel sucinos sibi aut suis adpendere." Trans. by Mueller, *Saint Caesarius of Arles: Sermons*, 1: 78.

136. Caes. Arel., *Serm.* 13.5.

137. Caes. Arel., *Serm.* 12.4 (*CCL* 103, 61): "De adulteriis vero vel homicidiis, rapinis vel testimoniis falsis quid opus est ut dicantur ad pompam vel ad opera diaboli pertinere...? Nam et auguria observare, et praecantatores adhibere, et caragios, sortilogos, divinos inquirere, totum hoc ad pompam vel ad opera diaboli non est dubium pertinere." Trans. by Mueller, *Saint Caesarius of Arles: Sermons*, 1: 70–71.

"spiritual medicine" available from his priests was that only the latter tended to the condition of the soul, because only it carried the authority of biblical sanction:

> Thus the Lord Himself deigned to promise through the Apostle James, saying: 'Is any one among you sick? Let him bring in the presbyters of the church, and let them pray over him, anointing him with oil. And the prayer will save the sick man, and if he be in sins, they shall be forgiven him [James 5:14–15].' Why, then, should a man kill his soul with sorcerers and seers, enchanters and diabolical phylacteries when he can heal both his soul and his body by the prayer of the priest and consecrated oil?[138]

For Caesarius, to seek an enchanter was tantamount to falling prey to the Devil's deception instead of embracing God's legitimate care. He insisted that whenever an *incantator* did successfully cure a patient, the result must be interpreted as the result of the Devil's deceit and a further indication of the soul's jeopardy. Caesarius explained:

> The Devil, indeed, does not want to kill the body as much as the soul. To try us he sometimes is permitted to strike our bodies with some infirmity; then, when we later agree to enchanters and phylacteries, he may kill our soul. For this reason the phylacteries sometimes seem to have power and beneficial effects; when the Devil has affected the soul with its consent, then he ceases to trouble the body.[139]

Thus Caesarius believed that those healers within his community who were not appointed from among the Arlésien clergy were associates of

---

138. Caes. Arel., *Serm.* 19.5 (*CCL* 103, 90): "Sic enim ipse dominus per apostolum Iacobum promittere dignatus est, dicens: SI QUIS INFIRMATUR, INDUCAT PRESBYTEROS ECCLESIAE, ET ORENT SUPER EUM, UNGUENTES EUM OLEO, ET ORATIO FIDEI SALVABIT INFIRMUM; ET SI IN PECCATIS FUERINT, DIMITTENTUR EI. Quare ergo per caraios et divinos, praecantatores et filacteria diabolica occidat animam suam, qui per orationem presbyteri et oleum benedictum potest sanare animam suam et carnem suam?" Trans. by Mueller, *Saint Caesarius of Arles: Sermons*, 1: 101–2. See also Caes. Arel., *Serm.* 13.3.

139. Caes. Arel., *Serm.* 50.1 (*CCL* 103, 225): "... etiam si per ipsas ligaturas aliqui sanitatem receperint, diaboli hoc calliditas facit; qui ideo aliquotiens de carne infirmitatem tollit, quia iam animam optat occidere: et ideo ad probandum nos permittitur aliqua infirmitate percutere carnem nostram, ut, dum illi postea consentimus ad praecantatores vel ad filacteria, occidat animam nostram. Et ideo interdum filacteria ipsa valere et prodesse aliquotiens videntur: quia, ubi diabolus per consensum percusserit animam, desinit persequi carnem." Trans. by Mueller, *Saint Caesarius of Arles: Sermons*, 1: 254.

Satan who offered only bodily remedies that sometimes worked, and whenever they did, threatened the condition of patients' souls. Even desperate mothers with infirm children should recognize that the grief and fear that compelled them to consult enchanters was motivated by "the deadly cunning of the unseen persecutor."[140] Caesarius pleaded for parents to entrust their children's care either to priests or to that other legitimate, albeit non-spiritual, kind of healer, physicians:

> If only they would seek that health from the simple skill of doctors! However, they say to themselves: Let us consult that soothsayer, seer, oracle, or witch. Let us sacrifice a garment of the sick person, a girdle that can be seen and measured. Let us offer some magic letters, let us hang some charms on his neck. In all this the Devil has one aim: either to cruelly kill the children by abortion, or to heal them still more cruelly by the charms.[141]

Here again Caesarius admitted to a shared belief with his congregation that enchanters often succeeded in their healing efforts. He was at pains to convince listeners that such cures were a danger to the eternal condition of their souls. It is notable that Caesarius perceived physicians' care as obviously legitimate; only the ministrations of *incantatores* were diabolical. Gregory, too, suspected that enchanters were motivated by Satan. For example, he speculated that a man from Bourges who displayed the ability to prophesy had been made to go insane –that is, he had had a demon inserted into his person – by the Devil.[142] Likewise, when he learned of an enchanter who was able to perceive the secret thoughts of others, the bishop wondered, "How else could he know this except through demons announcing it to him?"[143] Because prominent

---

140. Caes. Arel., *Serm.* 52.5 (*CCL* 103, 232): "... funestum ... occulti persequutoris ingenium."
141. Caes. Arel., *Serm.* 52.5 (*CCL* 103, 232): "Et atque utinam ipsam sanitatem vel de simplici medicorum arte conquirerent. Sed dicunt sibi: Illum ariolum vel divinum, illum sortilegum, illam erbariam consulamus; vestimentum infirmi sacrificemus, cingulum qui inspici vel mensurari debeat; offeramus aliquos caracteres, aliquas praecantationes adpendamus ad collum. Inter haec una diaboli persuasio est: aut per avorsum occidere crudeliter filios, aut per caracteres sanare crudelius." Trans. by Mueller, *Saint Caesarius of Arles: Sermons,* 1: 261–62.
142. Greg. Tur., *Hist.* 10.25.
143. Greg. Tur., *Hist.* 9.6 (*MGH*, SRM 1.1, 417): "... Et quid aliud nisi nuntiantibus daemoniis cognoscebat?"

ecclesiastics recognized reliance on enchanters as a popular alternative to clerically controlled healing, whether the latter was through Gregory and hagiographers' saints and relics or via biblically legitimized priests, à la Caesarius, they universally demonized rival claimants touting supernatural solutions.

Ecclesiastics complemented their verbal impugning of enchanters with actual opposition. Some clerics sought to thwart what they identified as *maleficium* by offering relics to patients who might otherwise be disposed to seek enchanters. As has been mentioned, days after Gregory discovered that his servants entrusted the care of one of their own to a *hariolus*, he promptly set them on the proper path by administering a potion containing dust from Saint Julian's tomb to another youth, thereby effecting a successful result. Similarly, when one of Gregory's field workers, the wife of Serenatus, became mute, the *harioli* descended and attended to her by prescribing "amulets of herbs and chanting" (*ligamina herbarum atque incantationum verba*), but to no avail.[144] Serenatus's son then rushed to inform Gregory's niece, Eustenia, who in turn sought out the servant and undid the damage: "Once she got rid of the amulets that the foolish [*harioli*] had applied, she poured some oil taken from the blessed tomb into [the patient's] mouth and added wax. Her speech soon returned, and with the deceit of the wickedness separated [from the patient], the ill woman was restored to health."[145] Like her uncle Gregory, Eustenia would have been raised in an atmosphere well attuned toward promoting saints as holy healers. She was the daughter of Gregory's anonymous sister and a certain Justinus. The latter once had benefited from the use of candles taken from Martin's tomb to overcome a fever, and on a separate occasion he recovered from an extended illness after his wife administered to him a potion containing a leaf of sage obtained from the church of Saints Ferreolus and Ferrucio.[146] Judging by her presence at Tours, it may be that Eustenia,

144. Greg. Tur., *VM* 4.36 (*MGH*, SRM 208).
145. Greg. Tur., *VM* 4.36 (*MGH*, SRM 1.2, 209): "... amotis ligaminibus quae stulti indiderant, oleum beati sepulchri ori eius infudit ceraque suffivit. Mox sermone reddito, nequitiae dolo dirempto, aegra convaluit."
146. Greg. Tur., *VM* 2.2, *GC* 70.

Gregory's youngest known relation, was being groomed to inherit her portion of the family's spiritual authority.[147] An aspect of augmenting that authority likely involved learning how to outperform common folk healers.

In addition to besting enchanters at healing, clerics with fewer scruples than the rigidly conventional Caesarius of Arles used Christianized divination techniques to show up soothsayers. For example, a contest of sorts in 577 over divinatory power took place at Saint Martin's basilica, where Duke Guntram Boso and the latest rebellious prince, Chilperic's son Merovech, were taking refuge.[148] The duke confided to Gregory that a longtime professional diviner, a *pithonissa*, had predicted that Chilperic soon would die, that Merovech would become king, and that Guntram Boso would become a general for five years before spending the rest of his long life as bishop of Tours! Gregory merely laughed off the duke's affront and cautioned his against relying on "what the devil promises" (*quae diabolus repromittit*).[149] Like the bishop, Merovech was not inclined to trust Guntram Boso's *pithonissa*, and so he determined to confirm the prognostication by placing three books—the Psalter, the Book of Kings and the Gospels—on Saint Martin's tomb. After three days and nights of fasting, vigil, and prayer, Merovech piously opened each tome and read the first passage his eyes lit upon. When each selection proved more disappointing than the previous one, the prince became so despondent, now knowing he would not become king, that he abandoned sanctuary at the basilica. Soon it happened that the *sortes* proved correct in every way, meaning that the soothsayer had erred. Chilperic survived the year 577, Merovech was dead within the year, and Guntram Boso neither replaced Gregory as bishop nor did he enjoy a long life.[150] Since Gregory was present for

---

147. Eustenia was wife of Nicetius, an upwardly mobile Austrasian courtier; Greg. Tur., *Hist.* 5.14. Nicetius was a *comes* and then *dux* in the Auvergne, *rector provinciae* at Marseilles, and *patricius*; *PLRE* 3: 945, s. v., "Nicetius 3." Eustenia's older sister Justina became prioress at the nunnery of the Holy Cross at Poitiers in 590; Greg. Tur., *Hist.* 10.15. It is not known whether Eustenia and Nicetius had any children.

148. Greg. Tur., *Hist.*, 5.14.

149. Greg. Tur., *Hist.*, 5.14 (*MGH*, SRM 1.1, 210).

150. Guntram Boso was part of the Austrasian faction that opposed Queen Brunhild. Kings Guntram and Childebert II arranged his execution in 587; Greg. Tur., *Hist.* 9.10. Gregory provided an obituary

Merovech's readings, and given that the bishop elsewhere revealed his approval of clerical use of divinatory media, it is very likely that he presided over this magical performance within Martin's church. Gregory gained a further appreciation of the wrongfulness of the *pithonissa*'s prediction when he was awakened one night by an angel who prophetically announced that none of Chilperic's sons (four were alive at the time including Merovech) would outlive their father: "When in the future these [utterances] were fulfilled, I then completely understood that whatever the *harioli* promised was false."[151] Thus, here Gregory participated in two magical exercises that he deemed legitimate by virtue of the holiness of the supernatural beings involved in them, a saint and an angel, and by the sanctity of the places where the heaven-sent messages arrived, Saint Martin's church and presumably the bishop's cathedral abode. Through all of this, Gregory was able to debunk the capabilities of one fortune-teller.

Besides simply touting instances whenever they bested *incantatores* at their own games of healing and divination, ecclesiastics sometimes employed their institutional might to stifle enchanters. Some enacted legislation expressly forbidding people from consulting enchanters, as did prelates attending the late sixth-century Council of Auxerre: "Let it not be permitted for people to look to soothsayers nor augurers, nor diviners, nor let them examine lots which they attribute to saints or which are made from wood or bread; but, no matter what a person wishes to happen, let him place all things in the name of the Lord."[152] One wonders what the prelates at Auxerre would have made of some of the goings on at Martin's basilica! In a similar prohibitive vein, ecclesiastics at the Council of Narbonne (589) decreed that diviners were to be not only excommunicated but also fined six ounces of gold payable to the count

---

of sorts that listed Guntram Boso's sins, which included his preoccupation with knowing future events and an over-reliance upon *harioli*.

151. Greg. Tur., *Hist.*, 5.14 (*MGH*, SRM 1.1, 211): "Cum autem haec in posterum inpleta fuissent, tunc ad liquidum cognovi, falsa esse quae promiserant harioli."

152. Council of Auxerre (561/605), c. 4 (*CCL* 148A, 265): "Non licet ad sortilegos vel auguria respicere nec ad caragius nec ad sortes, quas sanctorum vocant, vel quas de lignum aut de pane faciunt, aspicere, nisi, quaecumque homo facere vult, omnia in nomine Domini faciat."

of the city.[153] Furthermore, the canon decreed that corporal punishment be meted on diviners of low social station:

> Those who are filled with such iniquity that they [cast] lots and make divinations and seduce the people by colluding, whenever they are found or discovered, whether men or women, whether freed people or slaves or maidservants, let them be publicly and severely beaten and sold, and let the money be distributed among the poor.[154]

This canon's suggested use of bodily punishment confirms the strong measures some ecclesiastics were willing to take to eradicate this seemingly entrenched rival source of divine contact, which was being reached primarily by people of low rank.

The popularity of wonder-working individuals likely soared during periods of distress, as when plague afflicted communities. Gregory becomes the principal witness for regional appearances and even the trajectory of bubonic disease across Gaul during the first pandemic, the so-called "Justinianic plague," from the mid-sixth through mid-eighth centuries.[155] His anecdotes that illuminate these particularly anxious moments provide the most detailed accounts of clerics' actively responding to the challenge of *incantatores*. In most cases, Gregory portrayed bishops merely examining and confiscating practitioners' accoutrements and forcing them to leave their dioceses. The year 587 was one of those times when the reputations of enchanters might soar. Gregory recorded: "In this year the grape harvest was weak while the waters were mighty, rainfall was immense, and the rivers were increased to overflowing."[156]

153. Council of Narbonne (589), c. 14 (*CCL* 148A, 256–57).
154. Council of Narbonne (589), c. 14 (*CCL* 148A, 256–57): "Illi vero qui tali iniquitate repleti sunt et sortes et divinationes faciunt et populum prevaricando seducunt, ubi inventi vel invente fuerint, seu liberi seu servi vel ancille sint, gravissime publice fustigentur et venundentur, et pretia ipsorum pauperibus erogentur."
155. See Lester K. Little, "Life and Afterlife of the First Plague Pandemic," in *Plague and the End of Antiquity: The Pandemic of 541–750*, ed. Lester K. Little (Cambridge: Cambridge University Press, 2007), 3–32, especially at 9–11, who assesses the plague's entering Gaul through Marseilles and being transmitted to Cornwall and Ireland probably via Nantes. See further J.-N. Biraben and Jacques LeGoff, "The Plague in the Early Middle Ages," in *Biology of Man in History*, ed. R. Forster and O. Ranum; trans. E. Forster and P. M. Ranum (Baltimore: Johns Hopkins University Press, 1975), 48–80.
156. Greg. Tur., *Hist.* 9.5 (*MGH*, SRM 1.1, 416): "Vindemia eo anno tenuis, aquae validae, pluviae inmensae, flumina quoque granditer adaucta fuerunt."

As a result of this inclement weather, general anxiety ensued, and one Gallic *incantator*, Desiderius by name, amassed a sizeable following by virtue of his repute as a healer. The biased bishop described Desiderius' medical procedures as follows:

> Because I was not present, many of the rustics gathered about him bringing the blind and the disabled. Unable to restore them with sanctity, he proceeded to disgrace them with the error of necromantic crafts. For he ordered that those who were paralytics or hindered by other disabilities be stretched mightily, as if he could use physical labor to cure what he could not correct through the bestowal of divine power. Then his servants would apprehend a man's hands and others the feet, and they would pull in different directions, so that the nerves seemed about to burst. Those who did not recover they sent away almost lifeless. Whence it happened that many who had been given over to this torture exhaled their spirits.[157]

Because Gregory was not present at the city when this healer approached, it may be wondered whether he was fearfully hiding from the throng. I think this doubtful given that he did not shy away from other *incantatores*. By 587, the one supreme threat to his career, King Chilperic, was dead three years, and Gregory was in a strong social and political position. A folk healer posed no danger to such a bishop. Perhaps then he was avoiding the city because of the possibility of an outbreak of disease, or maybe he simply was tending to pastoral duties. Regardless of the reason for his absence, and despite it, the bishop knew he could rely on his minions to tend properly to an imposter: "When they detected his deceitfulness *our people* apprehended Desiderius and tossed him beyond the city lines."[158] Here we should suspect the operation of the bishop's

---

157. Greg. Tur., *Hist.* 9.6 (*MGH*, SRM 1.1, 417): "Ad quem, quia praesens non eram, rustici populi multa confluxerat, deferentes secum caecos et debiles, quos non sanctitate sanare, sed errore nigromantici ingenii quaerebat inludere. Nam hos, qui erant paralitici aut alia inpediti debilitate, iubebat valide extendi, ut quos virtutis divinae largitione diregere non poterat, quasi per industriam restauraret. Denique adpraehendebant pueri eius manus hominis, alii vero pedes, tractumque diversis in partibus, ita ut nervi potarentur abrumpi, cum non sanarentur, demittebantur exanimis. Unde factum est, ut in hoc supplicio multi spiritum exalarent."

158. Greg. Tur., *Hist.* 9.6 (*MGH*, SRM 1.1, 418): "Sed detecta dolositas eius et *a nostris* deprehensa, eiectus est extra urbis terminum," with my italics.

faithful lower clergy and the registered poor diligently assuring that their patron Martin maintained his controlling interest in local healing authority by expelling a rival from their territory.[159]

Another figure determined to remain the principal wonder-worker in his locale was the hermit Patroclus. When last we saw the *ingenuus* ascetic he was using the *sortes* to legitimize distancing himself from the village of Néris, and perhaps from its clergy as well. Despite the remoteness of Patroclus's new cell at Mediocantus, needy persons continued to seek him out for healings and exorcisms.[160] Meanwhile, during the plague of 571, a vision of Saint Martin appeared before a woman named Leubella and provided "offerings" (*oblationes*) by which she might alleviate the people's sufferings.[161] When she presented these healing tokens before Patroclus, the "truth" was revealed: "Not only did [the *oblationes*] disappear as the Holy Spirit uncovered [the deception], but also the true inciter of these crimes (i.e., Satan) appeared in a most abominable guise before the saint and confessed to what he wickedly had committed."[162] This admission included the fact that it was he, the Devil, who had materialized before Leubella looking like Martin and "wickedly" convinced her to attempt to heal plague victims. Here it appears Patroclus, bolstered by clerical status – he had been a deacon at Bourges – was using his spiritual authority to convince Leubella that her seemingly compassionate efforts were *maleficia*. This interpretation would have assured that the hermit would remain the only legitimate healer in the environs of Mediocantus. Interestingly, as a wonder-working non-aristocratic ascetic, Patroclus himself was in a liminal position for a churchman, for previously he had had his own problems with church hierarchy. His pursuit of a harsh, ascetic regimen had caused a breach with the clergy at Bourges even before he felt a need to disassociate himself from the clerics at Néris.[163] One way that Patroclus perhaps could maintain

---

159. For lesser clerics and *matricularii* performing the bishop's heavy work, see the discussion in Chapter Six.

160. Greg. Tur., *VP* 9.2.

161. Greg. Tur., *VP* 9.2 (*MGH*, SRM 1.2, 254).

162. Greg. Tur., *VP* 9.2 (*MGH*, SRM 1.2, 254): "... non solum, revelante spiritu sancto, evanuerunt, verum etiam ipse incentor malorum sancto teterrimus apparens, quae nequiter gesserat est professus."

163. Greg. Tur., *VP* 9.1.

legitimacy in the eyes of the more established clerics of his locale would be to discourage extraneous rustics from taking up wonderworking. Some time after his encounter with Leubella, Patroclus began to contemplate abandoning his cell and "returning to the world," but an angel appeared to him in a dream and convinced him to stay put.[164] Here the angel's line of thinking would have coincided with that of nearby clerics, who certainly were not partial to wandering Christian wonder-workers. In the end, Patroclus adopted a more respectable, stationary lifestyle. He built the monastery of Colombier, which he peopled with monks and a proper abbot. After eighteen years "in the desert," Patroclus died and was interred at the monastery, where the monks revered him as a saint.[165] As for Leubella, it appears that the cleric convinced – we cannot go so far as to say forced – her to renounce what she obviously initially thought was a holy calling to become a healer. Like virtually all *incantatores* of Barbarian Gaul depicted in the anecdotal evidence, she was a Christian who desired to assume a new identity by embarking on a well-trodden career path that might prove beneficial to herself and/or her neighbors' woes.[166] Unfortunately, Leubella ran afoul of a rural representative of an ecclesiastical establishment determined to make his "spiritual medicine" the locale's only available supernaturally based healing option. Although they shared the Christian faith with ecclesiastics, those healers not affiliated with churches would be deemed "diabolically" inspired.

---

164. Greg. Tur., *VP* 9.2.

165. Greg. Tur., *VP* 9.3.

166. *Contra* Valerie Flint's estimation that many, or most, Gallic *incantatores* were non-Christians; Flint, *Rise of Magic in Early Medieval Europe*, 47, 68, 70, 83, 189, 310–11, 361. The only enchanter found in Gallic *vitae* of our era whom I am certain was pagan was a decrepit weather-changer from Orange active during the tenure of Bishop Eutropius (ca. 450–475). This poor man did not even have the chance to amaze a crowd by preventing the approach of a storm before the bishop ushered him into the Christian faith; Verus of Orange, *Vita Eutropii, ep. Arausicani*, P. Varin, ed., *Bulletin du Comité Historique des Monuments Ecrits de l'Histoire de France* 1 (1849): 59–60; Mathisen, *People, Personal Expression, and Social Relations*, 1: 147–50. Notions of paganism continued flourish in Gaul are being diminished, as evidenced by new interpretations of archaeological material. For example, a once widespread belief that burial practices lasting through the sixth century such as the interment of grave goods and west-east burials were particular to pagans has been discarded; Effros, *Merovingian Mortuary Archaeology*, 133, 147. Not only did Christians bury their deceased with grave goods, but some also maintained what once would have been assumed to be pagan practices such as funerary feasting and mound burials; ibid., 163, 199–200. Facile "pagan" versus "Christian" interpretations of Gallic burials cannot continue to be used to argue for a strong non-Christian presence through the sixth century.

In 580, torrential rains again brought flooding to parts of Gaul, and an "earthquake" at Bordeaux presaged a great plague accompanied by dysentery.[167] That year also witnessed the emergence of another enchanter, unnamed but lowborn judging by his manner of speech, who traversed Gaul and gathered a following through an ostentatious Christian display: "carrying a cross from which dangled small flasks said to contain holy oil ... he professed he came from Spain and said that he possessed relics of the blessed martyrs, Vincent the deacon and Felix the martyr."[168] Here was a wandering Christian healer of the sort that stationary churchmen such as Gregory would not have wanted offering an alternative to the medicines available at local saints' tombs. At Tours, the enchanter became put off by Gregory's initial slights, so he entered the bishop's cell without his leave. Next the traveler revealed how he possessed some degree of liturgical competence by conducting morning prayer in the oratory, although Gregory was none too impressed by the delivery. After praying, the enchanter left the city. Note that in this instance, the bishop did not flinch at the arrival of the *incantator* despite his abrasive intrusion and lack of protocol. A short time later, the same character arrived in Paris and impudently challenged Bishop Ragnemod's scheduled Rogations processional by announcing that he would conduct his own tour of outlying holy places. As he was preparing to lead a column of "publicans and peasant women" (*publicanis ac rusticis mulieribus*), the city's archdeacon cordially invited the newcomer to set aside his relics and join the community feast, but the man responded by heaping insults on Ragnemod. In next to no time, the bishop, presumably having loosed his zealous bodyguards, was holding the man in a detention cell and examining his wares: "He found upon him a big bag filled with the roots of various plants; in it, too, were moles' teeth, the bones of mice, bears' claws and bear's fat. The bishop had all this thrown into the river, recognizing it as *maleficia*."[169] Ragnemod also confiscated the

---

167. Greg. Tur., *Hist.* 5.33.
168. Greg. Tur., *Hist.* 9.6 (*MGH*, SRM 1.1, 418): "... crucem ferens, de qua dependebant ampullulae, quas dicebat oleam sanctum habere. Aiebat enim se de Hispaniis adventare ac reliquias beatissimorum martyrum Vincenti levitae Felicisque martyris exhibere."
169. Greg. Tur., *Hist.* 9.6 (*MGH*, SRM 1.1, 418–19): "... invenit cum eo sacculum magnum plenum de radicibus diversarum herbarum, ibique et dentes talpae et ossa murium et ungues atque adipes

large cross and showed the man to the Paris border, but the enchanter afterward simply built another cross and carried on as before in the same vicinity. Again the archdeacon captured and confined the wanderer, this time with chains, but the culprit escaped the cell. Then, however, he happened across some wine and soon passed out on the floor of Saint Julian's church (this one at Paris), where who should discover him but a visiting Bishop Gregory of Tours, in town for a church council! Gregory hoped to pardon the wretch, so he ordered that he be brought before the assembled prelates. There Bishop Amelius of Bigorra recognized the culprit as his own runaway slave! Yet again a Gallic enchanter turned out to be a person of low rank trying to better his and others' lives through wonderworking. Although Gregory might have meant his description of the contents in the magical bag to demean the healer, the items may be representative of the kind of fearful and awe-inspiring *materia* that *incantatores* actually used in their craft.[170] The fact that the enchanter mixed Christian icons with traditional magic does not justify his, or those country people who acknowledged his powers, being character-ized as representatives of a "half-Christianized" peasant world.[171] First, he was the slave of a bishop and knowledgeable about the liturgy, so it would not be surprising if he actually were a cleric of freed or servile rank. Second, his conglomeration of Christian and traditional magi-cal *materia* confirms the extent to which Christian symbols had begun to represent awesome power, the very point Gallic ecclesiastics were

---

ursinos. Vidensque haec maleficia esse, cuncta iussit in flumine proici ..." Trans. based on Thorpe, *Gregory of Tours, History of the Franks*, 485.

170. Meeks, "Magic and the Early Medieval World View," 289–92.

171. Giselle de Nie, "Caesarius of Arles and Gregory of Tours," 174, refers to these bishops' communities as "usually only half-converted," and similarly, ibid., 195, to "the often only half-converted pagans who filled their churches." References to "half-converted" peasants are unhelpful in that they pre-suppose assumptions not unlike those of our elitist ecclesiastical authors who privileged their own theories about what behaviors were compatible with Christianity, and denigrated all others. Those deemed the "half-converted" basically were maintaining traditional social survival techniques, essentially rural in nature, alien to certain bishops' urban sensibilities and contrary to their central-izing city-based socio-religious agendas. Furthermore, comments about the "half-converted" con-vey a measure of historical inaccuracy commensurate with outmoded notions that only pagans and "less spiritual" Christians buried grave goods. Once commonly held theories that "greater Christian spiritualization" was responsible for drastic late seventh-century changes in burial customs, particu-larly the replacement of interment of grave goods with masses for the dead, are now deemed uncon-vincing; Effros, *Merovingian Mortuary Archaeology*, 86–88.

trying to establish.[172] The dilemma was that many among the mightier churchmen were attempting to channel all access to supernatural power through a smaller number of ecclesiastically approved disseminators. Perhaps this slave's patrons had refused to allow him a meaningful role in distributing supernatural largesse, and so he fled his masters to become the wonder-worker he wanted to be. Finally, notice that time and again ecclesiastics expelled this *incantator* from their dioceses. Neither Gregory nor Ragnemod perceived the man as a real threat to their spiritual authority; rather, they regarded him a nuisance who simply needed to be mildly encouraged to move along. In the end, Amelius forgave his servant and carried him back to Bigorra.

In Gregory's *Historiae*, one famous encounter between clerics and an itinerant *incantator* stands out above all others. Reportedly on the occasion of surviving an attack of swarming insects, a pauper from Bourges became an enchanter. He conducted prayers "like a religious" (*quasi religiosus*), and prophesied, all the while wandering southward for two years.[173] In 591, as the plague raged in southern Gaul, he arrived at Javols, where he proclaimed himself to be Christ. A female companion claiming to be his sister called herself Mary. Gregory, who thought the imposter obviously empowered by Satan, described how he acquired wealth and influence by playing on the people's distress:

> Great crowds flocked to see him and brought out their sick. He laid hands upon them and restored them to health. Those who gathered round him gave him clothes, and gifts of gold and silver. All this he handed to the poor, which helped in his deception. He would lie on the ground alone and say prayers with the woman... He foretold the future, prophesying that some would fall ill and that others would suffer affliction, while to a few he promised good fortune. All this he did by devilish arts and by tricks which I cannot explain. A great number of people were deceived by him, not only the uneducated but even priests in orders. More than three thousand people followed him wherever he went. Then he began to rob and despoil

172. Meeks, "Magic and the Early Medieval World View," 292.
173. Greg. Tur., *Hist.* 10.25 (*MGH*, SRM 1.1, 518).

those whom he met on the road, giving to the poor and needy all that he took.[174]

We already have witnessed the last moments in the life of this Pseudo-Christ from Bourges in relation to a consideration of bishops and their henchmen.[175] At Le Puy, the prophet challenged the authority of Bishop Aurelius, but a bishop need not flinch before an enchanter, even a very popular one. Aurelius merely sent his "strong men" to infiltrate the wanderer's camp, and one among them cut down the imposter with a sword. Afterward the clerics of Le Puy tortured Mary into revealing the prophet's tricks, and they dispersed the mob. I think it likely that the example of the Pseudo-Christ of Bourges reflects the highest degree of popularity an enchanter without sustained clerical backing could muster. No Gallic *incantator*, however, could pose a lasting threat to established ecclesiastics. Note, too, that what authority this prophet did accrue resulted from a combination of his being active during a moment of poignant duress, plague in southern Gaul, and effective exploitation of Christian behavior and expectations. Both his pious distribution of wealth to the downtrodden and the representation of himself as the returned Christ betray the enchanter as an apocalyptic millennialist. The historian Gregory included portrayals of the actual appearances of such persons toward the end of the *Historiae* to give credence in his text to his own eschatology: "'These were the beginning of sorrows,' as our Lord said in the Gospels: ... 'For false Christs and false prophets shall rise, and shall shew signs and wonders in the sky, to seduce, if it were possible, even the elect.' That is exactly what happened at this time."[176] For Gregory,

---

174. Greg. Tur., *Hist.* 10.25 (*MGH*, SRM 1.1, 518): "Confluebat ad eum multitudo populi, exhibens infirmos, quos contingens sanitati reddebat. Conferebant etiam ei aurum argentumque ac vestimenta hi qui ad eum conveniebant. Quod ille, quo facilius seduceret, pauperibus erogabat, prosternens se solo, effundens orationem cum mulierem... Praedicebat enim futura et quibusdam morbus, quibusdam damna provenire denuntiabat, paucis salutem futuram. Sed haec omnia diabolicis artibus et praestigiis nescio quibus agebat. Seducta est autem per eum multitudo inmensa populi, et non solum rusticores, verum etiam sacerdotes ecclesiastici. Sequebantur autem eum amplius tria milia populi. Interea coepit quosdam spoliare ac praedare, quos in itinere repperisset; spolia tamen non habentibis largiebatur." Trans. based on Thorpe, *Gregory of Tours, History of the Franks*, 585.

175. See the discussion in Chapter Six at pp. 238 and 239.

176. Greg. Tur., *Hist.* 10.25 (*MGH*, SRM 1.1, 517): "*Initia sunt* enim *haec dolorum* iuxta illud quod Dominus ait in evangelio: ...*et exurgent pseudochristi et pseudoprophetae et dabunt signa et prodogia in*

the Pseudo-Christ and his ilk represented the approach of end times, but what the non-apocalyptic, chronologically minded bishop realized that the false prophets did not was that the world had another two centuries and more remaining in its present torrid state.[177] Armed with this knowledge, Bishop Gregory knew that he need not fear the sight of false prophets.[178] As for the death of the Pseudo-Christ, he was slain not for practicing *maleficium* or for impersonating a saint, but rather because he was a thief and a heretic, deceitfully claiming to be Christ and agitating society with an errant millennial banter.[179] This Pseudo-Christ's behavior little resembled that of the run-of-the mill Gallic *incantator*. Likewise, his fatal end did not reflect what most enchanters could anticipate in terms of ecclesiastical intervention.

Most enchanters, if ever confronted by clerics, could expect forceful but not fatal treatment. As we have seen, clerics attempting to maintain local healing authority preferred simply to expel *incantatores* from their dioceses. Thus Gregory intimated that whenever he faced other less-colorful pseudo-prophets, he merely abjured them "to give up their error."[180] Otherwise, some clerics, imagining that the enchanters themselves were victims of demonic deception, performed exorcisms on them. For example, referring to the *pithonissa* from this chapter's introductory

caelo, ita ut electos in errore mittant, sicut praesenti gestum est tempore." Trans. by Thorpe, *Gregory of Tours, History of the Franks*, 584.

177. For Gregory's non-apocalyptic eschatology, see Richard Landes, "Lest the Millennium Be Fulfilled: Apocalyptic Expectations and the Pattern of Western Chronography 100–800 CE," in *Use and Abuse of Eschatology in the Middle Ages*, ed. W. Verbeke, D. Verhelst, and A. Welkenhuysen (Leuven: Leuven University Press, 1988), 166–68.

178. De Nie, *Views from a Many-Windowed Tower*, 53, suspected Gregory's inclusion of tales about false prophets toward the end of the *Historiae* to indicate the author's belief in an imminent end time.

179. Jacques Le Goff, *Time, Work and Culture in the Middle Ages*, 95–96, extrapolated from Gregory's stories about pseudo-prophets that there was emerging an elitist perception of peasants as a dangerous class: "... it was in the peasant masses that the *pseudo-prophetae*, the popular religious leaders, originated and recruited their followers. These Antichrists arose in the peasant world ..." But pseudo-prophets were not representative of all who wanted to preach or become clerics. As has been seen, such persons came from all social levels. The would-be prophets' worldview arose not from a popular peasant mentality; rather it derived from an essentially Christian notion of an imminent end time, sometimes latent but never completely forgotten. As with other millenarian movements, the activities of Gallic pseudo-prophets cannot be summed up tidily as popular movements. See Bernard McGinn, *Visions of the End: Apocalyptic Traditions in the Middle Ages* (New York: Columbia University Press, 1998), 29–32. McGinn exhibits Martin of Tours, Sulpicius Severus, and Pope Gregory – not a peasant among them – as expressing apocalyptic sensibilities; ibid., 51–52, 62–65.

180. Greg. Tur., *Hist.* 10.25 (*MGH*, SRM 1.1, 519): "revocare ab errore."

anecdote, when Bishop Ageric of Verdun learned that the prognosticator "daily was amassing gold and silver and parading about with jewelry so that the people thought her to be divine," he sent his deputies to retrieve the woman.[181] Having consulted Acts 16:16, he reasoned that she could prophesy because a demon had possessed her. Therefore the bishop took the necessary next step: "When Ageric performed the exorcism over her and applied holy oil to her forehead, the demon shouted out and the bishop recognized what it was."[182] But try as he might, Ageric failed to convince the spirit to depart the woman's body. With the ordeal concluded, the soothsayer "realized" (*cernens*) she must leave the region of Verdun.[183] Presumably this realization coincided with the bishop's insistence. Here, an ecclesiastic responded to a rumor that a non-church-affiliated wonder-worker had become prominent enough to demand clerical discretion. The bishop made what he would have considered a compassionate attempt to rid the *incantator* of demonic affliction. When the ritual failed, he assessed what he thought to be a lenient penalty, expulsion from the diocese, although one may wonder whether Ageric confiscated the enchanter's "diabolically" acquired wealth before he sent her away. For the diviner's part, it would seem that her vocation was too lucrative for an exorcism to be effective.

ENCHANTERS MAKING DO

Magical activity was as widespread in the last years of Barbarian Gaul as it had been in the first. Despite reservations, high ecclesiastics and secular magnates allowed much latitude for practicing wonder-workers. Beyond having to listen to the invectives of preachers and hagiographers, some *incantatores* doubtless encountered the occasional determined fiscal agent or cleric who meted out fines and beatings, or even conducted exorcisms. For an enchanter who settled in a region where ecclesiastics were sticklers to promote saints, or priests, as the only legitimate healers

---

181. Greg. Tur., *Hist.* 7.44 (*MGH*, SRM 1.1, 364): "Congregabat cotidie aurum argentumque, procedens in ornamentis, ita ut putaretur esse aliquid divinum in populis."
182. Greg. Tur., *Hist.* 7.44 (*MGH*, SRM 1.1, 365): "Denique cum exorcismum super eam diceret ac frontem oleo sancto perungueret, exclamavit daemonium et quid esset prodidit sacerdoti."
183. Greg. Tur., *Hist.* 7.44 (*MGH*, SRM 1.1, 365).

of the locale, forced relocation was a distinct possibility. Many people, however, desperately needed proximate healers with time-tested remedies, diviners who could identify wrongdoers, and also potion and poison manufacturers. Therefore the obstacles of zealous church and state officials could not deter everyone from persisting in the traditional, personally rewarding and potentially profitable business of working wonders.

For some, magic offered an invaluable boon, the self-satisfaction of bestowing benefits upon fellow disconsolate humans. As with some church-affiliated people whom clerics promoted as saints after their deaths, the common *incantatores'* most important skill was healing. Certainly poor Leubella felt inspired to help plague victims, just as Monegund needed to heal in order to overcome the grief caused by her daughters' demise. Unfortunately for Leubella, her nearest cleric, Patroclus, was determined to maintain his local healing authority at the expense of her dreams, whereas for Monegund, she was fortunate that the clerics of Tours regarded her as an asset in making Martinopolis an influential gateway to the supernatural. Besides desiring to cure others, some enchanters wanted to experience the joys associated with charitable works. Just as the holy recluse Senoch reveled in his ability to free people from servitude and debt by measuring out alms, so did the Pseudo-Christ of Bourges' penchant to "rob from the rich and give to the poor" reflect an obvious desire to level society through a redistribution of goods. In addition to exhibiting the influence of millennial thought, perhaps this prophet performed his "Robin-Hood act" because he was put off by the rhetoric of "defending the poor" that established churchmen were proclaiming at the same moment that they were hoarding church plate and amassing property, while their ecclesiastical leaders were vying economically and physically to outrank one another and be counted among the most socially prominent persons in Gaul.[184]

Some *incantatores* practiced magic to partake of the prestige that wonder-working conferred. Desiderius proclaimed that his *virtus* was equal

---

184. For the Pseudo-Christ being likened to Robin Hood, see Mathisen, *People, Personal Expression, and Social Relations*, 1: 232.

to Peter and Paul's and greater than that of Saint Martin's.[185] While Gregory was bound to label such an obnoxious critic of his holy patron a *maleficus*, Desiderius undoubtedly was hoping he could convince witnesses that his were "goodly" powers, perhaps so that he would become a saint. One senses a similar motive borne by the cross-wielding, runaway slave of Bigorra who toted his relics in a magic bag. Was this slave behaving much differently from Gregory of Tours, who when traveling donned about his neck a locket containing relics, and otherwise seemingly never left home without a bit of dust from the tomb of his alter ego, Martin?

In addition to acquiring prestige, some enchanters plied their trade to achieve socio-economic advancement. One career enchanter who established an influential clientele was Duke Guntram Boso's trusted diviner. The duke consulted her for a decade and more, and so she must have commanded a decent wage in exchange for her prophecies and expert advice.[186] The most materially successful *incantator* in the sources was the slave turned jewel-bedecked diviner from Verdun. That successful prognosticator was not about to allow Bishop Ageric's attempted exorcism to end her career. According to Gregory, when she departed from Ageric the diviner readily found refuge with Queen Fredegund.[187] Now there was a patron who could appreciate magic! It is unlikely that most enchanters enjoyed the "rags to riches" success of the Verdun *pithonissa*. But because many *incantatores* were of servile origin, perhaps it was not unrealistic for them at least to hope to achieve manumission after providing their masters with an extended period of faithful service and profit. Because Gregory always offered a hostile impression of Fredegund, one must regard his association of the queen with *maleficium* with some suspicion. But given that Merovingian courts were the most cosmopolitan settings in all of Gaul, perhaps with the exception of Arles, it would be unreasonable to think that enchanters could not

185. Greg. Tur., *Hist.* 9.6.
186. Guntram Boso's aforementioned consultation delivered to him while he was in sanctuary at Saint Martin's happened in 577. But Gregory related that the duke knew the diviner during the lifetime of King Charibert, who died in 567; Greg. Tur., *Hist.* 5.14.
187. Greg. Tur., *Hist.* 7.44.

realistically hope to secure patrons at such spots any less than, say, Italian poets. One hagiographer wrote that enchanters and augurers frequented King Chlothar I's royal banquets, and Hincmar of Reims imagined that magicians were present at Chlothar II's court.[188] But even if the few royal courts did welcome, or even somehow reward, talented enchanters, the number of such prominently placed persons would have been infinitesimal compared with the typical low-born, rural *incantator* whose healing and divinatory activities likely involved little more than a somewhat prestigious complement to his otherwise obligatory, mundane agricultural labors. Christian enchanters actively supplied the desperate demand, medical and otherwise, of the forsaken poor who subsisted throughout the Gallic countryside.[189] And urban ecclesiastics, suspicious of their motives, covetous of their clients, and bothered by their refusal to acknowledge the clerics' churches as the only proper locale to access the supernatural, were not about to stop them.

---

188. *Vita Vedasti* 8 (*MGH*, SRM 3, 422–23). At one banquet, Bishop Vedast of Arras embarrassed several magicians by making the sign of the cross and so causing them to spill their beer! Hincmar of Reims, *De divortio Lotharii et Tetbergae* (*PL* 125, 717–19).

189. Brown, *Poverty and Leadership*, writes that while urban privation was tempered by its proximity to the churches' "safety net," "[b]y contrast, real poverty, silent and untended, existed in the countryside."

CONCLUSION

CHAPTER NINE

Aristocratic authors, most of them clerics, controlled the written evidence for Gaul. Their sources projected visions for making and preserving a law and order, hierarchical Christian society. Meanwhile, makers of Salic law passed legislation that encouraged people of all ranks to look to the monarchy for privileges. Frankish kings sought to curtail establishment of a hereditary Gallic nobility, and toward this end, the Merovingians succeeded into the seventh century. Far from constituting a homogeneous group, Gallic aristocrats acted within multiple aristocracies distinguishable by region and behavior. Three important strategies by which aristocrats maintained and augmented local power were combining lands and resources through intermarrying with other elite families, acquiring high-level positions at court, and participating prominently at churches. Members of Gregory of Tours' family exemplify pursuit of each of these stratagems and reveal how the various aristocracies were not exclusive. The landed aristocrat Gregorius Attalus married the senatorial woman, Armentaria, by whom three children were born, and he acted as Count of Autun before becoming Bishop of Langres.[1] Gallic

---

1. Greg. Tur., *VP* 1–2; Heinzelmann, *Gregory of Tours: History and Society*, 17–19.

nobles were not limited to social strategizing inside a single region or subkingdom. Thus Gregory himself was the product of an Auvergnian father and Burgundian mother, while it was an Austrasian king who selected him to preside as metropolitan over a westward lying province, Lugdunensis Tertia. Ecclesiastical aristocrats such as Gregory composed most of the surviving literature for the Barbarian era, and these productions betray their authors' hopes for a society in which people of all social ranks would heed Christian leaders.

There was no single model for envisioning a Christian Gallic society. For example, Caesarius of Arles, heavily influenced by years spent at Lérins and by reliance upon Augustine's writings, promoted a text-based, monastic variety of piety intended for all Christians whose ears he could reach by disseminating model sermons. But the pieties that increasingly prevailed across Gaul were akin to that favored by Gregory of Tours, who promoted reverence for deceased saints.[2] Despite differences over particulars, ecclesiastical aristocrats imagined an orderly Christian society to include a stable, hierarchical social structure. Although powerful clerics frequently petitioned for the ransom of war captives, the liberation of slaves, and the release of prisoners, they did not oppose warfare in general, nor did they try to rid of slavery or the harsh incarceration system. Entering into clerical and ascetic communities afforded individuals what probably was the best chance to elude various difficulties such as the occasional marauding band of soldiers and the persistent brutality of secular slave masters. Churches and monasteries provided principal settings where magnates could perform social theater by acting as patrons and thereby building and consolidating local *potentia*. The blue-blooded Bordelais couple, Bishop Leontius and Placidina, erected and restored churches at Saintes to assert metropolitan authority in that city.[3] On the church walls, Venantius Fortunatus penned verses to ever remind those assembled in the edifices of the family of patrons to whom they should feel grateful for the opportunity to congregate there. Similarly, King Chlothar I looked to impress his kingdom's subjects, bishops

---

2. De Nie, "Caesarius of Arles and Gregory of Tours," 176–82.
3. Brennan, "The Image of the Merovingian Bishop," 125.

included, when he initiated the cult of Saint Medard by beginning construction of that holy man's church at Soissons.[4] In concert with the Merovingians, noble bishops gathered at royally sponsored synods and hammered out legislation that established urban clergies as the arbiters for proper Christian behavior. Prelates at the Council of Mâcon (585) issued a canon forbidding agricultural laborers from working on Sundays under pain of excommunication.[5] Similarly, Gregory of Tours and Fortunatus's solution for peasants caught in the act of tending fields on holy days was to invite them to return to good standing within a community by undergoing healing at a saint's basilica, through which process the paupers would become indebted to a holy patron. Churchmen sometimes secured clients of low rank by enacting ritual releases of prisoners, but the most common way they augmented a clientele beholden to saints was through healings. Gregory explained how people healed of blindness and paralysis by Saint Junianus of Limoges thereafter felt compelled to offer annual donations at their patron's basilica.[6]

According to late ancient systems of *patrocinium*, another way patrons bolstered their authority was through elevating protégés into higher occupational grades and social ranks. Thus, for example, six Merovingians who benefited from decades of dependable service from the agent Conda each interpreted the courtier's steadfastness as nobility, and he was welcomed to the *conviva regis*.[7] Similarly, Gregory of Tours repaid years of loyalty from his freeborn clerical disciple Plato by securing for him the bishopric at Poitiers, which office conferred nobility upon the holder.[8] But, of course, parvenus and others did not simply wait for patrons to grant social advancement; rather, many Gauls of middling and low status initiated, agitated, and persevered toward social improvement. Indeed, evidence from the sources indicates that Gallic society was very fluid. Furthermore, sources reveal how non-elites adopted strategies not dissimilar to those of aristocrats to rise socially and to secure

---

4. Greg. Tur., *Hist.* 4.19.
5. Council of Mâcon (585), c. 1.
6. Greg. Tur., *GC* 101.
7. Ven. Fort., *Carm.* 7.16.
8. Ven. Fort., *Carm.* 10.14.

local prestige. For example, the *ingenuus* father of Saint Leobardus expressed sentiments no different from those of Saint Gallus's aristocratic parents; both hoped to perpetuate their families' hold on sizeable properties by encouraging their children to marry advantageously.[9] Sidonius Apollinaris's wily client, the merchant Amantius, exhibited a talent for making an impression on the best possible patrons, and he fully established a lofty reputation by marrying into a wealthy family.[10] Similarly, Leudast, an upwardly mobile slave-turned-count married a woman from a prominent family of the Touraine and became an almost perpetual thorn in the side of Gregory of Tours.[11] The count's tenacious and bellicose character, plus his wealth and popularity among certain Tourangeaux and perhaps also an element of the Neustrian military, made it almost impossible for Chilperic and Fredegund to do away with him – almost. Another slave who achieved high status at court was the very educated lector Andarchius, who benefited mightily from his literary knowledge.[12]

Despite declining educational opportunities, literacy was not solely the reserve of aristocrats. Those who could show off some literary talent could benefit regardless of social station. Andarchius was acting no differently from Venantius Fortunatus when he displayed his literary skill before Duke Lupus and thereby gained access to the Austrasian court. Similarly, the Lombard Vulfolaic and the rural *ingenuus* Patroclus importantly acquired an education prior to attracting helpful patrons and going on to become leaders of ascetic communities.[13] Literacy was an attribute that Gallic aristocrats so admired, they perceived it to trump low birth and to confer an element of social respectability. Given evidence for so many late ancient physicians engaged in writing medical tomes and participating in literary circles, it is hard to imagine that literacy was not a prerequisite for becoming a physician in Gaul. Nobles such as Avitus of Vienne and Caesarius of Arles, friends

9. Greg. Tur., *VP* 6.1, 20.1.
10. Sid. Ap., *Ep.* 7.2.
11. Greg. Tur., *Hist.* 6.32.
12. Greg. Tur., *Hist.* 4.46.
13. Greg. Tur., *Hist.* 8.15, *VP* 9.1.

of the Bordeaux physician Helpidius, would have perceived mastery of language as a fitting complement to doctors' abilities to perform medical procedures such as phlebotomies and surgeries, which skills the powerful appreciated. While most doctors likely originated from *ingenuus* rank, even a physician of servile origin such as Marileifus could demand a high price for his expertise, and might become exceedingly wealthy.[14]

The examples of Leudast, Andarchius, Marileifus, and many others attest how Gauls beginning at the lower echelons of society needed not attune their lives to the imperceptible thrumming of a *longue durèe*. Rather, to achieve what they perceived would be meaningful lifestyles, they schemed and acted no differently from those originating at the upper end of society. From top to bottom, people played extant social systems and conditions to whatever advantage they could. For example, Gauls of every rank improved their lot by ostentatiously acting as church patrons. Thus the senatorial Gregory of Tours enlarged, refurbished, and rededicated the cathedral at Tours, repaired the basilica of Saint Martin, and built an adjacent baptistery; the *ingenuus* Aredius of Limoges erected several oratories in honor of Saints Martin and Julian about the Limagne; and an Auvernian peasant converted his hovel into a wooden oratory dedicated to Saint Saturninus.[15] Queens Clotild and Radegund became predominant religious figures at Tours and Poitiers, respectively, by founding convents, while the *ingenua* Monegund found solace at Tours, where she established a nunnery and joined the Tourangeaux clergy in promoting the *virtutes* of Saint Martin.[16] Similarly, the pauper Lupicinus enclosed himself within a cell at Lipidiacum and attracted a following of monks, although he relied upon a prominent matron for sustenance; and likewise, the slave-turned-monk Brachio founded several monasteries, but he depended mightily upon the generous support of the noblewoman Ranichild to do so.[17] According to the evidence regarding behaviors that lent themselves toward social improvement, there was no essential difference between the actions of aristocrats and

14. Greg. Tur., *Hist.* 7.25.
15. Greg. Tur., *Hist.* 10.28, 31, *GM* 47.
16. Greg. Tur., *Hist.* 2.43, 3.7, *VP* 19.2.
17. Greg. Tur., *VP* 12.3, 13.3.

"the rest." Indeed, the most significant disparity in pursuing opportunity appears to have been that between well-to-do *ingenui* and *pauperes*. For whereas people of *ingenuus* status and higher seemingly were able to follow socially advantageous stratagems of their own volition, paupers and slaves could proceed and succeed only with the consent and lasting support of patrons. Therefore, despite the presence of some behavioral constraints caused by social rank (e.g., paupers could not build the larger, more impressive church edifices that aristocrats and *ingenui* did), the similarity of pursuits among people trying to live meaningful lives and improve socially indicates that in fact there were no "two tiers," one elite and the other popular. In Barbarian Gaul, there was one culture in which all participated, each according to his means.

In town and countryside, powerful Christians dominated this single culture. Christianity was no "David" to the "Goliath" of an entrenched paganism, for by the Barbarian era, the age of mission in Gaul was long past.[18] Sometimes Christian aristocrats and peasants vied for control over potential new holy figures, but whenever such contests became spirited, the nobles usually won, as happened when the propertied *matrona* of Trézelle forcibly wrested the corpse of the holy recluse Lupicinus from peasants at Lipidiacum.[19] Otherwise, city dwelling ecclesiastics sometimes criticized certain activities, especially those of rural folk, which did not meet the clerics' criteria for proper conduct by belittling the behavior as "superstitious" and "pagan." For example, Caesarius of Arles deemed all wonder-workers besides himself and the priests who followed his design for appropriate healing techniques (i. e., prayer and anointing with holy oil) to be diabolically inspired, including clerics and religious who persisted in crafting ligatures and amulets.[20] In opposing magic-making priests, folk healers, diviners, and even relic-hawkers,

18. I derive the metaphors from Murray, "Missionaries and Magic in Dark-Age Europe," 93, who commented in reference to Flint's thesis on Christian magic that "the conversion of the Germanic kingdoms ... amounted to little more than the establishment of protected missionary stations. Christianity stood as David to Goliath." I contend that images of stalwart pagans and beleaguered Christian missionaries active within the Gallic interior simply do not correspond to the society in which Caesarius of Arles and Gregory of Tours participated.

19. Greg. Tur., *VP* 13.3.

20. Caes. Arel. *Serm.* 50.1 (*CCL* 103, 225), labeled the contrary clerics "the Devil's accomplices" (*adiutores diaboli*).

Caesarius was fighting a "one-man's battle" not against "popular habits" but against traditional behaviors that many people on all social levels practiced.[21] Gregory of Tours' personal involvement in episodes of dream interpretation, divination through the *sortes biblicae*, and healing with relics was mainstream to the culture from top to bottom.[22] More than Caesarius, Gregory allowed for greater latitude in imagining what constituted appropriate wonder-works; however, similarly to Caesarius, Gregory insisted that the only legitimate thaumaturges were those associated with established churches and clergies. For example, Gregory was pleased with the healing and liberating efforts of the suburban recluse Senoch, who accepted the office of priest and thereby acknowledged his proper place in the Tourangeaux clerical hierarchy.[23] But the bishop was less impressed with Anatolius, a slave of Bordeaux turned hermit who dwelt in a crypt.[24] When that young man began acting mad, he came to Tours, where Saint Martin successfully exorcized him. Apparently Gregory expected Anatolius to show the saint his gratitude by remaining in service at the basilica, but instead the youth scorned Martin's will and returned to his home city, where not surprisingly he reportedly again went insane. A more apposite recluse for Gregory was Patroclus, who cleansed demons from many possessed people who visited his cell at Mediocantus. Patroclus held the deaconate and founded a proper monastery at Colombier, and he was respectably educated, too![25] Unlike Senoch and Patroclus, and dissimilar to the thaumaturge Monegund, the peasant woman and would-be healer Leubella was not associated with a church. In an effort to initiate a career as a wonder-worker, she properly imagined how a vision of Saint Martin would legitimize her conduct.[26] But unfortunately she met up with Patroclus, who convinced her that the seemingly holy apparition had been the Devil, and

---

21. Quoting de Nie, "Caesarius of Arles and Gregory of Tours," 190.

22. As de Nie, ibid., 185–86, realized, healing, divinatory practices, and dreams had biblical as well as pagan precedents. For the era under consideration, such behaviors ought not to be characterized as "pagan" or the actors as "half-converted Christians."

23. Greg. Tur., *VP* 15.3.

24. Greg. Tur., *Hist.* 8.34.

25. Greg. Tur., *VP* 9.1–3.

26. Greg. Tur., *VP* 9.2.

so Leubella apparently quit what might have become a meaningful vocation. This story reflects how Gregory of Tours imagined rustics should comply with the designs of established clergy in rural parts.

However, I think that in actuality it would have been rare for prospective enchanters to accept interpretations that their vocation was without merit, or less inspired than that of clerics. Most probably were of a mind like the resourceful *pithonissa* of Verdun, who would not allow that her accommodating craft was the work of a demon.[27] *Incantatores* were not socially predominant on a par with urban clerical leaders and noble ascetics, nor were they necessarily as popular as some of the wonder-working religious operating from many dozens of rural ascetic retreats. But they realized that country people had a need for their useful ministrations, just as prominent urbane folk relied on physicians and saints.[28] Most rural healers were lay Christians not professionally attached to churches and shrines, but few among them would have followed the example of poor Leubella and acquiesced to a clerical competitor.

If bishops were fighting a losing battle to curtail indiscriminant access to the supernatural in the countryside, they used their spiritual authority to great effect in dominating the immediate environs of their cities. But bishops did not benefit simply by issuing threats of retribution by imaginary patron saints. Rather they cooperated with a variety of clients who assisted in making their churches the dominant cultural centers of Gaul. Consensus was a hard commodity to achieve or maintain in Gallic communities subject to sudden political changes and fraught with potentially contentious factions. Thus, after decades of distributing model sermons, the *pallium*-wearing bishop of Arles in the last years of his life scarcely held any political authority beyond his own city walls.

27. Greg. Tur., *Hist.* 7.44. It is unhelpful first to characterize the magical behaviors of Gallic peasants simply as crass survival strategies devoid of a compassionate intent and then to assert that these practices were inferior to the "religious" designs of prominent ecclesiastics. In countering Flint's use of the term "Christian magic" and in defending Caesarius and Gregory's wondrous behaviors as "biblically based" and "transformative," de Nie, "Caesarius of Arles and Gregory of Tours," 194–96, seems to insinuate such a contrast with non-elite wonder-workers presumably drawn from what she terms "the often only half-converted pagans" (p. 194).

28. Caesarius revealed that peasants tried to explain to him how enchanters healed them of poisonous snakebites. But the insensitive bishop apparently thought it safer for their souls that they die rather than consult folk healers; Caes. Arel. *Serm.* 54.3.

Meanwhile, at Tours the metropolitan Gregory over some twenty years consolidated his position as the dominant figure of his province. Late in life, he preached from a gleaming new cathedral, cooperated with a friendly count to effect occasional ritual releases of prisoners, and installed a loyal disciple on a cathedra situated beyond his own province. In order to get to this point, Gregory had to overcome kings desirous of taxing his churches' lands, a count eager to hold more local authority than he, and an element of his own clergy intent upon removing the Auvergnian interloper. As to his ability to survive and accomplish what he did, much credit goes to the repute of Saint Martin. But let us not forget the flesh and blood figures who like the bishop had their own stratagems to prosper socially through association with the saint. The *ingenua* healer Monegund presided over an urban ascetic community and credited her healing successes to Martin's power.[29] The freeman Senoch from his rural monastery healed peasants of snakebites, liberated prisoners, and amassed a crowd of humble clients loyal to himself and ultimately to Martin.[30] The pauper from Le Mans Sisulfus followed the advice of a distinguished looking vision of Martin and traveled to Tours while proclaiming the sinfulness of perjury, usury, and Sunday labor.[31] Last, but not least, numerous lesser clerics and *matricularii* manifested Martin's reputation for vengeance through their actions by meting wholesale slaughter upon a band of soldiers that defiled sanctuary and shed blood in the saint's basilica.[32] On a more diurnal level, these guardians earned their keep by reporting Martin's miracles to the bishop, fending off grave robbers, escorting the occasional puffed-up enchanter to the border of the diocese, and sheltering their episcopal patron from an aggressive count and overly ambitious high clerics. Along with urban prisoners and doctors and rural recluses and enchanters and a host of other Gallic *mediocres*, they converted a variety of opportunities into meaningful lives, all the while participating in a world without "two tiers."

29. Greg. Tur., *VP* 19.3.
30. Greg. Tur., *VP* 15.3–4.
31. Greg. Tur., *VM* 2.40.
32. Greg. Tur., *Hist.* 7.29.

BIBLIOGRAPHY

Primary Sources

ADALGISEL-GRIMO, *Testamentum*
Ed. by Wilhelm Levison. *Aus rheinischer und fränkischer Frühzeit: Ausgewählte Aufsätze von Wilhelm Levison*, 118–38. Düsseldorf: L. Schwann, 1948.

AMMIANUS MARCELLINUS, *Res Gestae*
Ed. with trans. by J. C. Rolfe. 3 vols. LCL. London: W. Heinemann; Cambridge, MA: Harvard University Press, 1963–69.

AREDIUS OF LIMOGES, *Testamentum sancti Aredii*
Ed. by J.-P. Migne. *PL* 71, 1143–50. Paris: J.-P. Migne, 1879.

AUGUSTINE OF HIPPO, *De Civitate Dei*
Ed. with trans. by William M. Green. 7 vols. LCL. London: W. Heinemann; Cambridge, MA: Harvard University Press, 1957–72.

AUGUSTINE OF HIPPO, *De Diversis Quaestionibus Octoginta Tribus*
Ed. by Almut Mutzenbecher. *CCL* 44A, 1–249. Turnholt: Brepols, 1975.

AVITUS OF VIENNE, *Epistulae* et *Homiliae*
Ed. by R. Peiper. *MGH*, AA 6. Berlin: Weidmann, 1883. Trans. by Danuta Shanzer and Ian Wood. *Avitus of Vienne: Letters and Selected Prose*. TTH 38. Liverpool: Liverpool University Press, 2002.

BAUDONIVIA, *Vita S. Radegundis*
Ed. by Bruno Krusch. *MGH*, SRM 2, 377–95. Hanover: Hahn, 1888.

BEDE, *Retractatio in Actus Apostolorum*
Ed. by M. L. W. Laistner. *Bedae venerabilis Expositio Actuum Apostolorum et Retractatio*, 93–146. Cambridge, MA: Medieval Academy of America, 1939.

BERTRAM OF LE MANS, *Testamentum*
Ed. by G. Busson and A. Ledru. *Actus Pontificum Cenomannis in urbe degentium*, 108. Le Mans: Au siège de la Société, 1901.

CAESARIUS OF ARLES, *Sermones*
Ed. by G. Morin. *CCL* 103–104. Turnholt: Brepols, 1953. Trans. by Mary Magdeline Mueller. *Saint Caesarius of Arles: Sermons*. 3 vols. New York: Fathers of the Church, 1956; Washington: Catholic University of America Press, 1964–73.

CAESARIUS OF ARLES, *Epistulae* and *Testamentum*
Ed. by G. Morin. *Sancti Caesarii opera omnia*. Vol. 2: *Opera varia*, 1–32, 283–89. Maretioli: G. Morin, 1942. Trans. by William E. Klingshirn, *Caesarius of Arles: Life, Testament, Letters*, 67–139. TTH 19. Liverpool: Liverpool University Press, 1994.

Capitularia Merowingica
Ed. by Alfred Boretius. *Capitularia regum Francorum*. *MGH*, LL sectio 2, 1, 1–23. Hanover: Hahn, 1883.

CASSIAN, JOHN, *Collationes*
Trans. by B. Ramsey. *John Cassian: Conferences*. Ancient Christian Writers 57. New York: Newman, 1997.

CASSIODORUS, *Chronica*
Ed. by T. Mommsen. *MGH*, AA 11, 109–61. Berlin: Hahn, 1894. Novus ed. 1961.

CASSIODORUS, *Variae*
Ed. by A. J. Fridh. *CCL* 96. Turnholt: Brepols, 1973.

Codex Theodosiana and *Sirmondianes Constitutiones*
Ed. by T. Mommsen, P. M. Meyer, and P. Krueger. *Theodosiani libri XVI cum constitutionibus sirmondianis*. Vol. 1, pars posterior. Berlin: Weidmann, 1905. Trans. by Clyde Pharr. *The Theodosian Code and Novels and the Sirmondian Constitutions*. Princeton, NJ: Princeton University Press, 1952.

Gallic Church Councils
Ed. C. Munier. *Conciliae Galliae*. *CCL* 148–148A. Turnholt: Brepols, 1963.

CONSTANTIUS OF LYONS, *Vita Germani ep. Autissiodorensis*
Ed. by W. Levison. *MGH*, SRM 7, 225–83. Hanover and Leipzig: Hahn, 1920.

CYPRIAN OF TOULON et al., *Vita Caesarii ep. Arelatensis*
Ed. by G. Morin. *Sancti Caesarii opera omnia.* Vol. 2: *Opera varia.* Maretioli: G. Morin, 1942. Trans. by William E. Klingshirn, *Caesarius of Arles: Life, Testament, Letters,* 9–65. TTH 19. Liverpool: Liverpool University Press, 1994.

Digesta
Ed. by T. Mommsen and P. Krueger, with trans. by A. Watson. *The Digest of Justinian.* 4 vols. Philadelphia: University of Pennsylvania Press, 1985.

Epistulae Austrasicae
Ed. by W. Gundlach. *MGH,* Epistulae 3, 110–53. Hanover: Hahn, 1892.

EUSEBIUS OF CAESAREA, *Ecclesiastical History*
Ed. and trans. by J. E. L. Oulton. LCL. 2 vols. London: W. Heinemann; Cambridge, MA: Harvard University Press, 1926–32.

FLODOARD, *Historia Remensis ecclesiae*
Ed. by J. Heller and G. Waitz. *MGH,* Scriptores 13, 409–599. Hanover: Hahn, 1881.

Formulae Turonenses
Ed. by K. Zeumer. *Formulae Merowingici et Karolini Aevi. MGH,* LL sectio 5, 128–58. Hanover: Hahn, 1886.

FREDEGAR, *Chronica*
Ed. by B. Krusch. *MGH,* SRM 2, 1–193. Hanover: Hahn, 1888.

GAIUS, *Institutes*
Ed. and trans. by F. Zulueta. *The Institutes of Gaius.* 2 vols. Oxford: Clarendon, 1946.

Gesta Piloti
Trans. by J. K. Elliott. *The Apocryphal New Testament: A Collection of Apocryphal Christian Literature in an English Translation,* 169–85. Oxford: Clarendon, 1993.

GREGORY OF TOURS, *Decem Libri Historiarum*
Ed. by B. Krusch and W. Levison. *Libri Historiarum X. MGH,* SRM 1.1. Hanover: Hahn, 1951. Trans. by Lewis Thorpe, *Gregory of Tours, History of the Franks.* Harmondsworth: Penguin, 1974.

GREGORY OF TOURS, *Libri Miraculorum*
Ed. by B. Krusch. *Miracula et Opera Minora. MGH,* SRM 1.2. Hanover: Hahn, 1885. Editio nova, 1969.

Liber de passione et de virtutibus S. Iuliani martyris
Ibid., 112–34. Trans. by Raymond Van Dam. *Saints and their Miracles in Late Antique Gaul,* 162–95. Princeton: Princeton University Press, 1993.

Liber de virtutibus S. Martini episcopi
Ibid., 134–211. Trans. by Raymond Van Dam. *Saints and their Miracles*, 199–303.

Liber in gloria confessorum
Ibid., 294–369. Trans. by Raymond Van Dam. *Gregory of Tours, Glory of the Confessors.*
TTH 5. Liverpool: Liverpool University Press, 1988.

Liber in gloria martyrum
Ibid., 34–111. Trans. by Raymond Van Dam. *Gregory of Tours, Glory of the Martyrs.*
TTH 4. Liverpool: Liverpool University Press, 1998.

Liber vitae patrum
Ibid., 211–94. Trans. by Edward James. *Gregory of Tours, Life of the Fathers.* TTH 1.
Liverpool: Liverpool University Press, 2d ed., 1991.

HINCMAR OF REIMS, *De divortio Lotharii et Tetbergae*
Ed. by J.-P. Migne. *PL* 125, 619–772. Paris: J.-P. Migne, 1852.

ISIDORE OF SEVILLE, *Etymologiae*
Ed. by W. M. Lindsay. *Isidori Hispalensis episcopi Etymologiarum sive Originum Libri XX.*
2 vols. Oxford: Clarendon, 1911.

JEROME, *Vita Hilarionis*
Trans. by C. White. *Early Christian Lives.* New York: Penguin, 1998.

JONAS, *Vita Vedasti ep. Atrebatensis*
Ed. by B. Krusch. *MGH*, SRM 3, 399–427. Hanover: Hahn, 1896.

The Jerusalem Bible
Garden City, NY: Doubleday, 1968.

Lex Romana Burgundionum
Ed. by L. R. de Salis. MGH, LL sectio 1, 2.1, 123–63. Hanover: Hahn, 1892.

Liber Constitutionum
Ed. by L. R. de Salis. MGH, LL sectio 1, 2.1, 29–116. Hanover: Hahn, 1892.

Lex Salica
Ed. by K. A. Eckhardt. *MGH*, LL sectio 1, 4.2. Hanover: Hahn, 1969.

Lex Visigothorum
Ed. by K. Zeumer. *MGH*, LL sectio 1, 1, 33–456. Hanover and Leipzig: Hahn,
1902.

LIBANIUS, *Orationes*
Ed. and trans. by A. F. Norman. 3 vols. LCL. London: W. Heinemann; Cambridge,
MA: Harvard University Press, 1969–77.

MARCELLUS OF BORDEAUX, *De Medicamentis Liber*
Ed. by M. Niedermann. Corpus Medicorum Latinorum 5. Leipzig and Berlin: B. G. Teubner, 1916.

MARIUS OF AVENCHES, *Chronica*
Ed. by T. Mommsen. *MGH*, AA 11, 225–39. Berlin: Weidmann, 1893.

MARTIAL, *Epigrams*
Ed. and trans. W. C. A. Ker. 2 vols. LCL. London: W. Heinemann; Cambridge, MA: Harvard University Press, 1919–20.

MARTIN OF BRAGA, *De Correctione Rusticorum*
Ed. by C. W. Barlow. *Martini episcopi Bracarensis opera omnia*, 159–203. New Haven, CN: Yale University Press, 1950.

MAXIMUS OF TURIN, *Sermones*
Ed. by A. Mutzenbacher. *CCL* 23. Turnholt: Brepols, 1962.

Pactus legis Salicae
Ed. by K. A. Eckhardt. *MGH*, LL sectio 1, 4.1. Hanover: Hahn, 1962. Trans. by Katherine Fischer Drew. *The Laws of the Salian Franks*, 57–167. Philadelphia: University of Pennsylvania Press, 1981.

Passio sancti Iuliani martyris
Ed. by B. Krusch. *MGH*, SRM 1.2, 429–31. Hanover: Hahn, 1885. Editio nova, 1969. Trans. by Raymond Van Dam, *Saints and their Miracles*, 196–98.

Passio [prima] Leudegarii ep. et martyris Augustodunensis
Ed. by B. Krusch. *MGH*, SRM 5, 282–322. Hanover and Leipzig: Hahn, 1910.

Passio Praeiecti ep. et martyris Arverni
Ed. by B. Krusch. *MGH*, SRM 5, 212–48. Hanover and Leipzig: Hahn, 1910.

PLINY, *Historia Naturalis*
Ed. and trans. by H. Rackham, W. H. S. Jones, and D. E. Eichholz. 10 vols. LCL. London: W. Heinemann; Cambridge, MA: Harvard University Press, 1938–62.

REMIGIUS OF REIMS, *Testamentum*
Ed. by B. Krusch. *MGH*, SRM 3, 336–47. Hanover: Hahn, 1896.

RURICIUS OF LIMOGES, *Epistulae*
Ed. by A. Engelbrecht. *CSEL* 21, 349–442. Vienna: C. Geroldi, 1891. Trans. by Ralph W. Mathisen. *Ruricius of Limoges and Friends: A Collection of Letters from Visigothic Gaul*. TTH 30. Liverpool: Liverpool University Press, 1999.

SALVIAN OF MARSEILLES, *De gubernatione Dei*
Ed. by F. Pauly. *CSEL* 8, 1–200. Vienna: C. Geroldi, 1883.

De septem ordinibus ecclesiae
Ed. by J.-P. Migne. *PL* 30, 148–62. Paris: J.-P. Migne, 1846.

SIDONIUS APOLLINARIS, *Carmina et epistulae*
Ed. and trans. by W. B. Anderson. 2 vols. LCL. London: W. Heinemann; Cambridge,
MA: Harvard University Press, 1936–65.

Statuta ecclesiae antiqua
Ed. by C. Munier. *Les Statuta Ecclesiae Antiqua: Édition – Études critiques.* Paris:
Presses Universitaires de France, 1960.

SUETONIUS, *De vita caesarum*
Ed. and trans. by J. C. Rolfe. 2 vols. LCL. London: W. Heinemann; Cambridge, MA:
Harvard University Press, 1970–79.

SULPICIUS SEVERUS, *Chronica, Dialogi, Vita sancti Martini*
Ed. by C. Halm. *CSEL* 1. Vienna: C. Geroldi, 1866.

VENANTIUS FORTUNATUS, *Carminum libri I-X* and *Appendices*
Ed. by F. Leo. *Opera Poetica. MGH*, AA 4.1, 1–292. Berlin: Weidemann, 1881. Trans.
by Judith George. *Venantius Fortunatus: Personal and Political Poems.* TTH 23.
Liverpool: Liverpool University Press, 1995.

VENANTIUS FORTUNATUS, *Vita S. Martini Libri IV*
Ed. by F. Leo. *Opera Poetica. MGH*, AA 4.1, 293–370. Berlin: Weidemann, 1881.

VENANTIUS FORTUNATUS, *Prose Vitae*
Ed. by F. Leo. *Opera Pedestria. MGH*, AA 4.2. Berlin: Weidemann, 1885.

Vita Albini ep. Andegavensis, ibid., 27–33.
Vita Germani ep. Parisiensis, ibid., 11–27.
Vita Hilarii ep. Pictavensis, ibid., 1–7.
Vita Marcelli ep. Parisiensis, ibid., 49–54.
Vita S. Radegundis, ibid., 38–49.

VERUS OF ORANGE, *Vita Eutropii ep. Arausicani*
Ed. by P. Varin. *Vie de S. Eutrope. Bulletin du Comité Historique des Monuments Ecrits
de l'Histoire de France* 1 (1849): 52–64.

Vita Boniti ep. Arverni
Ed. by B. Krusch. *MGH*, SRM 6, 119–39. Hanover: Hahn, 1913.

Vita S. Clotildis
Ed. by B. Krusch. *MGH*, SRM 2, 341–48. Hanover: Hahn, 1888.

Vita Eligii ep. Noviomagensis
Ed. by B. Krusch. *MGH*, SRM 4, 634–741. Hanover and Leipzig: Hahn, 1902.

Vita Gaugerici ep. Camaracensis
Ed. by B. Krusch. *MGH*, SRM 3, 649–58. Hanover: Hahn, 1896.

Vita Genovefae virginis Parisiensis
Ed. by B. Krusch. *MGH*, SRM 3, 204–38. Hanover: Hahn, 1896.

Vita Iuniani confessoris Commodoliacensis
Ed. by B. Krusch. *MGH*, SRM 3, 376–79. Hanover: Hahn, 1896.

Vitae patrum Emeretensium
Ed. and trans. by J. N. Garvin. Washington, DC: The Catholic University of America Press, 1946.

Vita Iurensium patrum
Ed. and French trans. by F. Martine. *Vie des pères du Jura. SC* 142. Paris: Cerf, 1968.

Vita Rusticulae sive Marciae abbatissae Arelatensis
Ed. by B. Krusch. *MGH*, SRM 4, 337–51. Hanover and Leipzig: Hahn, 1902.

Vita Severini abbatis Acaunensis
Ed. by B. Krusch. *MGH*, SRM 3, 166–70. Hanover: Hahn, 1896.

Secondary Material

ABEL, ANNE-MARIE. "La pauvreté dans la pensée et la pastorale de Saint Césaire d'Arles." In *Études sur l'Histoire de la Pauvreté (Moyen Age-XVIe siècle)*, 2 vols., ed. Michel Mollat, 1: 111–21. Paris: Publications de la Sarbonne, 1974.

AMORY, PATRICK. "Ethnographic Rhetoric, Aristocratic Attitudes and Political Allegiance in Post-Roman Gaul." *Klio* 76 (1994): 438–53.

AMORY, PATRICK. "Names, Ethnic Identity, and Community in Fifth- and Sixth-Century Burgundy." *Viator* 25 (1994): 1–30.

ARJAVA, ANTTI. "The Survival of Roman Family Law after the Barbarian Settlements." In *Law, Society and Authority in Late Antiquity*, ed. Ralph W. Mathisen, 33–51. Oxford and New York: Oxford University Press, 2001.

ARNHEIM, M. T. W. *The Senatorial Aristocracy in the Later Roman Empire*. Oxford: Clarendon, 1972.

ATKINS, MARGARET, and ROBIN OSBORNE, eds. *Poverty in the Roman World*. Cambridge: Cambridge University Press, 2006.

BACHRACH, BERNARD S. "The Education of the 'Officer Corps' in the Fifth and Sixth Centuries." In *La noblesse romaine et les chefs barbares du IIIe au VIIe siècle*, ed. Françoise Vallet and Michel Kazanski, 7–13. Paris: Association Française d'Archéologie Mérovingienne et Musée des Antiquités Nationales, 1995.

BACHRACH, BERNARD S. *The Anatomy of a Little War: A Diplomatic and Military History of the Gundovald Affair (568–586)*. Boulder, CO, San Francisco, and Oxford: Westview, 1994.

BACHRACH, BERNARD S. "Grand Strategy in the Germanic Kingdoms: Recruitment of the Rank and File." In *L'armée romaine et les barbares du IIIe au VIIe siècle*, ed. Françoise Vallet et Michel Kazanski, 1–9. Paris: Association Française d'Archéologie Mérovingienne et Musée des Antiquités Nationales, 1993.

BARB, A.A. "The Survival of Magic Arts." In *The Conflict between Paganism and Christianity in the Fourth Century*, ed. Arnaldo Momigliano, 100–25. Oxford: Clarendon, 1963.

BERGDOLT, KLAUS. "Die Kritik am Arzt im Mittelalter – Beispiel und Tendenzen vom 6. Bis zum 12. Jahrhundert." *Gesnerus* 48 (1991): 43–63.

BEUMANN, HELMUT. "Gregor von Tours und der Sermo rusticus." In *Spiegel der Geschichte. Festgabe für Max Braubach zum 10. April 1964*, ed. K. Repgen and S. Skalweit, 69–98. Münster: Aschendorff, 1964.

BIRABEN, J.-N., and **JACQUES LE GOFF**. "The Plague in the Early Middle Ages." In *Biology of Man in History*, ed. R. Forster and O. Ranum. Trans. E. Forster and P. M. Ranum, 48–80. Baltimore: Johns Hopkins University Press, 1975.

BLOCKLEY, R.C. "Doctors as Diplomats in the Sixth Century." *Florilegium* 2 (1980): 89–100.

BONNET, MAX. *Le Latin de Grégoire de Tours*. Paris: Hachette, 1890.

The Book of Saints. Compiled by the Benedictine monks of St. Augustine's Abbey, Ramsgate. Wilton, CT: Morehouse, 1989.

BOSL, KARL. "*Potens* und *pauper*: Begriffsgeschichtliche Studien zur gesellschaftlichen Differenzierung im frühen Mittelalter und zum 'Pauperismus' des Hochmittelalters." In *Alteuropa und die moderne Gesellschaft, Festschrift für Otto Brunner*, 60–87. Göttingen: Vandenhoeck & Ruprecht, 1963.

BOWDEN, WILL, ADAM GUTTERIDGE, and **CARLOS MACHADO**, eds. *Social and Political Life in Late Antiquity*. Leiden and Boston: Brill, 2006.

BOWERSOCK, GLEN W. "The Vanishing Paradigm of the Fall of Rome." In idem, *Select Papers on Late Antiquity*, 187–97. Bari: Edipuglia, 2000.

BRATTON, TIMOTHY. *Tours: From Roman "Civitas" to Merovingian Episcopal Center, c. 275–650 A.D.* Ph.D. diss., Philadelphia: Bryn Mawr College, 1979.

BRENNAN, BRIAN. "The Image of the Merovingian Bishop in the Poetry of Venantius Fortunatus." *Journal of Medieval History* 18 (1992): 115–39.

BRENNAN, BRIAN. "The Career of Venantius Fortunatus." *Traditio* 41 (1985): 49–87.

BRENNAN, BRIAN. "The Conversion of the Jews of Clermont in AD 576." *Journal of Theological Studies* 36 (1985): 321–37.

BRENNAN, BRIAN. "'*Episcopae*': Bishops' Wives Viewed in Sixth-Century Gaul," *Church History* 54 (1985): 311–23.

BRENNAN, BRIAN. "Senators and Social Mobility in Sixth-Century Gaul." *Journal of Medieval History* 11 (1985): 145–61.

BROWN, PETER. *The Rise of Western Christendom, Triumph and Diversity, A.D. 200–1000.* 2nd ed., Malden, MA and Oxford: Blackwell, 2003.

BROWN, PETER. *Poverty and Leadership in the Later Roman Empire.* Hanover, NH: Brandeis University Press/University Press of New England, 2002.

BROWN, PETER. *Power and Persuasion in Late Antiquity: Towards a Christian Empire.* Madison: University of Wisconsin Press, 1988.

BROWN, PETER. *Society and the Holy in Late Antiquity.* Berkeley, Los Angeles, and Oxford: University of California Press, 1982.

BROWN, PETER. *The Cult of the Saints: Its Rise and Function in Latin Christianity.* Chicago: University of Chicago Press, 1981.

BROWN, PETER. *The Making of Late Antiquity.* Cambridge, MA, and London: Harvard University Press, 1978.

BROWN, PETER. "Sorcery, Demons, and the Rise of Christianity from Late Antiquity into the Middle Ages." In *Witchcraft Confessions and Accusations*, ed. Mary Douglas, 17–45. London and New York: Tavistock, 1970.

BURY, J. B. *History of the Later Roman Empire from the Death of Theodosius I to the Death of Justinian.* 2 vols. New York: Dover, 1958.

BURY, J. B. *The Invasion of Europe by the Barbarians.* London: Macmillan, 1928.

CAMERON, ALAN, BRYAN WARD-PERKINS, and MICHAEL WHITBY, eds. *The Cambridge Ancient History*, Vol. 14, *Late Antiquity: Empire and Successors, A. D. 425–600.* Cambridge: Cambridge University Press, 2000.

CAMERON, AVERIL. "History and the Individuality of the Historian." In *The Past before Us: The Challenge of Historiographies of Late Antiquity*, ed. Carole Straw and Richard Lim, 69–77. Paris: Brepols, 2005.

CAMERON, AVERIL, ed., *Fifty Years of Prosopography: The Later Roman Empire, Byzantium, and Beyond*, Proceedings of the British Academy 118. Oxford: Oxford University Press, 2003.

CAMERON, AVERIL. *The Mediterranean World in Late Antiquity, AD 395–600.* London and New York: Routledge Press, 1993.

CHARLES-EDWARDS, T. M. "Law in the Western Kingdoms between the Fifth and Seventh Century." In *The Cambridge Ancient History*, Vol. 14, *Late Antiquity: Empire and Successors, A.D. 425–600*, ed. Alan Cameron, Bryan Ward-Perkins, and Michael Whitby, 260–87. Cambridge: Cambridge University Press, 2000.

CLARK, ELIZABETH. *History, Theory, Text: Historians and the Linguistic Turn.* Cambridge, MA, and London: Harvard University Press, 2004.

COLLINS, RICHARD. "Observations on the Form, Language and Public of the Prose Biographies of Venantius Fortunatus in the Hagiography of Merovingian Gaul." In *Columbanus and Merovingian Monasticism*, ed. H. B. Clarke and M. Brennan. Oxford: BAR, 1981,

CORBETT, JOHN H. "*Praesentium signorum munera*: The Cult of the Saints in the World of Gregory of Tours." *Florilegium* 5 (1983): 44–61.

CORBETT, JOHN H. "The Saint as Patron in the Works of Gregory of Tours." *Journal of Medieval History* **7** (1981): 1–13.

DALTON, O. M. *The History of the Franks, by Gregory of Tours.* 2 vols. Oxford: Clarendon, 1927.

DE NIE, GISELLE. "Caesarius of Arles and Gregory of Tours: Two Sixth-Century Gallic Bishops and 'Christian Magic.'" In *Cultural Identity and Cultural Integration: Ireland and Europe in the Early Middle Ages*, ed. Doris Edel, 170–96. Portland, OR: Four Courts, 1995.

DE NIE, GISELLE. *Views from a Many-Windowed Tower: Studies of Imagination in the Works of Gregory of Tours.* Amsterdam: Rodopi, 1987.

DE NIE, GISELLE. "The Spring, the Seed and the Tree: Gregory of Tours on the Wonders of Nature." *Journal of Medieval History* **11** (1985): 89–135.

DICKIE, MATTHEW W. *Magic and Magicians in the Greco-Roman World.* London and New York: Routledge, 2001.

DILL, SAMUEL. *Roman Society in Gaul in the Merovingian Age.* London: Macmillan, 1926.

DREW, KATHERINE FISCHER. *The Laws of the Salian Franks.* Philadelphia: University of Pennsylvania Press, 1981.

DRINKWATER, JOHN F., and **HUGH ELTON,** eds., *Fifth-Century Gaul: A Crisis of Identity?* Cambridge: Cambridge University Press, 1992.

DWELLE, FAY ROSS. "Medicine in Merovingian and Carolingian Gaul." Unpublished Ph.D. diss. Chapel Hill, NC: University of North Carolina, 1934.

EFFROS, BONNIE. *Caring for Body and Soul: Burial and Afterlife in the Merovingian World.* University Park, PA: Pennsylvania State University Press, 2002.

EFFROS, BONNIE. *Merovingian Mortuary Archaeology and the Making of the Early Middle Ages.* Berkeley and Los Angeles: University of California Press, 2002.

FAVROD, JUSTIN. *Histoire politique du royaume burgonde, 443–534.* Lausanne: Bibliothèque historique vaudoise, 1997.

FINN, RICHARD. "Portraying the Poor: Descriptions of Poverty in Christian Texts from the Late Roman Empire." In *Poverty in the Roman World*, ed. Margaret Atkins and Robin Osborne, 130–44. Cambridge: Cambridge University Press, 2006.

FLINT, VALERIE J. "The Demonisation of Magic and Sorcery in Late Antiquity." In *Witchcraft and Magic in Europe: Ancient Greece and Rome*, ed. Bengt Ankarloo and Stuart Clark, 277–348. Philadelphia: University of Pennsylvania Press, 1999.

FLINT, VALERIE I. J. *The Rise of Magic in Early Medieval Europe.* Princeton, NJ: Princeton University Press, 1991.

FLINT, VALERIE J. "The Early Medieval 'Medicus', the Saint – and the Enchanter." *Journal of the Society for the Social History of Medicine* **2** (1989): 127–45.

FONTAINE, JACQUES. "La culte des saints et ses implications sociologiques. Réflexions sur un récent essai de Peter Brown." *Analecta Bollandiana* **100** (1982): 17–41.

FOURACRE, PAUL, ed. *The New Cambridge Medieval History*, Vol. 1: *c. 500–700*. Cambridge: Cambridge University Press, 2005.

FOURACRE, PAUL. "Why Were So Many Bishops Killed in Merovingian Francia?" In *Bischofsmord im Mittelalter: Murder of Bishops*, ed. Natalie Fryde and Dirk Reitz, 13–35. Göttingen: Vandenhoeck and Ruprecht, 2003.

FOURACRE, PAUL. "Merovingian History and Merovingian Hagiography," *Past and Present* **127** (1990): 3–38.

FOX, ROBIN LANE. *Pagans and Christians in the Mediterranean World from the Second Century AD to the Conversion of Constantine*. New York: Alfred A. Knopf, 1986.

FRANKFURTER, DAVID. "Amuletic Invocations of Christ for Health and Fortune." In *Religions of Late Antiquity in Practice*, ed. Richard Valantasis, 340–43. Princeton, NJ, and Oxford: Princeton University Press, 2000.

GALINIÉ, HENRI. "Tours de Grégoire, Tours des archives du sol." In *Grégoire de Tours et l'espace gaulois*, ed. Nancy Gauthier and Henri Galinié, 67–80. Tours: Association Grégoire 94, 1997.

GARNSEY, PETER, and **CAROLINE HUMFRESS.** *The Evolution of the Late Antique World*. Cambridge, UK: Orchard Academic, 2001.

GARNSEY, PETER, and **RICHARD SALLER.** *The Roman Empire: Economy, Society and Culture*. Berkeley and Los Angeles: University of California Press, 1987.

GAUTHIER, NANCY. "From the Ancient City to the Medieval Town: Continuity and Change in the Early Middle Ages." In *The World of Gregory of Tours*, ed. Kathleen Mitchell and Ian Wood, 47–66. Leiden, Boston and Cologne: Brill, 2002.

GAUTHIER, NANCY. "Le paysage urbaine en Gaule au VIe siècle." In *Grégoire de Tours et l'espace gaulois*, ed. Nancy Gauthier and Henri Galinié, 49–63. Tours: Association Grégoire 94, 1997.

GEARY, PATRICK. "Barbarians and Ethnicity." In *Late Antiquity: A Guide to the Postclassical World*, ed. G. W. Bowersock, Peter Brown and Oleg Grabar, 107–29. Cambridge, MA, and London: Harvard University Press, 1999.

GEARY, PATRICK. *Before France and Germany: The Creation and Transformation of the Merovingian World*. New York: Oxford University Press, 1988.

GEARY, PATRICK. *Aristocracy in Provençe: The Rhone Basin at the Dawn of the Carolingian Age*. Philadelphia: University of Pennsylvania Press, 1986.

GEORGE, JUDITH W. *Venantius Fortunatus: A Latin Poet in Merovingian Gaul*. Oxford: Clarendon Press, 1992.

GEORGE, JUDITH W. "Portraits of Two Merovingian Bishops in the Poetry of Venantius Fortunatus," *Journal of Medieval History* 13 (1987): 189–205.

GERBERDING, RICHARD. "The Later Roman Empire." In *The New Cambridge Medieval History*, volume I, c. 500–c. 700, ed. Paul Fouracre, 13–34. Cambridge: Cambridge University Press, 2005.

GILLIARD, FRANK D. "The Senators of Sixth-Century Gaul." *Speculum* 54 (1979): 685–97.

GODDING, ROBERT. *Prêtres en Gaule mérovingienne*. Brussels: Société des Bollandistes, 2001.

GOFFART, WALTER. *Barbarian Tides: The Migration Age and the Later Roman Empire*. Philadelphia: University of Pennsylvania Press, 2006.

GOFFART, WALTER. *The Narrators of Barbarian History (A. D. 550–800): Jordanes, Gregory of Tours, Bede, and Paul the Deacon*. Princeton: Princeton University Press, 1988.

GOFFART, WALTER. *Barbarians and Romans (A.D. 418–584): The Techniques of Accommodation*. Princeton, NJ: Princeton University Press, 1983.

GRADOWICZ-PANCER, NIRA. "Femmes royales et violences anti-épiscopales à l'époque mérovingienne: Frédégonde et le meurtre de l'évêque Prétextat." In *Bischofsmord im Mittelalter: Murder of Bishops*, ed. Natalie Fryde and Dirk Reitz, 37–50. Göttingen: Vandenhoeck and Ruprecht, 2003.

GRADOWICZ-PANCER, NIRA. "De-Gendering Female Violence: Merovingian Female Honour as an 'Exchange of Violence.'" *Early Medieval Europe* 11 (2002) 1–18.

GRAF, FRITZ. *Magic in the Ancient World*. Trans. by Franklin Philip. Cambridge, MA, and London: Harvard University Press, 1999.

GRAUS, FRANTIŠEK. *Volk, Herscherr und Heiliger im Reich der Merowinger: Studien zur Hagiographie der Merowingerzeit*. Prague: Nakladatelství Československé akademie věd, 1965.

GRAUS, FRANTIŠEK. "Die Gewalt bei Anfängen des Feudalismus und die 'Gefangenenbefreiungen' der merowingischen Hagiographie." *Jahrbuch für Wirtschaftsgeschichte* (1961, teil I): 61–156.

GREY, CAM. "Salvian, the Ideal Christian Community and the Fate of the Poor in Fifth-Century Gaul." In *Poverty in the Roman World*, ed. Margaret Atkins and Robin Osborne, 162–82. Cambridge: Cambridge University Press, 2006.

GRIESER, HEIKE. *Sklaverei im spätantiken und frühmittelalterlichen Gallien (5.-7. Jh.). Das Zeugnis der christlichen Quellen*. Stuttgart: Franz Steiner, 1997.

GRIG, LUCY. "Throwing Parties for the Poor: Poverty and Splendour in the Late Antique Church." In *Poverty in the Roman World*, ed. Margaret Atkins and Robin Osborne, 145–61. Cambridge: Cambridge University Press, 2006.

HALSALL, GUY. "The Sources and Their Interpretation." In *The New Cambridge Medieval History*, volume I, c. 500–c. 700, ed. Paul Fouracre, 56–90. Cambridge: Cambridge University Press, 2005.

HALSALL, GUY. "Nero and Herod? The Death of Chilperic and Gregory's Writing of History." In *The World of Gregory of Tours*, ed. Kathleen Mitchell and Ian Wood, 337–50. Leiden, Boston, and Cologne: Brill, 2002.

HALSALL, GUY. "Childeric's Grave, Clovis' Succession, and the Origin of the Merovingian Kingdom." In *Society and Culture in Late Antique Gaul: Revisiting the Sources*, ed. Ralph W. Mathisen and Danuta Shanzer, 116–33. Aldershot and Burlington, VT: Ashgate, 2001.

HALSALL, GUY. "Social Identities and Social Relationships in Early Merovingian Gaul." In *Franks and Alemanni in the Merovingian Period: An Ethnographic Perspective*, ed. Ian Wood, 141–65. Woodbridge, Suffolk: Boydell, 1998.

HALSALL, GUY. "Violence and Society in the Early Medieval West: An Introductory Survey." In *Violence and Society in the Early Medieval West*, ed. Guy Halsall, 1–45. Woodbridge: Boydell, 1998.

HALSALL, GUY. "Towns, Societies and Ideas: The Not-So-Strange Case of Late Roman and Early Merovingian Metz." In *Towns in Transition: Urban Evolution in Late Antiquity and the Early Middle Ages*, ed. Neil Christie and Simon T. Loseby, 325–61. Aldershot: Scolar, 1996.

HALSALL, GUY. *Settlement and Social Organization: The Merovingian Region of Metz*. Cambridge: Cambridge University Press, 1995.

HANDLEY, MARK A. *Death, Society and Culture: Inscriptions and Epitaphs in Gaul and Spain, AD 300–750*. BAR International Series 1135. Oxford: Archaeopress, 2003.

HANDLEY, MARK A. "Beyond Hagiography: Epigraphic Commemoration and the Cult of the Saints in Late Antique Trier." In *Society and Culture in Late Antique Gaul: Revisiting the Sources*, ed. Ralph W. Mathisen and Danuta Shanzer, 187–200. Aldershot and Burlington, VT: Ashgate, 2001.

HARMENING, DIETER. *Superstitio. Überlieferungs- und theoriegeschichtliche Untersuchungen zur kirchlich-theologischen Aberglaubensliteratur des Mittelalters*. Berlin: Erich Schmidt, 1979.

HAYWARD, PAUL ANTHONY. "Demystifying the Role of Sanctity in Western Christendom." In *The Cult of Saints in Late Antiquity and the Middle Ages: Essays on the Contribution of Peter Brown*, ed., James Howard-Johnston and Paul Anthony Hayward, 115–42. Oxford and New York: Oxford University Press, 1999.

HEATHER, PETER. *The Fall of the Roman Empire: A New History of Rome and the Barbarians*. Oxford and New York: Oxford University Press, 2006.

HEATHER, PETER. "The Western Empire, 425–476." In *The Cambridge Ancient History*, Vol. 14, *Late Antiquity: Empire and Successors, A.D. 425–600*, ed. Alan Cameron, Bryan Ward-Perkins, and Michael Whitby, 1–32. Cambridge: Cambridge University Press, 2000.

HEATHER, PETER. *The Goths*. Oxford and Cambridge, MA: Blackwell, 1996.

HEINZELMANN, MARTIN. *Gregory of Tours: History and Society in the Sixth Century*. Trans. by Christopher Carroll. Cambridge: Cambridge University Press, 2001.

HEINZELMANN, MARTIN. "Heresy in Books I and II of Gregory of Tours' Historiae." In *After Rome's Fall: Narrators and Sources of Early Medieval History. Essays presented to Walter Goffart*, ed. A. C. Murray, 67–82. Toronto, Buffalo, and London: University of Toronto Press, 1998.

HEINZELMANN, MARTIN. *Bischofsherrschaft in Gallien: Zur Continuität römischer Führungeschichten vom 4. bis zum 7. Jahrhundert: soziale, prosopographische und bildungsgeschichtliche Aspecte*. Zurich and Munich: Artemis, 1976.

HEINZELMANN, MARTIN, and **JOSEPH-CLAUDE POULIN**. *Les Vies anciennes de sainte Geneviève de Paris: Études critiques*. Paris: Librairie Honoré Champion, 1986.

HEN, YITZHAK. "Paganism and Superstitions in the Time of Gregory of Tours: Une question mal posée!" In *The World of Gregory of Tours*, ed. Kathleen Mitchell and Ian Wood, 229–40. Leiden, Boston, and Cologne: Brill, 2002.

HEN, YITZHAK. *Culture and Religion in Merovingian Gaul, A.D. 481–751*. Leiden, New York and Cologne: Brill, 1995.

HERRIN, JUDITH. *The Formation of Christendom in Late Antiquity*. Princeton, NJ: Princeton University Press, 1987.

HERRIN, JUDITH. "Ideals of Charity, Realities of Welfare: The Philanthropic Activity of the Byzantine Church." In *Church and People in Byzantium*, ed. R. Morris, 151–64. Birmingham: Center for Byzantine, Ottoman and Modern Greek Studies, University of Birmingham, 1986.

HOPKINS, M. K. "Social Mobility in the Later Roman Empire: The Evidence of Ausonius." *Classical Quarterly* **11** (1961): 239–49.

HOWARD-JOHNSTON, JAMES, and **PAUL ANTHONY HAYWARD**, eds. *The Cult of Saints in Late Antiquity and the Middle Ages: Essays on the Contribution of Peter Brown*. Oxford and New York: Oxford University Press, 1999.

INNES, MATTHEW. *Introduction to Early Medieval Western Europe, 300–900: The Sword, the Plough and the Book*. London: Routledge, 2006.

INNES, MATTHEW. *State and Society in the Early Middle Ages: The Middle Rhine Valley, 400–1000*. Cambridge: Cambridge University Press, 2000.

JACKSON, RALPH. *Doctors and Diseases in the Roman Empire*. Norman, OK, and London: University of Oklahoma Press, 1988.

JAMES, EDWARD. *Gregory of Tours: Life of the Fathers*, 2d ed. TTH 1. Liverpool: Liverpool University Press, 1991.

JAMES, EDWARD. *The Franks*. Oxford and New York: Basil Blackwell, 1988.

JAMES, EDWARD. "'Beati pacifici': Bishops and the Law in Sixth-Century Gaul." In *Disputes and Settlements. Law and Human Relations in the West*, ed. J. Bossy, 25–46. Cambridge: Cambridge University Press, 1983.

JONES, A. H. M. *The Later Roman Empire, 284–602: A Social, Economic, and Administrative Survey*. 2 vols. Norman, OK: University of Oklahoma Press, 1964.

JONES, A. H. M., and J. R. MARTINDALE, eds. *The Prosopography of the Later Roman Empire*. Vol. 1, *A.D. 260–395*. Cambridge: Cambridge University Press, 1971.

JONES, ALLEN E. "Death and Afterlife in the Pages of Gregory of Tours." Forthcoming.

JONES, ALLEN E. "The Family of Geneviéve of Paris: Prosopographical Considerations." *Medieval Prosopography* 24 (2003): 73–80.

JONES, ALLEN E. *Gregory of Tours and His World: A Bibliography*. Online: http://spectrum.troy.edu/~ajones/gotbibl.html. 2002.

KASTER, ROBERT A. *Guardians of Language: The Grammarian and Society in Late Antiquity*. Berkeley and Los Angeles: University of California Press, 1986.

KEELY, AVRIL. "Arians and Jews in the *Histories* of Gregory of Tours." *Early Medieval Europe* 2 (1997): 103–15.

KESSLER, HERBERT L. "Pictorial Narrative and Church Mission in Sixth-Century Gaul." In *Pictorial Narrative in Antiquity and the Middle Ages*, ed. Herbert L. Kessler and Marianna Shreve Simpson, 75–91. Washington, DC: Gallery of Art, 1985.

KIECKHEFER, RICHARD. *Magic in the Middle Ages*. Cambridge: Cambridge University Press, 1989.

KITCHEN, JOHN. *Saints' Lives and the Rhetoric of Gender*. New York and Oxford: Oxford University Press, 1998.

KLINGSHIRN, WILLIAM E. "Defining the *Sortes Sanctorum*: Gibbon, Du Cange, and Early Christian Lot Divination." *Early Christian Studies* 10 (2002): 77–130.

KLINGSHIRN, WILLIAM E. *Caesarius of Arles: The Making of a Christian Community in Late Antique Gaul*. Cambridge: Cambridge University Press, 1994.

KLINGSHIRN, WILLIAM E. *Caesarius of Arles: Life, Testament, Letters*. TTH 19. Liverpool: Liverpool University Press, 1994.

KLINGSHIRN, WILLIAM E. "Charity and Power: Caesarius of Arles and the Ransoming of Captives in Sub-Roman Gaul." *Journal of Roman Studies* 75 (1985): 183–203.

LANDES, RICHARD. "Lest the Millennium Be Fulfilled: Apocalyptic Expectations and the Pattern of Western Chronography 100–800 CE." In *Use and Abuse of Eschatology in the Middle Ages*, ed. W. Verbeke, D. Verhelst, and A. Welkenhuysen, 137–211. Leuven: Leuven University Press, 1988.

LE BLANT, EDMUND, ed. *Inscriptions chrétiennes de la Gaule antérieures au VIIIe siècle*. Vol. 1. *Provinces gallicanes*. Paris: L'imprimerie imperiale, 1856.

LE GOFF, JACQUES. *Time, Work, and Culture in the Middle Ages*. Trans. by Arthur Goldhammer. Chicago: University of Chicago Press, 1980.

LESNE, ÉMILE. *Histoire de la propriété ecclésiastique en France aux époques romaine et mérovingienne*. Lille and Paris: R. Girard and H. Champion, 1910.

LIEBESCHUETZ, WOLF. "Violence in the Barbarian Successor Kingdoms." In *Violence in Late Antiquity: Perceptions and Practices*, ed. H. A. Drake, 37–46. Aldershot and Burlington, VT: Ashgate, 2006.

LIFSHITZ, FELICE. "Apostolicity Theses in Gaul: The Histories of Gregory and the 'Hagiography' of Bayeux." In *The World of Gregory of Tours*, ed. Kathleen Mitchell and Ian Wood, 211–28. Leiden, Boston, and Cologne: Brill, 2002.

LIFSHITZ, FELICE. "Beyond Positivism and Genre: 'Hagiographical' Texts as Historical Narrative." *Viator* 25 (1994): 95–114.

LITTLE, LESTER K., "Life and Afterlife of the First Plague Pandemic." In *Plague and the End of Antiquity: The Pandemic of 541–750*, ed. Lester K. Little, 3–32. Cambridge: Cambridge University Press, 2007.

LORREN, CLAUDE, and PATRICK PÉRIN. "Images de la Gaule rurale au VIe siècle." In *Grégoire de Tours et l'espace gaulois*, ed. Nancy Gauthier and Henri Galinié, 93–109. Tours: Association Grégoire 94, 1997.

LOSEBY, SIMON T. "Gregory's Cities: Urban Functions in Sixth-Century Gaul." In *Franks and Alemanni in the Merovingian Period: An Ethnographic Perspective*, ed. Ian Wood, 239–70. Woodbridge, Suffolk: Boydell, 1998.

LOSEBY, SIMON T. "Marseille and the Pirenne Thesis, I: Gregory of Tours, the Merovingian Kings, and 'Un Grand Port.'" In *The Sixth Century: Production, Distribution and Demand*, TRW 3, ed. Richard Hodges and William Bowden, 203–29. Leiden, Boston, and Cologne: Brill, 1998.

LUCK, GEORG. *Arcana Mundi: Magic and the Occult in the Greek and Roman Worlds, A Collection of Ancient Texts*, 2nd ed. Baltimore and London: Johns Hopkins University Press, 2006.

LUCK, GEORG. "Witches and Sorcerers in Classical Literature." In *Witchcraft and Magic in Europe: Ancient Greece and Rome*, ed. Bengt Ankarloo and Stuart Clark, 91–158. Philadelphia: University of Pennsylvania Press, 1999.

MacGONAGLE, SARA HANSELL. *The Poor in Gregory of Tours: A Study of the Attitude of Merovingian Society Towards the Poor, as Reflected in the Literature of the Time*. Ph.D. diss. New York: Columbia University, 1936.

MacMULLEN, RAMSAY. *Christianity and Paganism from the Fourth to Eighth Century*. New Haven: Yale University Press, 1997.

MARTINDALE, J. R., ed. *The Prosopography of the Later Roman Empire*. Vol. 3, *A.D. 527–641*. Cambridge: Cambridge University Press, 1992.

MARTINDALE, J. R., ed. *The Prosopography of the Later Roman Empire*. Vol. 2, *A.D. 395–527*. Cambridge: Cambridge University Press, 1980.

MATHISEN, RALPH W. *People, Personal Expressions, and Social Relations in Late Antiquity*. 2 vols. Ann Arbor: University of Michigan Press, 2003.

MATHISEN, RALPH W. "The Letters of Ruricius of Limoges and the Passage from Roman to Frankish Gaul." In *Society and Culture in Late Antique Gaul: Revisiting the Sources*, ed. Ralph W. Mathisen and Danuta Shanzer, 101–15. Aldershot and Burlington, VT: Ashgate, 2001.

MATHISEN, RALPH W. "La base de données biographique pour l'Antiquité tardive." In *Onomastique et Parenté dans l'Occident médiéval*, ed. K. S. B. Keats-Rohan and

C. Settipani, 262–66. Oxford: Occasional Publications of the Unit for Prosopographical Research, 2000.

MATHISEN, RALPH W. *Ruricius of Limoges and Friends: A Collection of Letters from Visigothic Gaul.* TTH 30. Liverpool: Liverpool University Press, 1999.

MATHISEN, RALPH W. *Roman Aristocrats in Barbarian Gaul: Strategies for Survival in an Age of Transition.* Austin: University of Texas Press, 1993.

MATHISEN, RALPH W. "Creating and Using a Biographical Database for Late Antiquity." *History Microcomputer Review* **5.2** (1989): 7–22.

MATHISEN, RALPH W. *Ecclesiastical Factionalism and Religious Controversy in Fifth-Century Gaul.* Washington, D.C.: Catholic University Press, 1989.

MATHISEN, RALPH W. "The Family of Georgius Florentius Gregorius and the Bishops of Tours." *Medievalia et Humanistica* **12** (1984): 83–95.

MATHISEN, RALPH W. *The Ecclesiastical Aristocracy of Fifth-Century Gaul: A Regional Analysis of Family Structure.* PhD diss. University of Wisconsin, 1979. Repr. Ann Arbor, MI: University Microfilms, 1980.

MATHISEN, RALPH W., and DANUTA SHANZER, eds. *Society and Culture in Late Antique Gaul: Revisiting the Sources.* Aldershot and Burlington, VT: Ashgate, 2001.

MATHISEN, RALPH W., and HAGITH SIVAN, eds. *Shifting Frontiers in Late Antiquity.* Aldershot and Burlington, VT: Ashgate, 1996.

MATTHEWS, JOHN W. *Western Aristocracies and Imperial Court, A.D. 364–425.* Oxford: Clarendon, 1975.

McDERMOTT, WILLIAM. "Felix of Nantes: A Merovingian Bishop." *Traditio* (1975): 1–24.

McGINN, BERNARD. *Visions of the End: Apocalyptic Traditions in the Middle Ages.* New York: Columbia University Press, 1998.

MEENS, ROB. "The Sanctity of the Basilica of St. Martin: Gregory of Tours and the Practice of Sanctuary in the Merovingian Period." In *Texts and Identities in the Early Middle Ages*, ed. Richard Corradini, Rob Meens, Christina Pössel, and Philip Shaw, 275–88. Vienna: Österreichischen Akademie der Wissenschaften, 2006.

MEENS, ROB. "Reforming the Clergy: A Context for the Use of the Bobbio Penitential." In *The Bobbio Missal: Liturgy and Religious Culture in Merovingian Gaul*, ed. Yitzhak Hen and Rob Meens, 154–67. Cambridge: Cambridge University Press, 2004.

MEENS, ROB. "Magic and the Early Medieval World View." In *The Community, the Family and the Saint*, ed. J. Hilland and M. Swan, 285–95. Turnholt: Brepols, 1998.

MITCHELL, KATHLEEN. "Saints and Public Christianity in the *Historiae* of Gregory of Tours." In *Religion, Culture and Society in the Early Middle Ages*, ed. T. F. X. Noble and J. J. Contreni, 77–94. Kalamazoo, MI: Institute of Medieval Studies, 1983.

MITCHELL, KATHLEEN. *History and Christian Society in Sixth-Century Gaul: An Historiographical Analysis of Gregory of Tours' Decem Libri Historiarum*. Ph.D. Diss.: Michigan State University, 1982.

MITCHELL, STEPHEN. *A History of the Later Roman Empire, AD 284–641: The Transformation of the Ancient World*. Malden and Oxford: Blackwell, 2007.

MOLLAT, MICHEL. *The Poor in the Middle Ages: An Essay in Social History*, trans. by Arthur Goldhammer. New Haven, CT: Yale University Press, 1986.

MOREIRA, ISABEL. *Dreams, Visions, and Spiritual Authority in Merovingian Gaul*. Ithaca, NY, and London: Cornell University Press, 2001.

MURRAY, ALAN V. "Prosopography." In *Palgrave Advances in the Crusades*, ed. Helen Nicholson, 109–29. Basingstoke and New York: Palgrave Macmillan, 2005.

MURRAY, ALEXANDER. "Missionaries and Magic in Dark-Age Europe." In *Debating the Middle Ages: Issues and Readings*, ed. Barbara Rosenwein, 92–104. Malden, MA, and Oxford: Blackwell, 1998.

MURRAY, ALEXANDER. "Peter Brown and the Shadow of Constantine." *Journal of Roman Studies* **73** (1983): 191–203.

MUSSET, LUCIEN. *The Germanic Invasions: The Making of Europe. A.D. 400–600*. Trans. by Edward and Columba James. University Park, PA: Pennsylvania State University Press, 1975.

NOBLE, THOMAS F. X., and THOMAS HEAD, eds. *Soldiers of Christ: Saints and Saints Lives from Late Antiquity and the Early Middle Ages*. University Park, PA: Pennsylvania State University Press, 1995.

NUTTON, VIVIAN. "*Archiatri* and the Medical Profession in Antiquity." *Papers from the British School at Rome* **45** (1977): 191–226, plates 31–32.

OSBORNE, ROBIN. "Introduction: Roman Poverty in Context." In *Poverty in the Roman World*, ed. Margaret Atkins and Robin Osborne, 1–20. Cambridge: Cambridge University Press, 2006.

PANCER, NIRA. *Sans peur et sans vergogne. De l'honneur et des femmes aux premiers temps mérovingiens*. Paris: Albin Michel, 2001.

PEARSON, KATHY. "Salic Law and Barbarian Diet." In *Law, Society and Authority in Late Antiquity*, ed. Ralph W. Mathisen, 272–85. Oxford and New York: Oxford University Press, 2001.

PÉRIN, PATRICK. "Settlements and Cemeteries in Merovingian Gaul." In *The World of Gregory of Tours*, ed. Kathleen Mitchell and Ian Wood, 67–98. Leiden, Boston, and Cologne: Brill, 2002.

PETERSEN, JOAN M. "Dead or Alive? The Holy Man as Healer in East and West in the Late Sixth Century." *Journal of Medieval History* **9** (1983): 91–98.

PIETRI, LUCE. *La ville de Tours du IVe au VIe siècle: naissance d'une cité chrétienne*. Rome: École française de Rome, 1983.

POHL, WALTER. "Perceptions of Barbarian Violence." In *Violence in Late Antiquity: Perceptions and Practices*, ed. H. A. Drake, 15–26. Aldershot and Burlington, VT: Ashgate, 2006.

POHL, WALTER. "The Construction of Communities and the Persistence of Paradox: An Introduction." In *The Construction of Communities in the Early Middle Ages*, TRW 12, ed. Richard Corradini, Max Diesenberger, and Helmut Reimitz, 1–15. Leiden and Boston: Brill, 2003.

POHL, WALTER, ed. *Kingdoms of the Empire: The Integration of Barbarians in Late Antiquity*, TRW 1. Leiden: Brill, 1997.

POHL, WALTER, with **HELMUT REIMITZ**, eds. *Strategies of Distinction: The Construction of Ethnic Communities, 300–800*, TRW 2. Leiden: Brill, 1998.

PRATSCH, THOMAS. "Exploring the Jungle: Hagiographical Literature between Fact and Fiction." In *Fifty Years of Prosopography: The Later Roman Empire, Byzantium, and Beyond*, Proceedings of the British Academy 118, ed. Averil Cameron, 59–72. Oxford: Oxford University Press, 2003.

RAPP, CLAUDIA. *Holy Bishops in Late Antiquity: The Nature of Christian Leadership in an Age of Transition*. Berkeley and Los Angeles: University of California Press, 2005.

REIMITZ, HELMUT. "Social Networks and Identities in Frankish Historiography. New Aspects of the Textual History of Gregory of Tours' *Historiae*." In *The Construction of Communities in the Early Middle Ages: Texts, Resources and Artefacts*, TRW 12, ed. Richard Corradini, Max Diesenberger, and Helmut Reimitz, 229–68. Leiden: Brill, 2003.

REYNOLDS, SUSAN. *Fiefs and Vassals: The Medieval Evidence Reinterpreted*. New York and Oxford: Oxford University Press, 1994.

RICHÉ, PIERRE. *Education and Culture in the Barbarian West, Sixth through Eighth Centuries*, trans. John J. Contreni. Columbia, SC: University of South Carolina Press, 1976.

RIDDLE, JOHN. "Theory and Practice in Medieval Medicine." *Viator* **5** (1974): 157–84.

ROBERTS, MICHAEL. "Venantius Fortunatus' Elegy on the Death of Galswintha (*Carm* 6.5)." In *Society and Culture in Late Antique Gaul: Revisiting the Sources*, ed. Ralph W. Mathisen and Danuta Shanzer, 298–312. Aldershot and Burlington, VT: Ashgate, 2001.

ROSENWEIN, BARBARA. *Emotional Communities in Early Medieval Europe*. Ithaca, NY, and London: Cornell University Press, 2006.

ROSENWEIN, BARBARA. "Inaccessible Cloisters: Gregory of Tours and Episcopal Exemption." In *The World of Gregory of Tours*, ed. Kathleen Mitchell and Ian Wood, 181–209. Leiden, Boston, and Cologne: Brill, 2002.

ROUCHE, MICHEL. "La matricule des pauvres: Évolution d'une inscription de charité du Bas Empire jusqu'à la fin du Haut Moyen Age." In *Études sur l'Histoire* *de la Pauvreté (Moyen Age-XVIe siècle)*, 2 vols., ed. Michel Mollat, 1: 83–110. Paris: Publications de la Sarbonne, 1974.

ROUSELLE, ALINE. "From Sanctuary to Miracle-Worker: Healing in Fourth-Century Gaul." In *Ritual, Religion, and the Sacred*, ed. Robert Forster and Orest Ranum, trans. Elborg Forster, 95–127. Baltimore and London: Johns Hopkins University Press, 1982.

SALZMAN, MICHELE R. "Elite Realities and Mentalités: The Making of a Western Christian Aristocracy." In *Élites in Late Antiquity, Arethusa* 33.3, ed. Michele R. Salzman and Claudia Rapp, 347–62. Baltimore: Johns Hopkins University Press, 2000.

SALZMAN, MICHELE R., and **CLAUDIA RAPP**, eds. *Élites in Late Antiquity, Arethusa* 33.3. Baltimore: Johns Hopkins University Press, 2000.

SAMSON, ROSS. "Slavery, the Roman Legacy." In *Fifth-Century Gaul: A Crisis of Identity?*, ed. John Drinkwater and Hugh Elton, 217–27. Cambridge: Cambridge University Press, 1992.

SAMSON, ROSS. "The Merovingian Nobleman's Home: Castle or Villa?" *Journal of Medieval History* **13** (1987): 287–315.

SCHACHNER, LUKAS AMADEUS. "Social Life in Late Antiquity: A Bibliographic Essay." In *Social and Political Life in Late Antiquity*, ed. W. Bowden, A. Gutteridge and C. Machado, 41–93. Leiden and Boston: Brill, 2006.

SCHEIBELREITER, GEORG. "Church Structure and Organisation." In *The New Cambridge Medieval History*, volume I, *c. 500–c. 700*, ed. Paul Fouracre, 675–709. Cambridge: Cambridge University Press, 2005.

SCHNEIDER, JOHANNES. "Die Darstellung der Pauperes in den Historiae Gregors von Tours: Ein Beitrag zur sozialökonomischen Struktur Galliens im 6. Jahrhundert." *Jahrbuch für Wirtschaftsgeschichte* (1966, teil 4): 57–74.

SETTIPANI, CHRISTIAN. "L'apport de l'onomastique dans l'étude des généologies carolingiennes." In *Onomastique et Parenté dans l'Occident médiéval*, ed. K. S. B. Keats-Rohan and C. Settipani, 185–229. Oxford: Occasional Publications of the Unit for Prosopographical Research, 2000.

SHANZER, DANUTA. "Gregory of Tours and Poetry: Prose into Verse and Verse into Prose." In *Aspects of the Language of Latin Prose*, ed. T. Reinhardt, M. Laidge, and J. N. Adams, 303–19. Oxford and New York: Oxford University Press, 2005.

SHANZER, DANUTA. "So Many Saints – So Little Time: The *Libri Miraculorum* of Gregory of Tours." *Journal of Medieval Latin* **13** (2003): 19–60.

SHANZER, DANUTA. "Laughter and Humour in the Early Medieval Latin West." In *Humour, History and Politics in Late Antiquity and the Early Middle Ages*, ed. Guy Halsall, 25–47. Cambridge: Cambridge University Press, 2002.

SHANZER, DANUTA. "Dating the Baptism of Clovis: The Bishop of Vienne vs the Bishop of Tours." *Early Medieval Europe* **7** (1998): 29–57.

SHANZER, DANUTA, and IAN WOOD. *Avitus of Vienne: Letters and Selected Prose*. TTH 38. Liverpool: Liverpool University Press, 2002.

SIVAN, HAGITH S. *Ausonius of Bordeaux: Genesis of a Gallic Aristocracy*. London and New York: Routledge, 1993.

SMITH, JULIA H. *Europe after Rome: A New Cultural History, 500–1000*. Oxford and New York: Oxford University Press, 2005.

STERNBERG, THOMAS. *Orientalium More Secutus: Räume und Institutionen der Caritas des 5. bis 7. Jahrhunderts in Gallien*. Münster: Aschendorffsche, 1991.

STRAW, CAROLE, and RICHARD LIM, eds. *The Past before Us: The Challenge of Historiographies of Late Antiquity*. Paris: Brepols, 2005.

TARDI, DOMINIQUE. *Fortunat. Étude sur le dernier représentant de la poésie latine dans la Gaule mérovingienne*. Paris: Boivin, 1927.

THEUWS, FRANS. "Introduction: Rituals in Transforming Societies." In *Rituals of Power: From Late Antiquity to the Early Middle Ages*, TRW 8, ed. Frans Theuws and Janet T. Nelson, 1–13. Leiden, Boston, and Cologne: Brill, 2000.

THEUWS, FRANS, and MONICA ALKEMADE. "A Kind of Mirror for Men: Sword Depositions in Late Antique Northern Gaul." In *Rituals of Power: From Late Antiquity to the Early Middle Ages*, TRW 8, ed. Frans Theuws and Janet T. Nelson, 401–76. Leiden, Boston, and Cologne: Brill, 2000.

THORPE, LEWIS. *Gregory of Tours: The History of the Franks*. Harmondsworth: Penguin, 1974.

TOCH, MICHAEL. "The Jews in Europe, 500–1050." In *The New Cambridge Medieval History*, volume I, *c. 500–c. 700*, ed. Paul Fouracre, 547–70. Cambridge: Cambridge University Press, 2005.

TREGGIARI, SUSAN. *Roman Freedmen during the Late Republic*. Oxford: Clarendon, 1969.

TROUT, DENNIS E. *Paulinus of Nola: Life, Letters, and Poems*. Berkeley, Los Angeles, and London: University of California Press, 1999.

ULLMANN, WALTER. "Public Welfare and Social Legislation in the Early Merovingian Councils." In *Councils and Assemblies*, ed. G. J. Cuming and L. G. Baker, 1–39. Cambridge: Cambridge University Press, 1971.

VAN DAM, RAYMOND. "Merovingian Gaul and the Frankish Conquest." In *The New Cambridge Medieval History*, volume I, *c. 500–c. 700*, ed. Paul Fouracre, 193–231. Cambridge: Cambridge University Press, 2005.

VAN DAM, RAYMOND. *Saints and their Miracles in Late Antique Gaul*. Princeton, NJ: Princeton University Press, 1993.

VAN DAM, RAYMOND. *Gregory of Tours, Glory of the Confessors*. TTH 5. Liverpool: Liverpool University Press, 1988.

VAN DAM, RAYMOND. *Gregory of Tours, Glory of the Martyrs*. TTH 4. Liverpool: Liverpool University Press, 1988.

VAN DAM, RAYMOND. "Images of Saint Martin in Late Roman and Early Merovingian Gaul." *Viator* **19** (1988): 1–27.

VAN DAM, RAYMOND. *Leadership and Community in Late Antique Gaul.* Berkeley and Los Angeles: University of California Press, 1985.

VAN OSSEL, PAUL. "Rural Impoverishment in Northern Gaul at the End of Antiquity: The Contribution of Archaeology." In *Social and Political Life in Late Antiquity*, ed. W. Bowden, A. Gutteridge, and C. Machado, 533–65. Leiden and Boston: Brill, 2006.

VIEILLARD-TROIEKOUROFF, MAY. *Les monuments religieux de la Gaule d'après les oeuvres de Grégoire de Tours.* Paris: Librairie Honoré Champion, 1976.

de WAHA, M. "À propos d'un article récent, quelques réflexions sur la matricule des pauvres." *Byzantion* **46** (1976): 354–67.

WALLACE-HADRILL, JOHN MICHAEL. *The Frankish Church.* Oxford: Clarendon, 1983.

WALLACE-HADRILL, JOHN MICHAEL. *The Long-Haired Kings and Other Studies in Frankish History.* New York: Barnes and Noble, 1962.

WARD, JOHN O. "Witchcraft and Sorcery in the Later Roman Empire and the Early Middle Ages: An Anthropological Comment." In *Witchcraft, Women and Society*, ed. Brian P. Levack, 1–16. New York and London: Garland, 1992.

WARD, JOHN O. "Women, Witchcraft and Social Patterning in the Later Roman Lawcodes." *Prudentia* **13** (1981): 99–118.

WARD-PERKINS, BRYAN. *The Fall of the Roman Empire and the End of Civilization.* Oxford and New York: Oxford University Press, 2005.

WEAVER, REBECCA HARDEN. *Divine Grace and Human Agency: A Study of the Semi-Pelagian Controversy.* Macon, GA: Mercer University Press, 1996.

WEBSTER, LESLIE, and MICHELLE BROWN, eds., *The Transformation of the Roman World, AD 400–900.* London and Berkeley: British Museum and University of California Press, 1997.

WEMPLE, SUZANNE FONAY. *Women in Frankish Society: Marriage and the Cloister, 500 to 900.* Philadelphia: University of Pennsylvania Press, 1981.

WICKHAM, CHRIS. *Framing the Early Middle Ages: Europe and the Mediterranean, 400–800.* Oxford and New York: Oxford University Press, 2005.

WOLFRAM, HERWIG. *History of the Goths.* Berkeley: University of California Press, 1988.

WOOD, IAN. "The Franks and Papal Theology, 550–660." In *The Crisis of the Oikoumene: The Three Chapters and the Failed Quest for Unity in the Sixth-Century Mediterranean*, ed. Celia Chazelle and Catherine Cubitt, 223–41. Turnhout: Brepols, 2007.

WOOD, IAN. "Liturgy in the Rhône Valley and the Bobbio Missal." In *The Bobbio Missal: Liturgy and Religious Culture in Merovingian Gaul*, ed. Yitzhak Hen and Rob Meens, 206–18. Cambridge: Cambridge University Press, 2004.

WOOD, IAN. "Deconstructing the Merovingian Family." In *The Construction of Communities in the Early Middle Ages: Texts, Resources and Artefacts*, TRW 12, ed. Richard Corradini, Max Diesenberger, and Helmut Reimitz, 149–71. Leiden: Brill, 2003.

WOOD, IAN. "The Individuality of Gregory of Tours." In *The World of Gregory of Tours*, ed. Kathleen Mitchell and Ian Wood, 29–46. Leiden, Boston, and Cologne: Brill, 2002.

WOOD, IAN. "Avitus of Vienne, The Augustinian Poet." In *Society and Culture in Late Antique Gaul: Revisiting the Sources*, ed. Ralph W. Mathisen and Danuta Shanzer, 263–77. Aldershot and Burlington, VT: Ashgate, 2001.

WOOD, IAN. *The Missionary Life: Saints and the Evengelisation of Europe, 400–1050*. Harlow, England, et al: Longman, 2001.

WOOD, IAN. "The Use and Abuse of Latin Hagiography in the Early Medieval West." In *East and West: Modes of Communication*, ed. Evangelos Chrysos and Ian Wood, 93–109. Leiden and Boston: Brill, 1999.

WOOD, IAN. "Conclusion: Strategies of Distinction." In *Strategies of Distinction: The Construction of Ethnic Communities, 300–800*, TRW 2, ed. Walter Pohl with Helmut Reimitz, 297–303. Leiden, Boston, and Cologne: Brill, 1998.

WOOD, IAN, ed. *Franks and Alamanni in the Merovingian Period: An Ethnographic Perspective*. Woodbridge, Suffolk, UK: Boydell, 1998.

WOOD, IAN. "Incest, Law and the Bible in Sixth-Century Gaul." *Early Medieval Europe* **7** (1998): 291–303.

WOOD, IAN. "Report: The European Science Foundation's Programme on the Transformation of the Roman World and Emergence of Early Medieval Europe." *Early Medieval Europe* **6** (1997): 217–27.

WOOD, IAN. *Gregory of Tours*. Bangor, Gwynedd, UK: Headstart History, 1994.

WOOD, IAN. *The Merovingian Kingdoms, 450–751*. New York: Longman, 1994.

WOOD, IAN. "The Code in Merovingian Gaul." In *The Theodosian Code*, ed. Jill Harries and Ian Wood, 161–77. Ithaca, NY: Cornell University Press, 1993.

WOOD, IAN. "The Secret Histories of Gregory of Tours." *Revue Belge de Philologie et d'Histoire* **71** (1993): 253–70.

WOOD, IAN. "Continuity or Calamity?: The Constraints of Literary Models." In *Fifth-Century Gaul: A Crisis of Identity?*, ed. John Drinkwater and Hugh Elton, 9–18. Cambridge: Cambridge University Press, 1992.

WOOD, IAN. "Forgery in Merovingian Hagiography." In *Fälschungen im Mittelalter* 5, MGH *Schriften* 33, 369–84. Hanover: Hahn, 1988.

WOOD, IAN. "The Audience of Architecture in Post-Roman Gaul." In *The Anglo-Saxon Church: Papers on History, Architecture, and Archaeology in Honour of Dr. H. M. Taylor*, ed. L. A. S. Butler and R. K. Morris, 74–79. London: Brill, 1986.

WOOD, IAN. "Disputes in Late Fifth- and Sixth-Century Gaul: Some Problems." In *The Settlement of Disputes in Early Medieval Europe*, ed. Wendy Davies and Paul Fouracre, 7–22. Cambridge: Cambridge University Press, 1986.

WOOD, IAN. "Gregory of Tours and Clovis." *Revue Belge de Philologie et d'Histoire* **63** (1985): 249–72.

WOOD, IAN. "The Ecclesiastical Politics of Merovingian Clermont." In *Ideal and Reality in Frankish and Anglo-Saxon Society. Studies Presented to J. M. Wallace-Hadrill*, ed. Patrick Wormald, 34–57. Oxford: Basil Blackwell, 1983.

WOOD, IAN. "Early Merovingian Devotion in Town and Country." In *The Church in Town and Countryside*, ed., Derek Baker, 61–76. Oxford: Clarendon, 1979.

WYNN, PHILLIP. "Wars and Warriors in Gregory of Tours' Histories I-IV." *Francia* **29.1** (2001): 1–35.

YOUNG, BAILEY. "Sacred Topography: The Impact of the Funerary Basilica in Late Antique Gaul." In *Society and Culture in Late Antique Gaul: Revisiting the Sources*, ed. Ralph W. Mathisen and Danuta Shanzer, 169–86. Aldershot and Burlington, VT: Ashgate, 2001.

INDEX

✺ ✺ ✺